Martin Heidegger and European Nihilism

European Perspectives

EUROPEAN PERSPECTIVES

A Series in Social Thought and Cultural Criticism
Lawrence D. Kritzman, Editor

European Perspectives presents English translations of books by leading European thinkers. With both classic and outstanding contemporary works, the series aims to shape the major intellectual controversies of our day and to facilitate the tasks of historical understanding.

Julia Kristeva	*Strangers to Ourselves*
Theodor W. Adorno	*Notes to Literature, vols. 1 and 2*
Richard Wolin, editor	*The Heidegger Controversy: A Critical Reader*
Antonio Gramsci	*Prison Notebooks, vol. 1*
Jacques LeGoff	*History and Memory*
Alain Finkielkraut	*Remembering in Vain: The Klaus Barbie Trial and Crimes Against Humanity*
Julia Kristeva	*Nations Without Nationalism*
Pierre Bourdieu	*The Field of Cultural Production*
Pierre Vidal-Naquet	*Assassins of Memory*
Hugo Ball	*Critique of the German Intelligentsia*
Gilles Deleuze and Félix Guattari	*What Is Philosophy?*
Karl Heinz Bohrer	*Suddenness: On the Moment of Aesthetic Appearance*
Alain Finkielkraut	*The Defeat of the Mind*
Elisabeth Badinter	*XY: Masculine Identity*
Julia Kristeva	*New Maladies of the Soul*

Martin Heidegger and European Nihilism

Karl Löwith
Editor Richard Wolin

TRANSLATOR GARY STEINER

Columbia University Press
NEW YORK

Columbia University Press
New York Chichester, West Sussex
Copyright © 1995 Columbia University Press
All rights reserved

Original German edition: Karl Löwith, Sämtliche Schriften Bd. 2, "Weltgeschichte und Heilsgeschehen" und Bd. 8, "Heidegger—Denker in dürftiger Zeit," published by J. B. Metzler Verlag 1983 and 1984.

   The Press gratefully acknowledges a grant
   from Inter Nationes toward the costs of translating this work.

Library of Congress Cataloging-in-Publication Data
Löwith, Karl, 1897–1973.
  [Selections. English. 1995]
  Martin Heidegger and European nihilism / Karl Löwith; edited and introduced by Richard Wolin; translated by Gary Steiner.
     p. cm.— (European perspectives)
  Includes bibliographical references and index.
  ISBN 0-231-08406-4 (cloth: alk. paper)
  1. Heidegger, Martin, 1889–1976   2. Philosophy, German—20th century.
  3. Nihilism (Philosophy)   I. Wolin, Richard.   II. Title.   III. Series.
B3279.H49L73213   1995
193—dc20   94-48411
                                                                                                      CIP

Casebound editions of Columbia University Press books are printed on permanent and durable acid-free paper.

Printed in the United States of America

c 10 9 8 7 6 5 4 3 2 1
p 10 9 8 7 6 5 4 3 2 1

Contents

Translator's Note   vii

Karl Löwith and Martin Heidegger—Contexts and Controversies:
An Introduction   1
Suggestions for Further Reading   27
Richard Wolin

One: Heidegger: Thinker in a Destitute Time
    Preface to the Second Edition   31
    1. Dasein Resolute Unto Itself, and Being
       Which Itself Gives   33
    2. History, Historicality, and Destining of Being   69
    3. The Interpretation of the Unsaid in "Nietzsche's
       Word 'God Is Dead'"   96
    4. On the Critical Appraisal of
       Heidegger's Influence   128

Two: The Occasional Decisionism of Carl Schmitt
    The Occasional Decisionism of Carl Schmitt   137
    Postscript: On Martin Heidegger's Political Decisionism
    and Friedrich Gogarten's Theological Decisionism   159

Three: European Nihilism: Reflections on the Spiritual and Historical Background of the European War

Part 1   173
The Unity of Europe and the Decline of that Unity   173
The End of Ancient Europe   181
European Nihilism   192

Part 2   209
Classical German Philosophy and the
    German Revolution   209
The Political Horizon of Heidegger's
    Existential Ontology   211
Germany: The Reich of Protest   225
Afterword to the Japanese Reader   228

Two Letters from Martin Heidegger to Karl Löwith   285

NOTES
Löwith and Heidegger: An Introduction   245
Heidegger: Thinker in a Destitute Time   249
The Occasional Decisionism of Carl Schmitt   271
European Nihilism: Reflections on the Spiritual and
    Historical Background of the European War   286
Two Letters   291

Index   295

Translator's Note

The essays included in this volume follow the German versions of the essays as they appear in Löwith's *Sämtliche Schriften*. "Heidegger, Thinker in a Destitute Time" and "The Occasional Decisionism of Carl Schmitt" follow volume 8: *Heidegger Denker in dürftiger Zeit* (Stuttgart: Metzler, 1984); "European Nihilism" follows volume 2: *Weltgeschichte und Heilsgeschehen* (Stuttgart: Metzler, 1983). The translation of the two letters from Heidegger to Löwith follows the presentation of those letters in the book *Zur philosophischen Aktualität Heideggers: Symposium der Alexander von Humboldt-Stiftung vom 24–28 April 1989 in Bonn-Bad Godesberg*, vol. 2: *Im Gespräch der Zeit*, ed. Dietrich Papenfuss and Otto Pöggeler (Frankfurt: Klostermann, 1990), pp. 27–39.

The translation includes two variations from the original texts. First, in a number of instances, exceedingly long paragraphs have been divided into shorter paragraphs; the aim here has been to make the text easier to read and comprehend. Second, in a great many instances, bibliographic citations have been provided for passages from Heidegger, Nietzsche, and other writers where Löwith had simply quoted textual passages without specifying the sources. Wherever possible, both English and original language editions of texts cited by Löwith have been included in endnotes. Where a number of successive references are made to a single work, for the reader's convenience the appropriate page numbers have been placed in parentheses in the text.

The reader will note that the "Postscript" at the end of "The Occasional Decisionism of Carl Schmitt" and the section entitled "The Political Horizon of Heidegger's Existential Ontology" in "European Nihilism" contain virtually the same set of remarks concerning Heidegger's National Socialism. This repetition has been necessary in order to preserve the continuity of the argument of each text.

In all cases, unless otherwise indicated, translations from original sources into English are my own.

Gary Steiner

Martin Heidegger and European Nihilism

Karl Löwith and Martin Heidegger—
Contexts and Controversies:
An Introduction

Richard Wolin

I

When one surveys the landscape of twentieth-century German philosophy, Karl Löwith stands out as one of its most significant personages. Löwith is perhaps best known in the English-speaking world for his landmark studies of modern historical consciousness. Two of his works have already achieved the status of minor classics: *From Hegel to Nietzsche*, a brilliant account of the decline and fragmentation of classical German philosophy; and *Meaning in History*, a fascinating reading of modern philosophies of history as they compare with their theological predecessors. When one combines these works with the more recent translation of his pathbreaking study of *Karl Marx and Max Weber* (first written in 1932), one begins to acquire a sense of the impressively original oeuvre that Löwith was able to assemble over the course of an extraordinarily prolific life of philosophical inquiry.[1]

The point of departure for so much of Löwith's thought was the profound dislocations and upheavals of modern historical life. In the venerable tradition of *Geistesgeschichte*, his inquiries circle around the question of the cultural and intellectual preconditions for the European catastrophe. For in Löwith's view, the European crisis was in the first instance a spiritual crisis. The fatal die had already been cast by the mid-nineteenth century, as European thinkers decisively turned their backs on the classicism of Goethe and Hegel. Increasingly, they grew impatient with values that were "timeless" or that transcended the finitude of human temporal existence. As a result, not God, but "man" became "the measure" of all value and meaning. It was a trend that reached its zenith with Marx's veneration of the proletariat and Nietzsche's enthronement of the "superman" as supreme categories of historical existence. For Löwith, this tendency represented a fatal misstep. It meant that there no longer existed any effective limitations or constraints upon the sovereignty of the human will. After all, had not Nietzsche felicitously described his later philosophy in terms of "the will to power"? In Löwith's view, the removal of all traditional constraints, along with the triumph of a radical historicism, loosened the floodgates of European nihilism. In many respects he remains today the unsurpassed chronicler of this trend.

In Löwith's estimation those who sought to exempt the Christian tradition from being implicated in the European crisis had not thought the situation through deeply enough. For Löwith was an adherent of the so-called secularization thesis, according to which the fundamental categories of modern historical consciousness were merely secularized versions of theological positions.[2] Hence, in Christian eschatology there already occurs a radical anthropomorphization of meaning that is far from unrelated to the "modern" developments with which Löwith is primarily concerned. The telos of redemption that plays such an important role in the foundational narratives of the Judeo-Christian tradition is merely secularized in modern theories of history, claims Löwith. This orientation toward the future or "eschaton" in post-biblical Western historical consciousness contrasts markedly with the cyclical view of history that was embraced in the world of classical antiquity. In his later writings Löwith, increasingly dissatisfied with the alternatives presented by the modern world, inclines toward the latter perspective.[3] In the worldview of the Stoics, cosmos and nature are viewed as superior to the fleeting vagaries of human historical life. It is this perspective alone which, according to Löwith, offers a proper corrective to the modern tendency to exalt the ontological status of the human world vis-à-vis the timelessness of nature and cosmos. As Hans-Georg Gadamer has described Löwith's perspective: "We should look at the eternal cycle of nature in order to learn from it the equanimity that alone is appropriate to the minuteness of human life in the universe."[4]

Proceeding from this assumption, one of the keys to understanding Löwith's later thought concerns his insistence that the difference between "world" and "human world" be preserved. This meant that it was essential that all historicist attempts to subsume the former by the latter be kept at bay. As has often been pointed out, Löwith's Stoicism has much in common with the "Oriental wisdom" he found so congenial during his five-year sojourn in Japan (1936–41) in flight from a Nazi-dominated Europe. Such sentiments materialize clearly in claims such as the following: "Once we have acceded to complete insight, then the mountain will simply become a mountain again and the river simply a river. In this final recognition of Being-so-and-not-otherwise, the world and man show what they are originally and ultimately."[5] In Löwith's view, much of Western thought—and, in particular, *modern* Western thought—failed to heed such insights. Instead, "world" and "human world" were conflated, resulting in the fatal anthropomorphism afflicting the post-Cartesian tradition. As subjected to human designs and intentions, the worldhood of the world, its original integrity and simplicity, can only be misconstrued. As Löwith remarks:

> World and human world are not equivalents. . . . The world is not simply a cosmological "idea" (Kant) or a mere "total-horizon" (Husserl) or a world-"project" (Heidegger), but it itself, absolutely independent: *id quod substat*. Only various world-pictures can be projected, never the world itself. . . . [The world] itself never appears as an object like other objects; it encompasses everything, without itself being comprehensible. It is what is greatest and richest, and at the same time as empty as a frame without a picture.[6]

II

Karl Löwith was born to an assimilated German-Jewish family in Munich in 1897. His father, Wilhelm Löwith, a convert to Protestantism, was a successful artist and stimulated his son's early interests in European cultural life. After attending high school in Munich, Löwith volunteered for World War I and was seriously wounded in the Italian campaign of 1915. He spent the next three years in a prisoner of war camp near Genoa, an experience that would inspire a life-long affection for the Latin sensibility. He was deeply impressed by the rather unGerman traits of his Italian captors—their spontaneity and warmth, their ability to live for the moment, their acceptance of fate. Löwith would return to Italy both during his student years and during his initial period of exile from the Nazi dictatorship.

In 1919 Löwith was privileged to hear Max Weber's famous Munich lecture "Science as a Vocation." The address was delivered during the height of Munich's short-lived and ill-fated *Räterepublik*. Weber's concluding plea for an "ethic of responsibility"—instead of chasing after false prophets, he soberly recommends that "We set to work and meet the 'demands of the day,' in human relations as well as in our vocation"[7]— would have a marked impact on the development of Löwith's own profoundly stoical ethical vision. It served as a sober, well-nigh prophetic warning concerning the perils of turning the academic lectern into a political platform and the dangers of political messianism.

Following the war, Löwith moved to Freiburg to study philosophy with the renowned founder of the phenomenological movement, Edmund Husserl. However, instead of continuing his studies with Husserl, Löwith soon found himself seduced by the phenomenologist's brilliant young assistant, Martin Heidegger, whom he followed to Marburg in 1924. According to Löwith, "the palpable intensity and impenetrable profundity of Heidegger's spiritual drive caused everything else to pale and made Husserl's naive belief in an ultimate philosophical method seem irrelevant."[8] In Heidegger, Löwith, like so many others, had found an exciting alternative to the sterile academicism of the reigning German school-philosophies.

In a series of autobiographical reflections, Löwith would go on to describe Heidegger in the following way:

> We gave [Heidegger] the nickname "the little magician from Messkirch." ... He was a small dark man who knew how to cast a spell insofar as he could make disappear what he had a moment before presented. His lecture technique consisted in building up an edifice of ideas which he then proceeded to tear down, presenting the spellbound listeners with a riddle and then leaving them empty-handed. This ability to cast a spell at times had very considerable consequences: it attracted more or less psychopathic personality types, and, after three years of guessing at riddles, one woman student took her own life.[9]

In 1928 Löwith would defend his "Habilitationsschrift," *Das Individuum in der Rolle des Mitmenschen*, which was written under Heidegger's direction. This "Jugendschrift," subtitled "A Contribution to the Anthropological Foundation of Ethical Problems," attempted to respond to the deficiencies of one of the key categories of Heidegger's great work of 1927, *Being and Time*, the category of "Mitsein" or "Being-with."

In *Being and Time* the hallmark of "authenticity" ("Eigentlichkeit") was a Self that was radically enclosed in its own Selfhood or "ownness" ("Jemeinigkeit"); a being—Dasein—that displayed all the traits of a Kierkegaardian, existential loneliness, culminating in the absolute, irreducible singularity of its own confrontation with death ("Being-toward-death"). However, the early Heidegger's Kierkegaardianism was of an emphatically post-theological variety. Having fully internalized Zarathustra's celebrated adage concerning the "death of God," Heidegger's reading of Kierkegaard was, moreover, radically *post-Nietzschean*. Thus, in Heideggerian "Angst," one discovers as it were a detheologized version of "fear and trembling." The modern "knight of faith" remains solitary and self-enclosed; but he or she has been divested of the redeeming power of salvation, which, qua possibility, alone made the Kierkegaardian wager meaningful.

Since in *Being and Time* the majority of individuals—the "They"—attempt to cover up and deny the rigors of authentic Selfhood via "busyness," "idle talk," "curiosity," "publicness," and other such ruses of social conformity, their Dasein is for the most part confined to the nether sphere of inauthentic existence. Yet, as a result of this a priori devaluation of the sphere of "being-with" or "Mitsein," in Heidegger's existential ontology, prospects for meaningful human intersubjectivity seemed to be either negligible or nonexistent.

It is this contradiction that Löwith wishes to remedy in his youthful study of philosophical anthropology, a treatise that is regarded by some (e.g., the philosopher Dieter Henrich) as an "as yet unsurpassed" exemplar of the genre.[10] In opposition to all claims concerning the ontological primacy of transcendental subjectivity (Heidegger's included), Löwith, in a manner that bears marked affinities with the dialogical philosophies of Buber and Levinas, not to mention the symbolic interactionism of Schütz and Mead, seeks to assert the centrality of *intersubjective relatedness*. The very concept of what it means to be a "Self," he contends, is essentially defined by a network of social relations—family, friends, associates, and so forth—in lieu of which the very concept of selfhood ceases to be philosophically meaningful. Principally, however, the "I" is formed and shaped by a world of human intimacy—the "thou." Or, as Gadamer would remark, "If one may put into an abbreviated form what Löwith's book sought to bring into philosophical discussion at this time, it was to shed light on what the 'thou' in its radical particularity signifies for Mankind."[11] Before it is my world, the human world is a "Mitwelt," a "co-world." Thus, the individual becomes him- or herself nonsolipsistically via a sophisticated process of "reflection": by seeing him- or herself in the other and the other in him or herself. Taking this insight a step further, Löwith goes on to claim that never—not even in the Heideggerian ultimate instance of Being-toward-death—does the individual stand in immediate relation to the Self. Instead, as a phenomenological construct, the self is always mediated. Löwith eloquently summarizes these insights as follows:

> Man returns to himself, not primarily from objects, but from subjects, i.e., from Beings who are like him; for the "world" to which he principally

> turns is the co-world [*Mitwelt*] that corresponds to him. From the outset and without his doing, his own world is ever and always determined through the Dasein of Others, such that it would not be there at all or in this way without the having-been-there of determinate Others. . . . When we inquire about the Other or the co-world, this question implies inquiring about one's own self, for whom others are "Other" and a "world"—i.e., one is making inquiries about Being-with-others [*Miteinandersein*].[12]

The concept of a "mediated self" stressed by Löwith was not a standpoint that had been embraced by modern philosophy. Hence, when one surveys the epistemological tradition from Descartes to Husserl (here, Löwith tactfully leaves Heidegger off his list), all leading representatives proceed from a "more or less abstractly conceived Self-consciousness," observes Löwith.[13] Much of the inspiration for his critique of this tradition would come from the anthropological humanism of Ludwig Feuerbach. For it was Feuerbach who, in his *Principles of a Philosophy of the Future*, would claim that, "The true dialectic is never a monologue of the solitary thinker with himself; it is a dialogue between I and thou."

To be sure, Löwith's Marburg *Habilitationsvater* had seriously called into question the adequacy of the standpoint of transcendental subjectivity as a basis for rigorous philosophical questioning. In Heidegger's view, this was a perspective that remained existentially impoverished, insofar as it falsely assumed the primacy of a theoretical standpoint (such as the Cartesian "I think") in trying to understand a being that was primarily defined by "care," "finitude," "ecstasis," and "temporality." Nevertheless, the young Löwith displayed ample precocity by insinuating that, in his attempts to disavow the philosophy of reflection, his master had not gone far enough.

III

Löwith belonged to a group of uniquely talented Jewish students who in the 1920s and 1930s were disciples of Heidegger. Among their number one would have to include Hannah Arendt, Hans Jonas, and Herbert Marcuse. In May 1933 they would all be faced with the conundrum of trying to reconcile their devotion to Germany's most gifted philosophical spirit of the interwar period with his triumphant conversion to Nazism. All were subsequently forced into exile by the Nazi dictatorship, where, following circuitous routes, they would take up teaching careers in the United States. None would disavow his or her earlier liaisons with Heidegger. But each in his or her own way sought to examine what it was about Heideggerian *Existenzphilosophie* that might have facilitated—or, at the very least, proved unable to prevent—his short-lived, though concerted, partisanship for Hitler's regime.

Their attempts to account for the (in their eyes) "unaccountable"— Heidegger's Nazism—often complemented one another. As Heidegger's students and as witnesses to Germany's unprecedented political tumult of 1929–1933, they shared a privileged perspective that enabled them to perceive the uncanny elective affinities between Heidegger's early philosophy and the "existential" version of politics propagated by the new regime. Thus, they were able to provide a *contextually informed* appraisal of Heidegger's commitment to Nazism that all late-comers to this problem would do well to heed.

With the exception of Löwith, Heidegger's former students (all of whom, of course, went on to become major philosophers in their own right) offered merely occasional, though insightful, diagnoses of the master's infamous political lapse. That there was something inherent to Heidegger's "philosophy of existence" that made it especially susceptible to a "national revolutionary"—i.e., pro-fascist—reading was, however, a point on which they would almost all agree.

For Herbert Marcuse, writing shortly after Hitler's accession to power, *Existenzphilosophie*'s emphasis on the concrete particularity of human Dasein suggested a fatal rejection of the universalist strivings of traditional philosophy. Though such strivings could present themselves— and often did—as "mere" ideals and, hence, as "ideological," they also contained a crucial utopian dimension: they emphasized the dialectical tension between the actual and the possible, between the real and the ideal. The ontological hiatus between these two moments therefore served to highlight the indigence of social reality as it was presently constituted. By abandoning this dimension of the Western philosophical legacy in favor of the specificity of self-existent Dasein, Heidegger's thought displayed telltale normative deficits. Thus, one was left with few substantive criteria by virtue of which one could differentiate *justifiable* existential commitments from *unjustifiable* ones—so far had Heideggerian existentialism departed, following the lead of Kierkegaard and Nietzsche, from the evaluative ideals pertaining to the concept of "normative rightness" that had been so essential to the heritage of Western metaphysics. In a strict sense, then, Heidegger's existentialism left him ideationally defenseless against the militaristic-heroic bombast of National Socialism. In his view, its potential for "authenticity" followed from its vehement rejection of the mediocrity of bourgeois "everydayness."

Marcuse's ultimate verdict on this theme is appropriately severe: "Existentialism collapses the moment its political theory has been realized . . . the struggle against reason drives it blindly into the arms of the powers that be." As an illustration of his point concerning existentialism's aversion to the universal, Marcuse concludes by citing a passage from one of Heidegger's 1933 political texts, in which the disastrous consequences of employing particularistic, existential criteria in the realm of political judgment are evident: "Let not doctrines and 'Ideas' be the rules of your Being," remarks Heidegger. "The Führer alone *is* the present and future German reality and its law."[14]

A remarkably similar appraisal of the philosophical bases for Heidegger's political engagement has been provided by Hans Jonas. Jonas sees the fatal link between philosophy and politics in Heidegger as deriving from the existential category of "resolve" or "decisiveness" ("Entschlossenheit"). According to Jonas, the problem with this concept is its contentlessness. It possesses virtually no evaluative components by virtue of which, for example, "ethical" versus "unethical" wordly commitments could be gauged. Instead, the determinants of authentic resolve are purely formal or (to highlight the important parallels Löwith will establish between the thought of Heidegger and Carl Schmitt) *decisionistic*. One's "resolve" is judged, therefore, purely by the quantum or degree of one's engagement on behalf of this or that cause, without regard to the specific ends of action. So formal is the level of analysis in *Being and Time* that I could be equally "resolved" as a Nazi, a Bolshevik, an anarchist, and so forth.

The contentless nature of "resolve" is crucial to understanding Heidegger's political commitment, according to Jonas. For it suggests that, in order to provide it with meaning and direction, one is both at the mercy of contemporary history and powerless to defend oneself against it. And in Heidegger's case, the radical alternative served up by contemporary historical circumstances was Nazism. As Jonas explains:

> As the hour of January 1933 struck, history offered the opportunity for decisiveness. . . . It was at this time that the enormous dubiousness of the Heideggerian outlook in its entirety became clear to me. Whereas he accused idealist philosophy of a certain idealism—it claimed to study the forms of thought, the categories, according to which the world is ordered, and thus [did] everything at a certain remove [from the world]—one could accuse him of something much more serious: the absolute formalism of his decisionism, where decision as such becomes the highest virtue.[15]

Arendt never made a concerted effort to come to grips with the dilemma of Heidegger's political engagement. She was more disposed to read Heidegger's Nazism in the manner of a character flaw than pertaining to his philosophy per se. Her estimations, moreover, differed from occasion to occasion. In a 1946 *Partisan Review* article in which she ponders this question, she referred to Heidegger as a typical German type, the "last romantic (we hope)," in the mold of Adam Mueller or Friedrich Schlegel. She attributes his "complete irresponsibility. . .partly to the delusion of genius, partly to desperation."[16]

Arendt is particularly unforgiving with regard to Heidegger's treatment of his former mentor, Edmund Husserl. According to Jaspers, it fell due to Heidegger as National Socialist Rector of Freiburg University to sign a decree banning Jews from university facilities. In Husserl's case, this meant he was forbidden on racial grounds to use the philosophy faculty library. On this point Arendt, who had no professional or personal ties to Husserl, proved particularly unforgiving: "because I know that this letter and this signature [i.e., Heidegger's] almost killed [Husserl], I can't but regard Heidegger as a potential murderer."[17] Indeed, in a letter of May 1933 to a friend, Husserl would lament his recent "woeful personal experiences." Most troubling among these were his relations with Heidegger, whose "increasingly strong anti-Semitism of recent years" had wounded the founder of the phenomenological movement deeply.[18] Yet, in her contribution to the Festschrift in honor of Heidegger's eightieth birthday, Arendt would insist that those who sought to relate Heidegger's philosophy to the political goings-on of the early 1930s were grasping at straws, since Nazism was a "gutter-born phenomenon" and had nothing to do with matters of "thought."[19]

How can one account for the apparently paradoxical fact that Heidegger, whom Husserl accuses of growing anti-Semitism in the years prior to 1933, had so many gifted Jewish students? The explanation lies in the fact that, for the most part, these students did not regard themselves as Jewish, nor did their teacher Heidegger so regard them. Instead, they viewed themselves as fully assimilated Germans. Heidegger never shared the Nazis' version of biological anti-Semitism. Rather, his dislike of Jews was of the traditional cultural variety—a mentality which, as a rule, was accepting of acculturated or baptized Jews. His German-Jewish students were of course in for a rude awakening with Hitler's racial legislation of April 1933 (the so-called Law for the Reconstitution of the German Civil Service), which, as we have seen, Heidegger fully supported in his capacity as university rector. For many Jews who stemmed from the milieu of

Germany's well-assimilated *Großbürgertum*, this was the first time they actually felt themselves to be Jewish—a fact to which Löwith attests quite eloquently in his autobiography.[20]

National Socialist ideology, especially in its early phases, was far from a homogeneous phenomenon. For a time (at least until the Röhm purge of June 30, 1934) it was able to coexist with the worldviews of national conservatives, conservative revolutionaries, national Bolsheviks, young conservatives, as well as its own "right" and "left" factions (on the "left," this meant those who, like the soon-to-be-purged Strasser brothers, took the "socialist" component of National Socialism seriously). What, then, remained of that ideology when one peeled away the veneer of rhetorical bluster? As the political theorist Franz Neumann has remarked:

> What is left as a justification for the Reich? Not racism, not the idea of the Holy Roman empire and certainly not some democratic nonsense like popular sovereignty or self-determination. Only the Reich itself remains. It is its own justification. The philosophical roots of the argument are to be found in the existential philosophy of Heidegger. Transferred to the realm of politics, existentialism argues that power and might are true: power is a sufficient theoretical base for more power.[21]

IV

It is Löwith's explorations of the intellectual origins of Heidegger's Nazism in terms of a re-reading of the key categories of the existential analytic of *Being and Time* that undoubtedly represent the most systematic and thorough discussion of this issue to date.

The publication history of his meditations on this theme (which of course would attain a new urgency following the great Heidegger debate provoked by the publication of Victor Farias' *Heidegger and Nazism*) is itself of no small interest. Löwith first set forth his ruminations on the political significance of Heidegger's existential ontology in his autobiography, "My Life in Germany Before and After 1933." The text dates from 1940. It was composed by Löwith in Japanese exile (after the Japanese attack on Pearl Harbor in December 1941, Löwith would be forced to emigrate to the United States) on the occasion of an essay competition of that title sponsored by Harvard University. The prize committee had made it clear that it was not interested in "philosophical reflections about the past," but in testimony that was "factual" ("wahrheitsgetreu"). Needless to say, Löwith failed to win the prize. His reflections on the great personages and events of the period undoubtedly proved too substantial for the tastes of the Harvard prize committee. The manuscript then lay dormant for some forty-six years and was first published in 1986.

Still, Löwith thought the Heidegger portion of the manuscript to be of sufficient interest that he proceeded to publish it independently immediately after the war. In 1946 it appeared under the title, "The Political Implications of Heidegger's Philosophy of Existence," in Jean-Paul Sartre's *Les Temps modernes*. The text was prefaced by a curious disclaimer to the effect that the journal's editorial board did not necessarily share the criticisms of Heidegger contained in the article. Clearly, it was Sartre himself who had authored the disavowal, which contended that, were one to judge a philosophy by the political convictions of its author, one would inevitably be selling the philosophy short—a claim that is indisputable as far as it goes. To support his assertion, Sartre invoked the well-known case of Hegel's justification of the Prussian state in the *Philosophy of Right* and other texts. In the same fashion, Sartre suggests, it would be unfair to judge Heidegger's philosophical contribution by the measure of his illfated embrace of Hitler and National Socialism. To be sure, the prefatory note was meant as a type of hermeneutical prophylaxis lest suspicions be directed toward Sartre's own version of existentialism, which clearly owed so much to his reading of Heidegger.[22]

Löwith's essay appeared at a tenuous point in Heidegger's professional life: a Freiburg University denazification commission had recently found him guilty of "having placed the great prestige of his scholarly reputation . . . in the service of the National Socialist Revolution and thereby contributing to the legitimation of this Revolution in the eyes of educated Germans."[23] As a result he was stripped of his *venia legenda*—his right to teach—and was banned from university life for a period of five years. It was a setback that affected him quite adversely: he suffered a nervous breakdown that required two months of hospitalization.

According to the testimony of Hannah Arendt, prior to this verdict in the fall of 1945, Heidegger had desperately sought to ingratiate himself among the French occupation authorities, offering his services (to no avail) for purposes of politically reeducating the German people. And since the political future of the province of Baden was in French hands, he desperately sought out contact with influential French intellectuals who might help him plead his case.

First, he tried contacting influential Sorbonne philosophy professor Emile Bréhier. Bréhier refused to respond: in his opinion Heidegger's letter had come five years too late.

Next, Heidegger tried contacting Sartre. The text of his letter of October 28, 1945 reads as follows:

My esteemed Mr. Sartre!

A few weeks ago I heard about you and your work. Mr. [Frédéric] Towarnicki kindly left your book, *Being and Nothingness*, here for me and I began to work through it immediately. In it I encounter for the first time an independent thinker who has fundamentally experienced the realm out of which I myself think. Your work is dominated by an immediate understanding of my philosophy the likes of which I have not previously encountered. I would be very pleased were we to enter into a fruitful exchange of ideas so that we might clarify some essential questions. Since writing *Being and Time* twenty years ago, the same problems have concerned me; I now see many things more clearly and simply; a number of misunderstandings can be eliminated.

I am in agreement with your critique of "Being-with" and your emphasis on "Being-for-another," and also in part with your critique of the explanation of death. *Being and Time*—or that part of it that was published—is only a path [*Weg*], and the decisive question that I only touched on in "The Essence of Reason" was not at all developed there. The "Introduction" and "Conclusion" of your work are very stimulating for me; I now think about these questions in their primordial relation to history—most of all in relation to the beginning of Western thought which, up until now, has been entirely concealed through the dominance of Platonism. I hope that I will have the occasion in the foreseeable future finally to publish my larger works.

It would be important for me to receive an additional copy of your work, for I could then work through it in an entirely different way; I would like to comment concerning several essential problems and thereby, with your help, to bring my thinking to the point where it can be experienced as a fundamental event of history, in order to bring contemporary humanity into a primordial relation to Being.

It would be nice if during the winter you could travel here. We could philosophize together in our little ski hut and use it as a base for ski tours in the Schwarzwald. . . .

I greet you as a *compagnon de route* and pioneer [*als Weggenossen und Wegbereiter*].

Yours, Martin Heidegger

Your main work must without question be translated into German.[24]

Nevertheless, the admiration Heidegger expresses for Sartre's philosophy jibes poorly with other accounts. Gadamer, for example, reports that, upon receiving *Being and Nothingness*, Heidegger "cut" merely the first forty pages of the book before hastily bequeathing it to his former student.[25] Moreover, when it became clear that his profession of interest in Sartre's work had remained unrequited, Heidegger would characterize Sartre's version of existentialism in much less charitable terms. In the pivotal "Letter on Humanism," written in the fall of 1946, Heidegger pillories Sartre's philosophy for remaining imprisoned in the categories of Western metaphysics: "Sartre expresses the basic tenet of existentialism in this way: Existence precedes essence. . . . But the reversal of a metaphysical statement remains a metaphysical statement." And in stark opposition to Sartre's attempt to reconcile existentialism and humanism via dicta such as, "We are precisely in a situation where there are only human beings," Heidegger responds, in keeping with his later doctrine of the "destining of Being," by celebrating a philosophy of *antihumanism*: "We are precisely in a situation where principally there is Being."[26]

V

Understandably, most devout Heideggerians have been at a loss to explain the master's partisanship for Hitler. Part of this explanatory incapacity is, one suspects, defensive-psychological: an example of the natural human attempt to rationalize facts that prove troublesome or inconvenient, a phenomenon that is especially commonplace when scholars have invested a considerable measure of "intellectual capital" in a given academic paradigm. Here, too, the time-honored maxim *amicus Plato, sed magis amicus veritas* should apply.

But there is another aspect to this commonplace intepretive failure which suggests, in addition, a more substantive basis. For those who prefer an exclusively textual or intraphilosophical reading of Heidegger's texts are bound to miss the profound historical-ideological dimensions of his work—a dimension that was self-evident for so many of his contemporaries.

It is in this respect above all that Löwith's understanding of the entwinement of philosophy and politics in Heidegger's work proves so enlightening. For as the account of a philosophically informed contemporary, Löwith's critique stands as an indispensable counterweight to the perils of a decontextualized, ahistorical misreading of Heidegger's thought—a misreading so characteristic of those interpretations that remain exclusively textual or philosophical. To employ a Heideggerian idiom: Löwith's meditations on his mentor's *Fall* (which in German means both "case" and "fall") provide us with a cohesive account of the way in which Heidegger's own life and thought became subject to the vicissitudes of the "historicity."

One of the commonplace reactions to the philosopher's partisanship for Hitler has been to claim that this support had nothing to do with his philosophy; that (echoing the defense of Hannah Arendt cited earlier) Nazism was too base and vulgar a phenomenon for there to have been any meaningful linkages with Heidegger's own elevated approach to philosophy, his "fundamental ontology."

Such reservations indeed point to some of the complexities involved in trying to account for Heidegger's controversial political stance; but they fall short of appreciating how Heidegger himself conceived of the imperatives of Germany's political situation circa 1933. For, in many ways, his case was paradigmatic for a great number of right-wing intellectuals in Germany who were convinced that democracy was in its essence *undeutsch*—unGerman. They came to believe that a "national authoritarian" political solution was required if Germany were to surmount the crisis-prone years of Weimar and hark back to the "great politics" (Nietzsche) of authentic German traditions.[27]

Such reservations also fail to account for Heidegger's own self-understanding as a nonconformist among Germany's professorial mandarinate. Given his own penurious background and origins, this provincial sexton's son always felt ill at ease among the largely upper-class professorate. Consequently, and strange as it may sound, Heidegger adopted the persona of an "anti-intellectual intellectual," who always felt markedly out of step with the dominant theoretical trends of the time, be they positivism, neo-Kantianism, or the sociology of knowledge. His self-understanding as an outsider, moreover, goes far in explaining his attraction both to philosophical and political radicalism. In his view, and following the extremely influential *Zeitdiagnosen* of Nietzsche, Spengler, and Ernst Jünger, contemporary European civilization had proceeded so far down the path of perdition that only solutions that were radical and total—that is, measures that demanded a wholesale *break* with the bourgeois universe of complacency and compromise—appeared to offer a possible way out.

No one has better understood the biographical-cultural origins of Heidegger's philosophical and political radicalism than Löwith. As he comments in his autobiography: "By birth a simple sexton's son, by profession

Löwith and Heidegger: An Introduction

[Heidegger] became the pathetic representative of a [professorial] estate that he negated. . . . The destructive radicalism of the [National Socialist] movement and the petty bourgeois character of all its 'strength-through-joy' institutions failed to make an impression on him because he himself was a radical petty bourgeois."[28] And to those who would claim that Heidegger somehow sullied the existential ontology of *Being and Time* by allowing its concepts to serve as a pseudophilosophical justification for the "inner truth and greatness of the National Socialist movement,"[29] Löwith rejoins that, insofar as Heidegger's thought itself is a species of *Existenzphilosophie*, a philosophy of existence, it is far from surprising that he would seek to actualize its terms in temporal-historical fashion in the sphere of the "everyday":

> Given the significant attachment of the philosopher to the climate and intellectual mood of National Socialism it would be inappropriate to criticize or exonerate his political decision in isolation from *the very principles* of Heideggerian philosophy itself. It is not Heidegger, who, in opting for Hitler, "misunderstood himself"; instead, those who cannot understand why he acted this way have failed to understand him. A Swiss professor regretted that Heidegger consented to compromise himself with the "everyday," as if a philosophy that explains Being from the standpoint of time and the everyday would not stand in relation to the daily historical realities that govern its origins and effects. The possibility of a Heideggerian political philosophy was not born as a result of a regrettable "miscue," but from the very conception of existence that simultaneously combats and absorbs the *Zeitgeist*.[30]

Of course, this leaves unanswered the question as to what it was substantively about "the very principles of Heideggerian philosophy" that bore such profound affinities with "the climate and intellectual mood of National Socialism." Here, too, Löwith's response is informed by an insight and sensibility that only a contemporary who simultaneously possessed a keen appreciation for the fine points of Heidegger's thought would be capable of articulating.

The key to Löwith's explanation is, as it were, twofold. It possesses both a cultural historical dimension centering on the phenomenon of "European nihilism" as well as a material aspect that concentrates on several of the key categories of Heidegger's early fundamental ontology.

The cultural-historical dimension analyzed by Löwith crystallizes in the nineteenth century. It was epitomized in Nietzsche's famous discussion of "European Nihilism" in *The Will to Power*, a concept the philosopher describes in the following memorable terms: "What does nihilism mean?

That the highest values devaluate themselves. The aim is lacking; 'why?' finds no answer."[31]

With these words, Nietzsche succinctly captures the fin-de-siècle mood of irredeemable decline and collapse that would become a virtual obsession in the literature and art of the period. Suddenly, it dawned upon the European *Bildungsbürgertum* that the values and beliefs they had taken to be the highest manifestations of the spirit of the West had lost their efficacy, their capacity to guide and inspire. Moreover, with the decline of these beliefs, a new radical and aggressive spirit of *Kulturfeindlichkeit*—of "hostility to culture"—began rapidly to gain currency. It was a spirit that was especially well represented in the Russian literature of the period: in Turgenev's poignant portrayal of generational conflict in *Fathers and Sons*; but also in Dostoyevsky's apocalyptical portrait of the ruthless anarchistic conspirators, personified by the figure of Kirilov, in *The Devils*. "If there is no God, then everything is permitted," asserts Dostoyevsky in *The Brothers Karamzov*. In other words, if God has died, then nihilism has triumphed. In Löwith's estimation, the delusionary excesses of the two world wars, of the Nazi regime, and of that generation of German antidemocratic thinkers who intellectually prepared the way for German fascism are all inseparable from the phenomenon of "European nihilism"— a nineteenth-century inheritance that was appropriated and radicalized in the twentieth. Over the course of the nineteenth century, argues Löwith, Europe lost touch with its traditional spiritual moorings, paving the way for a faithless political and intellectual radicalism. In this context, the Greek concept of *sophrosyne* (moderation) or the medieval Christian notion of the subordination of human purposes to a a series of superior, divinely ordained ends would become meaningless. Instead, as Löwith explains in "European Nihilism," "The Europe of the nineteenth century no longer lived with faith in a genuine mission; it simply disseminated its wares and its scientific-technological civilization in every direction."

In this connection, a citation Löwith culls from Nietzsche's *Untimely Meditations* marvelously captures the incipient "transvaluation of all values" that appeared so threatening to the nineteenth-century European literati. As Nietzsche observed:

> Now how does the philosopher see the culture of our time? Naturally quite differently than those philosophy professors who are satisfied with their state. When he thinks of the universal haste and the increasing speed with which things are falling, of the cessation of all contemplativeness and simplicity, it almost seems to him as if he were seeing the symptoms of a total extermination and uprooting of culture. The waters of religion are

ebbing, and they are leaving behind swamps or ponds; the nations are again separating from one another in the most hostile manner, and they are trying to rip each other to shreds. The sciences, without any measure and pursued in the blindest spirit of *laissez faire*, are breaking apart and dissolving everything which is firmly believed; the edified classes and states are being swept along by a money economy which is enormously contemptible. never was the world more a world, never was it poorer in love and good. the educated classes are no longer lighthouses or sanctuaries in the midst of all this turbulent secularization; they themselves become more turbulent by the day, more thoughtless and loveless. Everything, contemporary art and science included, serves the coming barbarism.[32]

Can there be any doubt that this is precisely the cultural predicament to which Heidegger sought to respond in the years following World War I, as his sense of the requirements for a type of radical philosophical questioning that would be truly appropriate to the age began to mature? This is the Heidegger so aptly described by friend, student, and intimate Löwith. It is an intellectual portrait that shows Heidegger to be as much influenced by the probing cultural meditations of Luther, Pascal, Kierkegaard, Van Gogh, Rilke, and Dostoyevsky as by the leading representatives of Western metaphysics; a Heidegger who readily accepted the nineteenth century's dispirited verdict on the totally of inherited western values—the verdict of "nihilism"—and who would go on in *Being and Time* to celebrate the nihilistic resolve of heroic-authentic decision in face of the Nothing. Or, as he would put it in a 1920 letter to Löwith: "I do only what I must and what I consider to be necessary, and I do this as I am able to—I do not slant my philosophical work toward cultural tasks for a universal present. . . . I work form out of my 'I am' and my spiritual, indeed factical heritage. With this facticity, existence rages!"[33]

Löwith perceives more than a passing affinity between the nihilistic spirit of revolution characteristic of the National Socialist movement and the same spirit as it infuses the existential analytic of Heidegger's philosophy.[34] Heidegger's transposition of the essential concepts of *Being and Time* such as authenticity, resolve, fate, potentiality-for-Being-a-Self, Being-toward-death, and *Jemeinigkeit* ("ownness") from the terrain of individual, self-subsistent Being to that of the Dasein of the German nation was, according to Löwith, but a very short step. In fact, the transition from an individual to a collective-political concept of authentic Dasein entails less of a conceptual leap than one might initially suspect. For if one pays heed to a number of the key categories proper to Division II of *Being and Time*—categories such as *Gemeinschaft*, destiny, historicity, choosing-one's-hero, and, at one point, the "das Volk"—one understands that a historical-political reading of the text, far from being alien to the spirit of Heidegger's enterprise, is virtually required. Far from being opposed, a doctrine of individual authenticity and a doctrine of political authenticity may be viewed as necessary corollaries. As the recent political biographies of Heidegger by Hugo Ott and Victor Farias show,[35] many of Löwith's suppositions concerning the parallels between Heidegger's thought and the Nazi movement have become a matter of historical record.

Hence, according to Löwith, the worldview of National Socialism and Heidegger's concept of "Being-in-the-world" possess a number of fundamental points in common. Both shared a concept of radicalism that related in a "nihilating" manner toward traditions and values that proved unserviceable for the ends of individual and historical greatness. Just as in his philosophy Heidegger sought to effect the "Destruktion" of the traditional categories of Western metaphysics, the radical political movements of his day sought to eliminate those aspects of the past that were deemed unserviceable for the ends of "total mobilization" (Ernst Jünger). As Löwith observes, "Instead of giving oneself over to the universal enterprise of education, as if one had been given the mission of 'saving the culture,' [according to Heidegger] one must [engage in] a 'radical dismantling and rebuilding' or a 'destruction.'. . . without concerning oneself with the idle talk and the bustle of those sensible and enterprising people who reckon time with clocks."[36]

VI

Given this analysis of the "existential decisionism" of resolute Dasein in *Being and Time*, Löwith is especially well-placed to pursue the relevant parallels with the "political decisionism" of Carl Schmitt—one of Germany's leading political philosophers and jurists during the Weimar Republic who, like Heidegger, became a wholesale supporter of the National Socialist Revolution in May 1933. Heidegger and Schmitt became the two most celebrated academicians of the Weimar period to lend their full support to the new regime. In fact, Heidegger, sensing their shared intellectual orientation and renown, would write to Schmitt in August 1933, urging that the two intellectual greats make common cause. "The gathering of the spiritual forces, which should bring about what is to come, is becoming more urgent everyday," Heidegger insists.[37]

According to Schmitt's political thought, all traditional concepts of political obligation have, regrettably, been delegitimated or lost their power. "Sovereignty," "king," "state," "majesty," "divine right"—even the concept of "the political" itself – have all (echoing Nietzsche's lament from *Untimely Meditations* cited above) forfeited their authority in the wake of the tremendous centrifugal energies of political modernity. The very ground has fallen away from our traditional modes of political legitimation and discourse. Like many German radical conservatives of his day, Schmitt attempted to forge new concepts of political order, authority, and legitimacy in order to counter the "eclipse of the political" in the modern age. In his view, responsibility for this eclipse must be attributed to the rise of a liberal democratic society, where socioeconomic "interests" have usurped the prerogative of politics proper.

Though compelling in many respects, Schmitt's depiction of the situation of modern politics forced him to adopt a number of positions that were either manifestly authoritarian or avowedly fascist. His 1920 book on the concept of dictatorship recommended that form of political rule as a method of keeping at bay those forces and interests that, in modern democratic societies, threatened to deplete the substance of political sovereignty. In *Political Theology* (1922) he would attempt to deny the legitimacy of the modern age by arguing that all modern political concepts were in essence secularized theological concepts. And his influential book on *The Crisis of Parliamentary Democracy* (1923) concluded with a glowing description of Mussolini's 1922 march on Rome. In his preference for direct action and glorification of the myth of the nation, Il Duce had truly understood the steps necessary to preserve the primacy of the political in the modern world.

During the concluding years of the German Republic, the fascistic elements of Schmitt's work came increasingly to the fore. In what was perhaps his most influential book of the period, *The Concept of the Political*, Schmitt coined the infamous "friend-enemy" distinction to define the essence of the political. In remarks that well illustrate Germany's burning desire to avenge the shame of Compiègne and the humiliation of Versailles, he observes: "The pinnacle of great politics is the moment in which the enemy comes into view in concrete clarity as the enemy."[38] For Schmitt, one does not kill the enemy for aesthetic, moral, or for other nonpolitical reasons. Rather, as Schmitt phrases it in a classical statement of the doctrines of political existentialism, he is to be killed on strictly "*seinsmässige*" or "existential-ontological" grounds. As Löwith shows, already in *The Concept of the Political* (that is, some six years before the advent of Nazi rule), Schmitt went to great lengths to justify the concept of *Artgleichheit*—"racial homogeneity"—as essential to the self-preservation of the modern state. Moreover, as a logical corollary to his concept of the "friend-enemy" distinction in politics, in the same work, Schmitt would emphasize the importance of rooting out and annihilating the "domestic enemy"—be it Communists, Jews, Social Democrats, or other undesirables. Needless to say, in an historical era whose signature would be concentration and death camps, whose barracks and crematoria were reserved for political and racial enemies of all stripes, theoretical recommendations of this nature quickly lose their innocence.

An admirer of the works of Jünger and the Soviet experiment in modernization from above, in the early 1930s Schmitt flirted with the notion of the "total state," according to which all domestic concerns must be subordinated to the primacy of foreign policy and, ultimately, preparation for war. The step from his authoritarian political doctrines of the 1920s to his active support of Hitler's dictatorship in the early 1930s (in addition to his many writings endorsing the new regime, Schmitt helped write crucial *Gleichschaltung* legislation during its initial months) was, to be sure, a short one.[39]

In Löwith's view the intellectual affinities between Heidegger's philosophical and Schmitt's political existentialism are far from fortuitous or uninteresting. As he expresses those affinities with characteristic discernment in "European Nihilism":

> It is no accident if Heidegger's existential ontology corresponds to a political "decisionism" in Carl Schmitt, a decisionism that shifts the "capacity-for-Being-a-whole" of the Dasein which is always on its own to the "totality" of the state which is always one's own. To the self-assertion of political existence, and to "freedom toward death" corresponds the "sacrifice of life" in the political exigency of war. In both cases the principle is the same, namely "facticity," i.e., what remains of life when one does away with all life-content.

The more one heeds Löwith's illuminating discussions of the intellectual mood pervading Germany in the late 1920s—a mood of *existential nihilism*, in which the pathos of resolute decision for its own sake appeared as an obligatory point of reference for philosophical and political discourse alike—the more one realizes that one is dealing with a profound and symptomatic generational phenomenon. Few analysts have better understood its import and ramifications than Karl Löwith.

VII

Though the question of the relationship between philosophy and politics in Heidegger's work has become extremely topical of late, Löwith's most enduring contribution to understanding his one-time mentor's intellectual legacy is undoubtedly contained in the powerful and brilliant essay, "Heidegger: Thinker in a Destitute Time." Since its initial appearance in 1953, this treatise has enjoyed the status of a minor classic: it went through three editions in Löwith's lifetime before being included in 1984 as the titular essay of volume 8 of his collected works.

The central theme of the essay concerns the change of perspective—some would call it an "epistemological break"—between the early and later Heidegger: the so-called *Kehre* or "Turn" in Heidegger's thought. Perhaps nowhere is this dramatic shift of focus more evident than in the specific terms Heidegger himself uses to describe his philosophical enterprise during these two phases: *Being and Time* is a study in "existential ontology," whereas he characterizes his later philosophical stance as that of "*Seinsgeschichte*" or the "history of Being."

At stake in this momentous metatheoretical transmutation of Heidegger's doctrines were far more than a few terminological subtleties. Instead, as Löwith was one of the first to discern, at issue was the viability of Heideggerianism as a mode of public discourse. For circa 1935, as Heidegger's own political radicalism began to wane, his mode of philosophical questioning underwent a process of radicalization that was permanent and profound. Whereas in his early work, Heidegger had engaged in an incessant and productive *dialogue* with the major representatives of the philosophical tradition (a fact to which the lecture courses from this period published in the *Gesamtausgabe* testify well), from this point hence, he began to treat the tradition in its entirety as a "*Verfallsphänomen*": as a phenomenon of degeneration and decay.

According to this new reading of the history of philosophy, Platonism, instead of being the foundation and guiding spirit of Western metaphysics, was viewed as its diabolical corruptor. With Plato there emerged the fatal ontological distinction between the "sensible" and "supersensible" realms, from which our historical understanding of Being has never recovered. Henceforth, the truth of Being would be conceived as "Idea," as "representation"—thus, as something subjective or proper to the "subjectum." This was a (mis)step that already foreshadowed the modern (i.e., from Descartes on) degeneration of philosophical contemplation to "calculative thinking." For Heidegger, calculative thinking or "reasoning" were merely the intellectual corollaries of the will to technological world-mastery that fundamentally characterizes the modern "world-picture"— an understanding of the world according to which Being (and beings) are merely grist for the purposes of scientific manipulation or control.[40]

There are several important consequences for Heidegger's later thought that result from this sweeping repudiation of the philosophical tradition—a repudiation that in many crucial respects prefigures Derrida's disparagement of the same tradition as "logocentric." For one, Heidegger's discourse loses its dialogical and argumentational character. Since he remains wedded to the firm conviction that the tradition in its entirety is contaminated by a type of progressively degenerative *Seinsverlassenheit*—"abandonment of and by Being"—there is little sense in engaging it in immanent or reasoned criticism. In fact, in his later texts, he becomes quite frank about his own abandonment of the standpoint of "philosophy" as such in favor of what he prefers to call "thought" or "*Denken*" (the etymological proximity between "thinking" and "thanking" [in German: "*denken*" and "*danken*"] is something he proceeds to make much of). According to this new reading of the history of Western thought, philosophy experienced a brief efflorescence with the Ionian Presocratics (Heraclitus, Parmenides, Anaximander, and so forth), in whose doctrines a fragile sense of the truth of Being qua "unconcealment" (*aletheia*) shone forth. But this approach to understanding the Being of beings was quickly covered up or "reconcealed" by onto-theologically inclined thinkers such as Plato and his descendants. Yet, as Löwith points out: "The other side of Heidegger's endeavor toward a reappropriation of the originary thinking and discourse of the Greeks is the disparagement and the elimination of the entire philosophical language and conceptual apparatus of the modern age."

Moreover, as part of his reevaluation of the status of philosophy in the history and course of Western Dasein, Heidegger would come to the conclusion that, given the unsavory parallels between metaphysics and the world-picture of modern technology ("*das Gestell*"), it has been *poets* rather than *philosophers* who have most faithfully given voice to the oblique ways in which Being "comes to presence." Thus, in the 1930s and 1940s, Heidegger would present significant lecture courses on the poetry of Friedrich Hölderlin in which he articulates the importance of poetry in the "setting-to-work of truth." His understanding of the historical mission of poetry could not be more removed from the aesthetic formalism of European modernism or of art for art's sake. Nor was it free of ideological taint. For Heidegger, it is the task of the poet to ground the historical existence of a people or Volk. He thus proclaims Hölderlin to be both the poet of "German destiny" and the "voice of the Volk."[41]

The philosophical perspective that Heidegger articulated in *Being and Time* was, neologisms and terminological difficulties notwithstanding, eminently wordly and practical. Even though in its author's eyes it remained only a partial success (the announced Part II on "Time and Being" was never written), it was a work that went far toward accomplishing the goal of reconciling the requirements of traditional philosophical inquiry with the demands of human practical life. It is far from accidental, therefore, that the thematic point of departure for Heidegger's landmark study are the multifarious world-relations of Dasein or human "Being-in-the-world."

However—and this is the basis for Löwith's incisive and powerful critique—in Heidegger's later thought, such worldly concerns become, at best, a dim and distant memory. He no longer speaks from the engaged standpoint of the this-wordly, practical involvements of human Dasein. Instead, his discourse proceeds from the hermetic standpoint of Being itself. It attempts to give voice to the mysterious "sendings of Being," a "*Seins-geschick.*" It seeks to articulate what is ineffable, that which defies the terms and requirements of meaningful public discourse. The history of Being is a story that can only be told via evocation and innuendo. Thus, in response to the question "What is Being?" in the "Letter on Humanism," Heidegger can only offer the feeble rejoinder: "It is It itself," "*transcendens* pure and simple"[42]—a self-identical, primordial substrate that resists the "logos," the philosophical method of providing coherent, intelligible accounts. Instead, with the later Heidegger, we are confronted with mandates and claims that possess the status of ex cathedra pronouncements, with positions that often defy the conventional terms of rational, intersubjective adjudication. The later Heidegger's "farewell to reason" is vividly expressed in his avowed conviction that, "Thinking begins only when we have come to know that *reason, glorified for centuries, is the most stiff-necked adversary of thought.*"[43]

As Löwith is quick to point out, the difficulty in reaching an intelligent verdict concerning the merit of Heidegger's approach "lies in following a thinking that fundamentally disapproves of arguments and a 'logical' development. . . . Instead of proof on the basis of demonstration and evidence, there are only cryptic 'gestures' and hints."[44]

Perhaps it is the tendency of Heideggerian "*Denken*" to lapse into a prophetic-oracular mode (a mode embodied in the oft-cited remark from the 1966 "Spiegel" interview, "Only a god can save us")[45] that moves Löwith to remark that it is a discourse that tends to provoke either fascination or repulsion; rarely, however, does it elicit the type of sober and considered evaluation that alone would be conducive to appraising its ultimate philosophical worth. The danger of a discursive mode such as

Heidegger's that depends on a "kind of Being that not only surpasses all beings (including humans) but, like an unknown God, lingers and 'essences' in its own truth," is that it risks forsaking the Kantian "bounds of sense" proper to the phenomenal world. And, as Kant knew long ago, it is solely via judgments proper to the sphere of immanent, non-noumenal knowledge that the distinction between sense and non-sense remains meaningful. Yet, as Heidegger observes in a portentous citation from Kierkegaard: "The time of distinctions is past."

In examining the cogency of Heidegger's later thought, the question of the relationship between philosophy and politics, broadly conceived, is never far removed. For at stake in the doctrine of the "history of Being" is an attitude toward history and the world that is anything but apolitical. For the later Heidegger remains essentially a philosopher of time and of historicity; as such, he is also *a philosopher of his time*, whose reflections on technology, world-politics, and history derive from his own factical historical situatedness. To the end, however, these reflections manifested an ambiguous character in which greatness and philosophical arrogance remained intertwined.

These are the reasons that his colleague and friend, Karl Jaspers, after much soul-searching, was forced to deliver a negative opinion as Heidegger's professional fate lay in the balance late in 1945. In Japsers' judgment, which was codified in a report to a Freiburg University denazification commission, Heidegger's manner of thinking was "in its essence unfree, dictatorial, and incapable of communication"; hence, to allow him to instruct German youth of the postwar period—who, after twelve years of totalitarian rule, remained intellectually "defenseless"—"would in its pedagogical effects be disastrous." "The youth of today," he continued, "must reach a point where they can think for themselves." Jaspers' recommendation was that Heidegger be denied emeritus status, which meant his effective ban from university life. Nevertheless, in view of Heidegger's considerable philosophical achievements ("In the torrent of his language he is occasionally able to strike the core of philosophical thought. In this regard, he is . . . perhaps unique among contemporary German philosophers"), Jaspers also proposes that Heidegger be granted a pension so that he might continue his philosophical work.

In Jaspers' estimation, with Heidegger, "the manner of thinking [was] more important than the content of political judgments." This "manner," Jaspers went on to observe, was "extraordinarily uncritical and at a remove from true science. [Heidegger] often proceeds as if he combined the seriousness of nihilism with the mystagogy of a magician. . . . His manner of speaking and his actions have a certain affinity with National Socialist characteristics which makes his error comprehensible."[46]

The conclusion to be drawn from the saga of Heidegger and politics is, needless to say, not that one should no longer read Heidegger. Instead, it is that one should no longer read him *naively*—that is, without careful attention to those aspects of his doctrines and philosophical habitus that facilitated his alliance with Nazis in the early 1930s. For one thing that the recent, contentious debates over the implications of Heidegger's Nazi past have taught us is that, in 1933, the philosopher himself believed there existed enduring affinities between his thought and the "inner truth and greatness" of the Nazi movement.

It is in this connection that Löwith's contributions prove so timely. As a Heidegger contemporary, student, and intimate, his reflections present a unique vantage point from which the complexities of Heidegger's case may be unraveled and illuminated. Without malice or prejudice, yet unflinchingly, he is able to expose those aspects of Heidegger's thought that were so inextricably related to the fateful *Zeitgeist* of the interwar period. Throughout Löwith's narrative it is not Heidegger's greatness as a thinker that is in dispute, but the uses to which that greatness allowed itself to be put. For his was a problematical greatness, one that remained wedded to the standpoint of an uncompromising and total critique of the modern world. And given his adoption of this standpoint—in Weberian parlance, that of an ethic of absolute ends (*"Gesinnungsethik"*) rather than an ethic of responsibility (*"Verantwortungsethik"*)—any means necessary proved justified in order to bring about the desired end of wholesale transvaluation of a degenerate historical present. With Heidegger's case we are presented with an exemplary parable concerning the perils of redemptory political paradigms. No one has better understood the ultimate implications and import of this parable than Karl Löwith.

Suggestions for Further Reading

Arendt, Hannah. "What is Existenz Philosophy?" *Partisan Review* 13, no. 1 (Winter 1946): 34—56.

Blumenberg, Hans. *The Legitimacy of the Modern Age*, tr. R. Wallace. Cambridge: MIT Press, 1983.

Farias, Victor. *Heidegger and Nazism*, eds. T. Rockmore and J. Margolis; trs. P. Burrell and G. Ricci. Philadelphia: Temple University Press, 1989.

Gadamer, Hans-Georg. "Karl Löwith," in *Philosophical Apprenticeships*. Cambridge: MIT Press, 1985.

Habermas, Jürgen. "Karl Löwith: Stoic Retreat from Historical Consciousness," in *Philosophical-Political Profiles*, tr. F. Lawrence. Cambridge: MIT Press, 1981.

Henrich, Dieter. "Sceptico Sereno," in *Natur und Geschichte: Karl Löwith zum 70. Geburtstag*. Stuttgart: Kohlhammer, 1967: 458—63.

Löwith, Karl. *From Hegel to Nietzsche: The Revolution in Nineteenth-Century Thought*, tr. David Green. New York: Columbia University Press, 1989.

Löwith, Karl. *Max Weber and Karl Marx*. London: Allen and Unwin, 1982.

Löwith, Karl. *Meaning in History*. Chicago: University of Chicago Press, 1949.

Löwith, Karl. *My Life in Germany Before and After 1933*. Champaign-Urbana: University of Illinois Press, 1994.

Löwith, Karl. *Nature, History, and Existentialism*, ed. A. Levinson. Evanston: Northwestern University Press, 1966.

Marcuse, Herbert. "The Struggle Against Liberalism in the Totalitarian Theory of the State," in *Negations: Essays in Critical Theory*, tr. J. Shapiro. Boston: Beacon Press, 1968.

Neske, Günther and Emil Kettering, eds. *Martin Heidegger and National Socialism*, tr. L. Harries. New York: Paragon House, 1990.

Ott, Hugo. *Martin Heidegger: A Political Life*, tr. Alan Blunden. New York: HarperCollins, 1993.

Riedel, Manfred. "Karl Löwiths Philosophischer Weg." *Heidelberger Jahrbuch* 14 (1970): 120—133.

Ries, Wiebrecht. *Karl Löwith*. Stuttgart: Metzler, 1992.

Riesterer, B. P. *Karl Löwith's View of History*. The Hague: Martinus Nijhoff, 1969.

Rockmore, Tom. *On Heidegger's Nazism and Philosophy*. Berkeley: University of California Press, 1992.

Rockmore, Tom and Joseph Margolis. *The Heidegger Case*. Philadelphia: Temple University Press, 1992

Sluga, Hans. *Heidegger's Crisis*. Cambridge: Harvard University Press, 1993.

Wallace, Robert. "Progress, Secularization and Modernity: the Löwith-Blumenberg Debate," *New German Critique* 22 (1981): 63—79.

Wolin, Richard. *The Heidegger Controversy: A Critical Reader*. Cambridge: MIT Press, 1993.

Wolin, Richard. *The Politics of Being: The Political Thought of Martin Heidegger*. New York: Columbia University Press, 1990.

Wolin, Richard. "Carl Schmitt, Political Existentialism, and the Total State," in *The Terms of Cultural Criticism*. New York: Columbia University Press, 1992.

Zimmerman, Michael. *Heidegger's Confrontation with Modernity*. Bloomington: Indiana University Press, 1990.

ONE

Heidegger: Thinker in a Destitute Time

Preface to the Second Edition

> Stranger: "Let us then examine one who seems to imitate the truth as we examine a piece of iron, when we see if it is a seamless whole or if instead it has a flaw in it." — Plato, *Sophist* 267e

I believe that I am not deceiving myself in assuming that the first publication (1953) of this critical assessment fulfilled its intention to the extent that it helped to break a spell of awkward silence and sterile repetition that had encumbered a group of adherents. Nonetheless, since that time a penetrating examination at Heidegger's request of the question concerning the relationship of human *Dasein* to *Being* and of *Being* to *time* has hardly been conducted.[a] In connection with such an examination, today's historically existing human beings lack any experience of Being as everlasting and living, of Being as remaining the same throughout the changes in its appearances. It is the enigmatic and manifest timeliness of Heidegger's thinking that secures for it a widespread impact in spite of all its apparent eccentricity. Nonetheless its radical challenge, which goes to the very limit of the European tradition and calls that tradition's rationality into question as a history of decline, remained without an appropriate response.

Similarly, this essay aroused both annoyance and agreement, but it received no critical opposition; hence there was also no occasion for its fundamental revision, with the exception that an untenable paragraph on

---

[a]Translator's note: In the following, *Sein* has been translated as "Being" and *Seiendes* as "being" (or "beings," as the context requires). When *seiend* is employed as an adjective, it has generally been translated as "extant."

p. 41 of the first edition was eliminated.[b] Naturally, however, in relevant places consideration has been made of those publications of Heidegger's which have appeared since 1953. As a conclusion, a lecture written for the thinker's seventieth birthday was added, which says of his own thinking that it corresponds to the "behest of Being" [*Geheiß des Seins*] which comes primordially to words only in the Greek and German languages.

"One repays a teacher poorly if one always remains only a pupil. And why don't you want to pluck at my wreath? You venerate me; but what happens if one day your veneration founders?"[1]

Heidelberg, Spring 1960

---

[b]Translator's note: The deleted paragraph to which Löwith refers here is included in translator's note, p. 67.

1 | Dasein Resolute Unto Itself, and Being Which Itself Gives

The following reflections, which concern Heidegger's path from *Being and Time* (1927) to the "Letter on Humanism" (1947) and the lectures from the years 1935 to 1946 gathered under the title *Holzwege* (1950), have the aim of discussing the question whether Heidegger's later talk of "Being" and finally of "event" [*Ereignis*] is the consequence of his point of departure or the result of a reversal. This question would be insignificant if it concerned nothing more than Heidegger's spiritual development. Why shouldn't a philosopher learn and rethink during the course of his life and write new prefaces or afterwords to his earlier works? But if we may assume that the second part of *Being and Time*, which was never completed, is de facto present in important fragments in all the later writings, then a critical discussion of these writings in relation to *Being and Time* changes from a biographical detail into a main philosophical theme that concerns nothing less than the question regarding the grounding of human Dasein: either on the basis of its own, "authentic" being, or on the basis of "Being" which is wholly other and which from out of itself "eventuates" [*ereignet*] the Dasein of human nature.

An expression of Rilke's from early in the First World War could be a motto for Heidegger's point of departure. Rilke writes on November 8, 1915, that it all depends on remembering, in the face of the pulmonary circulation of a world absorbed with itself and bent on progress, that the modern "trial of existence" is definitely overtaken from the start "by death and by God," so that at the end of progress and on the ground of our pyramid of consciousness "simple Being" could become like the "event" (letter, August 11, 1924). Heidegger characterized death, which overtakes and "over-knows" us from the beginning, precisely as Rilke did; of course, in *Being and Time* the talk is not of God. Heidegger had been too much of a theologian to be able to keep telling stories, like Rilke did, about loving God. "Whoever has experienced theology . . . on the basis of a developed heritage, prefers today to remain silent about God within the realm of thinking."

This is not contradicted by Heidegger's confession that without his theological heritage he never would have arrived on the path of thinking,[1] and that heritage always remains the future as well. Just as certainly as Heidegger's talk of "Being" does not evoke a Christian God, this talk does indeed point toward the realm of "healing" [*des* "*Heilen*"] and the "holy" ["*Heiligen*"], in terms of which God and gods are again to become thinkable.[a] Indeed the distinction of this age consists in the "closing off of the dimension of healing" ("Letter on Humanism"), whereas twenty years earlier, in *Being and Time*, the anticipation of one's own death and nothing else appeared to be the "highest instance" of an authentic existence.

We are involved in the attempt to call Heidegger into question, and we are doing so along with Heidegger rather than by criticizing him from the outside; nonetheless we are not doing so within the dimension that Heidegger invokes as the only essential one, though of course with this we do not want to say that we could move freely within that dimension if only we wanted to. Pupils who are more willing and more indentured, those who make pilgrimages from "Notschrei" (in the Black Forest) to the hut of the wise one,[b] have for a long time been engaged in parroting the master and speaking of "Seyn" as if they were his megaphone.[c2] The language

---

[a]Translator's note: The neologism *das Heile* admits of no direct English equivalent; it resonates with the notions of salvation, healing, wholeness, and well-being. In general I follow the translator of the "Letter on Humanism" in translating this term as "healing," though in some instances I have found it necessary to translate it as "that which heals." *Heillos* has been translated as "without healing" or "unhealed," as the context requires.

[b]Translator's note: Löwith is referring here to the tiny Black Forest ski hut, located in Todtnauberg in the mountains a short distance from Freiburg, in which Heidegger spent a great deal of time and in which he wrote *Being and Time*; this hut was also the site of part of the 1966 *Spiegel* interview.

[c]Translator's note: Heidegger employs the term *Seyn*, an archaic form of the term *Sein*, in "On the Essence of Truth" to signify "the distinction which holds sway between Being and beings."

of existentialism has found, especially through Sartre, a generally intelligible echo in the domains of hut-dwellers; and esoteric circles, for which the incarnate God of George's[d] New Reich has been lost with the Third Reich, stammer ecstatically about Da-Sein, in which Being projects a clearing for itself.[3] Others, who still believe in the knowing of the positive sciences, react instead with aversion to this new mysticism, which is reminiscent of Eckhart and to which—according to Heidegger's own account—" the most extreme acuteness and depth of thinking belongs." Genuine opponents, those who are not simply against Heidegger but rather could treat him as an adversary, can scarcely be found in the philosophical efforts of the most recent decades.

These two extreme reactions of fascination and repulsion bear witness, following a hint of Heidegger's in the "Letter on Humanism," that in its ethos "something un-canny" comes to presence.[4] In accordance with his idea of truth as a happening of truth, Heidegger is aware that the "setting-itself-into-work of truth," which is at stake for him, pushes forth the "uncanny" and overturns the seemingly canny.[5] At the beginning of Heidegger's influence, immediately after the First World War, it was in particular the will to overthrow or to "destruction" that attracted his hearers in a liberating way. Now, after the Second World War, when little remains to be toppled, it may be in particular the pushing open of a door to the concealed "truth" of healing Being that captivates.

Between the two extremes of fascination and repulsion, we are attempting to pursue a critical middle path. This is the path of common sense that Heidegger, by appealing to Hegel, attacks at every opportunity. But even Hegel did not simply place common sense on trial; instead, he also acknowledged that it is an outward sign of the truth of philosophical speculation that its results agree with the presuppositions of common sense. Let us make the attempt, within the bounds of intelligibility, to start a discussion of Heidegger's unique monologue with the Western philosophical tradition by proceeding from the point of departure specified at the outset. In order to do so it is unavoidable to move within the magic circle of Heidegger's language, though this does not mean that we must succumb to that magic.

An obstacle immediately places itself in the way of this, namely the

[d]Translator's note: In the days following January 30, 1933, the date on which Hitler was sworn in as chancellor by Hindenburg, the German poet Stefan George (1868–1933) was celebrated in a variety of publications as Germany's poet laureate. The last collection of his poetry to be published in his lifetime was entitled *Das neue Reich* (The New Reich).

difficulty of understanding Heidegger. This is not to say that it is not easy to follow step by step the presuppositions, consequences, and interruptions of an unusual train of ideas; rather, the special difficulty lies in following thinking that fundamentally disapproves of arguments and a "logical" development (in the sense of a consistent progression) in such a way that we avoid dealing with the same theme in ever newer variations. In Heidegger's later writings what corresponds to this is the confusing multiplicity of changing formulations for one and the same thing. Just as it is said of the "lighting middle" of Being that it, precisely like the Nothing, encircles all beings,[6] Heidegger for his own part encircles a lost middle; indeed he does so in a polemical countermove against what is supposedly the fundamental tendency of Western metaphysics, which in a forgetting of Being from Plato to Nietzsche increasingly revolves around the eccentric subjectivity of human beings to the point of completion and demise in the metaphysics of scientific technology and the language of "enframing."

In contrast to *Being and Time*, whose systematic structure is admittedly remarkably erratic, in his later publications Heidegger abandons not only systematic progress but also protracted demonstration. Here, instead of proof on the basis of demonstration and evidence, there are only cryptic "gestures" and hints. But the strength of spirit, Hegel tells us, is only as great as its expression, and spirit's depth is only as deep as it ventures to propagate and lose itself in its interpretation. The idea of a scientific philosophy as a "universal phenomenological ontology,"[7] which is presented programmatically in *Being and Time*, no longer provides guidance. The matter at stake, if one could still refer to it in this way, is no longer developed phenomenologically, but is instead expressed, stated thoughtlessly, and in the final analysis "passed over in silence" because it is no longer capable of expression.

But nonetheless, this Scholastic striving after a "saying non-saying" is far removed from any pure meditative reticence. The increasingly exclusive expectation and thinking of Being, which is said to "command" us to think, to "need" us,[8] and to wait for us, and whose "arrival" Heidegger designates as the "sole matter" (not of hope and faith, but of thinking),[9] explains this abandoning of phenomenological demonstration. The kind of Being that not only surpasses all beings (including humans) but like an unknown God lingers and "essences" [*west*] in its own truth by presencing and absencing—such Being cannot be explicated as a being and in terms of beings, but rather can only be evoked. Accordingly, Heidegger's thinking about Being changes directly into a "remembrance," and both of these change into a "thinking."[10] But the essence of thinking "and hence" of thanking is "noble-mindedness," in which thinking itself gives thanks to Being.[11] "The thinker says Being. The poet names the holy."[12] Both move within the element of "saying."[13]

This "that which is essential," namely that essentially religious thinking (though it is not attuned to Christianity) which is involved in seeking something which supports and binds it, wants to be neither philosophy nor theology. Already with Plato and Aristotle philosophy begins to succumb to a technological interpretation of thinking, in the attempt to explain everything on the basis of a highest cause, i.e., in a fundamental way; and traditional theology is not a theology of faith, but rather is derived from onto-theological thinking.

Essential thinking, which Heidegger claims for himself by endeavoring to hear the claim of Being, is neither theory, nor love of wisdom, nor absolute knowing, nor least of all scientific research and mere historical erudition. According to Heidegger's own statement, his "prospective thinking" of the arrival of Being has not yet found the abode proper to it; as a result this thinking is forced to proceed within traditional philosophy and science, though "to think in the midst of the sciences" means "to pass them by."[14] The "fall of thinking into science and faith" is the terrible destiny of Being.[15]

Fortunately, thanks to his extraordinary acquaintance with the entire philosophical tradition and his theological schooling, Heidegger is able to manage such a renunciation without having thereby to appeal to a mere "experience" of Being. Thinking itself is this experience. More obligatory than the rigor of science is the play of thinking and of language. Not unlike the sparse poetry of the modern poets, this thinking, wholly immersed in language, is "in a decline into the poverty of its provisional essence" and therefore gathers language into simple saying.[16] Of course its relationship to poetic naming of the holy is everywhere perceptible, though it remains just as undefinable as the philosophical results of Heidegger's interpretations of Hölderlin, which are as subtle as they are original.[17] It is not generally to be decided whether Heidegger composes poetry poetically or whether he thinks poetically, however much he may solidify a kind of thinking whose associations have loosened. The unheard claim of this thinking consists in its placing the entire history of Western philosophy on the scales, together with its prospect of helping an approaching turn in world history to come to language through the memory of the "originary," presocratic essence of truth.

Hegel, it was said in a lecture, was entirely right if he knew philosophy to be at its end; what came to an end in Hegel, however, was nothing more than a Greek beginning whose possibilities he could not exhaust, because in his dialectical circles he did not get back to the primordial center. At the same time Kierkegaard, who in *Being and Time* was acknowledged to have "grasped explicitly and thought through impressively" the problem of existence as an existentiell (if not as an existential-ontological) one,[18] is swept aside with two words in *Holzwege* because he is not a *thinker* but rather a "religious writer."[19] On the other hand Nietzsche, who for the young Heidegger was entirely inessential, counts as a great metaphysical thinker on the order of Aristotle and Plato. Nonetheless, what remains guiding in everything that Heidegger thinks and says is a motto from Kierkegaard: "The time of distinctions [*Distinktionen*] is past." The distinctions which Heidegger leaves behind are the traditional distinctions [*Unterscheidungen*] of the philosophical disciplines, e.g., physics, ethics, and logic.

Even the traditional distinction between thinking and acting is inessential; thinking itself is already action, and one can better experience what ethics is from Sophocles or from three words of Heraclitus than from the lectures of Aristotle. Only one single distinction is essential, namely that between Being and all beings. The time of distinctions is "past" because now, in this world-historical moment following the end of an epoch, what is at stake is once again beings as a whole, the whole existence that is always one's own, and Being as a whole and as such, whose "there" or dwelling-place is the ek-sistent human being.[20]

This is why Heidegger in principle always says one and the same thing and, albeit in a complicated way, something simple. This one, simple something of being and of Dasein is named and modified in a number of ways, by means of a sort of chemistry that has its origins in the school of Scholasticism and that is permeated by modern historical consciousness. Being is simply "it itself"; but it is also that which is open, that which clears, and that which heals. It is also that which sends and eventuates, that which temporally presences and prospectively arrives; it is a kind of advent. That which in a distinctive sense "is," is what announces itself in the world-historical moment of a "world need."[21] That which is one and essential is the One which is needful [*was not tut*], and it is solely on the basis of this need that Heidegger also grounds the "necessity" of his thinking.

The fascination with Heidegger's thinking is based primarily on this religious undertone of an epochal and eschatological consciousness. In fact he thinks *Being* on the basis of *time*, as a thinker "in a destitute time" whose destitution consists (according to his interpretation of Hölderlin) in its standing under a twofold lack: "in the no-longer of the gods who have fled, and in the not-yet of the one to come."[22] How distant is this eschatological-historical thinking, for which everything counts merely as seed-sowing and preparation for an arriving future, from the originary wisdom of the Greeks, for whom the history of time was philosophically insignificant because they directed their view toward eternal beings and beings-which-are-thus-and-not-different rather than toward what is in each case accidental, which could also be otherwise.

Heidegger says what he has to say with mastery and a moving profundity that is closely related to sophistry. Only occasionally (especially in the "Letter on Humanism," which is a single protest against the misunderstandings of those contemporaries who have abandoned Being) do false sounds of a subjectivity that is not completed interrupt the far-reaching course of his passionate investigation. This investigation seeks the One, that which is needful, that which heals and is a home for human Dasein, which has become without healing and homeless. The distinctive medium in which it seeks what is whole, is thinking and saying and hence language. And since Heidegger no longer understands language as he had in *Being and Time* (namely as the articulation of the intelligibility of our Being-in-the-world) but beyond this and above all as the "house of Being,"[23] his own dwelling in language becomes, more than in any other philosophy, the distinguishing characteristic of the proximity he claims to the truth of Being and to the Being of truth. He is far removed from the Socratic ponderings of the *Cratylus*.

In order to be able to satisfy fully the claim of Being, his apodictic linguistic thinking must in fact be an inspired language of revelation and a thinking that follows the dictate of Being. Just as Christian revelation of God's will points to an attentive and obedient will on the part of the faithful human, Heidegger's own claim to Being-addressed remains ambiguous. The uncontrollable gift of linguistic inspiration is united with a technologically completed art of linguistic formulation. The former may rest upon itself, while the latter cannot evade criticism.

The reproach which has already been issued from other quarters against Heidegger's linguistic art remains justified.[24] Heidegger builds his bridges of thought across long stretches with "basic words" and with word roots and their variations. For example, there is the derivation of the primordial meaning of truth from "war" as taking care of or protecting (perceiving, preserving, safeguarding),[e25] or the "essential" definition of technology as "enframing," derived from positing as representing, producing, and ordering.[f] Being "shocks" itself out of its truth into the "most squalid" essence of enframing and hence is itself that which posits. Where the transition from a basic or root word to its variations is not arbitrary, Heidegger's linguistic figures derive either from poetic possibilities of allusion or from an etymological dictionary and thus are subject to the question whether they are scientifically correct and capable of substantiation.

Certainly one would have to be a pedant to want to take umbrage when on occasion a thinker, by means of linguistic association, places the intended meaning of a word in a new and striking light, even if the connection he produces has no etymological justification. For instance, Hegel speaks of "opinion" [*Meinen*] and draws out of it the possessive pronoun [*mein*] in order thereby to bring to expression the subjectivity of mere opinion and hence to make clear that what is opined in a mere opinion is always in each case simply what I opine and contains no general truth. And yet it is something else when a thinker consistently and fundamentally claims that he is, in his own linguistic art, keeping intact and taking care of "the word of Being" and that he is thereby speaking the "language of destiny."

In spite of all care for words, it is often the case that the connections Heidegger establishes simply cajole rather than convince and in the most favorable case are [merely] probable. Thinking is connected with thanking; *ratio* with mere calculation and correctness with mere calculability; history [*Geschichte*] with destining [*Geschick*] and the latter with propriety [*Schicklichkeit*];[g] resoluteness [*Entschlossenheit*] with disclosedness [*Erschlossenheit*]; the "there is" [*es gibt*] (Being) with the gift of self-giving [*Sichgebens*];[26] love as "wanting" [*mögen*] with being capable [*vermögen*] as that which is authentically "possible" [*Mög-lichen*], on the basis of which

---

[e]Translator's note: The etymological connection between *Wahrheit* (truth) and the Middle High German *war* and the Old High German *wara* is lost in translation here; both of these terms signify attentiveness, and the latter is related to the Old High German term *biwaron*, which means to protect. Also lost in translation is the connection between *Wahrheit* and *in die Wahrnis nehmen* (translated as "protecting"), *wahrnehmen* (perceiving), *bewahren* (preserving), and *verwahren* (safeguarding). Löwith is alluding here to the fact that Heidegger is often at pains to relate truth not only to perceiving or disclosing but also to safekeeping. See also note 25.

[f]Translator's note: Again, the etymological connections have been obscured through translation. Heidegger's definition of technology as "Gestell" (enframing) relates it etymologically to the verbs *stellen* (to pose, place, set, or posit), *vorstellen* (to present or represent), *herstellen* (to produce or put here), and *bestellen* (to order or put in order).

[g]Translator's note: The terms *Geschick* and *Schicklichkeit* are related to the term *schicken*, which means to send. Heidegger is continually at pains to distinguish *Geschick* from *Schicksal*, which is typically translated as "fate."

Being is capable of thinking, so that at the end of these derivations Being, as "that which is capable and which wants" [*das Vermögend-Mögende*] is "that which is possible" [*das Mög-liche*]!^h27 As "that-which-regions" [*Gegnet*], the region [*Gegend*] becomes the concealed essence of truth, and the thinking of the truth of Being is "releasement toward that-which-regions" because the essence of thinking rests in the "regioning [*Vergegnis*] of releasement"!28

If one wanted to ask Heidegger whether this makes the matter clearer, he would give us the answer: "No, nothing is clear; but everything is significant!" Of course neither the subject matter nor the word makes it clear why, for example, correctness [*Richtigkeit*] could not be brought into an essential meaning-connection with justice [*Gerechtigkeit*] rather than with reckoning [*Berechnung*], and why *Wahrheit* could not be brought into such a connection with the English word "truth" (= "trust") or with "trow" (loyalty [*Treue*], to trust [*trauen, vertrauen*], to believe) rather than with the Greek word *a-letheia* (un-concealedness) or the Old German "war."^i The increasingly emerging tendency to let language not only speak for us but think for us as well unites itself in Heidegger with the opposed tendency to exploit in a deliberate way nothing but German possibilities of word construction, on account of which he is untranslatable. A Pentecost miracle would have to occur in order that his definition of the love of Being, or perhaps of the essence of technology as representable, producible, and orderable enframing, should become capable of being said in English.29

That which in Heidegger's language touches one as captivating profundity will strike another as wordplay, and this all the more as genuinely found words and merely invented ones get formulated with the same deadly seriousness. Heidegger's language is, as he himself says along with Hölderlin, "the most innocent of all affairs," a glass bead game with words, and at the same time "the most dangerous of goods."30 Its danger is that it is insidious and hence that it encumbers more than it liberates.

---

^h Translator's note: The German verb *mögen* has several meanings of relevance to the present remarks. As a modal auxiliary verb, it means "may" or "might," as when we say that something "may" or "may not" be the case; and it means to want or like. The hyphenated *das Mög-liche* at the end of the passage is a variation of the term *möglich*, which means "possible"; the hyphenation connects the notion of possibility with the notion of wanting or liking, as well as with the notion of capability or capacity (*vermögen*) discussed in the passage.

^i Translator's note: The Middle German *trouwe* and *trowe* are etymologically related to the Old High German and Middle High German *triuwe* and *triwe*, which signify trust or faith in someone (*Treue*), reliability, sincerity, and the quality of being well-intentioned.

The inner contradiction in Heidegger's language, namely that it is at once invention and discovery, characterizes his whole standpoint as an overcoming of the schism between rebelliousness and releasement, between challenging forth and restraint, between attack and being overcome with emotion, between wilfullness and sacrificing one's will, between reserve and resoluteness.

This schism manifests itself in the *one* concept of resolve and its later reformulation into re-solve as opening oneself for the Open.[31] In *Being and Time*, whose young readers were resolute without knowing what they were resolute about before the common story of "the anyone" [*das Man*] gave them content for their resoluteness, resolve is the fundamental attunement and the fundamental definition of an authentic Being-a-self in contrast to "Being-anyone." That to which one resolves oneself remains intentionally undefined in *Being and Time*, since this is first determined in the very resolution, which is a projecting upon factical possibilities. In resolve what is at stake for Dasein is its ownmost capacity-for-Being. Nonetheless this capacity is delimited by the certain imminence of death, by this end of all capacity, which means that the existentially understood future of that death which approaches us "closes" the capacity-for-Being and precisely through this makes possible an understanding of one's own nullity in which one resolutely comes back to oneself.

Of course in *Being and Time* resolve is at the same time a kind of disclosedness, though not as openness to Being but rather in relation to one's own Dasein and one's particular situation. After *Being and Time* the freedom of the self is no longer defined as the freedom of a *capacity-for*-Being but rather is defined as that of a *letting*-Be, and resolute conduct is accordingly recast as a "not-closing-oneself-off."[32] Now resolve is no longer supposed to be a decisive, resolute kind of conduct but rather the opening up of Dasein out of its predilection for beings and into the openness of Being. Resolve is now an opening-oneself-up-to the open, the unconcealed, that which is true in Being, in which all beings gain standing. It might be difficult to recognize anew in this receptivity to the dimension of Being the earlier resolve toward oneself.

Nobody will dispute that in spite of such linguistic art Heidegger, in dense trains of thought, succeeds in saying something essential in a consummate way. Through an energetic and persistent return to the "things" [*Sachen*] and the leap back to the primordial, he succeeded in infusing new life into the history of Western thinking, in summoning once again the exhausted naming power of traditional concepts, and in liberating, by means of the German language, basic words of Greek thinking (*aletheia, ousia, idea, logos, physis*) from a centuries-old habit of translation and toward their archaic meaning. Nonetheless, no classical philologist will be able to concur with his violent interpretation of the adage of Anaximander, an adage which becomes thoroughly obscured in Heidegger's Germanization, no matter what Heidegger may present as a justification for his violence.[33]

The other side of Heidegger's endeavor toward a reappropriation of the originary thinking and discourse of the Greeks is the disparagement and the elimination of the entire philosophical language and conceptual apparatus of the modern age. On the strength of a dogmatic distinction between authentic and inauthentic, existential and common, primordial and derivative, abiding beginning and transitory today, Heidegger managed to give a generation of students new measures and to persuade them that "logic" and "reason" must dissolve in the "whirl of a more primordial questioning";[34] that ethics, culture, and humanity, which for a long time we have only been writing in quotation marks anyway, are not a serious concern;[35] that human beings are not "rational animals" but rather ecstatic "shepherds of Being"(338/211); that all theoretical representing and technological producing, in which scientific thinking is grounded, is a decline of subjectivity to the objectivity [*Objektivität*] which corresponds to it and a decline to unconditioned objectification [*Vergegenständlichung*] (315/197).

And since according to Heidegger this fall of reification (Marx) and the fate of rationalization (Max Weber) already begins with Plato's subjugation of originary truth to the yoke of the "idea" and the viewpoint of ideas, he does not hesitate to maintain along with Gottfried Benn that "the fundamental movement of the history of the West" is nihilism,[36] which in the current world-historical moment takes shape according to the domination of the will to power as modern scientific technology.[j] This process is in no way brought about by human beings but is instead dispatched by Being—it is a "destining of Being [*Seinsgeschick*]."[37]

At the horizon of this ineluctable destiny and its greatest danger there surfaces the hope, which is not substantiated any further and which refers to Hölderlin's hymn "Patmos," that where danger is, that which saves [*das Rettende*] grows as well.[38] On this "path into the next epoch," before Being can eventuate itself in its originary truth, "Being in the sense of the will [must] be crushed, the world [must] be forced to collapse and the earth

[j]Translator's note: Gottfried Benn (1886–1956) was a German poet and critic who described the time period following the German defeat in 1918 as "postnihilistic" and who saw in the Third Reich the potential for realizing what he called an "absolute aesthetic."

forced to devastation, and human beings [must] be forced into mere labor."³⁹ What the "teacher" (in the "Conversation on a Country Path") really wants is "non-willing."⁴⁰

But how is that "which saves" supposed to be able to grow, if everything that has grown in the age of "enframing" gets replaced by what has been produced, and how is one supposed to be able to get through and endure full of hope the technological "constellation"⁴¹ of humans and Being as a mere "prelude" to the originary event, if at the same time it is prophesied that the demise of metaphysics and therewith the technological age will take longer than the whole prior history of metaphysics of two-and-a-half millennia? Is it more than wishful thinking when Heidegger, in a spirit of releasement, formulates the all too simple compromise that we must say Yes as well as No to technology, and that in the end a "new rootedness" could again emerge from these workings?⁴² Here the difficulty apparently lies not in language but rather in the matter: that a thinking of Being that is fundamentally oriented on the destining of time and not on what is at all times true, is by no means a thinking in the sense of a critical desire to know but rather corresponds at best to the "depth of world-shaking,"⁴³ where "world" nonetheless means only our human world.

What kind of experience underlies such thinking? What is the measure for this one-track construction of the history of the completion and demise of metaphysics and the whole Western tradition? What experience justifies the "destruction" of the history of Western philosophy,⁴⁴ its dismantling to the point of exposing its foundations, and beyond this the undermining of metaphysics as such, which itself, a *lucus a non lucendo*, is supposed to have forgotten not just the beingness of beings but Being from Plato to Nietzsche? To these questions only a specific discussion of Heidegger's historical self-consciousness can give an answer. Next we shall attempt to present his "turning" and the logic peculiar to it.⁴⁵

Philosophers who give measure have always been recognizable in virtue of finding the decisive word for their decisive ideas. The *Discourse on Method*, *Critique of Pure Reason*, *Phenomenology of Spirit*, *The World as Will and Representation*, and *The Will to Power* all describe in an incomparable manner what they want to show. With *Being and Time*, Heidegger found an outstanding title for his ideas. He does in fact think Being on the basis of time—on the basis of time as ours and as approaching us.⁴⁶ A different title, whose meaning surely betrays the interpretation which has been given, is *Holzwege*.ᵏ This title indicates first of all that Heidegger is entirely on the way, as he was already in *Being and Time*; occasionally he is also on "field paths" ["*Feldwegen*"], on which the native sound of Christian bells reverberates.[47] What he seeks along these paths is an answer to the "meaning of Being," which is left as a question in *Being and Time*. The talk is no longer of "meaning," which was made abstract in *Being and Time* as the "towards-which of a projecting."[48] In its place comes "truth" as the openness of a realm of projection. Meaning and meaninglessness are there only for a human Dasein. Being is neither meaningful nor meaningless. It "is" in that it "essences"; it can be present and absent, manifest and concealed, and it conceals itself and withdraws precisely when it reveals itself in a being.

This continually named Being is no mere way of Being, like human "existing" or the "Being-ready-to-hand" of a table or the "Being-present-at-hand" of a stone; it is precisely not an object which one could represent and produce; it is also not an idea, but rather—thought in terms of beings—the ultimate being [*das Allerseiendste*] and yet in itself just as unbeing and ungraspable and at the same time as present as time, which of course is also more a Nothing than a being. Nonetheless in a certain way Being is accessible—on woodpaths. It is said that woodpaths are paths that are overgrown because they are seldom trodden, and that they end abruptly in the untrodden. One can become lost on them. But they themselves always run their course within one and the same forest—that of the one and the same Being. "Woodworkers and forest keepers know the paths. They know what it means to be on a woodpath."[49]

The "forest keeper" reminds us of a "shepherd" and "guardian" of Being (in the "Letter on Humanism") who is at the same time the "place holder for the Nothing."[50] Like the shepherd, the "forest keeper" is the human being in its ek-sistent relation to Being, which for its own part is related to the human being.[51] It is not said explicitly what this keeper of the forest knows, and yet it can be guessed. Presumably he knows that he can go utterly astray in this forest of the truth of Being, "this sole matter of thinking." He can be broken by it and founder in connection with it. Of course woodpaths usually do not lead into the open and the illuminated, i.e., into the true.

Yet foundering in connection with the truth of Being and the Being of

---

[k] Translator's note: In 1950, Klostermann first published under the title *Holzwege* a collection of six essays written by Heidegger between 1935 and 1946: "The Origin of the Work of Art," "The Age of the World Picture," "Hegel's Concept of Experience," "Nietzsche's Word 'God is Dead,'" "What Are Poets For?" and "The Adage of Anaximander." The word *Holzwege* literally means "woodpaths," and Heidegger explains on a page immediately following the copyright page of *Holzwege* that this title is meant to signify paths of thought that do not lead to final destinations—what is at stake is not the endpoint but rather the path of thinking itself.

truth would not be a misfortune, but rather would be "the sole gift which could approach thinking from out of Being,"[52] just as the "breaking apart of the word" is the "most authentic step back" on the paths of thinking. But neither was the right kind of foundering successful, and Heidegger is sparingly vocal and is silent on the way [*unterwegs*] into the neighborhood of Being.[1] To be "on the way" belongs to the essential character and pathos of Heidegger's philosophical existence as a historically experienced existence. Thinking itself is a path to which we correspond by remaining on the way instead of positioning ourselves as viewers of the path and historically comparing the paths which others have trodden.

If nonetheless human Dasein and Being itself were not conceived from the start as temporal and historical, then the pathos of Being-on-the-way would lose its soil and ground; for why should a permanent Being-on-the-way to something distant and in the future be the right path to a lasting reflection on Being which is always the same? And so it is said already at the end of *Being and Time* that it remains to seek and to travel a path to the illumination of the question of Being;[53] whether it is the sole path and at all the right one, is to be capable of determination only after the trip. *Being and Time* is on the way, and Heidegger is still on the path, to an interpretation of Being.

Of course today he would no longer speak of an "interpretation" of Being, nor of an "understanding of Being" and least of all of a "science" of Being as such, of "its possibilities and variations." In fact no one will be able to maintain that he consciously understood what Being is, this mystery, about which Heidegger speaks. "The complete loss of the naming power of the word Being," which already Hegel brought about, to conceive of Being (= Nothing) as the "undetermined immediate" is also the catastrophe of Heidegger's saying of Being,[54] which was able generally to address his contemporaries only by means of the analytic of the Dasein which is always one's own. First of all it will be understood by faithful ones who mean to find in Heidegger's ontological talk of "revelation" and "unconcealment" access to the Christian revelation of a likewise nonextant God and who as faithful ones of course do not pretend to gain insight into the God of revelation by way of the understanding. They trust Him and listen to Him, without ever having seen Him as a being; they think of

---

[1] Translator's note: Here the etymological connection between *Weg* (path) and *unterwegs* (on the way) has been lost in translation; *Weg* has been translated as "path" rather than as its English cognate "way" for stylistic reasons. The reader should bear in mind that in the present context the term *unterwegs* brings with it the association of being in the midst of walking a path as well as the more general association of being on the way toward something.

Him, and they thank Him and experience His presence at work. In this way "remembrance" seems to encounter worship and prayer.

The unremitting perisistence with which Heidegger has pursued Being from *Being and Time* until today is unequivocal.⁵⁵ Indeed according to him the destiny of the West and with it the whole "earth" depends on the question of Being and on the translation [*Übersetzung*] of the Greek word for "to be," on the trans-position [*Über-setzen*]ᵐ to the truth of Being.⁵⁶ This is why he appears justified in protecting himself against the "anthropological" misunderstandings of *Being and Time* and in insisting on the seamless unity of his endeavor. "It is everywhere the opinion that the attempt in *Being and Time* wound up in a dead end. Let us leave this opinion alone. Even today the thinking which attempts a few steps in *Being and Time* has not gone any further than in that text. But perhaps in some respects it has made a start into its subject matter instead."⁵⁷

But of course the path that Heidegger takes has not remained the same, for when a path is trodden it gets defined by its direction, and this direction turned around after *Being and Time*. Inasmuch as Heidegger lets the "*condition humaine*," which is thought out by Pascal and Kierkegaard, be borne and determined henceforth by the "history of Being," the existentialia of *Being and Time* are by no means given up but are recast, rethought, and reversed in relation to the primordial meaning of their direction. Let us elucidate this by taking several concepts as examples. For this we select the relation between **existing Dasein** and **Being**, between the **projection of Dasein** [*Daseinsentwurf*] and the **throwing** [*Wurf*] **of Being**, between **existential facticity** and the **"there is"** Being, between **existential truth** and the **truth of Being**, between **finitude** and **eternity**; and finally the changed meaning of **fundamental ontology**, which bears all the existentialia.

In the end it was no mere misunderstanding when so many hearers of Heidegger's lectures and readers of *Being and Time* understood the author differently at that time than he understands himself today, namely as the author, attuned by Kierkegaard, Pascal, Luther, and Augustine, of a faithless "analytic of Dasein," and not as an initiate of Being who, supposedly already in *Being and Time*, left behind all human "subjectivity." And how indeed should one be able to abandon subjectivity, when the One which is needful demands nearness to Being, a "turning," and a "change in the human essence,"⁵⁸ and hence a kind of conversion and rebirth?

ᵐTranslator's note: "Trans-position" is a literal rendering of *Über-setzen*; without the hyphen, *Übersetzen* simply means "translating" or "translation."

Whoever permits himself to doubt the truth and correctness of Heidegger's later self-understanding of his first and foundational work will naturally have to consider that *Being and Time* in fact begins and ends with the question concerning *Being*. But the questions at the beginning and the end stand at the beginning and the end of a substantial middle with detailed analyses, the substance of which is a "fundamental analysis" of human subjectivity, i.e., of authentic and inauthentic Being-a-self as an existing *Dasein* which is always one's own.

Of course these funamental analyses are characterized as merely preparatory, i.e., with an eye toward the universal question concerning Being generally, but—and this is what is singularly distinctive in Heidegger's ontology—this question concerning Being can be asked and answered meaningfully only by taking as its point of departure and its goal "the most drastic isolation" or "most radical individuation" of the own-most Dasein of the one who asks about Being.[59]

Philosophy, it is said in *Being and Time*, is "universal phenomenological ontology, proceeding from the hermeneutic of Dasein which as an analytic of *existence* has fastened the guiding thread of all philosophical questioning at the point from which it *springs forth* and toward which it *rebounds*."[60] The ontological question concerning Being in general stands in need of a definite, extant, ontic foundation, and this foundation is that being which we ourselves are because only Dasein can ask about the meaning of Being in the first place. "The ontic distinction of Dasein lies in its being ontological,"[61] which means that it is extant in the sense that it relates itself toward and understands Being, which for its own part is always the Being of a being. Human Dasein understands its own Being, whose unique way of Being is "existing," and at the same time it understands all the other kinds of Being of beings which are not Dasein. Hence it is "the condition for the possibility of all ontologies" (13/34), the one universal ontology and the many regional ones. This ontic-ontological "priority" of Dasein was already noted by Aristotle when he said that in a certain manner the human soul is all beings, since only the human soul, through *aisthesis* and *noesis*, can sense and perceive all beings in terms of what and how they are. On the other hand, in Heidegger's later interpretation of Plato this priority of seeing, which senses and perceives, gets explained as the beginning of the decline of the truth of Being into the mere correctness of a subjective viewing.

How is Heidegger's later claim, namely that he abandoned all human "subjectivity" already in *Being and Time* because humans and all "humanism"—Roman, Christian, Marxist, existential—are not at all what is essential since humans alone are "from the standpoint of Being," compatible with these fundamental theses from *Being and Time*, which as a whole concern the existential relativity of Being and its truth to an existing human Dasein? Heidegger makes his point of departure compatible with the one arrived at later by consistently reinterpreting the existentialia of *Being and Time* with regard to the end which has been reached. Whereas in *Being and Time* Being is understood with regard to Dasein as the foundation because it is accessible only from out of Dasein, now on the other hand the human essence is thought in its "derivation from the truth of Being" and the existence of Dasein which is isolated unto itself in the face of death becomes transformed into an "ecstatic dwelling in the nearness of Being"![62]

The guiding principle of *Being and Time* that the so-called essence of Dasein lies in its existence, means there that its essence is no kind of general what-ness [*Was-sein*] but rather is a particular that-ness [*Daβ-sein*] which is always one's own, "that it is and has to be" (12, 42/32f., 67); in the "Letter on Humanism" the meaning of this definition becomes reinterpreted to mean that humans "essence" in such a way that they are the "There" [*Da*], i.e., the clearing "of Being" (323/205). Only this Being of the "There" has the fundamental character of ek-sistence, i.e., of the ecstatic standing-in of the truth or openness of Being (323/205). How is one to recognize in this new essential definition of Dasein the earlier one from *Being and Time*, according to which "Da"-sein is of course also a "clearing," though not because it is the "There" of a *Being* which is distinct from all beings but rather because as existentially disclosed Being-in-the-world it is there "for itself" and brings along *its* There "from the very start." Also, "care" no longer indicates, as in *Being and Time*, the essence of existing Dasein, about which it was said that it itself and its own Being are at stake, but instead it is care for *that* Being which is exclusively "it itself" in a distinctive and foundational way.

In *Being and Time* the existence of human Dasein, its own existential "There," is not attuned as the "There" of universal Being by the attunement of thanks for its "favor" and "grace," but rather is attuned by the experience of "burden."[n] Dasein burdens itself because it is absolutely without a whence and whither and "has to be." Indeed no human Dasein has ever freely decided whether or not it wanted to become Dasein. In

---

[n] Translator's note: The term *Stimmung* normally signifies the tuning of a musical instrument; the translators of *Being and Time* translate this term as "mood," though this translation loses the relationship between *Stimmung* and the related terms *Stimme* (voice) and *stimmen* (which usually means "to tune" a musical instrument but which I am translating as "to attune"). *Stimmung* has been translated variously in this text as "attunement" and "mood."

Being and Time Heidegger calls this character of Dasein's Being, that it is covered up in its whence and whither but disclosed in itself as all the more uncovered, i.e., its "that it is and has to be," Dasein's *thrownness* into its There. This indicates the "facticity" of being given over.

At the same time this thrown burden of facticity is also the basis for the *projection*-character of Dasein, which as an existence is no mere fact but rather is also a factical possibility, a "capacity-for-Being." Although in existing, humans constantly project possibilities on the basis of which they understand themselves, to the extent that they are up to something and are ahead of themselves they can of course never get behind their thrownness, which is the unfathomable ground of their existence. They can project upon possibilities only within their thrownness. Existing Dasein is a "thrown projection" of itself, which on the basis of blind facticity projects upon possibilities which have come into view. From this point of departure Sartre, with whose existentialism Heidegger wants to have "not the least" in common, thought further and made human existence transparent as a whole "*projet fondamental*," all the way down to biographical details.

In the "Letter on Humanism" the thrown character of projection, like the concept of existence, gets rethought both toward and from out of Being. Now existence no longer means a self-transcending in the projection of a world, but instead means ek-sistence as standing-out into the truth of Being. Being itself now supports ek-sistence, to the extent that Being "holds [ek-sistence] to itself and gathers [it] to itself" (329/211). Existing Dasein is no longer thrown, as in *Being and Time*, because it is and has to be placeless and homeless, without whence and whither, but rather because it essences in the "throwing of Being" as the throwing of that "which destines by sending" (324/207). Existence is no longer the point of departure and the goal, but instead Being itself is the whence and whither. The meaning of projection changes in a like manner. It is no longer a determination of Dasein's existence as thrown into its There, but rather is an "ecstatic relation to the clearing of Being" (325/207). That which throws in projection is by no means human beings but rather is Being itself, which sends human beings into ek-sistence as their essence. Far from continuing to characterize thrown projection as he had earlier, namely as the uncanny *factum brutum* or pure accident of human existence, he henceforth refers to our nearness to Being as nearness to home and to that which heals. Human beings are merely the ek-sistent "counter-throwing" of Being, called by Being and called upon to be its shepherds (338/221).

Hence the thrownness of existing Dasein is by no means a final ground and abyss in whose weight Dasein rests, but rather is thrown by Being itself. To this extent it loses the character of the burdensome facticity which was foundational for the analytic of Dasein. Heidegger's rethinking and further thinking of Dasein's thrown facticity as a "throwing by Being" indicates a foundational existentiell motive of his entire being on the way: the demand for the loss of heaviness and of being closed off, to which the recurring talk of opening oneself for the open stands in a direct relationship.

In *Being and Time*, *facticity* is a distinctive determination of Dasein's existence in distinguishing it from the non-existential fact of mere Being-present-at-hand. In "What is Metaphysics?" Heidegger broadens the problem of facticity to all beings as a whole by asking at the end: "Why are there beings at all and not rather Nothing?"[63] In the *Introduction to Metaphysics* this question, which was already asked by Leibniz and Schelling, is characterized as the highest in rank because it is the broadest, deepest, and most primordial. It does not occur to Heidegger that this question can be asked whatsoever only because it is preceded by the biblical story of creation according to which the totality of beings, as a creation out of Nothing, could also not be, though it would naturally remain to be considered that and why this "most primordial" question was never asked by the primordial thinking of the Greeks.[64] If instead Heidegger, as a thoughtful one, rejects the *creatio ex nihilo* and transforms it in a de-theologizing way into the statement "*ex nihilo omne ens qua ens fit*" ["all things that are come from nothing"], then he proceeds within Christian tradition against that tradition, but not in the realm of originary thinking, for which the Nothing is only the most extreme and empty limit of beings.

Questioning in Heidegger's manner requires that all beings be surpassed toward non-beings, toward the Nothing of beings. But this "not toward beings" touches upon *Being* in a positive way, insofar as Being is of course not supposed to be any being. The experience of the Nothing first opens up access to the experience of Being and lets the full "strangeness" of beings as such come over us. The expression "strangeness" mediates between the experience of Dasein's thrown facticity and "wonder" regarding the totality of beings, which finally—in the later "Afterword" to "What is Metaphysics?"—recognizes in the universal fact of Being the "wonder of all wonders" and thankfully acknowledges it. "Among all beings humans alone experience, called by the voice of Being (one would first expect: 'of the Nothing'), the wonder of all wonders: *that beings are*."[65]

Corresponding to this, the mood of anxiety that reveals the Nothing becomes transformed into a religious "shyness" before the mystery of Being (305). The thought of a "sacrifice" for the protection of the truth of Being ultimately takes the place of the self-assertion of a Dasein given over to itself, whose freedom was a "freedom towards death" (307f.). Yet this sacrificing and wasting of oneself in order to favor Being is not an achievement of Dasein, but is instead the "echo" of the prospective favor of Being and is no longer (307), as it still was in the text of the lecture, the expression of a "bold" Dasein which preserves its "final greatness" in a bold wasting of itself.[66]

But in what sense are we to understand the "is" of Being, which first of all and last of all stands in question, if it is in no way a being, not even the most extant and highest being? Is Being generally "In-itself," nonrelational, and independent of an extant Dasein which can relate to it and understand it? In *Being and Time* it is said: "Only as long as Dasein *is*, i.e., only as long as there is the ontic possibility of an understanding of Being, 'is there' Being. If Dasein does not exist, then 'independence' as well 'is' not, nor 'is' the 'In-itself'" (212/225). This assertion is really something obvious, to the extent that it is related to the *understanding* of Being.[67] For how should one be able to speak meaningfully of an independent In-itself, without understanding the meaning of such an In-itself and hence "presupposing" a Dasein which understands?

But on the other hand, talk of Being-in-itself means precisely a way of Being that is essentially independent of all human Dasein, relating, and understanding. Indeed in the understanding of Being and of Being-in-itself an understanding Dasein is presupposed, but of course this presupposition does not posit the Being and the Being-in-itself that are understood. Hence we are thrown back on the question whether it is essential to Being-in-itself that an understanding and perceiving Dasein be there and be cleared or not.

In his own way Hegel answered this question incomparably by means of the dialectic of the Being-in-and-for-itself of substantial subjectivity; but not Heidegger, who in *Being and Time* understands Being and its truth "fundamentally" on the basis of Dasein, though later on he understands the latter on the basis of the former without bringing the two modes of access into accord, unless this be through the postulate of a "correspondence" between the destining of Being and suitable Dasein, and generally between Being and the human essence.[68] As it is formulated three decades after *Being and Time*, they are assigned to and belong to *one another* because, on the one hand, only humans can let Being as presencing arrive and come to presence and because, on the other hand, it is precisely inasmuch as this Being "needs" humans that the latter can be assigned to Being.[69] Whereas in *Being and Time* the Dasein which is always one's own was assigned and given over *to itself*, the human essence is now defined by its being an obedient "listening" to the claim of Being and by belonging to it.[70] The requirement of *Being and Time* to take over one's ownmost There becomes transformed into the opposite requirement to "let go" of oneself into that into which we have already been admitted: into belonging to Being, which nonetheless for its own part belongs to us because it can dwell only with us.

According to the essay "On the Question of Being,"[71] the essence of Being, how it essences and presences, is already in itself the relation to the human essence and is nothing in and for itself, just as for the same token the human being is not a Dasein posited for itself but rather is founded upon its dwelling in the turning-toward and turning-away of Being. In the same spirit the lecture *What is Called Thinking?* says: "Every philosophical, i.e., thoughtful, theory of the essence of human beings is *in itself already* a theory of the Being of beings. Every theory of Being is *in itself already* a theory of the essence of human beings. But the one theory can never be reached through a mere reversal of the other. Why this is so, on what generally this relationship between the human essence and the Being of beings is founded, this question is of course the sole question before which prior thinking must first of all be brought."[72] But the *relation* to Being is at the same time its *withdrawl*, and "the event of withdrawl"—the absence of the healing, of the holy, and of the gods—could even be the "most contemporary among everything now contemporary."

On the other hand, this destined withdrawl is in itself already a relation to the human essence, without thereby becoming anthropomorphized. Hence Being is not cleared one-sidedly in the locale of human Dasein, but instead humans, in the relation of this withdrawl, likewise remain indigenous to the locale of Being. And this mutual relation of "correspondence" and of belonging to one another ultimately becomes overhauled and deepened to the extent that the domain through which humans and Being reach one another gets called the "event," in which the existential point of departure of the Dasein which is "always one's own" and "authentic" and given over to itself finally becomes sublated. The event is the "between" of the relation thought purely on the basis of it alone and as such, viz. the "relationship of all relationships."[73]

Already ten years earlier, in the "Letter on Humanism," Heidegger offers the statement from *Being and Time* that "Only as long as Dasein is, is there [*gibt es*]° Being" in order to say that the "it" which "gives" is Being itself!⁷⁴ Accordingly the statement from *Being and Time* gets turned into the completely different claim that only as long as Being gives itself, is there also Da-sein. The "gives" names that which does the giving, namely the essence of Being that grants the truth or unconcealedness of Being. Being itself is nothing other than this giving-itself into the open, which naturally entails that there is also a being that can open itself to the open and can receive its gift. Heidegger's initial question, "Why are there beings at all and not rather Nothing?" which could be asked but not answered within the dimension of thrown facticity, thereby meets with an unexpected answer, which might be formulated in the following way: There are beings (Dasein) because there is Being, and there is Being because it proceeds into the "There" of the clearing of a being. And ultimately even the "*es gibt*" of Being, which itself gives, stands in need of something that does the giving: the eventuating of an event, in order to arrive as presencing in that which is its own.

Just as ambiguous as the "*es gibt*," which stands facticity on its head, is the *truth* of Being, inasmuch as it resides in two places: in *Being itself*, which as the "clearing" is primordial truth itself in the sense of unconcealedness and, on the other hand, in the extant Dasein of humans, whose existence is the presupposition for any possible Being-true. Heidegger contemplated the question concerning the meaning of Being-true from the very start. Its first and unsurpassed treatment is the penetrating analysis of the interrelated concepts of *phainomenon* and *logos* in *Being and Time*.⁷⁵

A phenomenon is that "which shows" and manifests "itself in itself." In order to be able to appear, it must already stand in the radiance of a light. What belongs to this is the possibility of mere semblance and self-concealment. Phenomena become accessible in a logos which lets [things] be seen and which shows [things]. This logos can both uncover and cover up, be true or false. The logos lets extant phenomena be seen and be perceived truly or falsely. But that which is for the most part concealed and which therefore stands in need of an explicit phenomenological exhibition is Being, and it remains concealed in its very revealing. "The unconcealedness of beings, the radiance which is granted to them, darkens the light of Being."⁷⁶

The existential complement to this assertion about Being from

---

°Translator's note: The German *es gibt*, which literally means "it gives," permits no direct translation into English; the English "there is" loses the sense of an active conferring, which is crucial to Heidegger's and Löwith's meaning in the present discussion.

Holzwege is the thesis about Dasein in *Being and Time*, that humans understand themselves first of all and most of the time in terms of the world of the present-at-hand and the ready-to-hand and not on the basis of their own and ownmost Dasein and Being-in-the-world. In the lecture "On the Essence of Truth" the question concerning truth from *Being and Time* gets pursued further and becomes progressively transformed. A provisionally final view of truth is contained in the study of Anaximander's adage, where Heidegger's linguistic spirit thinks beyond all concepts and their substantiation. What gets said about truth here relates to a passage from Homer about the seer Kalchas. Like Heidegger himself, this seer is a "truth-sayer" to the extent that he protects or safeguards the truth of (literally understood) presencing, i.e., of Being, from out of the "true" in what is present (344/36). "Truth is the protection of Being" by humans as the shepherds of Being, where the genitive in the expression "protection of Being" is used in two senses, to mean on the part of Being itself and also to mean on the part of the seeing of the truth-sayer.

But what things depend on above all is no longer, as in *Being and Time*, the subjective and Dasein-oriented foundation of truth, but rather Being itself, which in its presencing and absencing is truth itself and gives and grants truth or withdraws and denies it, in contrast with which Dasein becomes reduced, or rather elevated, to the "locale" of the truth of Being.[77] What is at stake, it is said in the introduction to "What Is Metaphysics?" is exclusively the arrival or the nonappearance of the truth of Being.[78] We and our projections of Being do not determine Being-true and Being-false, but instead what is to be determined is "whether Being itself can, from out of its own truth, eventuate a relation to the human essence" and hence bring humans to "belonging to Being" (364/210). What the "can" in this eventuating of Being depends upon, remains obscure. It seems as if Being, indeed even "God" and "the gods," need the preparation by humans of a dwelling-place, in order to presence. They do not arrive if we do not meet them half-way. For some unknown reason, up to now Being apparently was not able to eventuate the relation to humans, at least not in the West; indeed Heidegger maintains that the decisive truth of Being remained concealed from Plato to Nietzsche. For over two thousand years we have been existing and thinking while having forgotten Being because we have abandoned it; nonetheless, this abandonment of Being is itself destined by Being, and it determines the destiny of our Western thinking and Dasein. Heidegger says that *Being and Time* was already on the way to opening up a path on which we can contemplate Being itself in its truth (367/212).

But in *Being and Time* the talk is not of the relation of the truth of Being to the human essence, but on the contrary it is of the relating of human Dasein to Being and to truth.[79] According to *Being and Time*, what is "primarily true," i.e., what uncovers and discloses, is extant Dasein (220/263). As a Dasein which is both thrown into its Da-sein and projecting itself out of this, Dasein uncovers and covers up, i.e., is in the truth and untruth, with equal primordiality (222/265). In accordance with their Dasein-oriented way of Being, all truth and untruth are relative to an extant Dasein. "There is" truth only "to the extent that and as long as Dasein is" (226/269). "Beings are uncovered only *when*, and they are disclosed (true) only *as long as*, Dasein *is* whatsoever. Newton's laws, the principle of contradiction, and every truth generally are true only as long as Dasein *is*. Before Dasein there was nothing at all, and after Dasein nothing at all will be any more, there was no truth and there will be none, because as disclosedness, uncovering, and uncoveredness they *cannot* be then" (226/269).

We must presuppose truth not because there are "eternal truths," but rather because we ourselves, as a Dasein which is finite and thrown into its There, which projects and discloses beings in their Being, are always already presupposed, i.e., we are factically there and have to be (227f./269ff.). "In itself it is by no means to be comprehended why beings are to be *uncovered*, why *truth* and *Dasein* must be" (228/271). Whoever extinguishes his life in suicide, thereby extinguishes truth as well (229/271).[80] Truth and Dasein are both "factically" existential, and the Being of truth stands and falls with extant Dasein. Heidegger concludes the discussion of the presupposition of truth by saying that "there is Being—not beings—only to the extent that truth is. And truth *is* only to the extent that and as long as Dasein is."[81]

It is hard to comprehend to what extent this radical formulation of the relativity of truth and its Being to an extant, factically existing Dasein is supposed to open a path for thinking on which it can contemplate Being itself in the truth proper to it. Of course even in Heidegger's later utterances the relation of the truth of Being to the human essence is never given up, but rather is recast in such a way that this relation to humans gets determined from out of Being itself. In the service of such a reconceived questioning, Heidegger assures us, a preliminary reflection on the human essence was necessary. But why was it necessary to work out an "analytic of Dasein," if the human essence in fact does not exist from out of itself but rather gets eventuated from out of Being? Would a definition of Being not instead have to precede the definition of Dasein, as Heidegger himself indicates at the end of *Being and Time*? (437/488). But how is "Being" to be capable of closer definition at all without reference to a definite being? And is it really at all true that the analyses of the essential phenomena of existence (Being-in-the-world, Being-with and Being-a-self, care, death, guilt, conscience) and their temporal interpretation prepare and sustain the understanding of Being? Must one have gone with *Being and Time* in order to be able to tread the *Holzwege* [woodpaths], or must one not instead forget the existential analyses of *Being and Time* in order to be able to follow the topology of Being? How, for example, should the radical independence of Dasein, which takes itself over, be able to provide illumination about Being itself—unless by means of a turning that takes as its point of departure and its goal Dasein's radical belonging to Being?

The existential analysis of an authentic "capacity-for-Being-a-whole," which presupposes that death is the "highest court of appeal" for our ownmost, resolute capacity-for-Being, is not simply unnecessary in order to experience the mystery of Being, but rather is incompatible with the entirely different thought that all of our resolute capacity is always already determined by the destiny of Being. How are these supposed to be compatible with one another: existence which is resolved upon itself in the face of death and which through its anticipation of the empty end can no longer be "surpassed" by anything, and ek-sistence that is eventuated by Being and that is always surpassed by the destiny of Being because from the very start every destiny of beings has already completed itself in Being?

The view that an analysis of Dasein is necessary in order to understand the meaning of Being could be maintained only if, as in *Being and Time*, an understanding of Being belongs primarily to Dasein. But if on the contrary our Dasein, which is always one's own, and our thinking belong primordially to Being and are sent and pre-thought by it, then it is unclear what an analysis of Dasein is supposed to be able to contribute and settle regarding the relation of the truth of Being to the human essence. In order to establish, without falling back into his initial standpoint of subjectivity, an essential relationship between Being and the reflection on the human essence necessary for Being, the sole "supposition underlying everything" to which Heidegger is entitled is that the relation of Being to the human essence "belongs entirely to Being itself" because Being "needs" humans.[82]

Yet this remains a mere supposition. For how should one be able not simply to wish, hope, and believe, but to know, that the Being of all beings is essentially interested in us humans, not to mention in the Europeans? The human essence, Heidegger maintains, is surely essential for the truth of Being, "though in such a way that it [Being] does not depend on humans as such," but rather on their ek-sistent essence, which becomes eventuated in advance from out of Being.[83] But what becomes, one would like to ask Heidegger, from out of Being, which is essentially related to ek-sistent humans, if one day human Dasein no longer exists, and what was there before there were humans?

Naturally Heidegger would not allow this question, since it presupposes once again that Being "is" analogous to a being and that time, its before and after, could come about without humans. Yet Being never "is" in the manner of a being, but instead "essences" prior to all beings as the event of the clearing. Accordingly, in the "Letter on Humanism" Heidegger articulates the assertion from *Being and Time* in the following way: "Only as long as the clearing (= the 'There') of Being eventuates itself, does Being give itself over to humans," and to this extent there is Da-sein (333/218).

If, however, the assertion from *Being and Time* "means" the opposite of what he says clearly enough, then such an interpretation is a reinterpretation that turns around the meaning of the assertion and that no longer wants to admit what was said earlier. The one word Da-sein, or da-Sein, solves only in a literal way the puzzle how Being, which itself is not a being nor a mere way of Being, is nonetheless supposed to be able to relate itself to beings, and indeed in an essential manner. In the relation of Being to the human essence, one would like to ask, what draws Being toward humans, and what attracts humans? Are, then, the "grace" and "favor" of Being not simply celebratory words, if ontological Being has no onto-theological foundation, be this in a natural manifestation of the "animatedly rich beauty" of a visible cosmos or in a supernatural and historical manifestation of an invisible God? Can the essence of Being be inquired about at all apart from a being that is to pose the questions, be this the questioning human as in *Being and Time*, or a God that creates humans and world, or a cosmos that sustains the human and the divine?

Since Heidegger revised his attempt to found universal Being in human Dasein individuated unto itself, it remains only to choose between illuminating Being in terms of Christian theology or in terms of Greek cosmology. An ontology without cosmology is like a human "Dasein" without nature [*Natur*] and lineage [*Geschlecht*].[p] But the basis upon which Heidegger's question about Being ignores the living Being of the world subsisting from out of nature and knows it only as a "project," is the existential narrowing of the natural world to world history and the human world, taking as its point of departure the human being as a historical existence.[84] In a different, anthropological manner, Theodor Litt took as his theme *human world-meaning*.[85]

In accordance with the relativity of Being and truth to a Dasein which is posited in advance [*im voraus setzt*] and which pre-sup-poses [*voraus-setzend*] itself,[q] Heidegger struggles in *Being and Time* against belief in *eternal truths* as a vestige of Christian theology within philosophy that has not yet been expelled. "That there are eternal truths will have been proved adequately only when it has been demonstrated that Dasein has existed and will exist for all eternity. As long as this proof is lacking, the assertion will remain a fantastic claim which does not gain legitimacy for being commonly 'believed' by philosophers" (227/269f.)

Together with Dasein, which is a finite existence, truth is essentially finite and temporal and hence historical. In *Being and Time* the *finitude of existing Dasein*, which is fixed by death, likewise determines the *finite temporality of Being* generally. In Heidegger's interpretation of Kant, the essential relation between Being and human finitude is taken as the theme, and the assertion is made that there is Being at all only where finitude has become existent.[86] And since an understanding of Being is constitutive for the existing Dasein of finite humans, this understanding itself is the "most finite in the finite" and is never to be taken absolutely (222). Both, extant Dasein and Being, find their "meaning" in finite time.

Still, the first half of *Being and Time* does not yet fulfill the promise of the title, but rather simply leads up to the interpretation of Being on the basis of time in the sense of the temporality of finite Dasein. That which is new, bold, and truly meaningful in the analyses presented in *Being and Time* is contained primarily in Division Two, on "Dasein and Temporality," where the temporal structures of our Being-in-the-world are exhibited with extraordinary power and incisiveness. In comparison with these analyses, everything said later concerning the relationship between Being and time is incomprehensible.

As meager as these utterances are, they are nonetheless indispensable

---

[p] Translator's note: Löwith's use of the term *Geschlecht* here is, like Heidegger's use of the term, somewhat ambiguous; it has a range of meanings, including species or kind, ancestry or lineage, generation, and gender. See "Die Sprache im Gedicht," p. 78; "Language in the Poem," *On the Way to Language*, p. 195.

[q] Translator's note: The term *voraussetzen* normally means to presuppose; literally it means to posit in advance, and Löwith stresses this literal meaning through the introduction of the hyphen.

for the discussion of the question: how is the finite temporality of human Dasein and its historicality related to the temporality and historicality of Being itself? Has a change taken place here as well, similar to the one discussed earlier, or does the later talk of a history of Being and a destining of Being maintain itself upon the foundation of *Being and Time*? Is the doctrine of *Being and Time* still envisaged as a "finite metaphysics of finitude," as it was in the book on Kant which followed *Being and Time* and at the end of which the question pops up whether human finitude can be understood apart from the presupposition of infinitude,[87] or is Heidegger, on his path to the overcoming of all metaphysics of subjectivity, on the path back to an acknowledgement of a kind of temporal eternity and hence ready to accept a kind of eternal truth of Being after all?

Being and Time never suggests that for Heidegger things could depend on something durable, lasting, indestructible, and remaining, unless this be in the form of the unconditional firmness of the certainty of death and hence of nothingness. This why it could not be foreseen that existence, which is individuated in the face of death and on whose finitude eternity founders, could in the end find an "abode" and a "home," a "healing" and even something "holy" after all. When Heidegger explains in the "Letter on Humanism" that homelessness now becomes a world-fate and that it is therefore necessary to contemplate this destiny in terms of the history of Being,[88] the experience of homelessness already points as such to an alienation and a possible homecoming to a home that is grounded in something that remains. But what remains is that which we usually call eternity. Hence when Heidegger rejects the Platonic-Christian thesis of temporality in *Being and Time* as a troubled likeness of eternity and allows only the question how inauthentic, *in*-finite time proceeds out of "primordial," i.e., finite temporality, this confinement of Being and time to the finite Being of a finite time thus stands in need of a revision in the light of the later publications, if not a revocation.

The few indications of this that are about to be examined are, however, by no means clear and unambiguous. In "What is Metaphysics?" the belonging together of Being and Nothing is substantiated, in agreement with *Being and Time* and the book on Kant, on the grounds that Being itself is finite in its essence and manifests itself only in the transcendence of Dasein, which is held out into the Nothing. On the other hand, in the subsequently written afterword to this essay it is said that where anxiety draws near to timidity, the latter "lights and looks after the locale of the human essence, within which this essence remains at home in that which remains."[89] In the same sense it is said of the timidity of the spirit of sacrifice, a timidity which is prepared for anxiety, that it takes on "proximity to the indestructible" (308f.). This proximity can only be what is also called nearness to Being. In the end, then, is Being nothing merely finite after all, but rather *something which remains* and *which is indestructible*?

But even thus, Being retains a temporal character. Time is the "first name" for the truth of Being,[90] and indeed it is so from the beginnings of Greek thinking on, where "Being" (*ousia, parousia*) amounts to presencing, Being-present, and abiding, up to Nietzsche's doctrine of the eternal recurrence of the same Being. Yet the temporality of Being does not exclude but rather accommodates the fact that in Being Heidegger is searching for an "abode" which grants the experience of what is durable. The support (protection) for all conduct is a gift of the truth of Being, which protects and shelters ek-sistent humans. Given that the truth of Being, as Heidegger says, gives support to the human essence, one must assume that in spite of its temporal-historical character this truth is itself something durable and not simply a varying happening of truth and a changing history of Being.

In the guise of the Hölderlin interpretation as well, reference is made to that which remains and is homelike. That which remains is nothing above and outside of time, but rather is an extension of time. "It is only since they placed themselves in the present of something which remains, that humans are able to expose themselves to that which is variable, to that which comes and goes; for only that which persists is variable. Only since the 'time which races along' was torn apart into present, past, and future, has there been the possibility of agreeing on something which remains."[91] This is said even more distinctly in connection with the interpretation of Hölderlin's assertion: "Yet what remains, the poets establish," namely that that which remains is not something imperishable and everlasting, nor a persisting of permanent presence, however desirable such a thing might appear to be [citing the final line of Holderlin's poem "Andenken" ("Remembrance")] (40f./304f.). On the contrary, it is a matter of "something" which remains, and it is a proper remaining or reposing in what is proper, "on the way to the source."[92] It is said of this source that it is the one origin from which all native dwelling of the sons of the earth springs forth. That which remains is "a movement into the nearness of the origin," and whoever dwells in this nearness serves the essence of remaining (145).

Of course it thereby remains the case that Heidegger's Being-on-the-way is an abode to the extent that it springs forth from a primordial nearness of Being. To that which remains in the source of the origin there corresponds a Being-on-the-way to it from out of a distant and foreign place for which nearness to home is the measure. The "source" of Being, which lets all beings primordially spring forth, is paradoxically the sole "solidity," inasmuch as it constantly retreats into its own ground in order to "solidify" it (146). "To dwell near the origin" means to exhibit it from a distance (146f.). The timid drawing near of this exhibiting remains at a distance which is appropriate to that which primordially remains. The poet dwells near the origin by exhibiting the distance "which draws near in the coming of the holy" (148). And the thinker as well, one can add, by announcing the distance that draws near in the *Parusie* of Being.ʳ The essential thinker is a prophetically gifted truth-sayer.

Hence the imminence of death is no longer, as it was in *Being and Time*, the highest authority for the interpretation of finite Dasein, but instead the mortal "sons of the earth" can find an abode in the primordial language of Being if remaining and dwelling near the origin is granted to them (148). From the beginning, there is only *one* Either-Or for Heidegger: "Are we primordially historical in our Dasein—or are we simply relying . . . on established knowledge of what has passed?"[93] For deciding between these alternatives there is an unmistakable sign which "hardly abandons" what "dwells near the origin, i.e., which hardly abandons the locality" (Hölderlin).[94] What this absolute-historical origin is, this origin which is at the same time a "leap ahead" because from the beginning it has already decided about what is to come,[95] naturally remains as dark and mysterious as Being and the destining of Being and is supposed to remain concealed in its announcement as well.

Being and Time only appears to have dispensed with the question concerning an eternal truth. In actuality Heidegger posed it anew by thinking onward, in a turning, from the finite temporality of Dasein to an origin that remains. The existential-temporal standpoint of *Being and Time* is thereby "sublated." In the end Heidegger the thinker, who in the "Country Paths" speaks of a "gate to the eternal,"[96] is today not at all far removed from the religious writer Kierkegaard. For who established already a hundred years ago, leaving aside Kierkegaard, that what is essential for time is the opposite of what time demands, namely reforms and changes? Time

---

ʳTranslator's note: The term *Parusie* is a cognate for the ancient Greek *parousia*, a term which Heidegger often invokes (together with the term *ousia*) in arguing that the Greeks conceived of Being in terms of presence. In the present context *Parusie* has this meaning as well as a religious overtone, inasmuch as in both biblical Greek and in German the term is also used to siginify the return of Christ on Judgment Day; cf. Matthew 24.27 and I Corinthians 15.23. See "Hegels Begriff der Erfahrung," *Helzwege*, pp. 187, 200.

needs something that stands unconditionally firm and that brings time to standing by holding up for it something that remains or that is eternal.

Along with these consistent transformations of the analytic of finite Dasein into a saying of an indestructible Being, a saying which is no longer divided up but which instead gathers together, the concept of a *fundamental ontology*, which sustains all the existentialia, becomes modified. Fundamental ontology is no longer an analysis of Dasein which provides the foundation for the question of Being, but instead it is an attempt to expose the concealed ground of ontology. For the traditional principles or beginnings of metaphysics are not yet the ultimate roots of beings. Indeed metaphysics always thinks beings *as* beings, and yet with respect to Being it does not know that it owes its view of the Being of beings to the concealed light of Being itself. For this reason it is a matter of experiencing, through a "return into the ground of metaphysics," the soil from which the roots of the tree of metaphysics, whose branches are the sciences, nourish themselves.[97] In this thinking about Being which is no longer metaphysical and no longer humanistic, traditional metaphysics is supposed to be overcome. For this it is necessary that the human being become transformed from an "*animal metaphysicum*" and "*animal rationale*," i.e., from a foundational subject, into a "shepherd of Being."[98]

But how is such a decisive transformation supposed to take place or be capable of happening? On the basis of one's own choice or on the basis of inspiration and grace, or on the basis of both together? In contrast to Nietzsche, Heidegger says almost nothing about this decisive "transformation," unless this be that the modern will to will must change and become "more willing."[99] Hence the subjectivity which has been abandoned inevitably seeks a new opportunity to speak, inasmuch as even the essential thinking of Being is not simply "eventuated" by Being but instead requires its own act of appropriation which can correspond to Being. Of course Heidegger's thinking does not mediate the distinction between subject and substance with a Hegelian dialectic in the medium of absolute spirit and with a view toward a historical mediator, though even for Heidegger a circular dialectic is the final information source for making intelligible the relation of Being to the human essence and the relationship of Dasein to Being, albeit according to his own assertion it is at this very point that all dialectic founders and no longer has any place.[100]

But in accordance with the subject matter, nothing changes if one thinks ambiguously instead of dialectically. In the thinking "of" Being, the genitive is intentionally ambiguous;[101] thinking is "of Being" to the extent that thinking, eventuated by Being, belongs to Being. Thinking is at the same time "thinking of Being" to the extent that thinking, belonging to Being, listens to Being. "As that which belongs to Being by listening, thinking is what it is according to its essential heritage."

For Heidegger a dialectic of "corresponding," which one can suppose along with Heidegger to be "a pure philosophical predicament" like all dialectic,[102] takes the place of Hegel's dialectic of mediation, though it naturally does not achieve the conceptual determinacy, historical grounding, and phenomenological development of Hegel's dialectic. A few examples may clarify this merely verbal suggestion of a dialectic of correspondence: Being in its arriving waits for us, just as we prepare an arrival for Being and await it; Being grants us to itself, just as we protect Being; being protected by Being corresponds to our calling as guardians and shepherds of Being, and to the "insight" [*Einblick*] or "flashing-in" [*Einblitz*] into that which is,[s] corresponds the Heraclitean "sight" or "flash" of Being;[103] truth itself is an ambiguous protection of Being; Being is a self-clearing and openness for a human Being-disclosed and Being-opened; as something which clears, Being, whose veil is the Nothing, is equally a nihilating; to the "ecstatic" character of Dasein corresponds the "epochal," i.e., the self-sustaining, character of Being; to the errancy of humans corresponds the self-concealing of the clearing of Being; to the claim and the unspoken "word of Being" corresponds our capacity-for-hearing and our bringing to language; to language as the house of Being corresponds language as the abode of humans; to the history of Being corresponds our historicality, and to the destining of Being corresponds our propriety.

Philosophy itself is nothing other than "corresponding to the Being of beings."[104] Hence in every case there are two kinds of grounds, foundations, and substantiation: "Dasein" as foundation, on whose ground there is Being, and "Being" as foundation, on whose ground there is Da-sein. And to the extent that Heidegger wants to understand Being, indeed wants to say Being, even his supra- and submetaphysical thinking cannot avoid seizing upon humans and their subjectivity, and it cannot avoid demanding a transformation in the essence of humans and their thinking and language which corresponds to Being.

Thus the essential distinction between *Being and Time* and the later

---

[s] Translator's note: "Einblick in das was ist" ("Insight into that which is") is the title Heidegger gave to a series of four lectures first read in 1949: "Das Ding" ("The Thing"); "Das Gestell" ("Enframing," which was subsequently expanded and retitled "The Question Concerning Technology"); "Die Gefahr" ("The Danger," which has never been published); and "Die Kehre" ("The Turning"). A note on this lecture series is provided as the "Vorbemerkung" to Martin Heidegger, *Die Technik und Die Kehre*, p. 3.

writings is focused in a subtle displacement of emphasis in the relationship between Being and Dasein. Though this displacement may at first appear to be as irrelevant as a hardly noticeable change in a tone of voice, in actuality it changes the heart of the matter which is in question. In "What is Metaphysics?" as well as in the book on Kant, the relationship of Dasein to Being is characterized as a "breaking-in" of human existence into the totality of beings, by means of which beings "break open" into what and how they are and manifest themselves in their Being.[105] On the other hand, later it is said that first of all, together with self-giving Being, a "clearing" eventuates and opens itself in the totality of beings, and makes human ek-sistence possible, in accordance with its essence.[106]

In *Being and Time* human Dasein relates itself to Being independently, through its understanding of Being; *after Being and Time* it is above all a matter of a relation of Being to the human essence, and the relationship between the two, which is in and for itself ambiguous and reciprocal, is ultimately fastened to Being, which in contrast to Dasein is not a being. Dasein no longer primarily discloses the meaning of Being, but instead Being itself clears itself in the There of the human essence. Being is that which is, or rather "essences," prior to all positive beings, just as the Nothing nothings prior to all negation of beings on the part of an extant Dasein. Formulations like Being "is," the Nothing "nothings," the essence "essences," time "completes [*zeitigt*]," world "worlds," the thing "things," language "speaks," and the event "eventuates" indicate not simply a verbal dynamic but rather a proper Being-from-out-of-itself. This also, and above all, holds for the definition of *Being*. Seen from out of ourselves, the "there" of Being is a human Dasein, a *humanum*; seen from out of Being itself, this *humanum* is the "locale" of the truth of Being, of *Being's* da-Sein.

In this way, humanity becomes deprecated on the one hand and ennobled on the other. The existential structures of Dasein from *Being and Time* become transformed into a topology of Being, the persistent discussion of which is supposed to determine the "locality of all localities" in which even all questioning Being-on-the-way gets sublated toward a kind of rootedness.

That one can look at one and the same state of affairs from two mutually opposing sides would nonetheless be merely an apparent solution to the problem contained in the dialectic of corresponding. The possibility of a double view from here and from there would signify a mere shift of standpoint in the subjective line of sight, in point of view, and hence would not signify a fundamental change in the human essence. The supposed or actual obscurities and discrepancies in Heidegger's formulations cannot be explained on the basis of a mere shift in perspective, but on the contrary are thereby only explained away. The dialectical contradiction between the existential analytic of extant Dasein and the topology of nonextant Being is instead constitutive, because the "correspondence" between Being and Dasein does not do away with their distinction but, on the contrary, encompasses it. In contrast to the absolute, theological difference between eternal creator and finite creation, the ontic-ontological difference between Being and beings, this core element of Heidegger's thinking, surely signifies more than each being's distinctness from and connection with its beingness or manner of Being, and yet it also signifies less than an unconditioned transcendence of Being.

But there is *one* contradiction that is not to be resolved through a perspectival difference in viewing, nor through dialectical correspondence. In the afterword to the fourth edition of "What Is Metaphysics?" it is said in connection with the truth of Being that Being "surely" essences without beings, "but" that there are never beings without Being. In the fifth edition, which appeared six years later, the "but," and hence the stress on a contrary clause, is deleted and the "surely" is replaced with a "never," that is to say the entire meaning of the assertion gets changed into its opposite, indeed without this change being indicated as such. What would one say to a theologian who maintains at one time that God surely essences without a creation, and at another time that He can never essence without it? How is it to be explained that a language-thinker like Heidegger, who weighs his words so carefully, makes such a radical change at such a decisive point?

Of course it appears that only the one or the other formulation can be the true and "suitable" one. Hence, one must conclude, Heidegger erred regarding what is decisive in the ontic-ontological difference, by maintaining that Being is distinguished from beings inasmuch as beings are of course always dependent on Being even though Being cannot essence without beings. But how was he able, in the presentation of such a fundamental thesis, to be on such dubious woodpaths?

An answer regarding the meaning of this change seems to be suggested by the following consideration. In *Being and Time* Being is characterized as the "*transcendens* pure and simple" (38/62), and it is thoroughly distinguished from beings, though it is by no means detached from them. It is and remains the "Being of a being" (6/26), and it is a *transcendens* to the extent that a presupposed being surpasses toward it. In *Being and Time* the distinctive and sole subject of this surpassing is the extant Dasein of humans, which itself, as existence, crosses over to the world. When Heidegger later stresses Being in its Being-it-itself, this surely can mean only that he found it necessary to press the ontic-ontological difference beyond the distinction between beings and their beingness or manner of Being, and out to the distinction between both (beings *and* their beingness) and Being itself,[107] in order to secure the priority of Being, though not ultimately in contrast to the transcending Dasein, which previously had methodological priority. Being thereby moves into a dubious nearness to the divine, analogous to the "sight of Being" and the "flashing of God." With respect to all beings, it gets characterized as the "entirely other dimension" and as "the Other pure and simple."[108] Hence even the thinking of the Being in beings can seek "no stopping point," but instead it expends itself for the truth of Being in the sacrifice which is a "departure from beings."[109]

Similarly, it is said at the end of the interpretation of Plato that one must "save" the truth of Being from all subjectivity of the logos, of reason, and of spirit, and that for this what must first of all arise is the need in which it is not merely beings but Being which becomes questionable.[110] Likewise it is said in the "Letter on Humanism" that thinking cannot free itself from thinking about Being, once Being announces itself in the current world-moment through the "shaking of all beings."[111] What announces itself in this way is never a being. Just as Augustine, in a dramatic place in the *Confessions*, asks whether God is somewhere in the entire universe and receives from the heavens and the earth, from the ocean and the air, the answer that they are not God, Heidegger as well says: "Wherever and however far all research may search beings, it will never find Being"—it always contacts only beings.[†][112]

But in spite of the elucidation attempted here, the ambiguity of the ontic-ontological difference, which comes to expression in the contradiction between these two opposed formulations, remains unclarified. In fact this ambiguity is unavoidable, if Being is neither a being's manner of Being nor a highest being but is nonetheless supposed to be able to relate

---

[†] Translator's note: It is at this point in the text that Löwith originally included the subsequently deleted paragraph to which he alludes in the "Preface to the Second Edition" above; the text of that paragraph (see *Heidegger: Denker in dürftiger Zeit*, 1st ed., [Frankfurt: Fischer, 1953], p. 41) reads as follows: "The sense of all these expressions is to draw out Being and bring it into relief, not simply in contrast to the whole of beings but rather in opposition to them. And for this reason, in connection with our question the answer seems to suggest itself that Heidegger retracts his radical formulation of the unconditioned character of Being as a cautionary measure; in a literal way this measure takes the ground out from under the authentic project of bringing Being itself, in its unconditionally ruling independence, to language and validity, though this measure does not do so substantively."

itself to beings. To his question regarding what is wholly other than all beings, where the latter are taken as a creation, Augustine was able to receive the answer: we are surely not God, but "He made us." Such an unambiguous answer on the basis of faith in God's creation is denied to Heidegger as a thinker. Nonetheless Being, this "what is wholly other than all beings," is supposed to clear itself and give itself into the "There" of an extant Dasein.

But how is it possible to think, let alone to "experience," that Being gives and grants the Being of a *being*, if it itself, in its nonextant Being, does not ontologically have a part in its gift and does not, like the Christian God, incarnate itself and sacrifice itself as a human, out of love for humans? And how, on the other hand, is our thinking supposed to be able to "help" Being, "save" it, "care" for it, and even "occasion" a new destining of Being, if thinking itself is merely indebted to the favor and care of Being, which takes care of it and by which it is "pre-thought" and "sent"? Does the "truth of Being" stand in need of a Dasein that protects it, in the same manner and to the same extent that Dasein conversely stands in need of Being? Is the "it" which "gives" so helpless that it stands in need of humans as guardians, shepherds, and forest keepers, in order not to go astray in its own forest? Or is Being not instead essentially free of need and independent of our destitute human essence? If anywhere, it is on this most essential of all philosophical questions that the rigorous decisiveness of Heidegger's thinking appears to be remarkably undecided, as undecided as the question at the end of "Der Feldweg" whether it is God or the world or the soul in which Being speaks.

Heidegger's self-stylization into a shepherd, thinker, and sayer of "Being" and, at the same time, into a protector of the "West," goes hand in hand with a modesty that is as ambiguous as the condescending acknowledgement that the previous epoch of the forgottenness of Being, which extends from Plato to Nietzsche, was surely great and significant in its own way even though it never contemplated and interrogated the concealed truth of Being.

2 | History, Historicality, and Destining of Being

In a lecture on time from the year 1924, Heidegger explained that the philosopher knows nothing of God and consequently also knows nothing of eternity.[1] The philosopher does not have faith, and if he asks about time then he is "resolved to understand time on the basis of time."[2] Even the Ever-extant [*Immer-Seiende*] thought in Greek terms, which looks like eternity, is in actuality a mere derivative of temporal Being. Heidegger remained true to this first projection of the problem of time, though today he might not formulate the opposition between temporality and eternity so unambiguously any more because even the precipitous destining of Being, which is in question, shows something selfsame and self-constant.

Nonetheless the "turning" in the question regarding time is not a turning away from *Being and Time* and from "Dasein" *and* "happening" [*Geschehen*],[3] but instead changes only the Whence of their possible explication. In *Being and Time* historical time gets explicated in terms of the so-called happening of finite Dasein, *after Being and Time* in terms of Being itself as a happening of Being. In both cases that which "is" is a temporal-historical happening to which linguistic expression is given by many verbalizations. In fact Heidegger thinks Being on the basis of the time that shelters and conceals it, as a historical thinker "in a destitute time." Its privation consists in its standing in a double lack: "in the no-longer of the gods who have fled and the not-yet of the one to come."[4]

In the light of this indecision concerning God and the gods, Heidegger asks whether Being will again become capable of a God. Hence as a destitute time, time apparently has something to do with God and gods after all, though not with a timeless eternity. Whatever the singular God and the many gods of the poet Hölderlin or even the "godly ones" of the "fourfold," which are only one of the four domains of the world, might mean philosophically, Heidegger thinks toward one to come, toward the anticipated *parusie* of Being that is supposed to open up the healing and holy and make possible in it something like a God.

In consequence of the current manner of speaking we are accustomed to characterizing such an epochal and eschatological thinking with regard to the future as a "historical" thinking, although the primordial and natural meaning of history suggests the exact opposite of such a futurism. By history [*Historie*] the Greek historians understood an investigation of what has happened, in connection with which they presupposed that human nature remains essentially the same through all variations in the destinies that accidentally befall us.[a] That which is, is the same as what already was and what will be. When on the contrary Heidegger, as a modern, post-Christian thinker, speaks of human existence as a historical one and expects, on the basis of a turn in the destining of Being, a transformation in the human essence, he thereby presupposes that there is no human nature that is always the same. Humans ek-sist by being on the way toward something. Accordingly even Heidegger's thinking is not an Eastern meditation nor a Greek beholding of Being as always the same, but instead is a historically conditioned Being-on-the-way that wills in a modern sense.

The movement of his thinking is determined by a Whence and Whither and above all by an In-connection-with-which [*Wogegen*][b] which gets this

---

[a]Translator's note: Heidegger often distinguishes the terms *Historie* and *Geschichte* (and likewise *historisch* and *geschichtlich*), employing the former to signify "history" in the sense of a chronological recounting of events and the latter to signify "history" in the sense of an unfolding that is unified or (in the language of Heidegger's later writings) that has been "destined" or "sent." Except as noted, I follow the translators of *Being and Time* in translating *Historie* as "historiology" and *Geschichte* as "history," and in translating *historisch* as "historiological" and *geschichtlich* as "historical." Some translators render *Historie* and *historisch* as "historiography" and "historiographic," respectively.

[b]Translator's note: The term *wogegen* expresses three different senses: the sense of being opposite or across from something and hence different than but related to it; the sense of being against or opposed to something; and the sense of being in exchange for something. The "Opposite-which" to which Löwith refers here is that in connection with which or in response to which the movement of Heidegger's thinking takes its point of departure.

movement going. The Whence of his "originary" and at the same time "prospective" thinking is the Greek origin of the Western tradition; the Whence is the highest moment or *eschaton* of an arriving world-turn;[c] the In-connection-with-which is the decline of the historical origin into our present. Beginning and end, what is earliest and what is latest, are *one* "one day" [*Einst*][d5] with two meanings, inasmuch as what is earliest in the beginning determines and outstrips in advance what is latest in the end. The history of Being, it is said in the discussion of Anaximander, gathers itself in this leave-taking of what has so far been its essence and its heretofore concealed destining in a historical "eschatology of Being" (323/18).

But the immediate point of departure for Heidegger's thinking, which looks forward and backward, is the experience of the present. It is the characteristic of decline in our time that orients his essential-historical thinking on the future and at the same time motivates it as a thinking which dismantles and which descends from Hegel's pinnacle of Western metaphysics. Nonetheless, in principle Hegel's constructive progress and ascent and Heidegger's destructive retreat and descent are not different. Both move within the same modern eccentricity of a historicism with regard to the history of spirit and the history of Being, inasmuch as they historize spirit's absolute and Being respectively. The contemporary of Napoleon thought his completion of the European history of the Notion as the attained wealth of an undeveloped beginning; the contemporary of Hitler thinks this same history of Western spirit as a self-completing emergence of nihilism.

The experience of the civil-Christian world's Being-at-the-end was already proclaimed immediately after Hegel's completion by Marx and Kierkegaard. Their critique of the present, a critique in which they are mutually opposed but also belong together, is implicitly alive in Heidegger's historiological consciousness. Kierkegaard's "moment of vision" is, in de-theologized form, also decisive for Heidegger's understanding of history, and his construction of the history of the West up to now is, like that of the Hegelian Marx, the construction of a "prehistory" prior to a coming world-turn. Like all radical critics of the nineteenth century, Heidegger thinks at the outer limit of a tradition which subsists merely

---

[c] Translator's note: The term *eschaton* comes from the Greek *eskatos*, which means that which is last or farthest; in the present context the term is meant to awaken associations of a historical end point as conceived in eschatology. See "Der Spruch des Anaximander," p. 323/ "The Anaximander Fragment," p. 18.

[d] Translator's note: *Einst* can mean "one day" or "once," either in the sense of a time long past or in the sense of "some day" in the future.

for the moment and which he wants to call into question down to its very foundations.

But at the same time his thinking certainly moves exclusively within that tradition. The destining of Being confines itself to the early and late history of the West, as if universal Being as such and as a whole had a predilection for the Occident. But when Heidegger speaks of the Occident and the West he thinks, in an evasion of Christianity, primarily of the origins and beginnings of the West in Hellenism. "Greek" is not simply the unique character of a people but rather is "what is early in destining," where destining means that in terms of which Being itself clears itself in beings and "claims an essence of humans," though this is of course only *one* definite, historical essence among other possible essences [*Wesensmöglichkeiten*] that Heidegger ignores. Even Being cannot withdraw itself in this historical conception of historiological relativity.

In the effort to illuminate the intellectual history of the West exclusively and to evaluate it, Heidegger had originally taken Dilthey as his point of departure. *Being and Time* was supposed to serve the work of Dilthey. In reality Heidegger thought in opposition to Dilthey's historiological meaning, and he apparently solved the problem posed by Dilthey of a philosophical overcoming of historicism by radicalizing it and thereby eliminating it. Heidegger carried Dilthey's historiological relativism too far by tracing it back to the unconditioned historicality of the Dasein, which is always one's own and finite. A Dasein that exists temporally and historically in its essence, as opposed to one that is merely "in" time and "has" a history, is no longer relative to time and history. This historicality, which is existentially absolutized and is tied to "Being toward the end," is supposed to make the "common" [*vulgär*] history of the world first of all possible and intelligible.[e]

But even this existentially interpreted historicality is still not the last one. In Heidegger's later writings it is thought in terms of a "destining of Being" which, as an ultimate court of appeal, is no longer relative to anything else, not even to an existence which is resolved upon an empty end. By means of this obscuring of history, which crosses Hegel's historiological meaning with Kierkegaard's concept of the decisive moment of vision, Heidegger carries the modern problem of historicism into the essence of Being itself, an essence which is "up to now" and "prospective." Likewise, truth becomes a "happening of truth" which from time to time turns in "precip-

---

[e]Translator's note: The term *vulgär* means "common" in the sense of being ordinary or everyday; it also means "common" in the sense of being crude, low, or vulgar.

History, Historicality, and Destining of Being 73

itous epochs of truth."[6] Yet the truth of Being no longer has the tendency, as it did in Hegel, to develop ever more richly into an "empire of spirit," but instead has the opposite tendency increasingly to withdraw itself.

In *Being and Time*, time is understood as the temporality of human Dasein. The Being of Dasein finds its meaning in temporality. Temporal existence is at once the place for the problem of history and the condition for the possibility of historicality. This existentially interpreted historicality is more primordial than what one commonly calls history, in connection with which one thinks of world-historical events. World-history is founded instead in the "happening of Dasein, which brings itself about [*sich zeitigt*] in the three extensions of temporality. What is primarily historical is Dasein as Being-in-the-world; secondarily historical are the beings, and the things we encounter in events, which are "within time" and "within the world" and which in a narrower sense are what is "world-historical." What is world-historical is historical only because and to the extent that it takes a place in the happening of worldly Dasein. And because the Dasein of the one who questions about Being is historical, the question of Being as well can be posed only historically and historiologically. But because in addition human Dasein is inclined to fall prey to its historical world and tradition as something present-at-hand, the mere preservation of tradition becomes uprooted from genuine history, whose appropriation requires a destruction of the prevailing tradition; this will "repeat" for the future the unexhausted possibilities of what has been.

In the fifth chapter of Division Two of *Being and Time*, the question of historicality, in contrast to the "common" understanding of history as world-history, is developed in greater detail in an existential-ontological manner. The guiding thread for the existential construction of history, a guiding thread that determines everything, is human Dasein's project of an authentic "Capacity-to-be-a-whole." Dasein can be whole only when it anticipates death in the sense of the end as something outstanding and impending, and consigns itself to existence. "Being toward death," which is to be understood in an existential manner but also attested to in an existentiell manner, is supposed to be the concealed ground not only of primordial temporality but also of historicality. Being-free for death, as the finite *eschaton*, is supposed to give Dasein "its goal pure and simple."[7] In this way, temporal extension into the arriving future of this finite goal receives a fundamental priority over the other dimensions of time.

In the resoluteness of factical Dasein, in which resoluteness "runs ahead" toward the still outstanding end and Dasein hands down its inheritance to itself and takes itself over, authentic historicality and historical fate become constituted together with authentic temporality. Heidegger distinguishes fate [*Schicksal*] from "destining" [*Geschick*], a word which *Being and Time* attaches to the narrower meaning of "happening along with" in Being-with others (384/436), whereas later, in the talk of a destining of Being, it loses this special meaning. In *Being and Time*, what is more essential than any destining with others is *fate* and its relation to individual *resoluteness*. The resolute anticipation and importing of death into existence pushes existence into its finitude, discloses to existing Dasein its essential "situation," and makes Dasein first of all capable of fate. To exist resolutely "in the mode of fate" means "to be historical in the ground of one's existence" (385/437). Fate is the "There" of the "moment of vision," and the moment of vision is the authentic present.

Hence in Heidegger's analysis resoluteness, self-chosen fate, and historical situation form a unitary structural whole which is tied to resolute freedom towards death. "Only beings that are essentially *futural* in their Being in the sense that, as free for their death, they can be thrust back upon their factical There . . . can take over their own thrownness and be *in the moment of vision* for 'their time.' Only authentic temporality, which is finite, makes possible something like fate, i.e. authentic historicality" (385/437). In these assertions Heidegger summarizes the essential content of the analyses of "temporality and historicality."[8]

The question arises: can world-history, as humans in the West from the Persian Wars up to the last World War have in a thousand ways experienced and endured it, and have contemplated it, reported on it, and thought it through philosophically—can world-history be recognized once again in this self-willed project of history on the basis of "Being toward the end,"[9] which is always one's own? Does this existential interpretation of history on the basis of the historicality of finite Dasein render comprehensible what we commonly call history? Does not the experience of Being-mortal, without which there would also be no freedom towards death, instead connect us with the nature of everything living? And does not the transition from the finite temporality of a Dasein that is individuated unto itself in the face of death remain a leap which, rather than illuminating the shared destinings of history, simply leaps over them?

The quotation marks in which Heidegger places "their time" in the above citation are presumably supposed to indicate that what is at stake here is not an arbitrary "engagement" [*Einsatz*] with a contemporary present that intrudes momentarily, but rather the decisive time of a pure moment of vision, whose character of decision results from the distinction between common and existential time and history. But how can one

History, Historicality, and Destining of Being

determine unequivocally in a given case whether the time of decision is a "primordial" moment of vision or merely a "present" that obtrudes in the course and passage of a world-happening?

The resoluteness that does not know what it is resolute about gives no answer to this. It has certainly happened more than once that highly resolute individuals commited themselves to something which demanded that they be fateful and decisive, and which was nonetheless common and not worthy of the sacrifice. How is one supposed to be able to draw the line within a thoroughly historical thinking between "authentic" happenings and that which "commonly" happens, and be able to distinguish unequivocally between self-chosen fate and the destinings which are not chosen and which befall humans or seduce them into a momentary choice and decision? And did not common history wreak vengeance clearly enough on Heidegger's contempt for what is merely present-at-hand today, by seducing him in a crudely decisive moment of vision into assuming under Hitler the leadership of Freiburg University and transferring his resolute ownmost Dasein into a "German Dasein" in order to apply the ontological theory of existential historicality upon the ontic soil of the happenings that are actually historical, i.e., political?

Heidegger's rectoral address of 1933 on "The Self-Assertion of the German University" attests unequivocally to the ambiguous confusion of actual history and the authentic happening of Dasein.[10] The thinker expected from the National Socialist movement "a complete upheaval of German Dasein,"[11] hence apparently the same as what he calls a change in the human essence in the later writings. The language of this discourse (existence and resoluteness, Dasein and capacity-for-Being, the interpretation of this capacity as a fate and a Having-To [*Müssen*], the insistence upon the capacity-for-Being which is always one's own and is German) is drawn entirely from the concepts of *Being and Time*, and also from the vocabulary of the political movement.[12] The whole is a philosophy of existence, of radical change and awakening, which has become political.

Almost simultaneously with Heidegger's call to "armed service" and "knowledge service," Karl Barth's reflection on *Theological Existence Today* appeared.[f] Barth did not become a "German Christian," but rather remained a Christian theologian with a steadfast sense of what actually happened, in order to proclaim, "now as ever," a truth of faith that is not

---

[f] Translator's note: The Swiss theologian Karl Barth (1886–1968), the leading exponent of "crisis theology," argued for the superiority of Christian revelation over the comparatively "fallen" character of human reason. This position led him to develop a "dialectical theology" which emphasizes the contradiction between God and the world.

merely temporo-historical—"perhaps in a gently augmented tone, though without direct reference . . . something like the Benedictines' song of the Horae . . . continues in an orderly manner . . . without a doubt in the Third Reich as well."[13] Thanks to this incomparable freedom from the power of time, Barth was able to understand the multiple grounds and backgrounds of the "downright astonishing lack of resistance" in the face of the assault of the political movement (55), and in connection with it he was able to remark that a deeply philosophical account of events is most surely to be found when one has let oneself be overrun most thoroughly by "actuality" (56).

But why should such a free distance with regard to the happening of time, which is right for the theologian, not also be reasonable for one who does not "have faith" but rather "thinks"—unless one is resolved to understand time on the basis of time, without a philosophical measure for the evaluation of this happening.

It was necessary to make reference Heidegger's rectorial address, not because political action could in any given case coincide with philosophical thinking, but rather because under certain circumstances thinking brings about practical consequences in which definite presuppositions of this very thinking expose themselves. What manifests itself in Heidegger's call is a decisive readiness to believe in historical fate as such. The "moment of vision" appeared to have come in which authentic history, i.e., a destining of Being in the emphatic sense, happened and in which one had to be in terms of the moment of vision. In Heidegger there is no talk of Plato's question regarding the just state. In a confused and confusing way, he thinks "historically" and at the same time completely apolitically, because his historical thinking uncritically lost its way.

Of course, thirteen years later Heidegger offered a philosophical explanation and justification even for this mistaken decision, one co-attuned with the pathos of resoluteness, for a definite historical movement. In *Holzwege* we are told that, as well as why, what arises historically must "necessarily" be misinterpreted. For Being withdraws precisely when it reveals itself in beings, and it thereby confuses [*beirren*] beings; indeed this "error" [*Irre*] is part of the very essence of truth![14] Above all this applies for the beings of history. The "essential space" of history is in fact a domain of error. For world-history happens when Being maintains itself, along with its truth, in that which it sends.

Using a Greek word, Heidegger names this self-maintaining the "epochal" character of Being (333/27). In consequence of this character, that which happens historically does not get misinterpreted on the basis

History, Historicality, and Destining of Being 77

of personal mistakes in judgment, for which the individual would be responsible, but instead gets misinterpreted "necessarily," in consequence of a destining of Being. It is Being itself which holds itself back and conceals itself in extant history. Hence "making a mistake" in humans corresponds to the "self-concealing" of Being. "Throughout this misinterpretation, destining awaits that which grows from its sowing. It brings the interpretation concerned with it into the possibility of the fateful and the un-fateful" (333/26).

In this regard, Heidegger's own un-fatefulness [*Ungeschicklichkeit*] contains a deeper meaning without any irony.[g] His "leadership" of Freiburg University demanded that one be "led" by the "inexorability" of a historical "mission" which "forces the fate of the German people into the imprint of their history."[15] But in the same way the misinterpretation of the "magnificence" of the German awakening was sent by Being itself, and beyond the destining of Being there is no further authority to which humans could appeal and could be allowed to appeal. Even the leadership of the Third Reich is defended, in a subsequently published critique of the present age written in 1939,[16] as being "onto-historical" [*seinsgeschichtlich*]. It is not simply the case that the total state is a kind of errancy, but instead the "earth" has become the "un-world of error"—"onto-historically [*seynsgeschichtlich*], it is the star of error"—and within this environment the leaders are the necessary consequence of beings having proceeded into the manner of error. Only those who do not yet know "what is," will for this reason become indignant about arbitrariness and the claim of dominion on the part of the leaders, whereas those who know comprehend such a "moral indignation" as "the most fatal form of constant appreciation" and of being caught up in an annoyance.

Heidegger, who knows what is, does not express such an inferior kind of indignance but instead sees that the state which is totally planned and led, together with the leadership of literature and a manufacture of humans which is equally controlled by a plan, is the historically necessary consequence of the abandonment of Being. —One asks oneself whether such a total claim is the result of a historical knowledge and a philosophical thinking, or whether it is not instead the translation of the doctrine

---

[g]Translator's note: The reader should bear in mind here that the terms *geschicklich* and *ungeschicklich* normally mean "adroit" and "clumsy," respectively, and that Heidegger uses these terms in connection with the idea of *Geschick* or destining; here Löwith's use of the term *Ungeschicklichkeit* is intended to convey both the everyday and the specialized senses of the term. Cf. "Der Spruch des Anaximander," p. 333/ "The Anaximander Fragment," p. 26.

of the Fall into falling into the world of beings. When Christians believe that everything evil in this world is the necessary consequence of the abandonment of God and the forgottenness of God, this is more understandable than when a thinker derives the error of the epoch from a destining of Being and takes its "history" as the absolute measure.

What changed after *Being and Time* was not faith in history as fate, but rather the grounding of history. Whereas it is said in *Being and Time* that the question of Being can be posed only historically because the questioning Dasein of humans is of a historical kind, it is said conversely in the "Letter on Humanism" that the thinking of Being is historical because there is a history of *Being* into which thinking belongs, as a remembrance of this history which is eventuated by this very history. In *Being and Time* the grounding of history follows from the temporality of our ownmost temporal Dasein, whereas *after Being and Time* it follows from this entirely other Being itself, which essences beyond and behind all beings and sends us the essential destinings, so that the locale and meaning of history and fate become reoriented and modified. History authentically emerges already with the "es gibt" of the Being which gives and sends itself. "Being comes to destining in that It, Being, gives itself,"[17] or respectively withholds itself. History does not first happen as a happening rich in events, but rather essences as the simple and essential "destining of the truth of Being" from out of Being (332/215), i.e., history is first and last the emergence of what is concealed into the truth as unconcealedness. As an unconditioned prehistory of Being, history becomes not only undatable, but also unexplorable and unrecognizable. History is rare, which is to say that it is only when a destining of the truth of Being abruptly eventuates itself.

In accordance with this displacement of the problem of history from extant Dasein to Being, Heidegger no longer wants to be in terms of the moment of vision for his time, on the basis of his own resoluteness; instead he wants to attune his resoluteness toward fate into the "essential path" of a world-destining and into the "world-moment-of-vision" of a "world-need" (337, 360/220, 242). Now the world-historical moment of vision ultimately points toward a "sight [*Blick*] of Being," to which there corresponds an "insight [*Einblick*] into that which is."[18]

Heidegger's insight formulates anew what had been seen and said throughout Europe with growing urgency from the beginning of the nineteenth century up to Nietzsche and Léon Bloy.[h] What is new here is that Heidegger claims that the movement of nihilism is the fundamental movement of the entire history of the West, and that he brings this sup-

History, Historicality, and Destining of Being

posedly fundamental happening into a system in a philosophico-historical manner by tracing back to their incomprehensible origin, in a forgetting of Being, all appearances of a progressive decline [*Verfall*], on the basis of the original falling [*Verfallen*] into beings.

In seeming accord with world-spirit as the destining of Being, Heidegger lets world-history proceed as the history of decline, in connection with which he, like Hegel[19]—the "sole thinker of the West to experience thoughtfully the history of thinking"[20]—interprets retrospectively what has been, in the blinding light of its supposedly necessary consequences, and unifies seamlessly the intellectual history of Being, the history of metaphysics, with the history of the world. Onto-historical thinking and the essence of world-history must correspond entirely with one another, just as for Hegel the history of philosophy and the philosophy of history are essentially the same, if thinking corresponds to a behest of Being which for its own part is a historical-destining one.

The question of Being, it is said in 1935 in the lecture *An Introduction to Metaphysics*, is one of the essential conditions for a primordial world of historical Dasein and "hence for an assumption of the historical mission of our people to be the middle of the West."[21] And because Heidegger's "authentic attack" is aimed at the "fundamental position of Western spirit," i.e., at the "divorce of Being and thinking" (125/117) and he himself assumes that essential thinking and its history repose in the destining of Being and correspond to it, for him the history of thinking is "the dispatching of the human essence out of the destining of Being."[22] Even the technological world of the modern age, which is coming to completion, is nothing made by humans, but rather is, in its essence, an onto-historical destining of the truth of Being. It is grounded in the history of metaphysics, which is now coming to completion, a history which for its own part is not lined up on the "countertop of historiological representing," but rather corresponds to a constantly and precipitously changing destining of Being itself.

Similarly, one may not judge communism all too shortsightedly as a political *Weltanschauung*,[23] but rather must understand it as a destining of Being. For whatever position one takes toward it, it is "onto-historically" certain that what expresses itself in it is something world-historical. Of course several years earlier Heidegger granted this same onto-historical

[h]Translator's note: Léon Bloy (1846–1917) was a staunch defender of Catholicism (with a special emphasis on asceticism) and has been widely received as an implicit exponent of literary Naturalism; his intimate contemporaries included Jacques Maritain and René Martineau.

sanction to National Socialism. And why not, if ever-changing world-history were always to emerge from the essence of a "history of Being," and neither a materialistic nor a Christian or humanistic metaphysics but rather only an onto-historical thinking could thoughtfully reach what "now is" in a fulfilled meaning of Being. It is this momentary Now which bears forth Heidegger's historical construction of the beginning of an *eschaton* and motivates his critique of the present.

In the introduction to *Being and Time* it is noted briefly that the destruction of the history of ontology is related negatively not to the past but rather to the "present" [*Heute*].[24] It is indirectly a critique of the present [*Gegenwart*] which was originally inspired by Kierkegaard's critical differentiation between edifying reflection and existential decision. Heidegger's critique is made explicit for the first time in the rectoral address, which concludes with the question whether we, as a historical people, still and once again will [*wollen*] ourselves,[i] or whether we do not will ourselves.[25] Whether the spiritual strength of the West fails and its dissipated excuse for culture collapses into itself so that everything gets ripped into confusion, or whether we shall begin anew in Europe, depends entirely on this self-willing.

Back in 1933, Heidegger's outlook was still that the answer to his question had already been decided positively by the "greatness" and the "magnificence" of the German awakening (19/38). Three years later, in a lecture on Hölderlin, the tone is essentially more resigned. Now things no longer depend on an awakening but rather on standing firm in the "Nothing of this night."[26] In the essays in *Holzwege*, in which the critique of the present age becomes thematic, in connection with the encroaching "world-night" Nietzsche's question is repeated regarding whether we late-born can be called on to recover once again the beginnings of Western thinking and to be the premature first-born of a new beginning.[27] A series of rhetorical questions suggests itself, to the effect that we are not only late ones but rather for that very reason are also premature ones. "Do we stand on the eve [*Vorabend*][j] of the most tremendous change of the entire earth and of the time of historical space in which it hangs? Do we stand before the evening [*Abend*] of a night prior to a new dawn? Do we

---

[i]Translator's note: The verb *wollen* means to "want," but it also carries overtones of willing, which are especially strong not only in this statement but in the rectoral address generally.

[j]Translator's note: In this and the following questions, Heidegger progressively weaves the everyday meaning of *Abend* as evening together with the cultural meaning of *Abend* and *Abendland* as the Occident or the West.

History, Historicality, and Destining of Being 81

set out just in order to immigrate to the historical land of this evening of the earth? Does the land of the evening [*Land des Abends*] first arise? Does this evening-land [*Abend-Land*], beyond Occident and Orient and throughout the European, first become the locale of the coming originary history, which has been sent? Are we of today already Western [*abendländisch*] in a sense that first arises through our crossing into the world-night? . . . *Are* we the late-born who we are? But are we at the same time also the premature ones of the dawn of an entirely new age which has left behind our current historiological representations of history?"[28]

Heidegger certainly does not want to "calculate" the decline of the West, but who could fail to see that this very timely eschatology of Being bears the mark of Spengler[k] and above all of Nietzsche, who, according to Heidegger, surely experienced "several features" of nihilism but did not recognize the "essence" of nihilism.[29] Indeed the truth of Being remained concealed from metaphysics throughout its entire history, from Anaximander to Nietzsche! And because metaphysics, which represents beings and forgets Being, is the historical ground of Western world-history, this world-history itself is nihilistic in its essence.

What happens in this way as a destining of Being and consequently what happens in this epoch, is so unfathomable that all our political and sociological perspectives, as well as all our scientific and technological ones and our metaphysical and religious ones, do not manage to think truly "what is." Expelled from the truth of Being, modern humans revolve around themselves unhealed, as individuated individuals or perhaps as an enormous collective, privately and publicly. Not only does the holy as the trace of divinity remain concealed, but even the trace of the holy, namely that which heals, appears to be extinguished—unless a few mortals are still there "in the right moment" and are capable of seeing the danger because they reach into the abyss and, as Rilke put it, are "more venture-

---

[k]Translator's note: Oswald Spengler (1880–1936), German philosopher of history and author of *The Decline of the West* (2 vols., 1918, 1922), borrowed the distinction between "culture" and "civilization" from Nietzsche. He conceived of "culture" as the creative phase of a society's history, and he believed that in this phase the bucolic "soul" is preeminent. He contrasted culture with "civilization," which he conceived as the historical phase in which the theoretical consequences of cultural creativity are drawn out and in which there is an emphasis on material comfort; he believed that in this phase the urban "intellect" is preeminent. Ludwig Klages (1872–1956), founder of a center for the study of "characterology" in Munich, maintained that human life consists in a struggle between spirit (which he identified with rationality) and both body and soul (the soul being identified with creative forces).

some."[30] Salvation, it is said in Heidegger's interpretation of Rilke, can come only where there is a turn in the relationship of humans to Being.

What complements this eschatological construction of world-history as his history of Being is the construction of the main epochs of metaphysics. In the interpretation of Plato's cave allegory, Heidegger sketches out the stages of its decline with reference to the concept of truth as unconcealedness.[31] Already in Plato truth comes under the yoke of the "Idea." With this the primordial meaning of truth as the unconcealedness of beings shifts to viewing Ideas in the right way. The correctness of subjective viewing, perceiving, and asserting gets priority over the emergence of beings themselves from concealedness into unconcealedness. Even more definitely than Plato, Aristotle says that true and false are not in things but rather are in the understanding. From now on, the stamp of the essence of truth as the correctness of representations which assert becomes the measure for all of Western thinking. According to St. Thomas, truth is found in the human or the divine understanding. Truth is no longer *a-letheia* but instead is *adequatio*, the correct conformity of the understanding and the assertion to the matter [*Sache*]. Descartes sharpens this thesis, and in the epoch of the completion of subjectivity Nietzsche says, in a further sharpening, that truth is an error which is necessary for life, i.e., a subjectively necessary falsification of reality by means of our objectifying representation. Hence Nietzsche's thesis is the most extreme consequence of the change in truth, which already began in Plato,[32] from the unconcealedness of beings to the correctness of viewing.

In his discussion of Nietzsche, Heidegger develops Nietzsche's supposed Platonism more completely. His concept of value (which can be demonstrated historiologically to stem from the economic theories of the nineteenth century) is, according to Heidegger, supposed to be a final legitimate formulation of Plato's doctrine of Ideas. In accordance with his destructive tendency, Heidegger accepts without restriction Nietzsche's thesis of the decay of the suprasensible world of Ideas and ideals, in order on the basis of this to classify and interpret the Christian history of spirit as a comparable history of decline. "In the place of the diminished authority of God and the Church, the authority of conscience steps in, the authority of reason presses itself. Against these, social instinct presents itself. The flight from the world and into the suprasensible gets replaced by historiological progress. The otherworldly goal of an eternal beatitude becomes transformed into the earthly happiness of the many. The caring of the cult of religion gets replaced by enthusiasm for the creation of a culture or for the expansion of civilization. Creativity, which was previously proper to the biblical God, becomes the distinction of human doing. This creating [*Schaffen*] ultimately merges into business affairs [*Geschäft*]. That which seeks in this way to put itself in the place of the supersensible world, is a variety of modifications of the interpretation of the world in the Christian Church and in theology, an interpretation which took over its conception of the *ordo* or the hierarchical order of beings from the Hellenistic-Jewish world, whose fundamental structure was established by Plato at the beginning of Western metaphysics."[33]

What really happens in the entire history of Western metaphysics is an unequivocally nihilistic occurrence, namely the destining of Being that "the suprasensible world, the Ideas, God, the moral law, the authority of reason, progress, the happiness of the many, culture, civilization, and their formative energy forfeit and become null. We call this essential decay of the suprasensible its decomposition [*Verwesung*]" (217/65). Nonetheless, in Heidegger's account this process of decomposition also takes on a remarkable attractiveness. He refers to something in the future which is coming, a new day after the "world-night" which has been manufactured technologically. To this there correspond only recurring, mysterious intimations of that which humans "today" are naturally "not yet" able to know—though perhaps some other day. What we "today" are only just able to presage, what for us "still" remains to be thought, what "so far" is still concealed because we ourselves "still" belong to an epoch which "one day" will be followed by an entirely different one—these and similar words regarding time in Heidegger's discourse create an atmosphere of tension and allow a concealed knowledge to be presaged that goes beyond what has been said previously.

Who can be surprised, in hearing such a radical critique of the present and of the entire past, and in hearing such a prescient prophecy of an indeterminate future, when attentive pupils of a master who imposes his idea and masters language ask what sort of "necessary" turn history must make, if "the Freiburg philosopher's counter-movement which grasps all of Western thinking" is one day to take effect?[34] Already a hundred years ago, a similar situation had resulted in Germany with Hegel's culmination of the Western history of spirit, when his pupils, and not least Marx, asked in all seriousness how history could continue at all after Hegel. The liberation from Hegel's definitive system was provided first of all by Schelling. Even as level-headed a Hegelian as Rosenkranz noted in 1841, on the occasion of Schelling's inaugural lecture on the positive philosophy of existence and revelation: "Schelling's inaugural speech has come. I devoured it. If he fulfills only half of what he promises, then he will end the course of his life in an infinitely greater way than he began it. He possesses, in the highest degree, the art of enthralling. He wants to 'move' humanity 'beyond the consciousness it has reached up to now.' If he succeeds in doing this, then he is more than a philosopher, he is the founder of a religion."[1]

Heidegger too understands the art of enthralling, he too wants to move us beyond the consciousness we have reached up to now, and in this regard he too initially gives the impression of being a soothsayer who turns the need of time in a preparatory way, by turning back toward Being as the place of a possible God. If one asks whether Heidegger's passionate effort to bring Being to language reaches beyond personal seriousness and stands under a "law," then in the sense which is most proper to Heidegger the answer can only be: under no other law than that of need [*Not*] and of a "need-fulness" [*Not-wendigkeit*] which he interprets historically with reference to world-need. Certainly everyone has more or less experienced the general need of our destitute time. Whether and how this is to turn, can neither be known nor said. This is why Heidegger's claim to the necessity [*Notwendigkeit*] of his thinking can convince only those who believe along with him that his thinking of Being has been sent, that it is a destining of Being and hence that it says "the decree [*Diktat*] of the truth of Being."[35]

About this nothing can be said rationally. Still, one surely can and must raise the question whether a historical need, however great and pressing it may be, can be the essential ground for the movement of a philosophical reflection on the essence of Being and of truth. Indeed already in his early consideration of historiology Nietzsche himself, who like no other philosopher was a child of his time in the sense of being an "untimely one," defined the task of the philosopher in terms of having to think beyond history, and hence into the ubiquity of an eternally returning Being, from the standpoint of which our overestimation of history and of historiological consciousness is an "Occidental prejudice."

A reflection on the essence of modernity does as a matter of fact place thinking and decision within the "scope of the essential forces of this epoch," and in the face of these Heidegger can rightfully insist on the

---

[1] Translator's note: Johann Karl Friedrich Rosenkranz (1805–1879) was a leading adherent of Hegel who argued for the inner compatibility between Hegel's philosophy and that of German thinkers like Kant and Schleiermacher. He also advocated the autonomy of the church and the university from the influence of the state, though he believed that these are united in terms of an underlying *Volksgeist* or spirit of a people.

alternative: either "preparedness to convey" historical fate, or "evasion into the ahistorical." But assuming that there were something older, more lasting, and more permanent than an epoch, namely a cosmic world-aeon, then Heidegger's historico-philosophical project could appear to be right while nonetheless being untrue, namely if the realm of the historical is circumscribed by the Being of a being which cannot be reached through the mere negation of the historical toward the ahistorical. Even in the epoch of the "completion of subjectivity," "nature" is still the same as two thousand years ago, and it is mightier than all variations in the realm of the historical human essence.

A late Roman thinker and poet, in whose work the knowledge and the wisdom of early Greek thinking once again gather themselves, concluded his didactic poem on the "nature of all things" with a depiction of human need which spares us nothing—"hopeless," if it were a matter of speaking about hopelessness where nothing is hoped for, least of all a "salvation" from deepest need. Lucretius knows that even human need belongs to the nature of things and is the same at all times, as is the creative *voluptas* of the lust for life with which his didactic poem commences. The logos of the physical cosmos, to which even humans belong, is and remains, throughout all generation and corruption, always one and the same. No classical philosopher turned to reflection on the true essence of Being as a preparation for the arrival of Being and of future history. Historiological futurism was first made possible by Christian eschatology.

But doesn't Heidegger struggle explicitly against our prior, merely historiological representations of history and against the historicism which gets organized ever more permanently through radio and the press, inasmuch as these constitute a demolition of our historical relation to Being, whose authentic happening is an "exclusive nearness of the same"? And doesn't he even characterize the happening of truth, with reference to the fundamental Greek experience of *physis*, as an emergence of what is concealed into unconcealment, thereby not characterizing it at all historically, in the historiological sense of this word? But to what extent does this association of true history and ubiquitous *physis* harmonize with the claim that history rarely is, namely in the rare instants of a world-destining which turns precipitously?

Physis and historiology have as little in common in Greek as beings-which-are-always-thus have in common with the mere investigation (*historein*) of varying human destinings. Greek historians did indeed record histories and explain the seemingly lawful diversity of historical destinings on the basis of the encompassing nature of all things, but no Greek philosopher devised, with an eye toward the future, a philosophy of the one and universal history; but of course all of them made ever-present *physis* into the object of "physics" and metaphysics. In Greek thinking historiology did not have, in a sense which befits the word nor in a sense which befits the subject, a subject area that expressly belonged to it and that was comparable to physics. As an investigating and becoming acquainted, it is related to everything that can be investigated and known. An effort like that of Heidegger to think Being onto-*historically* is as far removed as possible from the physical beginnings of Greek thinking. Hence a critical discussion of his concept of history must ultimately take into account his concept of nature as well, although in comparison with the former the latter is remarkably precarious and undeveloped.

Together with his concept of history, Heidegger's conception of nature changed in a number of ways without coming to complete determinacy. In *Being and Time* nature and history are entirely distinct, whereas later, as *physis* and the happening of Being, they nearly collapse into one another. In *Being and Time* nature in its naturalness gets ignored and, in contrast to the "readiness-to-hand" of equipment and the historical "existing" of human Dasein, becomes subject to the lowest concept of the merely "present-at-hand." Humans are not nature but are instead, as for Pascal, a "*condition humaine*." Even birth and death are not natural, but rather are incorporated into the care of temporal existence. Dying, which from a biological standpoint is a mere "perishing," is, understood existentially, a free "Being toward the end" in which one's demise is a sublated moment.[36] Similarly, it is in ready-to-hand equipment (in paths, bridges, buildings) that nature is merely "co-uncovered" by our concern.

On the whole, in *Being and Time* nature is a being "within the world" which is encountered by human Dasein in its world, but it is nothing in itself and it is by no means the Being of all beings.[37] Nature is simply a "limiting case of the Being of possible beings within the world."[38] Nonetheless, "world" is part of the manner of Being of Dasein, which as Being-in-the-world is an issue for iself. The world's manner of Being, its worldliness, cannot be grasped on the basis of nature, but instead one must interpret nature in terms of the existential structure of our Being-in-the-world. Hence nature as such is absent from Heidegger's project of a "natural concept of world."[39] It is the ahistorical and nonexistential Other in relation to the Being of historical Dasein. This negative definition of nature is a product of the modern tradition, having been first of all established in Descartes' distinction between *res extensa* and *res cogitans* and having persisted from that time up to Vico and Dilthey under various titles (nature and spirit, nature and culture, nature and history, the explicable and the intelligible).

In the essay "On the Essence of Ground," where the concept of world gets further developed to the point that it finally loses its existential meaning and thereby comes to mean the same as the "clearing of Being," Heidegger protests against the objection that nature is missing in *Being and Time*.[40] The reason for this is that nature is found neither within the scope of the environment of the ready-to-hand nor as something "towards which" we "relate" ourselves. But in spite of this insight into nature as something which permeates everything including humans, even here Heidegger holds to his existential point of departure when he says that nature manifests itself primordially "in Dasein" to the extent that Dasein is situated "in the midst of" beings (154n/81n). And because situatedness [*Befindlichkeit*][m] belongs to the essence of Dasein, the "basis" for the question concerning nature is "care" as the fundamental existential constitution of humans. The human being is not an *animal rationale*, but rather is an ecstatic existence.[41] It cannot be understood why the workings of nature in its naturalness are supposed to be capable of being experienced on this basis, unless it is understood negatively as that which is ahistorical, which lacks care, and which is not "existent," in comparison with our caring, historical existence.

A new approach to grasping nature is found in the essay "On the Essence of Truth," in connection with the discussion of truth as freedom. Here freedom is no longer defined, as in *Being and Time*, as a *capacity-for-Being* and ultimately as freedom toward death, but instead it is defined as a *letting*-Be. Human freedom lets beings manifest themselves in what and how they are, by letting itself into the unconcealed (the true). The freedom of letting-Be is the condition for the possibility of truth, because it opens itself up and exposes itself to the Open. It is ex-position (ek-sistence) into the revealedness of beings. With it begins the "historical" ek-sistence of humans. "Only where beings themselves are expressly raised into and preserved in their unconcealedness, only where this preservation on the basis of questioning after beings as such is grasped, does history begin. The originary privation of beings as a whole, the question con-

---

[m]Translator's note: In *Being and Time*, Macquarrie and Robinson translate *Befindlichkeit* as "state-of-mind," though it should be noted that the notion of mind is misleading here; the term signifies "situatedness" in the sense of one's relation to things generally, i.e., how things stand with a person, and it can also signify where something is located. The expression "Wie befinden Sie sich?" is commonly translated as "How are you?" or "How are you doing?"

cerning beings as such, and the beginning of Western history are the same and are simultaneously in a 'time' which itself, immeasurably, first opens up the Open for every measure."[42]

This most unusual use of the word "history" signifies that true happening does not happen in world-history nor in the so-called happening of Dasein, but instead "history" is first and last the originary privation of beings as a whole. But the whole precedes and goes beyond the distinction between nature and history as special regions of Being. Nonetheless this history of Being, grasped as absolute, is supposed to ground metaphysically a very definite and historiologically graspable history, namely that of the West. How is this conceivable? How are the rare decisions of history to be capable of emerging from the manner "in which the primordial essence of truth essences" (188/130), if this essence is the revelation of beings as a whole and this whole knows nothing of the distinction between nature and history? But even if we assume that the distinction between nature and history, according to which nature is the ahistorical, is not essential because essential happening relates itself to beings as a whole and thereby to Being as such, how were beings as a whole able nonetheless to reveal themselves primordially as *physis* in the early thinking of the Greeks,[43] and *not* as history in a historiologically definable sense?

Apparently the Being of all beings cannot be defined more precisely, i.e., immediately and purely as such, but instead can be defined only with respect to its concrete mediation. And supposing that the most natural concretion of beings as a whole, or rather of the Being of all beings, is still nature just as it was earlier, then we would have to ask in addition why the arising of the concealed into unconcealedness, which appears in the growth of everything living, i.e., in its generation and corruption, together with the retreat into concealedness is supposed to be capable of grounding the "rare decisions" of *history*, given that these decisions certainly appear to be part of a historiologically definable history which is not of a physical kind. How for example is the fate of technology, which is decisive for modernity, supposed to be capable of emerging from a physical happening of Being, if *techne* is as different from *physis* as what is produced artificially is from what is grown naturally?

In the guise of one of his interpretations of Hölderlin, Heidegger attempts to show that the primordial meaning of nature as *physis*, which continues to resonate in Hölderlin, signifies neither a being in contrast to other beings nor a definite being's manner of Being, but rather the clearing of Being pure and simple.[44] Heidegger thinks this Being, which for him is distinct from all beings, into Hölderlin's poetizing of nature, in order to read out of it the "concealed truth" of the originary, fundamental word *physis*, which is already "ruined without healing" by its Latin rendering as *natura* and nature. Nature is present in everything actual, in rocks, plants, and animals, in rivers, storms, and stars, but also in the destinings of peoples and in the gods. It is, in Hölderlin's words, the wonderfully "ubiquitous [*Allgegenwärtige*]" (52ff.), in Heidegger's translation Being itself, which is not a being.

Accordingly he maintains that nature, in spite of its ubiquity in everything that is, cannot "even be intimated" by an actual being. Nature is that which is present [*Anwesende und Gegenwärtige*] in advance in everything and which is at the same time something coming. It is "Being" and the arrival of Being. Prior to everything else, nature is "the same as ever," which means in Heidegger's interpretation: it is "some time" [*einstig*] in the dual sense of the oldest of all and the youngest of all, indeed in such a way that what is in its future comes from what was longest ago (73). Thus it can also never become antiquated. The first before everything and the last after everything, nature is that which is primordially originary, and as such it is that which remains or which is eternal. It is also that which is holy, mighty, and all-creating. As a consequence of this indifference of nature as Being toward natural and historical beings, even the years in Hölderlin's poem are as much natural seasons of the year as they are historical years of peoples.

Corresponding to this assimilation of *physis* to Being, Heidegger, with reference to the concept of truth as a revealing, also formalizes the fundamental sense of growth contained in the Greek word for nature (*physis*, *phyein*; *natura*, *nascor*) into emergence and arising into the Open. Hence in Heidegger's interpretation *physis* becomes the "clearing" pure and simple, in which something can first of all appear and be present as this or that. Together with the emergence which opens itself (*genesis*), a withdrawing retreat (*phthora*) in this emergence takes place. "*Physis*" is thus "going-back-into-itself which arises and designates the presencing of that which lingers as the Open in the arising which essences in this way" (56). This nature, interpreted as "Being," is "older than the ages" which are meted out to historical peoples and also "beyond the gods of the Occident and the Orient," though it is not older than time as such (59). It is not extra- and supra-temporal, but rather is the most originary and hence also the most futural time. The "now" at the beginning of the seventh strophe names the coming of nature as the coming of the holy, and only this coming, on Heidegger's interpretation, fixes the time at which "it is time" for history "to face up to essential decisions" (76).

Heidegger concludes his interpretation with the suggestion that nature, the fundamental word of Hölderlin's poem, says the holy and thereby names "the sole time-space of the originary decision in favor of the essential composition of the coming history of the gods and of the varieties of humanity" (77). In its coming, that which is holy in unscathed nature is grounded in "a new [*anderen*] beginning of a new [*andern*] history" (76).

One can accept Heidegger's spirited elucidations of Hölderlin's poetry from a distance, as an impressive whole; or one can examine them in their particulars from the standpoint of literary historiology. One must call this elucidation into question, as a thinker's elucidation of a poet, with respect to the problem of history. For what is allowed to the poetic word, is for the same token not valid in thinking that makes critical distinctions. Indeed on the occasion of his interpretation of the adage of Anaximander and in connection with his fundamental calling into question of "science," Heidegger guards against the "common opinion" that in order to proceed scientifically [*wissenschaftlich*] one must distinguish subject areas [*fachwissenschaftlich*], e.g., the physical from the moral and judicial. But getting rid of substantive demarcations between areas does not signify a blurring into the indefinite; instead it first of all brings to language the "free structure" of the matter, thought purely.

But is Heidegger's artistic language system really able to illuminate the essence or nonessence [*Unwesen*] of history,[n] if history, with respect to Being as such, coincides with nature as *physis*? It is obvious that in Hölderlin's poetry, as in all pure poetry, the word "nature" resonates beyond its immediate semantic content and does not name the nature of natural science. But to every impartial reading of the poem it is equally clear that Hölderlin, in naming nature in the whole breadth and multiplicity of its poetic meanings, constantly has in mind the actual nature with which the first stanza begins. But if the poet relates this one nature, which is ubiquitous and holy and which is beyond the gods of the Occident and Orient, indiscriminately to the growing of plants and to the destinings of peoples, then no thinking that makes critical distinctions can match him.

Whoever thinks, cannot avoid thinking the year of natural seasons and the years of popular history or the storm at the beginning and the storm at the end of the poem as distinct from one another, and whoever thinks

---

[n]Translator's note: The term *Unwesen* normally signifies an awful or dreadful event or state of affairs; but Heidegger sometimes uses this term as a negation of the term *Wesen* (essence). Cf. e.g., "Vom Wesen des Grundes," *Wegmarken*, 2d ed., p. 171 / *The Essence of Reasons*, p. 127.

History, Historicality, and Destining of Being 91

will have to refuse to go along with Heidegger in applying to nature the ambiguous "one day" of the early time and the late time of historical decisions. The time in which it is time for history to pose decisions, the decisive "moment of vision" as it was put in *Being and Time* in a language that was in no way oriented on nature, cannot be reckoned and measured; but even if essential history could not be worked out in terms of dates, surely on the basis of its decision-character alone it is as unfathomably different from nature as that which is intact in nature is from *the* healing and holy, the expectation of which arises from the lack of healing in a historical experience. In the words "epoch" [*Zeitalter*] and "aeon" [*Weltalter*], a poet may name the world and time of humans together with the world and time of nature; a thinker who insists on the rigor of reflection and on care in saying will have to decide whether nature is ahistorical and merely co-discovered in our historical Being-in-the-world, or whether instead our historical world and human beings are grounded in the *physis* which brings forth everything and hence in the Being of all beings.

History, which for Heidegger was at issue from the beginning, loses all definite and demonstrable meaning if, like *physis*, it is a ubiquitous emergence into the Open and a retreat into what is closed off. Assuming that the ground of all essences is nature in this broad sense, the ground of humans would in fact not simply be "like" the ground of plant and animal (since only distinct things can be alike and comparable) but rather would be the same ground. Then nature, as the Being of all beings, would be the ground for history, art, and natural kinds [*Gewächse*]. But how can *physis* be the essential ground of an actually extant nature and history, if it is not itself a being which emerges into the Open and returns into what is closed off? How can one, along with Hölderlin, call nature that which is ubiquitous in everything that is, and say at the same time that it can "not even be intimated" through something actual, without depriving this poetic naming and intellectual saying of its basis? A Being which is defined by nothing extant and which is thereby undefinable, and which with respect to actual nature and history is neutral and indifferent, can ground and define neither nature nor history. In the end even the "clearing," as that which Being is named, is not thinkable and demonstrable apart from the experience of an actual source of light, of the rising and setting sun in whose light all extant things stand and into which they emerge and grow.

If one surveys the path from *Being and Time* to the later writings, then in connection with the problem of history a three-tiered "*Aufhebung*" of historicism becomes evident. Heidegger first sublates [*hebt . . . auf*] historiological relativism by grounding the possibility of Being-historiological in human Being-historical, and by basing human historicality in the "Being-toward-the-end" of existing Dasein and thus positing historicality absolutely. This radicalization of historiological relativism into an existential historicality is possible, however, only because Dasein's end is of an ahistorical kind: the unchanging fact of natural death. With the anticipation of death, Dasein acquires a "prehistorical stability."[45] Then Heidegger also sublated the historicality of the Dasein which is rooted in Being-towards-death, by shifting the starting point from humans and all "humanism" to the question of the truth of Being and by defining truth as the happening of truth in a history of Being. The historicality of existing Dasein thereby becomes reduced to a "proper" or "improper" correspondence of ek-sistent Dasein to the destinings of Being which have been sent.[46] "History" is now the word for the "destining of a sending."

Nonetheless, even in this conception of history historicism is maintained in an absolute manner. In this way Heidegger can reject Hegel's historically conceived system, which makes the law of thinking into the law of history, and at the same time say that Hegel's definition of history as the development of spirit is not untrue. It is also not partly true and partly false, but instead is as true as the whole metaphysics of subjectivity which in Hegel brings its essence, thought absolutely, to language. If Being, in precipitous epochs of the history of Being, sent itself to and at the same time withdrew itself from Heraclitus as *logos*, *kosmos*, and *physis*, to and from Plato as *Idea,* Aristotle as *energeia*, the Christian thinkers as *ens creatum*, Kant as the *objectivity* of the object of experience, Hegel as *absolute notion* and as the *spirit of willing*, Nietzsche as the *will to power* which eternally wills the same—if Being in general is as it is only in an ever-historical stamp and tradition, and if it can be experienced only in its passage through the history of Western thinking, then the question of the truth of what has been thought dissolves into the indiscriminate acknowledgement of the epochs of a history which is always true because it always reveals, even if one no longer speaks of it in a "common" way but instead speaks of it onto-historically as a mysterious destining of Being. For Being is not what is universal to all beings, but rather is a Being which is always defined in terms of history and destining.

As little as Heidegger recognizes a universal human nature, i.e. one which is common to all, just as little does he understand Being to be a Being which is common to everything which is by nature extant; but of course he cannot avoid speaking in the most universal terms of the historical existence which is always one's own and of Being which always destines. The metaphysics which from Plato to Nietzsche was denied the

History, Historicality, and Destining of Being 93

truth of Being, belongs to the history of a *happening* of truth in which truth gives itself and denies itself. Historiological relativism is by no means overcome with this, but instead gets onto-historically sublated, as it was already in Hegel himself, who first made such relativism possible by proceeding from the assumption that truth has the "tendency" to develop along with time. And finally, Heidegger also defined the history of Being as a history of *physis*. As an emergence and arising into the Open, *physis* is the "clearing" pure and simple.

Thus the "common" history of occurrences has completely foundered within Being, about which no more can be said than that It is "it itself."[47] And nonetheless, in decisive moments of actual world-history, historiologically definable histories of the world are supposed to emerge from out of this clearing. Hence it is no accident if Heidegger's essential-historical thinking can be interpreted in opposing ways: as an extreme consequence of historicism to the extent that, in a historiologically definable way, it thinks in an excessively historical manner, and as a nonhistoriological thinking to the extent that it distances itself from all merely historiological "representing" and thinks essential history as a destining of Being.[48] If it is not only temporal Being in the manner of finite Dasein which is historical, but instead, in a sense still to be clarified, Being itself is Being *and* time because time and history essence [*wesen*] primordially in the clearing of Being, then nothing, and this means no definite being, is distinguished by historicality but instead everything is subsumed into the one pseudohistorical and historiologically undefinable Being.[49] Then not only can history no longer be reckoned in terms of dates, it can also no longer be known nor specified according to its contents, since there is history "originarily" only to the extent that there is not yet any distinction between nature and history. The modern opposition of nature and history may in fact be dubious and invalid, though this is not because with respect to the Being of all beings generally there is no history in contrast to nature and its history, but rather because modern historical thinking is a distant Event of Christian eschatology and an immediate consequence of Vico's reversal of Descartes's mathematical natural science.[50]

According to Heidegger history, which is true but concealed, ultimately reduces itself to the *one* destining of the forgottenness of Being, to the forgottenness of the distinction between Being and beings. But this forgottenness, Heidegger says, is not the result of an all-too human forgetfulness, but instead is the very destining of Being, its concealedness. From the beginning, Being holds to itself along with its essence—up to a new *parusie* and apocalypse of Being. But this primordial, exclusive, and singularly essential history of Being is at the same time supposed to be defined as Western world-history. "The forgottenness of the distinction, with which the destining of Being begins and with which it will come to completion, is nonetheless not a lack but instead is the richest and broadest Event, in which Western world-history comes to the fore."[51] The fate of Western metaphysics, a fate which is sent by Being, is a world-destining. Heidegger is convinced that it announces itself preeminently in the poetry of Hölderlin, whose "world-historical" thinking is essentially more originary and hence more futural than the "mere cosmopolitanism" of Goethe.[52] The question whether for Goethe, who himself was a healing nature and a "son of the earth," nature and history were not more unconcealed than for Hölderlin's worldless existence, will have to be allowed in spite of Heidegger's dictum.

But what is at issue is neither the authority of Goethe nor that of Hölderlin, but rather the question whether we, the heirs of the historiological thinking which arose around 150 years ago and which can thus also pass away again, do not immoderately overestimate history in all of the possibilities for its apolitical interpretation—as "spiritual," "existential," and "onto-historical"—ever since its experience was emancipated from both its natural delimitation by the *logos* of the *cosmos* and its supernatural delimitation by the will of God, in such a way that it became absolutized. The transition from the analysis of *time* to the time of *history*, which is characteristic for Heidegger's analyses of temporality, is not to be found in Aristotle and Augustine. In Greek philosophy time is discussed within physics, because it is oriented on the eternal circular movement of the *cosmos*, movement which is without beginning and end. In Christian theology it is related, with respect to the question of the timeless eternity of God, to the world as creation, and to the human soul. According to Aristotle, knowledge of history is less philosophical than poetry, because in each case it deals only with what has happened accidentally and not with what is always possible and necessary. According to Augustine, the profane history of the *saeculum*° is a hopeless sequence of empires and generations dominated by arrogance and foolish desires. If an "essential ground" of history must be asked about at all, then for an understanding of profane history the biblical story of creation is still more

---

°Translator's note: A *saeculum* is a generation, either in the sense of a person's lifespan (about 33-1/3 years in Roman antiquity) or in the sense of the people who compose a given generation; it can also signify, as in the present context, an age or an indefinitely long period of time.

illuminating than an onto-historical speculation about the "condition of the possibility" of common history.

According to the Old Testament, human history begins with the fall from grace and in particular with Cain's fratricide. Cain was the first founder of a town, who because he was restless and itinerant wanted to settle himself on the earth, whereas Abel was a pilgrim who trusted in God. Only the post-Christian modern age was able to hit upon the idea that the movement of history, rather than being a *procursus*[p] (Augustine) toward judgment and salvation, is a constant progress toward something better or is even, in the overturning of faith in progress, a history of decline, a progress toward nihilism which, when the danger is greatest, is supposed to turn, together with a change in the human essence. In relation to the untimely intuition that in known history humans remain the same in the ground of their essence, there is no essential difference whether one experiences such a change in the human essence in a Christian way as rebirth in faith and prepares this change by means of a repentant conversion, or whether one anticipates it in an un-Christian way as the anonymous destining of a nameless fate and approaches it "suitably."

Jakob Burkhardt,[53] who knew what actual history is, was of the view that what is "interesting" in history is what is seemingly uninteresting, namely that which is constant and which repeats itself in all change, because humans are as they always already were and always will be. Neither the soul nor the understanding of humans has improved demonstrably in historiological times; in any case our faculties were "complete" long ago, and if in olden times one sacrificed one's life for others then we have not gotten beyond this ever since.

---

[p] Translator's note: A *procursus* is a running forward or advance, especially a military advance or charge.

3 | The Interpretation of the Unsaid in "Nietzsche's Word 'God Is Dead'"

Heidegger is a thinker who has excited his contemporaries, just as Fichte and Schelling did in their time, and for similar reasons: the force of his philosophical thinking is bound to a religious motive. Hence peculiar to his "remembrance" is a pathos that draws willing readers and hearers into its spell and that seduces them into a false devotion. The intensity of this thinking becomes all the less palpable, the more it proceeds within interpretations in which Heidegger articulates his own ideas only indirectly, through the thinking of others, so that his thinking merges imperceptibly into that of the other.

In order to present and to call into question this process of interpretation with respect to Heidegger's account of Nietzsche, it is indispensable to employ reason and rational arguments. If essential thinking were in fact to begin only where it has bidden farewell to reason as "the most stubborn adversary" of thinking and where it has "passed up" logic and the sciences,[1] which according to Heidegger's dictum do not think,[2] then from the very start the aim of a critical engagement with Heidegger's manner of thinking, in order to clarify the matter in question, could not be satisfied. Instead of coming together with Heidegger's thinking and engaging it, one could then take his remembrance only as a half-poetic system of language. But in the end, even "essential" thinking is not as irrational, nonconceptual, and unassailable as it might appear, but instead is bound to rational thinking and is open to it.

Nietzsche said that what is new in our view of philosophy is the conviction "*that we do not have truth*."³ Because "nothing is true any more" and as a result "everything is permitted,"⁴ for him everything depended on making a final "experiment [*Versuch*] with truth."⁵ In accordance with the fact that we do not have truth, the will to true knowledge shifted into the will to a creative "interpretation"; and there are as many interpretations as there are possible perspectives regarding a state of affairs which in itself is unknowable. Historiological relativism has let itself be satisfied with this impossibility of ascertaining what is always true in and for itself, and it has thereby been content to "understand" that every philosophical truth is an expression of the life of a particular epoch and is relative to time.

What is new in Heidegger's thinking is that he drew the final consequences from historiological relativism, by first attaching the truth of Being to the finitude of existing Dasein and its understanding of Being, and by ultimately grasping truth itself and Being itself as a historical happening of truth and of Being. But because in manifesting itself in beings the truth of Being at the same time conceals itself and withdraws, in Heidegger too the knowledge and assertion of this truth shifts into a historical understanding and interpretation. Even Being, this *transcendens* pure and simple, is to reveal itself to an "interpretation." Indeed the thinker now "says" Being, but he does not assert its mystery in a scientifically testable assertion. The renunciation of scientific knowledge corresponds to the withdrawal of Being-true. But in contrast to Nietzsche, for Heidegger our not having truth is nothing "new," but instead is something very old: the whole history of Western thinking, from Plato up to and including Nietzsche, has never experienced nor contemplated what the truth of Being itself is.

In keeping with the withdrawal of Being and its truth, already in 1923 in a lecture on the "Hermeneutics of Facticity"⁶ (the first title for the "Analytic of Dasein") Heidegger gave merely "formal indications"; and in his last writings suggestive "hints" take the place of demonstrative proof. The impetus for this retreat from communicable knowing to formal indication, which in Jaspers' philosophy corresponds to an "appeal" to existence, was given by Kierkegaard, who in opposition to Hegel's claim to absolute knowing devised the method of "indirect communication of existence" and who summarized the aim underlying his impact as an author in terms of seeking only one thing: "to call attention" to the Christian definitions of existence "without authority." Of course in the one case as in the other, this modesty has its own kind of arrogance. Kierkegaard thought that he was the only one who knew, at a turning point of European history, what is truly and exclusively Christian; Heidegger claims to know what in general "now is" and happens in a fulfilled meaning of Being, and he claims to know that the essence of Being remained concealed from all prior philosophy. His own dictatorial saying of Being, about which it can only be said that it is "it itself" and is wholly other in regard to all beings, derives its authority from the "dictate" and "appeal"[7] of Being,[8] which guides the pen of the onto-historical thinker.

Nonetheless the inspirational force of this thinking is not the certainty of a prophetic knowing, but instead is its experimental questioning and searching, its attempting and Being-on-the-way. Heidegger's steadfast but highly unsocratic questioning has priority over every answer, which is simply "the final step" of questioning.[9] *Being and Time* seeks first of all to reawaken an understanding of the meaning of the *question* of Being, and it finds this meaning—prior to the planned "turning" from "Being and *Time*" to "Time and *Being*"—in time as the horizon of every understanding of Being. The interpretation of Being on the basis of time, which for its own part grounds history, sees itself as being dependent on the history of a prior understanding of Being and understands itself as a critical appropriation of the history of philosophy.

The appropriation of ancient ontology begins already with the translation of particular Greek texts into one's own language, namely into German. For this it is not sufficient to have a knowledge of the foreign language and an understanding of the thinking which is expressed in it. Translation [*Übersetzen*] requires a *trans*-position [*Über*-setzen] into the Western tradition; and from out of the philological-historiological task there emerges, unexpectedly, an onto-historical fate which has world-historical consequences. Indeed according to Heidegger the destining of the West depends on the appropriate translation of the word *eon*. The right—even if not the necessarily correct, i.e., literally correct—translation presupposes an onto-historical relationship between early thinking and our late thinking, and hence a kind of dialogue between thinkers, but one in which the genuine speaker is supposed to be Being itself.

The meaning of such a dialogue between thinkers who have been called by Being must be understood to include the introductory statement of *Being and Time*. He cites a statement from Plato's *Sophist*, just as Hegel concludes his *Encyclopedia of the Philosophical Sciences* with a citation from Aristotle. Both think in a fundamentally historiological and historical way, inasmuch as they ponder "Being" and "spirit" respectively. Even the seemingly nonhistoriological system of phenomenological analyses in

Being and Time is directed toward a destructive interpretation of the history of Western thinking and is in itself "hermeneutics." From the first formal indications of the "hermeneutics of facticity" up to his final mysterious hints, Heidegger is a historical interpreter who contemplates what has already been thought and who, at the end of the history of metaphysics, translates it anew and interprets it with an eye toward something unsaid.

Wilhelm Szilasi has pointed out that, apart from Schelling and Hegel, no significant philosopher has devoted as large a proportion of his life's work to the interpretation of philosophical texts as Heidegger.[10] He is a lover of the intended word [*des gedachten Wortes*],[a] and precisely for this reason he is against philologists, who simply seize upon the text without also perceiving what is unsaid in it. *Prior to Being and Time* Heidegger interpreted Duns Scotus, and in courses and recitations he interpreted Aristotle, Augustine, and Aquinas; *after Being and Time* he interpreted Kant, in courses and recitations he interpreted the presocratics and Plato, Descartes, Fichte, Schelling, Hegel, and Nietzsche, and in lectures he interpreted Hölderlin, Rilke, Stefan George, and Trakl. His pupils—the author of this work included—replaced philosophy entirely with interpretations of the history of philosophy; and they turned the need of a destitute time, in which the Socratic will to knowledge and its accompanying acknowledgment of ignorance were lost, into the virtue of understanding. Even the thinking of earlier times, which in itself was thought nonhistoriologically, counts for the modern historiological consciousness as a historiologically conditioned and historically determined understanding which for its own part needs to be interpreted. It gets neither recognized as perceptive and true nor rejected as imperceptive and false; rather, in line with Hegel, beyond true and false, it gets conceived as a historically necessary phase in the development of truth.

Whatever Heidegger interpreted in the course of four decades, what is philosophically decisive is not the scope of the themes but rather the uniform process of interpretation. What does Heidegger understand by "understanding," and what is the measure for his interpretations? In contrast to Dilthey, who assigned the concept of understanding to the *Geisteswissenschaften* as a definite way of knowing and developed it epistemologically and psychologically on the basis of spiritual life, Heidegger

---

[a]Translator's note: The term *gedacht*, apart from being the past participle of the verb *denken* (to think), can mean "imagined," "assumed," or "intended." Löwith's point here is that Heidegger is sensitive not only to what a text actually says, but equally to what remains elliptical or implied in a text.

defines understanding in terms of Fundamental Ontology, on the basis of the constitution of the Being of human Dasein, in accordance with a universal intention. The possibility of understanding is grounded primordially in the fact that, as a "There," Dasein is itself both disclosed and disclosive, and it discovers beings which do not have Dasein's manner of Being. Even Being itself and the Being of truth can be understood only because Dasein is "disclosedness, i.e., understanding" from the ground up. Dasein is cleared in itself, not by another being and also not—as it is *after Being and Time*—by Being; rather, it is cleared in such a way that it is its own clearing. As disclosedness which is extant there, Dasein is a Being-which-understands, prior to any distinction between "explanation" and "understanding" in the narrower sense. Because in addition Dasein is, as "existing," a *capacity-for*-Being, the understanding which belongs to Dasein shares with Dasein this existential definition. It can understand itself in terms of something, which is to say: it understands itself from out of and toward its possibilities.

In accordance with the existential priority of the possible over the actual—a thesis which comes from Kierkegaard's concept of existence,[11] though without taking over its Christian-ethical presuppositions and aims—understanding is a "pressing forward into possibilities." Understanding, defined existentially, does not know the permanent nature of anything; rather, understanding has the character of the "projection" of a being toward something. Projection which understands, which together with Dasein is a factically thrown projection, "throws possibilities ahead of itself."[12] However Dasein conducts itself for its own sake and understands itself toward something, as a capacity-for-Being it is "wholly permeated by possibility" (146/186), or, in Sartre's language, it transcends every "Being-in-itself" by way of "negation." As a result of this orientation of the concept of understanding on a possible for-the-sake-of and towards-which of understanding-toward-something, even the "sight" of understanding is not primarily a purposeless, theoretical viewpoint but instead is circumspection, consideration, and above all fore-sight.[b] The temporal meaning of foresight is the future, which is already contained in every understanding of something "toward something" and is primordially posited along with the Dasein which understands and hence with a capacity-for-Being which projects itself. But the possibility of existence which is most one's own, highest, and inescapable is the anticipation of

---

[b]Translator's note: The terms *Umsicht*, *Rücksicht*, and *Vor-sicht*, translated here as "circumspection," "consideration," and "fore-sight" respectively, all have the notion of sight (*sicht*) as their root; in everyday usage, the word *Vorsicht* means "caution."

death as the final towards-which of the projection of an authentic capacity-for-Being-a-whole.

The development of the possibilities contained in the understanding is *interpretation [Auslegung]*. For example, in our understanding of the world, a being which is ready-to-hand get explained circumspectively in terms of its in-order-to in our dealings with it. What gets explicitly understood here has the formal character of an understanding of "something as something."[13] When, for example, a table gets understood "as" a table, it gets understood on the basis of its in-order-to and hence on the basis of its being e.g., something for writing. Such a circumspective interpretation of ready-to-hand equipment is grounded in a "fore-having"; this in turn is guided by a definite viewing, a "fore-sight," which brings the content of the fore-having into view with regard to a definite possibility of interpretation. And because in addition interpretation has always already decided on a definite conceptualization (e.g., on conceiving of a being as a present-at-hand "thing" with "qualities" which are present-at-hand in it), fore-having and fore-sight also have a "fore-conception." "Interpretation is never a presuppositionless grasping of something pre-given" (150/191f.). Hence the "meaning" which is determined in every understanding of something "as" something is "*the towards-which of projection, which is structured by fore-having, fore-sight, and fore-conception, and on the basis of which something as something becomes intelligible*" (151/193).

What holds for our everyday understanding of the world in our dealings with beings within the world, applies to the understanding and interpretation of a philosophical text as well. Such a text cannot be grasped without presuppositions, like something pre-given. "When the specific concreteness of interpretation in the sense of an exact textual interpretation seeks to make reference to what 'is there,' then that which first of all 'is there' is nothing other than the obvious but unarticulated preconception of the interpreter, which is necessarily contained in every attempt at interpretation as that which is 'posited' with interpretation generally, and this means that which is pre-given in fore-having, fore-sight, and fore-conception" (150/191).

Hence the manner in which Heidegger approaches the analysis of understanding is determined in advance by the "fore-structure" of understanding, which always already presup-poses [*voraus-setzend*] itself. But the necessity of this presupposing does not lie prior to the understanding of something in the sense that it gets cast aside in the process; rather, it is constantly co-present and guides the process. All interpretation must have somehow understood what is to be interpreted in advance, and it must maintain itself in such a pre-understanding. But because scientific proof may not presuppose what it is supposed to establish, the fore-structure signifies that all understanding, in opposition to the demands of science, moves in a "circle," and according to the rules of scientific logic this circle is a *circulus vitiosus* which needs to be avoided. "*But*," Heidegger says, "*to see a vitiosum in this circle and to seek a way to avoid it, indeed to 'perceive' it as simply an unavoidable imperfection, is to misunderstand understanding in a fundamental way*" (153/194). What is at stake is not to get out of the circle of understanding, but rather to come into it in the right way; and this means to "secure" explicitly the scientific theme of an understanding for oneself by not allowing the fore-conception to be misled by what "one" commonly presupposes without knowing it, and by instead making the presuppositions of one's understanding explicitly one's own and transparent.

The circle of understanding which has been secured in this way is not a cycle in which a particular kind of knowing happens to move; instead it is the expression of the existential fore-structure of Dasein itself. A being for whom, as caring Being-in-the-world, its own Dasein is at issue, has a circular ontological structure. The fore-structure of understanding is grounded in the Being of Dasein, inasmuch as Dasein, as care for its ownmost capacity-for-Being and capacity-for-Being-a-whole, is a "Being-ahead-of-itself" and an "anticipatory resoluteness." Whoever does not grant this circular structure which is grounded in the character of projection and care, simply proves thereby that he has fallen into the common-sense "Anyone" which maintains itself in "factually" present-at-hand beings and refuses to go beyond them.

On the basis of this interpretation of understanding, which employs the measure of a definite idea of "existence" (43, 310, 312/68f., 357f., 359f.), it is to be expected from the start that even Heidegger's interpretation of philosophical texts will be secured *a priori* by fore-having, fore-sight, and fore-conception, and that it will go beyond what "is there" in order to project what is to be interpreted onto something which is not there and which has not been said. But for Heidegger the first and last towards-which of all essential interpretation of former metaphysics is the "ontological difference": the distinction between Being and beings, the adherence to the latter and the forgetting of the former. The ultimate measure of Heidegger's interpretations of the history of philosophy is the standpoint of questioning presupposed in *Being and Time*. It is only natural and part of the meaning of Heidegger's own interpretation of the circularity of Dasein's understanding, when this presupposition again comes forward as a product of his interpretations. The assertion which has been wrested from the most diverse texts is one and the same, and at the same time it is Heidegger's own.[14] But with this, does the closed circle of disclosive understanding not defeat itself in the attempt to understand what others have thought, supposedly in a different way, or does this secured understanding simply want to encounter itself in the text of another?

The fore-conception of understanding is indeed an unavoidable starting point; but this approach is not to be secured, since the task can only be one of calling one's own starting point into question in the light of the text to be interpreted, in order to be able to understand another, without presuppositions, in terms of what is *his* own. This requires an openness to the claim of another and to the objection and contradiction which he may pose against our self-understanding which rushes toward him. In order not to turn the necessity of the circle into the virtue of an ever-superior understanding, one must move freely within the circle and also be able, if need be, to abandon one's own approach. The "problem" of the circle in understanding is not that the Dasein which is at issue for itself in a circular way is beyond question, but rather that every relation between oneself and another is relative, and that there is a sharp line to be observed between one's own appropriation of another's idea and the estrangement of that idea. *Te totum applica ad textum, rem totam applica ad te* (Bengel); this means that one must turn oneself entirely to the text, in order to apply the entire text to oneself; or, as Rudolf Bultmann said: "It is a matter, in questioning the text, of letting oneself be questioned by the text."[15] The presuppositions which have been brought along cannot be secured, just as there is no requirement that the presuppositions of the text to be interpreted be recognized and acknowledged in order that we be able to understand the text without presuppositions.

What Heidegger has expounded with laudable incisiveness under the title of "circle" is the prejudice, which has gained general ascendancy, not only that there cannot be a presuppositionless understanding, but that such an understanding would be contrary to the meaning of understanding. The modern reader of modern interpretations is prepared to accept as something obvious the relativity of what is to be interpreted to the particular interpreter. When for example Jaspers interprets Nietzsche's philosophy as a "philosophizing" which itself is a "transcending" that places every definite position and its corresponding negation in the "balance" so that no "doctrine" and no "fundamental words" remain which one might seize upon, and when on the other hand Heidegger's interpretation of Nietzsche leaves nothing in the balance and ultimately establishes that

Nietzsche understood the essence of Being and of the Nothing as little as had the metaphysics before him—then, more than anything else, the contemporary reader will draw the conclusion that Jaspers' Nietzsche is not Heidegger's Nietzsche, and that both interpreted Nietzsche in their own way, just as one does generally in order to understand others, namely from the standpoint of one's own presuppositions, on which each must "decide" for himself. In spite of all the historiological reflection on the part of modern understanding, the question of how Nietzsche himself decided and understood remains unasked because it is assumed that only such a presuppositionless movement beyond the text is capable of interpreting it. The mere text is assured at all points but supposedly remains "mute" when we do not interpretively bring it to speech—as if in general a text did not speak from and for itself.

The need to interpret a text as it was understood by its author, and to clarify what he himself said more or less clearly as well as what he did not say,[16] is grounded in the authority of the matter to be interpreted, a matter which was at issue for the author. Whoever does not attempt to understand the ideas of another in the way that the other understood them himself, can also not adopt a critical posture toward the other in which one distinguishes oneself from the other, but instead will carry out the critique within an interpretation which is really a reinterpretation. One may call such a reinterpretation a "productive transformation," but this changes nothing in the fact that it is not a proper, critical interpretation. The requirement of understanding another as he understood himself, apart from its difficulty, remains justified if one does not assume *a priori* that the process of history places us beyond all prior thinking.

It is difficult enough to fulfill this requirement among the living, where in dialogue one gives another unanticipated answers to his questions, answers which are not simply the final step of our questioning. In conversation the other can correct us when we understand him only according to our own meaning and measure and thereby obstinately misunderstand him. Then at least—and this little is surely a lot—we will be able to make ourselves understood regarding the decisive point of our nonunderstanding and misunderstanding. When the conversation partner is absent and the "dialogue" between thinkers is factically a monologue because the other is there only in the text, the possibility becomes greater that in the appropriation of the text to be interpreted we will get back only what is our own and that we will miss what is proper to the other. But the text, which is pre-given even to the pre-understanding, is not there in order to substantiate our implicit or even transparent preconceptions. Instead we must presuppose that it has something to say to us and to teach us which we do not know of our own accord.

Assuming that it could be shown that Heidegger's interpretation of a philosophical text understands it differently than it was understood by its author, indeed not as a result of a specific misunderstanding but instead as a consequence of the whole manner in which his interpretation proceeds, then along with the demonstration of what has been missed in a particular interpretation the questionable character of its methodological presuppositions would be proved indirectly. But its ultimate presupposition lies in the "analytic of Dasein" and its fundamental proposition that the human "essence" is nothing natural but instead is a capacity-for-Being which is always one's own and which is at stake for itself in a circular manner, in projecting and understanding. And because the understanding of a text is an understanding of the other through oneself, more than anything else things depend on the way in which the existential analysis of Dasein understands authentic "Being-with" others, namely as the "release" of the other to the possibilities which are always *his* own.[17] But such a "release" is not the expression of a pure bondage and obligation, but rather a reinforcement of the capacity-for-Being which is always my own and unlike anybody else's. It releases the other for being independent and nonrelational. In *Being and Time* the most authentic capacity-for-Being is one's own capacity-for-Being-a-whole, which is "unrelated" to others and "inescapable" because death is the highest and unsurpassable instance of a free existing.[18]

In his own way, Heidegger is aware of the nonrelational and individualistic character of his interpretations. In order to justify this he protests against the objection of violence, by pointing out that an intellectual dialogue among other, more vulnerable principles constitutes mere historiologico-philosophical interpretation.[19] But the distinction between philosophico-historiological research and onto-historical dialogue is as questionable as the comparable distinction between a nondatable history of Being and a historiologically datable world-history, whose actual catastrophes are supposed to emerge from the nonextant happening of Being. Even the intellectual experience of the history of thinking cannot avoid proceeding from texts which have been historiologically handed down and edited, and it cannot avoid examining such texts; and it cannot do so any less, indeed it must do so more, than the philologist whose interest is merely historiological. Ultimately Heidegger does of course want to understand the "unsaid" in a *present-at-hand text*, by turning to what is said explicitly and to what was intended by the author, in order on its basis to understand what was said indistinctly or not said at all. The more things depend on something unsaid, the more the one contemplating the text will have to listen to what was said.

Nobody will be able to dispute that Heidegger is more perceptive than practically any other contemporary interpreter, and that he is an expert in the art of reading and interpreting when it comes to carefully taking apart an intellectual or poetic system of language and assembling it anew. But neither will anyone be able to overlook the violence of his interpreting. In fact his interpreting goes entirely beyond the clarification of what is there. It is an inter-pretation that construes, in which something is inserted, and it is a trans-position of the text into another language which purports to think "the same." Hence his subtle disclosedness for the text is just as great as the resolute decisiveness with which Heidegger carries out his fore-having. One can find fault with his violence and admire his subtlety, and yet they complement one another. His violence in carrying out his fore-having is concealed in the subtlety of the interpretation, in such a way that the subtlety serves the violence. They determine, to an extent that is different for each, what is appropriate and helpful in the interpretations.

The discussion of "Hegel's Concept of Experience"[20] is more an accompanying commentary than an interpretation that construes. The discussion of a poem by Rilke ("What Are Poets For?") is—apart from some specific violations[21]—a masterwork of subtle interpretation which goes beyond what Rilke said only to the extent that it over-poeticizes what Rilke said and thinks it further. The discussion of Anaximander is an interpretation which does not simply go far beyond the adage to be interpreted, but instead goes right past it by interpreting something which has not been said so as to render unrecognizable the adage which was to be interpreted. The discussion of Nietzsche's word "God is dead" is just as penetrating on selected texts by Nietzsche as it is violently beyond Nietzsche's own ideas. Particular interpretations, and sometimes translations, are just plain violent. Plato's assertion "ta . . . megala panta episfalh," with which Heidegger closes his rectorial address, undoubtedly does not say that everything great stands "in the storm,"[c] as he translated it during a

---

[c] Translator's note: The passage from Plato, and Löwith's translation of it into German, can be rendered in English in a number of ways. The term *gefährdet*, related to the term *Gefahr* (danger) and translated here as "endangered," can also mean jeapordized or exposed (e.g., to a threat). The term *hinfällig*, translated here as "precarious," can also mean weak, infirm, or null-and-void. The term *bedenklich*, translated here as "dubious," can also mean grave, hazardous, precarious, or alarming. The original passage is from Book VI of the *Republic* (497d9) and literally means "all great things are precarious."

stormy time, but says instead that everything great (noble) is endangered (precarious), or as Schleiermacher translated it, "dubious."[22]

Heidegger often took a position regarding Nietzsche—in *Being and Time*, in a discussion in *Holzwege*,[23] in the lecture "Who is Nietzsche's Zarathustra?"[24] and in the lecture *What is Called Thinking?* At the conclusion of the analysis of the existential origin of historiology on the basis of Dasein's historicality (*Being and Time*, section 76), he gives a brief interpretation of the authentic meaning of Nietzsche's Untimely Meditation "On the Use and Disadvantage of History [*Historie*] for Life."[d] Apart from an incomparably sharper conceptual execution, the course of his thinking is to a great extent aligned with that of Nietzsche. Common to both is the critique of historiology and historicism which moves toward a historicality which is part of "life" or "Dasein," together with the relation of this historicality to the prospective possibilities of our own capacity-for-Being. The thesis of this critique is that historiology is alienated from a pure relationship to history, and that times which live non-historiologically are not for that reason alone ahistorical. Inasmuch as historical conduct and understanding "repeat" past possibilities of life, they let past events approach us once again and thereby bring what has been into our own possibilities.

In agreement with Nietzsche's fundamental statement that only as "architects of the future" and as "initiates of the present" can we decipher an adage of the past, Heidegger says that the pure historiological disclosure of the past comes to fruition in the current moment on the basis of the future.[25] Its structural connection with the past and the present and the corresponding trinity of historiology as "monumental," "antiquarian," and "critical,"[26] is not explicitly shown by Nietzsche to be necessary, but the beginning of his Meditation gives rise to the presumption that he "understood more than he expressed."[27]

Heidegger wants to understand this "more," and to this extent he wants to understand Nietzsche better than Nietzsche understood him-

---

[d]Translator's note: Whereas Heidegger's use of the term *Historie* has customarily been translated as "historiology" in order to distinguish it from his use of the term *Geschichte* (history), Nietzsche's use of the term *Historie* has generally been translated as "history" and his use of the term *historisch* has generally been translated as "historical." In translating the present discussion, except where noted, I have translated *Historie* as "historiology" and *historisch* as "historiological." The related term "historiography" appears in translations of Nietzsche, but it generally is used as a rendering of *Geschichtsschreibung*, which literally means "the writing of history"; cf. *Untimely Meditations*, tr. R. J. Hollingdale and intro. J. P. Stern (Cambridge: Cambridge University Press, 1983), p. 70.

self. The result of this interpretation is that the unitary foundation of the three ways of historiology is authentic "historicality," and that its origin is "temporality" as the existential meaning of care. But Heidegger's presupposition, namely that the human being is essentially a Dasein which historically "exists," projects itself, and cares, is not shared by Nietzsche. If anything at all distinguishes the beginning and the end of Nietzsche's Meditation, it is his view of an ahistorical way of pure Being [*Dasein*]^e that can "forget" what "was" and which can carelessly be consumed in the present moment without a trace: the animal and, "in close proximity," the child.[28] Both are unlike the grown human, which is "something imperfect which can never be completed" and which on that account is concerned with its capacity-for-Being-a-whole; instead they are playfully perfect and whole in what they are, and for this reason they are happy.

The historically living, incomplete human being likewise demands such perfection. For Nietzsche, the child, which is akin to the animal, is so little a merely prehuman way of Dasein that in *Zarathustra* it instead becomes the symbol for the kind of human which has overcome itself and, after the final metamorphosis, becomes a child of the world which is "innocence" and "forgetting," a "new beginning" and a "wheel rolling of its own accord."[29] Beyond this positive relation of childlike Dasein to the Heraclitean child of the world,[30] childlike Dasein has a polemical relationship to the Word of God's kingdom, which is open only to those who trust as children do. In the same way, *Zarathustra* develops the complete meaning of the "moment" [*Augenblick*] without which there can be no happiness. It is the "highest time," neighboring on despair and after that on bliss, and it is a time in which time "stands still";[31] as the moment of a "noon" it signifies "eternity."[32] For Heidegger's definition of Being on the basis of time, there is only the choice between authentic and inauthentic temporality and historicality; for Nietzsche what is at stake is the reacquisition of a lost world by means of a sublation of the historiological process within a Being which eternally means the same.

Hence already in his Untimely Meditation, Nietzsche's critique of historiology is twofold. Heidegger takes into consideration only that aspect of the critique which maintains itself within historiological consciousness and which Nietzsche himself calls the ahistoriological ability-to-live. For one who lives historically, it is a matter of being able to remember (historiologically) as well as to forget (ahistoriologically), in order to appro-

^eTranslator's note: For Nietzsche, *Dasein* is not a technical term signifying exclusively human being, in the way that it is for Heidegger. Translators of Nietzsche generally translate *Dasein* as "being" or "existence."

priate from the "it was" only as much as is consonant with one's own ability. But beyond this Nietzsche's Meditation contains a repeated reference to a suprahistorical [*überhistorisch*] way of living,[33] for which nothing essentially new is to be learned from the process of history, because in the moment of the successful completion of pure Dasein the world is already "finished" or completed in each of its moments. In opposition to all three historiological ways of meditating, such a suprahistorical human will see the past and the future, the "formerly" and the "one day," together with the "present" as one and the same,[34] as a "ubiquity" of undying types, which "always have the same meaning." Only this would be "wisdom," i.e., completed knowing.

From the very beginning, Nietzsche was on the way to such wisdom, in connection with which our estimation of historiology is merely an "occidental prejudice." Nonetheless, for those who live historiologically and those who live relatively ahistoriologically, this wisdom is first of all something "loathsome" because it seems to contradict the kind of life which busily moves forward. Wisdom, which knows that in truth only that is which eternally means the same, entrusts Untimely Meditation to "art and religion," i.e., to the sole "eternalizing powers."[35] Only as the teacher of the eternal return of the same does Nietzsche-Zarathustra change from a critic of his time to a proclaimer of eternity who is no longer bound, in an untimely manner, to time and history.

Hence the beginning and corresponding end of Nietzsche's Meditation do not allow us to suppose that Nietzsche already implicitly understood himself in the way that Heidegger interprets him; instead we must suppose that Nietzsche understood himself differently. The "life" which Nietzsche takes as the criterion for the use and disadvantage of history [*Historie*] is not historical "existence" but instead is related to the *physis* of the *kosmos*, in the same way that "culture" is a new "physis"[36] and the "wisdom" that Nietzsche seeks is not historical understanding. Nietzsche's last and first problem, which is specified already in the two schoolboy essays on "History" (or "Freedom of the Will") and "Fate,"[37] and which is developed further in the second Untimely Meditation and solved in *Zarathustra* through a "deliverance" from every "it was," is not *Being* and *time* but rather *becoming* and *eternity*.

The motif of eternity as an eternal return of the same defines Nietzsche's philosophy from the very beginning and up to the end. It manifests itself first of all in an autobiographical sketch by the nineteen-year-old, which asks about the "ring" which could embrace humans after their liberation from all prior historical authorities; it defines the distinction between an ahistorical and a suprahistorical position regarding history; it is clearly audible in the question mark at the end of *The Dawn* and it completely dominates *Zarathustra*. But even the critique of time in *The Will to Power* as a history of nihilism is grounded in the "yes" which is prior to the "eternal yes of Being."[38] To the extent that in Nietzsche there can be any talk of an ontological questioning in the rigorous sense, that which he occasionally calls "Being" and for the most part calls "the total character of life" is not essentially related to the Nothing but instead is the Being of all beings, which is eternally the same and which as a becoming both annihilates and creates, though to the extent that it is a Being which eternally becomes it is simply affirmative. For Heidegger, that which is "supposedly eternal" is merely "something transitory which has been cast off, cast off into the emptiness of a now which has no duration."[39]

In the discussions in *Holzwege*,[40] Heidegger becomes a belated disciple of Nietzsche to the extent that his thinking can be grasped as historical. In both, the consciousness of the epigone turns into a will to the future. Nietzsche's historico-philosophical construction of the decay of suprasensible values ("How the 'true world' finally became a fable") is adopted without reservation and is simply paraphrased. Of course Heidegger does not speak as unequivocally as Nietzsche regarding a history of the oldest "error" which ends with an "incipit Zarathustra"; but in accordance with the matter at hand, his position on the whole prior tradition likewise aims toward a new beginning and a re-valuation of the oldest error, as if one contemplated Being itself by thinking beings as beings.

In order to examine whether, on the basis of his proximity to Nietzsche, Heidegger does justice to the texts to be interpreted, I shall ask the following three questions: 1) What in general does Nietzsche mean for him? 2) What is his conception of an interpretation of Nietzsche? 3) How does he interpret Nietzsche's word regarding the death of God?

1. For him Nietzsche is not simply "the last German philosopher, who passionately sought after God";[41] rather, he is a "metaphysical thinker" who, as such, preserves his proximity to Aristotle and thinks "no less substantially and rigorously" than Aristotle. The layman will wonder why the author of the *Untimely Meditations*, a *Gay Science*, a *Thus Spoke Zarathustra* and *Beyond Good and Evil*, *The Will to Power*, *The Antichrist*, and *Ecce Homo*, who attempts to form his ideas in aphorisms, allegories, and unfulfilled plans and who thus always brings himself to language, should have a close relationship to the rigorously scientific works of Aristotle, to his physics and metaphysics, his ethics and politics, his geology and astronomy. Does Nietzsche's thinking really demonstrate a different, modern sensibility in nothing but a "histori-

ological and superficial way," or is it as essential for Nietzsche to have written his discourse on the "madman"[42] as it is essential for Aristotle that his God is neither living nor dead but instead is the eternal principle of natural movement in the highest heavenly sphere, and hence nothing for which one could cry *de profundis*. In the end the association of Nietzsche and Kierkegaard which "has become customary" is still more appropriate than the thinking, called for by Heidegger, which draws together the author of an inverted Sermon on the Mount with Aristotle, Leibniz, Schelling, and Hegel.[43]

2. Heidegger begins his interpretation of Nietzsche with the statement: "The following elucidation attempts to point toward the place from which it may one day be possible to pose the question concerning the essence of nihilism." What he means by an "elucidation" [*Erläuterung*] is stated beautifully and simply in the preface to his *Elucidations of Hölderlin's Poetry*: it seeks to make the poetry "clearer in several respects," and for the sake of the poetry it must strive to render itself superfluous.[44] "The final step of an interpretation, which is also the most difficult one, consists in disappearing along with its elucidations, in the face of the pure presence of the poem" (8). When this is successful, then on a subsequent reading we have the impression that "we always understood the poem in this way" (8). In general, this devoted aim does not characterize Heidegger's interpretation of what has been thought. There could hardly be a reader of his interpretation of Nietzsche for whom, after repeated reading, Heidegger's idea is not present in the guise of Nietzsche—for which part of the reason may naturally be that Nietzsche's own idea is not thought purely.

Heidegger's interpretation explicitly seeks to go beyond what is said by Nietzsche, so as not to remain a mere "report which repeats in an empty way"; and in keeping with its aim and import it maintains itself within the scope of that *one* experience on the basis of which *Being and Time* is thought. Nietzsche's idea gets included in the history of the forgottenness of Being, and it gets interpreted with regard to that history. In order to elucidate Nietzsche's word concerning the death of God against this background of a presupposed two thousand year history of Being, Heidegger must in addition present what is his own "on the basis of his [own] subject-matter."[f] Of course the "layman" will perceive such an addition to be interpretive, and will criticize it as violent caprice in relation to what he takes the factual content of the text to be. In contrast with

---

[f] Translator's note: In order to interpret this obscure statement, it is helpful to consider the statement from "The Word of Nietzsche: 'God Is Dead,'" which Löwith is paraphrasing here: "Of course every elucidation must not simply draw the subject-matter from the text but must also, without being insistent, imperceptibly contribute something of its own on the basis of its [own] subject-matter." "Nietzsches Wort 'Gott ist tot,'" p. 209/ "The Word of Nietzsche: God is Dead,'" p. 58.

this non-understanding on the part of common understanding, Heidegger insists that an essential elucidation does not understand a text "better" than its author understands it; but it does indeed understand it "differently," although this different manner must be such that it encounters "the Same" which is contemplated by the text being elucidated.[45]

The attempt to grasp Nietzsche's ideas more clearly than he himself was able to say them, presupposes that he has first become "more significant" to us. But that which is more significant is the unsaid, which is the authentic "doctrine" of a thinker.[46] In the interpretation of the adage of Anaximander,[47] it is further said that all onto-historical dialogue with another thinker is based on an appeal from Being. Of course whoever thinks within such a bond can errantly move right past the idea of the other, and in doing so can nonetheless, or "perhaps even only in this way," think the Same. Who would want to decide whether Heidegger interprets the word regarding the death of God on the basis of an appeal from Being? All that is certain is that he thinks beyond what is said by Nietzsche, from out of what is his own and into what is his own: the ontological difference.

3. An initial reference to Nietzsche's word "God is dead" occurs in Heidegger's rectorial address of 1933. One must come to grips with this "forsakenness of contemporary human beings in the midst of beings [*inmitten des Seienden*]."[48] In what does coming to grips with this being forsaken by God consist, if what is at stake here is a forsakenness of Being in the midst of beings? Nietzsche certainly sought passionately after "the" God, namely after the "unknown" God, when in his youth he liberated himself from his Christian heritage,[49] and when he ultimately attacked the God of the Old and New Testament with an "Antichrist." At that time Nietzsche believed that he had found in Dionysus the unknown God, i.e., the God who had both been killed and had risen again, and he believed that he had distinguished the Christian God from the pagan God by appealing to the measure provided by a contrary "interpretation of suffering" (*The Will to Power*, paragraph 1052).

But what does Nietzsche's passionate seeking and seemingly blessed finding mean for Heidegger, who, with unmistakable sympathy, recounts the story of the madman who announces the death of God, but who for his own part brings the question of God back to the question of the ontological difference? For the hardest blow against God is not struck by those who do not believe in God, but rather by the believers and their theologians, who talk of God as the "most extant" of all beings without thinking of "Being itself."[50] But because Heidegger thinks of Being as the possible locale of something healing, holy, and divine, and because he asks whether

Being will "once again" become capable of a God, the neutral position of *Being and Time* may no longer be adequate,[51] namely the position according to which the existential analysis proves nothing either *for* or *against* the possibility of sin, because testimony on the part of faith is closed off from all "philosophical experience"; and the same holds for the equivalent position in *On the Essence of Ground*,[52] according to which the ontological interpretation of Dasein makes neither a positive nor a negative determination about the possibility of God's Being.

Indeed Heidegger's discussion concludes with a pronounced distancing from those who publicly stand about and who are without faith "because they themselves" have given up "the possibility of faith" to the extent that they are no longer able to seek God. But it is also said that "they can no longer seek [God], because they can no longer think." Nonetheless, only Being truly needs to be pondered, and in order to be able to think it one must bid farewell to "reason."[53] The thinking of Being is indeed a perceiving, it is even an "ear" of thinking; but this perceiving which hearkens and hears is not, as it is in Hegel, the shared ground of reason and belief. On the other hand, Heidegger's farewell to reason is made for the sake of thinking, and hence it is not identical with Luther's struggle to provide justification on the basis of faith alone, which is a struggle against that "whore reason."

One will ask, what does it mean for Heidegger on the one hand to advocate the possibility of faith that seeks, and on the other hand to reduce such faith to an antirational thinking? If faith has no place in thinking,[54] and the "decline of thinking into the sciences and into faith" is the evil destining of a Being,[55] which is now supposed to turn, how can the "loss of the gods"[56] be thought essentially as the loss *of the gods*, unless the place of investigative, "skeptical" knowing and obedient faith is taken by a "thinking" which in itself is devout and pious but which is neither philosophy nor theology. Then the truly faithful one would be the one who— this side of faith and non-faith in an extant God—binds oneself back to Being and is "religious" to the extent that he adheres to "questioning" as the "piety of thinking."[57] Of course, later on even questioning gets taken back into the accommodation [*Zusage*] of Being and language, and it is no longer claimed to be the authentic gesture of Being.

The ambivalent distinctions and connections which Heidegger makes between thinking and faith are all the more precarious, given that both the thinking of the essential thinker and the faith of the truly faithful claim to know that Being, or in the case of the latter, God, reveals and conceals itself in a historical manner. Is faith in revelation perhaps thought by Heidegger, the former Christian theologian, in a suprametaphysical way, and are the theologians thus left with a thoughtless kind of faith, as if Christian theology and mysticism had not from the beginning considered that God cannot "be" in the same manner as what He has created? It would not be the first time in the history of German philosophy, which according to Nietzsche's dictum is an "insidious theology," that a philosopher considered himself to be the better theologian and took over the task of theology into philosophy, though on the other hand there are still theologians who think that faith in revelation can benefit from the experience of the Nothing and the thinking of Being.

Nietzsche's word of the death of God does lie at the center of Heidegger's interpretation, though not as an individual doctrine but instead as a leitmotiv on the basis of which the other fundamental words in Nietzsche get illuminated: "nihilism," "life," "value," "will to power," "eternal return." The fifty pages of Heidegger's essay are a summary of five semesters of lectures on Nietzsche, and to this extent they may be taken seriously.[g] According to Heidegger, "God is dead" means that the metaphysical world of ideas, ideals, and values is no longer alive and that metaphysics is thereby entirely at its end. Of course Heidegger does not dispute that Nietzsche's word refers to the Christian God of biblical revelation, but the word "God" embraces above all a recognition of the decline of the authority of a suprasensible world. Nietzsche by no means understands Christianity in terms of the primordial Christian life which was influential for a short time, but understands it instead in terms of the world-political appearance of the Church.

Nonetheless there is no need for exhaustive demonstration of how little Nietzsche, in contrast to Kierkegaard, fought the Church, not merely the "latent" Christianity of moral values but rather the Christianity of the New Testament and St. Paul. From beginning to end, *Zarathustra* is an anti-Christian gospel. The overman Zarathustra, who wants to drain the cup of the excess of eternal desire and who is accompanied by a proud eagle, is from the very first sentences a counter-image to the God-man Christ, who suffers meekly like a sacrificial lamb and who empties the chalice of suffering; and he concludes his speeches with the blasphemous worship of an ass which repeatedly says "hee-haw" and which is given wine to drink by the ugliest man who killed God, because in opposition to the Christian kingdom of God, Zarathustra wants an "earthly kingdom." A look at *The*

---

[g]Translator's note: These lectures comprise volumes 43, 44, 46, 47, and 48 of Heidegger's *Gesamtausgabe*; to date, all but volume 46 have been published.

The Unsaid in "Nietzsche's Word 'God Is Dead'"   115

Antichrist and Nietzsche's relationship to Pascal makes it clear that for him the Christian soul, suffering understood in Christian terms, and the Christian God were at issue, and that in contrast to "God" what was at issue was the "world" and thereby the ultimate abolition of the suprasensible "hidden worlds" of Christian Platonism as well. Nietzsche's unfathomable distance from the natural theology of Aristotle, and his proximity to Pascal and Kierkegaard, can scarcely show itself more penetratingly than in the fact that at the end of *Ecce Homo* he characterized himself as "Dionysus against the Crucified" and at the outbreak of insanity called himself "the Crucified."

What Nietzsche actually sought from beginning to end was by no means a "theoretical" knowing in the sense of Greek philosophy, nor a modern kind of understanding, but rather "deliverance" and an answer to the "cry of distress" issued by the higher human beings, among whom is to be counted even the "ugliest" man, who did not want God to be a witness to his contemptuousness and who therefore killed Him out of revenge. Zarathustra is "the godless one," pure and simple. So obvious is it that Nietzsche did not preach any ordinary, free-thinking atheism,[58] that it simply cannot be denied that he understood himself as a "turning point" within the history of modern atheism and that he understood his task to be one of "bringing about a kind of crisis and final [*höchste*] decision regarding the problem of atheism."[59]

Heidegger's interpretation goes far beyond and behind this, by interpreting Nietzsche's word on the basis of a two thousand year history of Being and the world; for the word of the death of God has been said, "always implicitly,"[60] within the whole, metaphysically determined history of the West. How so? Perhaps to the extent that the later ancients already spoke of the death of the great Pan, or to the extent that the Christian West is based on faith in a crucified God? But what has the great Pan got to do with the biblical God, and what has Christ, who was crucified according to God's will for the sake of healing human beings, got to do with the ugliest man's killing of God? Heidegger gives only a meager indication of this when he claims that the death of God which Hegel has in mind in appealing to Pascal (*Pensées*, section 441) and in speaking of the "infinite pain" over the death of God, surely thinks "something different" than does Nietzsche, though he claims that "all the same" there is an "essential connection" between the two assertions, and likewise one between these and the talk of the death of the great Pan, a connection which is "concealed in the essence of all metaphysics" (210/59).

Hence the connection between the pagan (Plutarch), Christian (Pascal), religico-philosophical (Hegel), and anti-Christian (Nietzsche understandings of the death of God supposedly lies in the fact that for Heidegger, the entire history of the West, from its pre-Christian beginnings up to and including Nietzsche, is the kind of forgottenness of Being in which "nothing is going on with Being" [*mit dem Sein nichts ist*] (254, 260f. / 104, 110f.), and that consequently even Christianity could be a mere after-effect of this primordial "nihilism" (217/65), whereas for Nietzsche nihilism is on the contrary a consequence of our having killed the Christian God, or a consequence of faith in Him having become untenable [*unglaubwürdig*]. Heidegger does not want to orient his thinking about Christianity on God's revelation through Christ, as Pascal does; nor does he want to give the death of God a philosophical existence by means of a "speculative Good Friday," as Hegel does; nor does he claim that the history of Christianity is a "two thousand year lie," as Nietzsche does. But he does say along with Nietzsche, though for different reasons, that Christianity has the greatest share in modernity's "loss of the gods"[61]—a thesis which does not go together well with the thesis that Christianity itself is merely the shape taken by a nihilism which essences in Being. Who is thinking more clearly and unequivocally here: Heidegger, whose thinking draws its nourishment from Christianity just as much as it deprives Christianity of its ground, or Nietzsche?

Nietzsche's mature thought is a continuum of thought, at the beginning of which stands the *death of God*, at its middle the *nihilism* which emerges from that death, and at its end the self-overcoming of nihilism toward the overman's *eternal return of the same*. Zarathustra's first speech, "On the three metamorphoses," is in accord with this continuum: the "Thou shalt" of biblical faith metamorphoses into the liberated spirit of the "*I will*"; and in the desert of this faith's freedom toward the Nothing, the final and most difficult metamorphosis takes place from the "I will" to the "I am" (*The Will to Power*, section 940) of a childlike world-play's eternally returning existence [*Dasein*]. With this final metamorphosis of freedom toward the Nothing, a freedom which prefers to will the Nothing rather than not to will it, into the freely-chosen necessity of an eternal circulation of all things, Nietzsche thinks that his temporal fate is achieved as an "eternal" one: for him, his "*ego*" becomes "*fatum.*"

Under the "sign of necessity," under the "highest star of Being," which makes no requests and never brooks [*befleckt*] a "No," the accident of one's own Da-sein is once again at home in the whole of worldly Being. The path on which Nietzsche finds this deliverance from the accomplished fact of an existence [*Dasein*] which in each case already "was" before it

The Unsaid in "Nietzsche's Word 'God Is Dead'" 117

willed itself, is a way of avoiding the Christian doctrine of creation. He characterizes it as the "self-overcoming of nihilism." Zarathustra is the "conqueror of God and the Nothing" which had temporarily assumed the place of God.[62] On the basis of this unequivocal connection between the "soothsaying" of nihilism and the completely different "soothsaying" of the eternal return—both of these are, though in opposed senses, an "all for naught" and an "everything is the same," a lack of meaning, purpose, and value—Nietzsche's whole doctrine has two faces: it is a self-overcoming of nihilism, in which "the one who overcomes and that which gets overcome are one." They are one in the same sense as the "dual" will of Zarathustra, the Dionysian "dual view" of the world and the Dionysian "dual world" which are *one* will, *one* view, and *one* world. This unity of nihilism and return are a result of Nietzsche's will to eternity being the "reversal" of his will toward the Nothing.[63]

For Heidegger, Nietzsche's reversal signifies something merely negative, because all reversals move within the domain of what has been reversed.[64] Nietzsche's reversal inverts metaphysics into its perversion [*Unwesen*], inasmuch as the removal of the suprasensible brings with it the elimination of the merely sensible and thereby the distinction between the two. But for Nietzsche himself, the abolition of the "true world" together with its sensible obverse by no means comes to an end in the insubstantial, but instead comes to an end in a new beginning, at "noon," when the "shadow" is shortest and the sun of Being and of knowledge is at its highest.[65] This self-interpretation on the part of Nietzsche does not prevent Heidegger from claiming that Nietzsche so little overcame metaphysics, i.e., Christian Platonism, that on the contrary his mere "countermovement" against nihilism left him irretrievably entangled in metaphysics and its nihilistic presuppositions and consequences. Indeed according to Heidegger, along this path of reversal Nietzsche experienced "several characteristics" of nihilism, though he interpreted nihilism itself nihilistically and recognized the "essence" of nihilism, i.e., the concealedness of the truth of Being, just as little as metaphysics before him ever did.[66] His transvaluation of prior values simply concludes a previous devaluation of what had been the highest values. Within the purview of the self-willing will to power, i.e., guided by the perspective of value and the positing of value, Nietzsche did not recognize his new positing of value to be a killing and to be nihilism.

One wonders how a thinker who underwent a "turning," who insisted on a circular structure to all disclosing and understanding, and who pushed aside formal-dialectical refutations such as that of skepticism (*Sein und Zeit*, p. 229/ *Being and Time*, p. 271f.) as mere "attempts to take by surprise," is not able to acknowledge that even an attempt to overcome nihilism cannot begin without presuppositions and history, this side of nihilism, but instead sublates within itself what is to be overcome, just as Nietzsche knew and said. "Overcoming has many paths and ways: just *you* wait and see! But only a buffoon thinks: 'human beings can also be *skipped over*.'"[67] And who among all modern thinkers does not move, in a timely as well as in an untimely manner, within the scope of an "Against Which," to the extent that he still thinks historically and, like Heidegger, wants to "confront" [*entgegenwärtigen*] his "now" or, like Nietzsche, wants to make a decisive "moment" eternal? If any historically thinking philosopher of modernity, which is coming to its conclusion, came so far as to have thought past all historical thinking within ages, epochs, and world-needs, and toward something which is eternally the Same and whose necessity proceeds not from a "prospective need" but rather from the eternal law of Being in which everything becomes, then it was Nietzsche when he attempted "to transpose" human beings, who had become eccentric, into the eternal "foundational text" of nature.

In opposition to Nietzsche's overcoming of nihilism, Heidegger says that it is really only the completion of nihilism because it does not let Being be as such. Nonetheless, so little does he himself let Nietzsche's thought be what it is, that he establishes his point of view "already in advance" of his discussion of what Nietzsche himself says about nihilism,[68] just in order to be able to inquire into nihilism in *his own* way. From within this anticipatory point of view he establishes, in agreement with what is said in "What is Metaphysics?" that nihilism, thought essentially, is a history which unfolds along with Being itself and which solely on this account takes place in the history of the West and its modern age. Here one will surely ask: how is a point of view which is so clearly preferred in advance supposed to let us see what Nietzsche himself thought, when he speaks of the death of God, of nihilism, and of Being as a "Yes to Being" which cannot be touched by any "No?"

Heidegger's primary concern is to interpret several selected statements from *The Will to Power*, particularly in connection with the "thinking of value," in order to work out the main assertion concerning the death of God from the standpoint of value and the positing of value. "The positing of value has brought beneath itself and killed everything which is extant in itself and which thus is extant for itself" (258/107).[69] It is superfluous to stress along with Heidegger that the academic philosophy of value was not a philosophy, that "values" are not what possesses the greatest value,

The Unsaid in "Nietzsche's Word 'God Is Dead'"   119

and that nobody "dies for mere values" nor by any means for the word "Being." Heidegger remarks in the same place that one must attempt to grasp Nietzsche's thinking independent of his representations of value, in order to get into the right position for understanding his work.

Remarkably, though, his own critical interpretation adheres completely to Nietzsche's thinking on value, which is conditioned by time inasmuch as it derives from the national economics of the nineteenth century. Against his own tendency to bring the unsaid to language, in this case he takes Nietzsche's discourse on value literally in order to proceed critically, within this presupposed thinking on value and onward to the killing of God, and this means: within Being, which by means of the thinking of value gets appraised as a mere value and thus gets crushed. But was Nietzsche really inclined toward thinking on value, and did he ever grasp Being as value? Or did he not liberate himself from all positing of values, goals [*Ziele*],^h and ends, from every "towards-which" and "for-the-sake-of" when, in thinking through the question of the "value" (the "meaning" or "end") of existence [*Dasein*] which emerged from the decline of the Christian interpretation of existence, he came to the conclusion that the "total character" of life or of becoming, hence of that which on the ontological formulation is the "Being of all beings," in fact can *not* become appraised and evaluated?⁷⁰ Even Nietzsche's critique of the biblical concept of God depends on the idea that this creative God is essentially will, that He made the world into something for the sake of human beings, and that in doing so He deprived the world of its "eldest nobility," which consists in its being there "by chance."⁷¹ Being in its entirety is beyond our evaluations, and it is thereby "beyond good and evil" and "beyond man and time," an eternally repeating world-play of becoming and passing, of Being and semblance, of necessity and play, into which man has been drawn.⁷²

For Nietzsche, "to posit values" does not mean to transpose Platonic Ideas into values; rather, it means to propose ends and goals, so that "positing values" is a part of willing. But the will first of all becomes free by liberating itself from itself, and it does so by "willing back" toward everything which always already was; and the "world" which the will thus reacquires gets characterized in *Zarathustra* and *The Will to Power* as being *without* will and purpose, "if" a ring does "not" have good will toward itself and "if" there is "no" goal in the happiness of the cycle. The Dionysian

---

^h Translator's note: In this paragraph *Ziel* has generally been translated as "goal," though in a few instances it has been translated as "purpose."

world, which is described in the final aphorism of *The Will to Power*, is not the world and the time which Heidegger is thinking of when he speaks of historical epochs and world-needs, but rather is a world of *physis* or of life, whose time is "without purpose."[73] If the eternal Being of the living world is a constant becoming and if time is a repeating cycle, then in the total character of life or of becoming Being there can be no future-oriented purposes of the will, ends, or positings of value. And even less can the "eternal return" of life, whose power is ever the same, be understood in terms of the essence of modern technology and its gyrating machines.[74]

Against all this, Heidegger interprets Nietzsche's philosophy as a "metaphysics of value," and he interprets value as a "standpoint" whose simple meaning he artfully misconstrues. What Nietzsche understands by "value" is contained in aphorism 715 of *The Will to Power*. Its first paragraph, which is interpreted by Heidegger, says: "The standpoint of 'value' is the standpoint of the conditions of preservation and augmentation, as regards complex forms of the relative duration of life in the course of becoming." From the statements which follow upon this one and from pertinent fragments of *The Will to Power*, it becomes clear what is meant by this statement and what it is said against.

Contrary to Heidegger's interpretation, it does not mean that the "essence" of value is itself a "standpoint" and that value is to be understood "as" a standpoint inasmuch as it is posited in a representational manner by a looking-at, looking-away-from, and calculating; rather, the standpoint "of" value means here, as in other places (e.g., sections 567 and 1009), that one must pose the question of value essentially from the standpoint of conditions for preservation and augmentation, and this means fundamentally from the standpoint of "becoming" and growing, increasing and decreasing, but never from the inessential standpoint of a "Being" which is unitary and uniform and which stands fast, as in the case of "atoms" and "monads" or even (section 708) "the thing in itself" and the "true world." For Nietzsche it is a matter of "devaluing" the evaluation of life's becoming that proceeds from a false standpoint, or of "devaluing" the "hypothesis" of a "being," which means the "hypothesis" of something that stands fast and merely preserves itself; he calls for this "devaluing" in order to justify becoming, because judgments regarding becoming that proceed from the standpoint of mere beings are the "source of all world-defamation" (section 708; cf. section 617).

But the standpoint of "value" is fundamentally inapplicable to this becoming (section 711), which in itself is "innocent," i.e., groundless and purposeless or without "why" and "towards which," and which characterizes the total character of life; it is inapplicable because in general becoming has no "end state" (section 708; cf. section 1062) and does not culminate in a non-becoming "Being" in relation to which becoming would be merely a "semblance-state." "Becoming has the same value at every instant: the sum of its value remains the same: *put another way: it has no value at all*, because there is no Something against which it could be measured and in relation to which the word 'value' would have meaning. *The total value of the world cannot be evaluated.*"[75] The "conception of the world" that Nietzsche had in mind and that he attempted to develop on the basis of *Zarathustra* in *The Will to Power*, is characterized by the idea that life as will to power cannot be evaluated because "at every instant" life is entirely what it is, and has the same value throughout all its changes (section 1050) and has the same significance—without vestiges of the past and without reference to the future [*ohne künftige Ausstände*].[i] "The present is absolutely not to be justified as being for the sake of the future, nor the past as being for the sake of the present."[76]

According to Nietzsche, in order to arrive at such a conception of the world, what is needed is not only the exclusion of our human estimations of the world, but above all the elimination of the kind of "total consciousness" of becoming which posits ends and means, i.e., of becoming as it is taken into account in God. The world that is conscious of itself cannot qualify as the point of departure for value, and "if" in general we seek to posit a goal and value for the total life, then this goal might not coincide "with any category of conscious life"[77]—nor, therefore, with the categories of looking-at, looking-away-from, representing, and calculating.

Accordingly the "one thing [*das Eine*]," that "which is essential" for Nietzsche's concept of value, cannot be that value is always posited by and for a seeing, as if the value of the "center of vision" which has been posited and represented were for seeing and the doing which is led by it; rather, the special character of Nietzsche's doctrine of value is that, beyond positing value in a fundamentally new way, he calls into question the applicability of the concept of value to the total character of life, which is why in the statement taken by Heidegger as his point of departure Nietzsche puts the word "value" in quotation marks. Nietzsche did not deprive Being of its worth by appraising it as a "value";[78] rather, Heidegger deprived Nietzsche's essential idea of its special character by interpre-

---

[i] Translator's note: In the present context, *Ausstand* means "something outstanding" in the sense of, e.g., an outstanding debt; *ohne künftige Ausstände* literally means "without anything outstanding as regards the future."

tively placing it back into the "age of the completion of subjectivity",[79] and in doing so he lets Nietzsche's idea merge imperceptibly into that of Descartes, or to put it more precisely: into that of Cartesianism.[80] Heidegger puts his interpretation of Descartes ("The Age of the World Picture") into Nietzsche, so that he can construe the beginning and the completion of "modernity" as being unified and on the same path.

But when Nietzsche, contradicting his final intention and insight, says that even life itself, as will to power, is a life which appraises and in which we confer value, namely "*when*" we posit values,[81] i.e., to the extent that he never completely got past the thinking about value that prevailed in his time, all this proves is that he was not capable of developing his idea purely, free from his polemical orientation on Schopenhauer's devaluation of the "will to live" and on Dühring's "value of life." If his thinking had ever been as substantive, clear, and rigorous as that of Aristotle, then the many obscurities and the corresponding misinterpretations of his thought would not have been possible. But at the same time it is clear that for Nietzsche the Being of all beings, or "life" as will to power and becoming, is never a "value" but instead is the living, natural ground of our valuing, and hence in itself it is incapable of being devalued. It is by no means in the notes of *The Will to Power*, which remain entangled in the modes of questioning regarding the theory of knowledge and of value prevalent in his day, that Nietzsche thinks in an exact manner; rather, he does so in the allegorical speeches of *Zarathustra*, which are a well-formed system of "thought-experiences."

From Nietzsche's assertion that the measure-giving standpoint for the "value" of life is the standpoint of the "conditions of preservation and augmentation,"[82] Heidegger also interpretively derives the consequence that preservation, "i.e., the self-securing of constancy [*die Bestandsicherung seiner selbst*],"[83] is part of the essence of the will to power, indeed as a necessary value. The will to power justifies the necessity of "securing" on the part of all beings, and thus it remains within the Cartesian definition of truth as "certainty" (234/83). This is supposed to make it clear how modern metaphysics completes itself in Nietzsche's doctrine.

But in the context of section 715, the assertion concerning the conditions of preservation and augmentation places unequivocal stress on the conditions of augmentation, or on the increase and decrease of the dominant centers of life, rather than on preservation as the securing of constancy. The need for mere preservation is "relative" to "the smallest world [*die kleinste Welt an Dauer*]." The essential character of life lies in its going out beyond itself, i.e., in creativity, in opposition to all securing of constancy and all certainty; and in order to bear the thought of the eternal return, even the Cartesian concept of truth must become revalued: according to Nietzsche, it is not the desire for certainty but rather the desire for uncertainty and for a lack of security which characterizes constancy creativity.[84] It is the desire for uncertain "accident" which characterizes Zarathustra's soul and its world as the "most necessary"[85] and which characterizes Nietzsche's philosophy as a voyage of discovery toward the uncertain.

Nietzsche's thinking does not complete the self-certain subjectivity of modernity, but instead is a "new beginning" after the end of the Christian interpretation of existence [*Daseinsauslegung*]. If there was a thinker in the nineteenth century who, being cognizant of "old origins," thought both in terms of beginnings and in terms of the future by seeking "new origins" and "sources of the future," it was Nietzsche, to the extent that he made his way to Being and thereby escaped from the freedom of the will toward the Nothing, and to the extent that as a courageous seafarer he "*hoped to reach an India by steering westward*" but ran aground on "infinity" in the process[86]—"the only gift that could come to thinking from Being."[87]

Heidegger's anticipatory starting point for his interpretation, namely the concept of value, is decisive for everything that follows. According to Heidegger, value must even be the basis for understanding what Nietzsche meant when he said that God is dead.[88] For Heidegger this assertion signifies the abandonment of all suprasensible values by human beings, who rise rebelliously into the subjectivity of their essence and the subjectivity of beings by objectifying everything and finally forgetting Being, so as to accord with the will to power (257/107). For this reason, Nietzsche's metaphysics is itself still supposed to be nihilism. But in actuality, Nietzsche made a last "experiment with truth"[89] when, with a decision which was also an inspiration,[90] he devoted himself to the Being of all beings and taught the eternal return of all beings. The uprising of the overman, who wants to command himself and who has freedom towards death, is only the *immediate* consequence of the death of God, who previously defined the "Thou shalt" and all values. The final and most difficult step on the "path to wisdom," i.e., to perfect knowledge regarding the whole of beings, is the transition which liberates us from willing itself and liberates us to a simple "Yes and Amen," i.e., to the "eternal Yes of Being"; it is with this transition that Nietzsche closes *Zarathustra* and concludes the poem "Fame and Eternity."

This final metamorphosis to the "play" of creating, by means of which one who has lost his world is to reacquire it, occurs in the section of

Zarathustra entitled "On the Vision and the Riddle";[91] it occurs between the "stillest hour" (4:187ff./145ff.) of desperation and "involuntary bliss" (4:203ff./160ff.), so as to lead to a "convalescence" (4:270ff./215ff.). This final critical transition is completed at noon and eternity (4:342f./275f.). For Nietzsche, at this highest instant, which corresponds to the "highest kind of all beings," time was fulfilled in an anti-Christian sense, so that "all the words and the word-shrines of Being" burst forth from that instant, as if Being itself wanted to become word.[92] It is hard to grasp how Heidegger can maintain with such certainty that Nietzsche never experienced the mystery of Being and that he represented eternity as a securing of constancy on the part of the will to power.

Coerced by his own will to power, Heidegger does not interpret the noon which is eternity as Nietzsche experienced and understood it, namely as the "abyss" of "light"—"noon" is also "midnight"[93]—in which all time and all temporal willing sink into the "fountain of eternity" and in which all things are baptized; instead he interprets it simply as the time of the brightest light of consciousness, a consciousness which has become conscious of itself as the knowing which is supposed to consist in "deliberately willing the will to power as the Being of beings and, as such willing, to supersede rebelliously every necessary phase of the objectification of the world, thereby securing the enduring constancy of beings for the most uniform and steady willing possible."[94] But according to Heidegger the condition for willing, which itself must also be willed, is the positing of value and every estimation pursuant to values. In this way, value determines all beings in their Being.

Whoever simply reads attentively what Nietzsche says regarding "noon" can only be astonished by what Heidegger reads out of what is neither said nor meant. His interpretation of what is "essential" in Nietzsche's doctrine does not take into consideration that Nietzsche concludes the third and fourth parts of *Zarathustra* with a remembrance of eternity rather than with the determination of contemporary history: "the desert grows." This "eternity" is neither timelessness nor the securing of constancy. The eternity of the eternal return is not timeless, for it concerns an *ever*-again; and it is not temporal in the historical sense of a momentary decision and an abrupt change, for it concerns an ever-the-*same*. The fulfilled time of eternity is the time which gathers together as a whole that which in the temporality of unfulfilled, everyday time is dispersed into the dimensions of future, past, and transitory present. As an eternal return "of the same," it shows up quite inadequately in Heidegger's interpretation, when Heidegger says that the will to power, on the basis of which he one-sidedly interprets the doctrine of eternal return, secures its own enduring constancy for a "most uniform and steady willing possible." As the same, the will constantly comes back to itself as the Same; and "the manner in which beings as a whole, whose *essentia* is the will to power, exist, i.e., their *existentia*, is the eternal return of the Same" (233/81).

In Nietzsche's doctrine, the eternal return is a return of the Same because such a Sameness lies in the naturally necessary coming-over-and-over-again of all beings which have been brought into the circle; for Heidegger, the eternal return is "the manner of making-constant in which the will to power wills itself and in which it secures its own presencing as the Being of becoming."[95] But because Heidegger left behind the traditional metaphysical distinction between *essentia* and *existentia*, his interpretation of the two fundamental words of Nietzsche's metaphysics, namely the will to power and the eternal return, comes to the conclusion that Nietzsche thought absolutely nothing essentially new but instead simply completes what guided metaphysics since ancient times: the definition of beings in their Being in terms of a still unthought "essence" and a still unthought "existence." And yet the essential relationship which is thus to be thought between the will to power and the eternal return of the Same does not get discussed further.

Whoever seeks to contemplate Nietzsche's disparate attempts to ground his doctrine of return as attempts to ground an ethical "imperative" and necessary "fact" rather than simply disregarding them, cannot fail to see that the will to power and the eternal return do not belong together like the *essentia* with its *existentia* but on the contrary are forced together, in order to unify the division between eternally natural Being and human willing and valuing. With regard to willing or intention, the "ring" of the physical world which eternally wills itself, and which takes the place of God, includes only the ring of a human Dasein which eternally wills itself. Nietzsche himself succeeded in "becoming betrothed to" "the ring of all rings" only when he became insane and the sun sank into "blue forgottenness." But the search for this accord between man and world already defined the thought of the eighteen-year-old Nietzsche when he considered whether the antagonism between "freedom of the will," or "history," and the "fate" of natural necessity might not be capable of resolution through our conceiving of freedom of the will as the "highest potency of fate."[96]

Heidegger is in agreement with Nietzsche that all prior human goals and measures, above all Christian love, have lived out their lives. "Here and there, there will be Christian faith. But the love which rules in such a world is not the effective and influential principle of what is now occurring."[97] The suprasensible ground of the suprasensible world has become unreal. In the face of this knowledge of what is now occurring, knowledge which has been secured world- and onto-historically, the question arises whether a suprasensible principle—and what is more suprasensible than the "Being" which is not only not sensible but in addition is nothing extant?—was ever the "infallibly influential power of action" in that which happened, always in an epoch-making way, in the history of the world. And does such a principle perhaps lose its truth if it is not, or is no longer, epoch-making, but instead is alive merely "here and there"? Assuming that the will to power is the measure-giving, nihilistic power of action in present world-history, would not every great thinker *before* Hegel have asked whether this power of action is the True and the Right, or whether it is a contemporary error beyond measure?

Heidegger cannot pose such a naive question regarding the True and the Right, because for him truth itself, as appearing *and* seeming, as manifesting *and* concealing, is an ambiguous happening of truth which changes in precipitous epochs of truth. Accordingly the will to power as well, as the historical truth of a definite age, is neither affirmed nor denied by Heidegger, but instead is characterized as the utterly unhealing, though it is at the same time proposed by him as that which is necessary [*Notwendige*] pure and simple, and also as that which may bring healing and which addresses need [*die Not Wendende*]. The world is rushing toward the "fulfillment of its essence,"[98] but it is precisely through this that the nutritive ground for a primordial questionableness of Being can grow and the space of decision can open up regarding whether Being will once again become capable of a God and the truth of Being will claim the human essence in a more originary manner (109f. / 153).[99] "Unhealing, as unhealing, traces out the healing for us" and thus finally draws "the" God near.[100] The more carelessly the modern age completes itself in its own, unhealing expanse, the greater the chance that "that which saves" will come out of the growing danger and Being will "reverse" its forgottenness[101]—an enticing thought[102] which, considered onto-historically, repeats the thought of Nietzsche, a thought rejected by Heidegger, that only the most resolved-upon devaluation makes new values necessary and leads to a revaluation, so that the "final danger" becomes the "final refuge."[103]

"Being," Heidegger said already in the introduction to *Being and Time*, though he took as his point of departure a Dasein which is resolved upon itself, is "the *transcendens* pure and simple." It essences beyond extant Dasein and all beings within the world; said in Nietzsche's language: it is a suprasensible "hidden world" which sends us our destinings, which pre-thinks our thoughts for us, and which in general claims us. "But 'that world' is well concealed from humans, that inhuman world deprived of humans, which is a heavenly Nothing; and the belly of Being does not speak to humans at all, unless as a human. —Indeed, all Being is hard to prove and hard to bring to speech" (4:36/32). All the harder, when one exists as a thinker of Being in a destitute time, understands Being on the basis of time, and in doing so sees in the cessation of time, as Nietzsche experienced it, only an "arrested transitoriness."[104]

4 | On the Critical Appraisal of Heidegger's Influence

Go and endure
Errors and questions
Along your one path.

The native of Messkirch, Martin Heidegger, who prefers "wood paths" and "country paths" to heavily traveled thoroughfares and whose seventieth birthday is the occasion for this critical appraisal of his influence, is widely known as a magnificent teacher at the Freiburg University, who throughout four decades knew how to provide young students and independent researchers with guidelines and measures. Beyond this he disclosed anew, with masterful interpretations, the history of Western spirit, as a whole and in its particulars; and with his strange translations of fundamental Greek words, he made our habits of thought evident as habits. Above all he is a primordial, enduring, and gathered force of intensive knowing and of intellectual penetration, a force that does not automatically accept any of our worn-out concepts but instead critically calls into question all traditional philosophical thinking with regard to its heritage and significance.

The same man who, forty years ago as a *privatdozent*, said that we pupils do wrong to measure him against standards like Nietzsche and Kierkegaard or any other creative philosopher, since he has nothing comparatively positive to offer and is by no means a "philosopher" but rather is a "Christian theo*logian*" (with the accent on logos) who has the sole task, one that is wholly unsuited to schooling by installments, of critically destructing the traditional conceptions of Western philosophy and theology, in connection with which it could naturally come to pass that he is sometimes simply threshing "empty straw"—this same man, who in the ground of his essence was modest, simple, and restrained, and who from the very beginning placed himself outside of all business activities and never took part in a conference, has since become a public speaker whose name fills the largest halls, whose voice can be heard on phonograph records, and whose words define contemporary philosophical thinking far beyond Germany. On his own account as well, he has become a "thinker" whose work is more than a book. In a kind of *retractio*, in 1947 Heidegger interpreted that work of his which appeared in 1927, in order to show that the misunderstandings of *Being and Time* are not mere nonunderstandings of a book, but on the contrary sprang from his contemporaries' "forsakenness of Being."

For Heidegger, the "somnambulistic certainty" with which contemporary philosophy has passed by *Being and Time* is simply a demonstration of the power of the forgottenness of Being!—Whether misunderstood or understood correctly, for whatever reason, the fact is that Heidegger's writings, unlike anything else that has appeared in philosophy, have gained an extraordinary influence. Fragments of their language can be found not only in philosophical dissertations but also in theological and psychiatric discussions and even in daily newspapers. Heidegger's writings have been translated into French, Spanish, Italian, and Japanese, and even in Korea I met Heidegger specialists. When I was in Japan a Japanese traveled from Hiroshima to Kyoto in order to ask me, with reference to Heidegger's "Letter on Humanism," how "Being" is related to God.

The force of Heidegger's influence expresses itself above all in the fact that intellects are both in accord and in disagreement about him. This dual reaction of attraction and repulsion, veneration and suspicion, became publicly apparent in recent years, particularly following the Munich lectures on the essence of technology and the essence of language. The discussions appearing in the newspapers ranged from the highest to the lowest intonations, between uncritical admiration of the incomparably deep thinker and angry deprecation of the sophist and charlatan who captivates his hearers with linguistic artistry and oracles. In itself, such a mixed reaction is nothing special or strange. Even if it is not characteristic of truly great individuals, it is characteristic of almost all significant persons who sought and carried out something new and who thereby had no lack of followers or of adversaries, or of adherents who became turncoats. Kant did not simply produce Kantians but also had passionate opponents; Fichte was attacked in a sarcastic manner in Schelling's polemical writings; like no one else Hegel engaged in schooling, and like no one else he fell into disrepute as an "absolute professor."

The distinction between the situation then and today is, nonetheless, that in the great time of German philosophy each was able to seize upon his predecessor as an equal partner, and a Kant and a Hegel did not consider themselves too good to consider responsively the objections of subordinate contemporaries; but Heidegger's willful monologue conducts itself in a space without discussion, a space on whose edge there stand those who are fascinated, those who parrot Heidegger, and those who are reluctant, though on the other hand there are also those who negotiate Heidegger's achievements like hard currency.

But when Heidegger (in the preface to the third edition of *On the Essence of Ground*) poses the bitter question, "What would it be like if meditative ones finally began to approach this matter thoughtfully, a matter which has been waiting for two thousand years?"[1] it is natural to answer this together with the additional question: How can we expect others to follow a thinker as his traveling companions, when it is part of that thinker's essential character to reject all community and cooperation and to proceed in isolation along paths that end precipitously in what cannot be traversed? All of Heidegger's previous work is fundamentally one single, great challenge and an attack on a "world which has grown old,"[2] an attack which was not countered with a defense. And nonetheless, the man and his work became influential in a manner that is hard to define. This influence is not limited to his pupils; even today it embraces and stimulates a broader circle, and it is relatively independent of a substantive understanding of the path of thought, as broad as it is intensive, which is characterized by the words "Being" and "time" and "Being" and "beings." One may ask how many or how few have understood the extent to which Heidegger's question of "Being" has to do not simply with "time" generally but also with the *specific* time in which he posed the universal question of Being; that time was the 1920s, after the First World War, when the "eternal values" of the philosophy of value and culture, and the traditional content of our so-called culture generally, had become threadbare and fragile, and Dilthey's historiological critique of reason and of traditional metaphysics became generally accepted.

A friend, whose judgment has the virtue of not being caught up in the "for" or "against" concerning Heidegger's work and personality engaged in by his personal disciples, wrote to me regarding the thought-provoking 1920s, whose catchword was "upheaval" and "uprising" and hence a break with tradition: "On what basis has Heidegger surpassed in influence all others like him? How does success of this kind ever come to pass? Granted, above all in *Being and Time* there are several magnificent phenomenological analyses. But the whole is surely an ontology without Being, and hence it has no right to this name. Why do we accept from him something that we would let hardly anyone else get away with? Heidegger's success reminds me of that of another "master," Stefan George. In both I often find banality on stilts and a profundity that touches on the grotesque. And of course we did not get rid of George and are not getting rid of Heidegger, and this means that we need to be rid of something that cannot be reckoned. It would be fair to say that something would be nothing if it exerts an influence of this kind. Do you have an answer to this?"

Rather than giving *the* answer to this I would like to attempt to give *an* answer, without solving the dark puzzle of an individual's ability to captivate. In doing so we can put aside the question whether Heidegger's steadfast and persistent question of Being admits of an answer in the sense of traditional "ontology," and to what extent the affiliation he claims between thinking and Being is "philosophy" at all and to what extent it seeks to be philosophy in the traditional sense. We can also leave aside the fact that these two masters are comparable only in the respect that a dictatorial power to impress is proper to both, although in George's case the impression itself concerned the life path of embodied human beings while in the other case it concerned only the thinking of brains schooled in science and literature and the thinking of speculative minds. What remains in spite of this distinction is the general question of the basis for such influence, an influence which nonetheless is ambiguous, for *who* is influencing *whom*, and *when* does a potential influence factically take effect?

At a time when Spengler's *Decline of the West* had appeared, a German poet and a German thinker exerted their influence on Germans who were and are particularly receptive to pathos and leadership, and who were and are unreceptive to empty skepticism, spiritual thoughtlessness, and common sense. But why was the one's power to impress not confined to the poetry of poets, and why was the other's not confined to the thinking of philosophers? Why does this highly exacting "thinking of Being" have such general appeal, in the same way that the existential-ontological "destruction" of traditional metaphysics previously had a liberating influence, even if one did not know what its positive aim was and one has only an obscure sense of that to which the talk of the forgottenness of Being and the destining of Being refers? Is Being, which pre-thinks itself to and addresses the thinker in a destitute time, not finally Being thought in a Greek manner as something ever-extant and indestructible, but instead a word for the *"which is,"* namely "now" and "in the future" and hence a reference to the *world-historical moment* of our age, an age which is in the midst of upheavel? Indeed thirty years ago it was said in *Being and Time*: "Only beings that are essentially *futural* in their Being . . . can . . . take over their own thrownness and be *in the moment of vision* for 'their time.' Only authentic temporality, which is at the same time finite, makes possible anything like fate, i.e., authentic historicality."[3]

In keeping with these statements from *Being and Time*, twenty years later in the "Letter on Humanism" the world-historical situation in the current "world moment" is invoked as the driving motive for the question of Being; according to Hedegger this is a moment in which all beings are in flux [*erschüttert*], and hence it is a moment that does not permit us to think exclusively of beings and to adhere to them instead of letting them go and questioning after Being as such, which from the standpoint of beings appears as Nothing because it is nothing extant. And again a decade later, in the lecture *The Principle of Reason*, the discussion of the tradition's fundamental principles of thinking is not broached by chance in the midst of dramatic references to our historical situation, but instead is essentially inspired by that situation, indeed in such a way that the appeal to the need of our time—the manufactured danger of the atomic bomb—is supposed to elucidate the unfathomable danger of thinking by turning to the measure of the principle of sufficient reason [*Satz vom Grunde*][a] (according to which all beings must have their ground in another being which is ultimately the highest one). Even more directly and decisively than in these instances of relating thinking to the contemporary situation, in 1933 Heidegger thought the return to the Greek beginnings of Western thinking together with Hitler's leadership, which Heidegger understood as the "law" of "current and future German reality."[4]

Hence if even such an abstract problem as the "ontological difference," the distinction between beings and Being, was able to address the hearer and reader and exert an influence, this must surely be due to the connection between "Being" *and* "time," i.e., to the interpretation of the meaning of Being on the basis of the horizon of time and to the essential relation of Heidegger's thinking of Being to the world-historical situation of

---

[a] Translator's note: In this passage, the term *Grund* has been translated variously as "ground" and "reason," as the context requires. *Der Satz vom Grund(e)* literally means "the principle of ground" or "the principle of reason," though particularly in connection with Leibniz it has historically been translated and understood as "the principle of sufficient reason."

our time as it has always been understood. What is distinctive and characteristic throughout Heidegger's interpretations and analyses is that even in his abstract discourses the sign of our time is evident, because in Heidegger even the most incisive and subtle conceptual distinction is never suspended in emptiness but instead springs from the experience of "historical facticity" which he now calls the "destining of a sending." And as long as Heidegger does not contemplate something that is ever-extant and everlasting, *Being and Time* remains the measure-giving title even for all of the later writings in which the phenomenon of temporality comes to appearance merely in the concept of the "presencing and absencing" of the self-concealing truth of Being. Along with the preeminent pathos of what is mysterious in a self-concealing revelation, what may be of no little significance in connection with Heidegger's contemporary influence is his negative relationship to the rationality of "representational" and "productive" *science*, which objectifies things into objects, and on the other hand his positive relationship to *poetry*, particularly to Hölderlin, to whom he dedicated a series of interpretations and entreaties.

But the basis that serves as the background for everything said by Heidegger, and that permits many to take notice and listen attentively, is something unsaid: the *religious motive*, which has surely detached itself from Christian faith, but which precisely on account of its dogmatically unattached indeterminacy appeals all the more to those who are no longer faithful Christians but who nonetheless would like to be religious. Although there are only a few sparse statements in which there is talk of the healing and the holy, of the mortals and the immortals, and of God and the gods, they still suffice to make it clear that Heidegger in fact thinks "Being" in terms of "time," i.e., in terms of our own time and its "destitution," which according to Heidegger-Hölderlin consists in its standing under a twofold lack: "in the no-longer of the gods who have fled and in the not-yet of the one to come." Of course according to Heidegger himself the "futural thinking" of the arrival of Being has not yet found the abode proper to it, and occasionally a doubt announces itself regarding the scope of our Western, European thinking; but even if Heidegger himself is still on the way, one thing seems certain for him: the conviction that his questioning thinking of Being is literally need-ful [*not-wendig*] and that, as a questioning, it is a kind of "piety."[5]

This thoughtful piety, which is supposed to turn the need of time, might also be the essential ground for Heidegger's broader influence, namely on those who are upset by the thesis of the "death of God" because they do not yet think *subsequent to* Nietzsche's turning point in the problem of atheism. Perhaps nothing is as characteristic of Heidegger's questioning position as the conclusion to the autobiographical "Country Path," which does not decide between God, world, and soul, and where, with reference to the "appeal" of the field path which points into Being, it is said: "Does the soul speak? Does the world speak? Does God speak?"[6]

The Christian thinker Augustine said unequivocally and decisively in his *Soliloquia* that he is not interested in the world but only in the relationship of his soul to God. In contrast, the post-Christian thinker Heidegger defines human Dasein as "Being-in-the-world," and the question whether Being speaks primarily as world to human Dasein or as God to the soul remains undecided and ambiguous.

TWO

The Occasional Decisionism of Carl Schmitt

The Occasional Decisionism
of Carl Schmitt

> In the same measure that the race worsens,
> Action takes on the character of decision.
> *Ernst Jünger, Blätter und Steine*

When a specialist in constitutional law as intelligent and as practically influential as the Counselor of State Carl Schmitt addresses the question of what the political is, the aim and impact of his ideas will extend far beyond his area of substantive specialization. Nonetheless, the essay *The Concept of the Political*,[1] in which Schmitt deals with this question, can be understood only in connection with a substantively related discussion of the now-past "age of neutralizations and depoliticizations" and with two earlier essays entitled *Political Romanticism* and *Political Theology*.[2] For Schmitt's own concept of the singular essence of the political is characterized generally by the fact that it is first of all a polemical counter-concept to the romantic concept and that in addition it is a secularized concept derived from the theological one. The basic concept in terms of which Schmitt characterizes political romanticism, and especially that of Adam Müller, is ironic *occasionalism*; and that with which he characterizes political theology, especially that of Donoso Cortés, is sovereign *decisionism*.[a] It will become

---

[a]Translator's note: Adam Müller (1779–1829) was the Austrian general consul in Leipzig early in the nineteenth century and a thinker in the German romantic tradition; Schmitt considered Müller and Friedrich Schlegel (1772–1823) to be the preeminent figures of political romanticism. Schmitt discusses Müller and Schlegel at length in *Political Romanticism*.

apparent that even Schmitt's antiromantic, atheological decisionism is simply in keeping with his conduct, which in each case has been dictated by opportunity and circumstance.

Schmitt's remarks are essentially "polemical," i.e., in the process of clarifying his opinions it is not merely from time to time that he directs his remarks critically against this and that, but instead the "correctness" which is proper to these remarks is based wholly on that against which they are directed. His opponent is the liberal state of the nineteenth century, whose apolitical character Schmitt understands within the context of a general tendency of the modern age toward the *depoliticization* of the state.³ To the extent that this tendency toward the depoliticization of the state, particularly by means of economy and technology, seeks a politically neutral ground, Schmitt characterizes this tendency toward depoliticization as one toward *neutralization* as well.

Since the emancipation of the Third Estate and the formation of civil democracy and its refinement into industrial mass democracy, this neutralization of distinctions which are measure-giving for politics, together with the postponement of decisions regarding these distinctions,ᵇ has developed to the decisive point where it is now changing into its opposite: into a *total politicization* of all areas of life, even those which would appear to be the most neutral. Thus there emerged in Marxist Russia a worker-state "which is more intensively civil [*staatlich*] than any state of the absolute monarchs ever was"; in fascist Italy there emerged a corporate state which standardizes not just national labor but the *dopolavoro* and all of spiritual life as well;ᶜ and in National Socialist Germany there emerged a thoroughly organized state whose politicization extends, by means of racial laws and the like, into those areas of life which had previously been private.

But Schmitt sees the negative presupposition of this politicization in the "spiritual Nothing" that prevailed at the end of the age of neutralizations.⁴ This situation, as we moved into the twentieth century, was merely "provisional," and the "final meaning" of our so-called technological age can be

---

The Spaniard Juan María de la Salud Donoso Cortés (1809–1853) was a diplomat and Catholic political philosopher; his decisionism called for a civil authoritarianism modeled on the hierarchy of the Catholic Church. Schmitt discusses Donoso Cortés in *Politische Theologie*, pp. 65ff. / *Political Theology*, pp. 51ff.

ᵇTranslator's note: Schmitt frequently uses the terms *Dezision* and *Entscheidung*; in this essay both have been translated as "decision," though in a few instances *Entscheidung* has been translated as "determination." *Entscheidung für* has generally been translated as "decision in favor of."

ᶜTranslator's note: The *dopolavoro* was an Italian Fascist institution that organized the workers' leisure time activities.

realized only "when it becomes apparent which kind of politics is strong enough to master the new technology and which of the groupings that are growing on the new soil are genuinely friends and which are enemies."[5] Nonetheless Schmitt does not believe that this new centralization of politics signifies that politics is now coming forth as the *central domain* and is becoming the "substance" of the state, in place of those "spiritual spheres" in which the Europeans of the past four hundred years found "the center of their human existence [*Dasein*]."[6] Of course [Schmitt believes that] in the course of the past four centuries the spiritual center of human existence has changed four times, from *theology* to *metaphysics* and from *humanistic morality* to *economy*, and [that] the meanings of all specific concepts have shifted accordingly;[7] but [for him] even the *state* derives its "reality and power . . . from the prevailing central domain, because the foundational [*maßgebenden*][d] matters of dispute among the groupings of friend and enemy are themselves determined by the foundational substantive domain."[8]

But the political itself is by no means a special substantive domain, and hence it never has the prospect of being the central domain.[9] Still, Schmitt never says which specific substantive domain is foundational today, for our time. He simply describes the historical development of the past four centuries, and all that becomes clear is the negative insight that the central domain of life fundamentally can *not* be *neutral*; it does not become clear from which domain the total state of the twentieth century draws its spiritual power and reality—unless perhaps from a "myth of the twentieth century."[e] Of course on one occasion,[10] Schmitt distinguishes the "intellectual music of a political program" from the "irrationality" of political myth which, in the context of a "real war," emerges out of "political activity." But apart from the fact that it remains romantic and unclear what this "real," true, and genuine war consists in, *The Concept of the Political* also provides no indication of the kind of new myth which could serve as the spiritual foundation of modern, political activity.

Within this conception of history, which was supported by Vico and Comte, Schmitt ascribes a special role to *romanticism*. For it is in romanticism that the problematic transition from the eighteenth to the nineteenth century takes place, namely from the preeminence of humanitarian morality to that of technological economy. "In reality the romanticism

---

[d]Translator's note: The term *maßgebend* literally means "measure-giving"; in this essay I have translated this term variously as "measure-giving," "authoritative," "foundational," and "that sets the standard," as the context requires.

[e]Translator's note: This is a reference to Alfred Rosenberg's *The Myth of the Twentieth Century* (1930), a work of Nazi propaganda that argued for Nordic superiority.

of the nineteenth century signifies ... nothing more than an intermediate, aesthetic stage between the moralism of the eighteenth and the economism of the nineteenth century, i.e., it was simply the transition by means of which all spiritual domains became aestheticized, indeed quite easily and successfully. For the path from the metaphysical and the moral to the economic proceeds by way of the aesthetic."[11] Hence this aestheticization of all the domains of life was simply a prelude to that radical neutralization which then took place by means of economy and technology. The vehicle of the romantic movement is the new bourgeoisie. "Its epoch begins in the eighteenth century; in 1789 it triumphed with revolutionary force over monarchy, nobility, and church; already in June 1848 it stood on the other side of the barricades, when it defended itself against the revolutionary proletariat."[12] Carl Schmitt has an unmistakable affinity for this romanticism and its adroit political representative Adam Müller, the creator of the theory of the total state; this affinity enables his perceptive critique to illuminate "how in general German romanticism, which was recently said to stand in need of being overcome, is an immense reservoir in which everything that does not think in a trivially exact manner has its spiritual source."[13]

On Schmitt's analysis, what is characteristic of the romantic in general is that for him *anything* can become the center of spiritual life, because his own existence has no middle. What is always central for the true romantic is simply his ego, which is clever and ironic but which is fundamentally unstable. "In the liberal, bourgeois world, the individuated, isolated, and emancipated individual becomes the final court of appeal, the absolute."[14] But because it lacks a substantial world, this absoluteness of one's own is itself an absolute Nothing.[15] From this most extreme isolation and privatization of human existence, it is but a step to its very opposite, namely an extreme, public kind of commitment, for instance to the community of the Catholic Church or to national politics, which itself then becomes a form of religious involvement.[16] But as long as the romantic is a romantic, the world becomes for him a mere occasion, a mere opportunity or *occasio*, in romantic terms a "vehicle," "incentive [*Inzitament*]," and "elastic point," for the productive activity of his ironic, scheming ego. This romantic concept of *occasio* negates—as does Schmitt's concept of decision!—"every commitment to a norm."[17]

The form of discourse peculiar to romanticism is not the imperative or any kind of apodictic dictum, but rather the "eternal conversation," the kind of discourse which from time to time is stimulating but which has no definite beginning or end. The romantic mixes up all categories; he is incapable of making unequivocal distinctions and determinations, of making decisions that are quite beyond discussion.[18] Political romanticism is merely pseudopolitical, because it lacks moral seriousness and political energy. But because at all times decisive human beings determine the course of human events, what this means for the indecisiveness of romanticism, an indecisiveness which lacks substance, is that against its own will it is in servitude to decisions which are *foreign* to it.[19] With this conception of romanticism Schmitt is not ultimately characterizing himself as well, since his own decisionism is an occasional [*okkasionell*] one.[f]

Marx and Kierkegaard were the first to oppose this kind of "decision" to the bourgeois and to romantic existence.[20] At the end of the first chapter of *Political Theology* there is a brief reference to Kierkegaard, whereas "dictatorship in Marxist thinking" is treated thoroughly and penetratingly in the essay on "Die geistesgeschichtliche Lage des heutigen Parlamentarismus" [The Place of Contemporary Parlamentarianism in Intellectual History] (1923 and 1926) and in the book on *Die Diktatur von den Anfängen des modernen Souveränitätsgedankens bis zum proletarischen Klassenkampf* [Dictatorship from the Beginnings of the Modern Idea of Sovereignty to the Proletarian Class Struggle] (1921 and 1928). Of course Schmitt's own theory of politics lacks not only an underlying central domain, but also a metaphysics of decision, which he rightfully recognizes to be the sustaining foundation of Marx's "scientific" socialism, and it further lacks the theological foundation which sustains Kierkegaard's religious decision in favor of an authoritative government.[21] Hence it will remain to be asked: by faith *in what* is Schmitt's "demanding, moral decision" sustained,[22] if he clearly has faith in neither the theology of the sixteenth century nor the metaphysics of the seventeenth century and least of all in the humanitarian morality of the eighteenth century, but instead has faith only in the power of decision?[23]

In reading Kierkegaard, Schmitt places exclusive emphasis on Kierkegaard's apparent apology for "exceptions" because, as the first sentence of *Political Theology* states, "he is sovereign who makes a decision about the exceptional situation."[24] What appeals to him in Kierkegaard is that the latter orients himself on the extreme "limiting case" rather than

---

[f] Translator's note: *Okkasionell* literally means "occasional" in the sense of "that which occasions" or causes something; it should not be confused with the notion of things that take place "from time to time."

[g] Translator's note: "Normal case" is a literal translation of *Normalfall*; the contrast between a marginal or emergency situation and the *Normalfall* is one between the "exception" and the "rule."

on the "normal case";g for Schmitt this corresponds to a "philosophy of concrete living."[25] It is of no consequence for Schmitt that the "*extremus necessitatus casus*," understood in the juridical sense and considered in relation to politics, has nothing in common with Kierkegaard's existential-religious decision in favor of the "one thing that is needful," because for Schmitt it is simply a matter of securing the nonnormal right of decision purely and as such, quite apart from what is decided upon. Authority as such, which in virtue of its authority makes a decision in the eminent sense about an exceptional situation, proves for him "that in order to establish right, [authority] need not be right." *Auctoritas, non veritas facit legem* [authority, not truth, makes law].

But for him the exceptional case which is politically decisive is war, which precisely as an exceptional case is the one "that sets the standard [*maßgebend*]" and which consequently cannot be measured against anything beyond itself. The exception, Schmitt says with a suspiciously romantic turn of phrase, is "more interesting" than the normal case;[26] and it does not simply confirm the rule, but instead it is only on the basis of the exception that the rule can live. And it is for this reason alone that he is interested in Kierkegaard, though Kierkegaard never meant to justify the exception *as such* when he says that it explains the universal as well as itself and that if one wants to study the universal then one need only look for a genuine exception.

Quite apart from the fact that Kierkegaard did not want to make a *political* decision about the exceptional political situation of 1848 but instead decided in favor of *Christian* authority, it is telling that in citing Kierkegaard Schmitt leaves out, in a sovereign manner, a passage which does not fit together with his own ideas and which says: "The *legitimate* exception is reconciled with the *universal*" and "the universal, *in contrast with the exception*, is polemical from the ground up" (italics mine), whereas Schmitt conversely poses the exception polemically against the universal. Kierkegaard himself by no means refused to think the normal and universal; on the contrary, he did not want to think it "superficially" but instead wanted to think it with "energetic passion," and for him the exception has its rights only in relation to the universal. For him the particular is to make evident what "anyone" can be. In order not to deceive himself, "he transforms the particular into the universal." He comes "to the aid of the particular by giving it the meaning of the universal," inasmuch as "the universal is a strict lord and judge of the exception."[27] Hence Kierkegaard does not simply elevate the exception and the limiting case above the rule and the normal case, but instead he knew how to distinguish between

The Occasional Decisionism of Carl Schmitt 143

mere mediocrity and that which is the measure for Being human; for him, the eternally valid standard for the latter was the claim of Christianity.

But in connection with the problem of decision, what is at stake is a political *theology*, because the exceptional situation, about which a decision must be made in a sovereign manner, has "a meaning for jurisprudence which is analogous to the meaning of miracles [*Wunder*] for theology."[28] Schmitt wants to show that all juridical concepts that are the expression of a sovereign decision, power, and dominance are secularized ones which do not simply make linguistic reference to theological notions but are also substantively developed from out of such notions. It was only under the predominance of modern democracy, of thinking in the natural sciences, and of the kind of economy that thinks in terms of natural scientific concepts that decisionistic thinking, which reaches its apex in the determination of a personal will, became replaced by faith in anonymous laws of a natural scientific kind. The system of modern democracy is, understood theologically, the political expression of a scientific framework [*Wissenschaftlichkeit*] which has been liberated from miracles and dogmas and which is grounded in human understanding (55/42). For "the metaphysical image of the world which a specific epoch constitutes for itself, has the same structure as the image that straightforwardly presents itself to that epoch as the form of its political organization. The establishing of such an identity is the sociology of the concept of sovereignty. This shows that . . . metaphysics is the most intensive and clearest expression of an epoch" (60/46).

And yet this clearest expression cannot be found in Schmitt himself, because his own historical construction of the modern totality of the political lacks a transparent metaphysical foundation and a genuine "*subject* of dispute," i.e., it lacks a foundational "substantive domain." And as a consequence, his adherence to the idea of decision as beyond question in the political theology of the philosophers of the counterrevolution (de Maistre, Bonald, Donoso Cortés) is not obligatory.[h] Whereas these thinkers, remaining within Catholic faith, decided against the political con-

[h]Translator's note: Joseph Marie Comte de Maistre (1753–1821) was an advocate of orthodox Catholicism and is typically taken to be an advocate of political romanticism (but cf. translator's introduction to *Political Romanticism*, p. xiv); of special relevance to the present discussion is his *Étude sur la souveraineté* (1794–96). Vicomte Louis-Gabriel-Ambroise de Bonald (1754–1840) was a statesman and political philosopher who, along with de Maistre, was an apologist for "Legitimism," which rejected the values of the French Revolution and advocated monarchical and ecclesiastical authority. Schmitt discusses the counterrevolutionary thought of de Maistre, Bonald, and Donoso Cortés in chapter 4 of *Political Theology*.

sequences of the French revolution, Schmitt's profane decisionism is necessarily occasional because he lacks not only the theological and metaphysical presuppositions of earlier centuries but the humanitarian-moral ones as well. Thus it is not simply now and then that decision in his sense, which is free-floating because it is self-sustaining and hence sustained by nothing, is in danger of missing the "stable Being" which is to be found even in every great political movement, a danger which is familiar to Schmitt and which arises through an "emphasis [*Punktualisierung*] on the moment";[29] on the contrary, decision in this sense is unavoidably subject to such danger at all times, because *occasionalism* is essential to it, though in *unromantic-decisionistic form*. What Schmitt defends is a politics of sovereign decision, but one in which content is merely a product of the accidental *occasio* of the political situation which happens to prevail at the moment; hence content is precisely not a product "of the power of integral knowledge" about what is primordially correct and just, as it is in Plato's concept of the essence of politics, where such knowledge grounds an order of human affairs.[30]

So little does Schmitt return to "unscathed, uncorrupted nature" that on the contrary he leaves human affairs in their corrupt condition; and from out of himself he "makes a decision" one way or another about this condition, though at all events he does "make a decision." This will become more clearly apparent through an examination of this problematic in terms of Schmitt's foundational distinction.

Schmitt's presentation of the political philosophy of the counterrevolution begins once again with a contrast between romantics and decisionists, in which he considers the former to be the classic example of the liberal indecisiveness of the bourgeoisie, which debates and negotiates.[31] He construes de Maistre's statement that "tout gouvernement est bon lorsqu'il établi [every government is good when it is established]" to mean that "a decision resides in the mere existence of a governmental authority; and the decision as such is worthy because in the most important affairs it is more important that a decision be made than how the decision is made."[32] What is essential is "that no higher court of appeal reviews the decision."[33] And "just as revolutionary radicalism is infinitely deeper and more consistent in the proletarian revolution of 1848 than in the revolution of the Third Estate in 1789, the intensity of decision increased in the political thought of the counterrevolution. Only in this manner can the development from de Maistre to Donoso Cortés—from legitimacy to dictatorship—be understood" (72/56). Dictatorial decision poses the most extreme contrast to romantic conversation and parliamentary discussion.[34]

But when, in the preface to his essay on parliamentarianism, Schmitt prophesies the end of the epoch of discussion and at the same time has the "pessimistic suspicion" and "fears" that his own "substantive discussion of political concepts" will encounter little interest or understanding, we must ask him whether with his essay he himself has not made a leading contribution to the fact that today "a steadfastly scientific discussion which distances itself from all the exploitations of party politics and which does not serve to propagandize for anyone" is in fact an "anachronism" (5/1). That there can be and has been a kind of political discourse and rejoinder that is different than a so-called discussion, namely in the public polity of the Greek *polis* and in Platonic dialogue, is something that Schmitt does not see because his fundamentally polemical position takes its measure from the modern party politics of the liberal partisan state and because he "recognizes," in explicit opposition to liberalism, "the political as the total."

What especially impresses him about Donoso Cortés is the "confident greatness of a spiritual descendant of the Grand Inquisitors."[35] Nonetheless, Schmitt's discussion leaves out of consideration the fact that Donoso Cortés, as a devout Catholic, ultimately subordinated his own decisions in every case to the dictum of the pope, and the fact that it was only on the basis of his orthodox faith that Donoso Cortés was able to be a decisive statesman who could have the faith to decide *rightly*.[36] Schmitt sees the historical significance of Donoso Cortés above all in the fact that this statesman, recognizing the time of the sovereign kings to be at an end, radicalized his decisionism to the point of entailing "*political dictatorship*."[37] His most serious opponent was no longer the "*clasa discutidora*" [discussing class], the bourgeoisie, but rather anarchistic socialism as it was advocated by Proudhon and later, in more radical form, by Bakunin.[i] But when in this connection Schmitt says that the essence of the state thereby necessarily reduces itself to an absolute decision which is "created from out of Nothing" and is not to be justified,[38] he is characterizing his own position rather that of Donoso Cortés, who as a

---

[i]Translator's note: In *Political Theology*, Schmitt explains that Donoso Cortés' strict advocacy of dictatorship left him severely critical of the bourgeoisie as that class which would rather "discuss" than "decide"; *Politische Theologie*, p. 75/ *Political Theology*, p. 59. Pierre Joseph Proudhon (1809–1865) was a French libertarian socialist whose "federalism" (the rejection of centralized political organization) had a great influence on subsequent anarchist thought. Mikhail Aleksandrovich Bakunin (1814–1876) was a Russian political theorist and anarchist, and was the author of *Staat en anarchie* (1873). On Cortés' relationship to Proudhon and Bakunin, see *Politische Theologie*, p. 81ff./ *Political Theology*, pp. 64ff.

Christian had the faith that it is never humans but only God who can create something from out of Nothing. This *active nihilism* is exclusive to Schmitt and like-minded twentieth-century Germans.[39] In a decision created from out of Nothing, Donoso Cortés would have seen the same "horrible comedy" he would have seen in the eternal conversation of romanticism.

This nihilistic ground of the kind of decision that is not bound by anything beyond itself becomes completely clear in the concept of the political.[40] If, like Schmitt, we abstract from all central subject areas in order to define the political in terms of the concept of a sovereign decision, then the only thing that logically remains as the goal of decision is the kind of war that extends beyond all subject areas and calls them into question; that is, all that remains is readiness for the Nothing, namely death, understood as the sacrifice of one's life for a state whose own "presupposition" is that which is decisive and political. Schmitt's decision in favor of the political is not a decision in favor of a definite and authoritative subject area, as it is in religious, metaphysical, moral, or spiritual decisions generally; rather, it is nothing other than a *decision in favor of decisiveness*—regardless of what this is actually in favor of—because this is the specific essence of the political.

But this formal conception of decision does not negate that which makes such decision concrete and free, since part of this conception is that one decides on something definite and that one is forever bound by that on which one has decided. And yet the readiness for death and for killing,[41] rather than any kind of ordering of social life as is proper to the primordial meaning of the *polis*, becomes the "highest court of appeal" for Schmitt's concept of the essence of politics; according to this concept, the normal case of living together in a public community is not what is distinctive [*das Spezifische*].

By way of introduction, Schmitt offers the following definition: "According to its linguistic meaning and its historical manifestations, the state is a special situation of a people; indeed it is that situation which is authoritative in the decisive case, and hence in contrast to the kind of particular status which many find conceivable, it is status *per se*. More cannot be said in the first instance. All characteristics of this picture—status and people—get their meaning from the further characteristic of the political, and they become unintelligible when the essence of the political is misunderstood" (7/19f.). The decisive case, in which the political status of the people becomes the measure for all comrades of the state [*Volksgenossen*], is the state of extreme *emergency* or, as Schmitt tends to say, the political "exigency" ["*Ernstfall*"] of war, which demands of people that they sacrifice their lives.[j]

Schmitt's analysis of the political, like Heidegger's analytic of Dasein, considers itself to be secured beyond question by this highest and unsurpassable court of appeal which concerns our Dasein as such, namely the fact *that* we are here at all, i.e., our "facticity"; and it considers itself to be secured in this manner in contrast to every determination which concerns itself with the *what* of our political Dasein. The sheer fact that in war the readiness for death and for killing is something ultimate, confers on it a sovereignty over everything that is, a sovereignty which is analogous to the "superiority" which the *romantic politician* has in virtue of his principle of *occasio*[42] and which the *liberal bourgeois* has in virtue of the relativity of his multiple commitments, none of which is unconditionally binding.[43]

This politically conceived "freedom toward death" presupposes that there are a number of states that confront one another in a hostile manner. Therefore, according to Schmitt's theory of decision, the fundamental distinction to which all political actions and motives are to be traced is the *enemy-friend distinction*—or rather, because the political friend does not dispute his own Being, the distinction between *one's own Being* and *foreign Being*, where foreign Being completely negates one's own Being.

But what is the meaning here of one's own and of a foreign "*way of Being*," and what is the meaning of "*ontological* [*seinsmäßig*]" (3d ed., 14, 20, 23, 37) in general, if indeed political Being is not one kind of Being among others but instead is the protection of one's own Being and the complete negation of foreign Being as such, i.e., if it is political "*existence*"? Is there a natural distinction here between foreign Being and one's own Being which makes [possible] a determination regarding the possibility of war, or is it instead the case that the very distinction between one's own Being and foreign Being follows only from the fact of an actual decision to enter into war? In other words, does the political exigency of war exist because there are essentially different peoples and states or political "*forms of* existence" which accord with a way of Being; or is it only when a war happens to take place, hence accidentally or occasionally, that even the most extremely tense and purely existential commitments and divisions emerge, which according to Schmitt are the distinctive and essential characteristic of the political?

[j]Translator's note: The term *Volksgenosse*, or national comrade, was a term specific to National Socialist rhetoric.

I have translated *Ernstfall* variously as "exigency" and "exigent circumstances," as the context requires.

To this second case would correspond the fact that, e.g., in the last war the Turks were Germany's "friends" and the English its enemies, which could just as well be different in a different war. For these factical "groupings"—a concept from liberal sociology—are, precisely in exigent circumstances, defined above all by their commitments as these are occasioned by the historical situation and the political constellation at the outbreak of a war rather than being defined by an enduring "way of Being."

Now it is significant that Schmitt's formulations are amenable to *both* of these possible interpretations. In some places it appears as if the enemy is "precisely" nothing but someone foreign and other, someone "of another kind,"[44] so that in the extreme case a conflict with him is possible which can be decided only by the participants as a matter of life and death, because the political opponent is neither an "antagonist" nor a mere "competitor" and "opponent in a discussion" (16/28). Even more explicit is the statement that war is not a spiritual struggle or a symbolic wrestling, but instead is an "ontological primordiality" that proceeds from the differences between one's own Being and foreign Being. War *follows* from enmity; it is simply the highest "realization" and "consequence" of an ontological distinction (20, 23/32f., 35).

But on the other hand, a real state of mutual enmity gets portrayed not as a naturally given reality but rather as an essential possibility of political existence, as a capacity-for-Being rather than as a naturally determined Being-thus which is as it is and which cannot be otherwise. It is even explicitly denied that the friend-enemy distinction is supposed to signify that "a specific people would have to be the eternal friend or enemy of another specific people," and it is denied that this distinction is supposed to signify that a state of neutrality could not be politically meaningful and that the avoidance of war could not be politically right (22, 3d ed., 16/x34f.). On the contrary, war seems even more meaningless when one judges its meaning in terms of life's concrete aims and possessions rather than in terms of its naked presupposition: the demand [*Behauptung*] for and receipt of political existence.[k] With a reference to Grotius, Schmitt rejects out of hand the idea of a just war as well as all moral justification (37/49).

But the fact that as a result all that remains as a possible basis for war is the "ontological assertion" of one's own existence, a demand which needs no justification and which amounts to war against a "real" enemy, does not mean that Schmitt's concept of the political has *no* moral and metaphysical presuppositions *whatsoever*, not even those of an immoral

[k]Translator's note: *Behauptung* also means an assertion in the sense of asserting one's rights or interests.

and nihilistic kind. On the contrary, even in Schmitt these presuppositions remain obscured by a polemical commitment to humanitarian morality and liberal positivity.[45] Schmitt does indeed maintain that on his definition the political is "neither belligerent nor militaristic, nor imperialistic, nor pacifistic";[46] and yet his definition is not neutral but instead is antipacifist, so that as a consequence of this polemical negation it is, in itself, belligerent.[47] We should not let Schmitt's captious Neither-Nor prevent us from recognizing that the crux of all his remarks, from his dedication on, is a manifest sympathy for the "high points of great politics," i.e., for war as that which is dangerous and risky.[48]

But from the indisputable fact, which not even a pacifist would dispute, that war over life and death is and always has been a real possiblity in which all concrete oppositions lose their authoritative meaning, does there not follow some *concept* of the political, not to mention a conception of the essence of Being-in-the-*polis* which is not merely an acknowledgment of the simple fact that war is, "when called for," the "*ultima ratio*" that cannot be rationally grounded? And in order to be consistent, would Schmitt not have to reject all talk of the possible "meaning" of war and of *knowledge* of the political? For how could it be possible to know the political situation as a whole "correctly" and to distinguish "correctly" between friend and enemy,[49] if such knowledge is limited *de facto* to the recognition that in exigent circumstances each of the participants must decide in a sovereign manner whether or not this exigency prevails as well as who is to negate, "when called for," their own manner of political Dasein (15, 33, 36, 36, 57/27, 45f., 48, 50, 70f.). But if it is only *in* the given case of conflict that it can be decided whether this ultimate consequence, namely physical killing and physical sacrifice, is necessary, then does this ontological enemy—which surely must mean more than that someone or other happens "to be" my enemy—not get defined in a merely occasional way, that is to say on the grounds that he is calling my political existence into question and negating it, though he is doing so quite independently of my particular kind of Being? But then this enemy is not negating my "*form* of existence" or "manner" of Being, but instead is negating nothing more or less than my naked existence, the *factum brutum* of public, political Dasein, which is prior to more precise definitions in terms of various ways of Being such as nation, race, religion, morality, civilization, and economy, irrespective of whether these pertain to enemies or to friends.

But in that case the fundamental distinction between enemy and friend has no special characteristic in itself. On the contrary, this fundamental distinction reaches through and beyond all special distinctions and commonalities in human Being; it is meant in a "purely" existential sense (37/49), because it is "simply" the highest "degree of intensity" of a potential commitment and division, even though it cannot be specified *what this intensity is an intensity of*.[50] Of course one can say that political tension is all the more intensively "political" in Schmitt's sense the more impersonal and insignificant the substantive content of enmity is, because this intensity has nothing to do with anything definite and unique in the political Dasein of human beings, but instead has to do with pure *Being or Non-Being*.

Schmitt makes this most extreme *sharpening* of the political situation, which comes to pass in the exigent circumstance of war, into the *basis* of his concept of political Being; here he is in agreement with Heidegger's existential ontology, according to which Dasein's "fundamental disposition" consists in its "*that* it is" and—one does not know for what purpose—"has to be."[51] This "that" I am at all rather than not being, or rather that there is a political unity at all, counts here as in Heidegger as what is authentically fundamental, because it is the total and radical, in relation to which all what-ness [*Was-Sein*] is a matter of indifference. As long as it is evident from the start that what things depend on is "never anything but" the existential case of conflict, "what things depend on" is not whether a human being or a state is constituted and ordered in this or that way—whether for example it is an imperialistic and capitalistic nation-state or a communist proletarian-state, a state of priests, dealers, soldiers, officials, or some other kind of political unity[52]—but instead things always depend simply on this one thing, *that* the state in question *is* an "authoritative unity," one which in exigent circumstances gives rise to "groupings" in terms of friend and enemy and decides in a sovereign manner about the lives of human beings. This radical *indifference* [*Gleichgültigkeit*] of purely formal decision to any kind of political *content*, as a consequence of which any particular content has the same value as any other [*einander gleich-gültig*],[53] is characteristic of Schmitt's fundamental, existential-political concept of war as the high point of great politics.

The Protestant Englishman Cromwell's implacable enmity against papist Spain seems to Schmitt,[54] even more than Baron von Stein's hatred of the French,[1] or Lenin's contempt for the bourgeoisie, to be the preem-

---

[1]Translator's note: Oliver Cromwell (1599–1658), Lord Protector of the republican Commonwealth of England, Scotland, and Ireland from 1653–1658, advocated sovereignty in the form of shared government consisting of a single individual ("protector") and a parliament whose members swore allegiance to the protector.

Baron Heinrich Friedrich Karl vom und zum Stein (1757–1831) was a Prussian statesman.

inent example of great politics. Indeed the Nothing characteristic of the sustaining content, i.e., the nihilistic ground in Schmitt's concept of politics, is again evident in his reference to Cromwell. For Cromwell Spain was not *the* enemy simply because he believed that in this case it just happened to be Spain that was challenging his nation's existence; on the contrary, for him Spain was by nature the given, eternal, destined, and divinely willed enemy which never could have come into a different "grouping," [i.e., the Spaniard exhibited] a "providential" and "natural enmity put into him by God."[55] And [on Cromwell's view] whoever considers the Spaniard to be merely an "accidental enemy" fails to know the Holy Scripture and God's affairs—of which there is no talk in Schmitt. Similarly, according to one of his own footnotes, for the Greeks the "barbarians" were not simply others and foreigners whose otherness first had to be "defined"; rather, they were given as enemies in their very nature, and only a conflict with *them* was a war (*polemos*) whereas conflict with other Hellenes was *stasis*.[m][56]

Schmitt, in contrast, winds up in an ambiguous situation. In order to be able to establish his war-oriented concept of politics as something distinctive and independent,[57] on the one hand he must seize upon a substantiality which no longer befits his own historical situation and from which enmity derives substantive content; on the other hand, as a modern, postromantic human who thinks far too occasionally to be able to believe in divinely willed and naturally given distinctions, he must again relativize these substantial presuppositions and shift his whole fundamental distinction back into a formal existentiality. As a consequence his decisive formulations of the enemy-friend distinction shift indecisively back and forth between a *substantial* and an *occasional* understanding of enmity and friendship, so that we do not know whether what is at stake here is those of like kind and those of a different kind, or whether instead what is at stake is simply those who—either with one or against one—are occasionally allied.[58] Upon the shifting ground of this ambiguity Schmitt builds up his concept of the political, whose essential feature is no longer life in the *polis* but instead is simply the *ius belli*.

But together with the question concerning the order of public life, the necessarily related question concerning the relationship of the *polis* to the *individual* is excluded as well. In virtue of Schmitt's manner of avoiding

---

[m]Translator's note: *Polemos* signifies war in the sense of hostility between enemies; in this connection *stasis* (plural *staseis*), whose primary meaning is standing stationary, signifies sedition, discord, or civil war. See Plato, *Republic*, Book V, ch. xvi, at 470.

Baron Heinrich Friedrich Karl vom und zum Stein (1757–1831) was a Prussian statesman.

the totality of the individual by means of a polemical privatization, his claim to genuine totality cancels itself out. Paradoxically, his total concept of political Being captures neither the order of human affairs in a *polis* nor the constitution of the individual in itself;[59] instead, everything that is simply gets totalized with reference to the exigent circumstance, namely the potential annihilation or even the claim to sheer existence on the part of the state and the individual. At one point Schmitt does touch upon the fact that a human being lives within multiple and varied commitments and associations, *as* a member of his family and his work situation, *as* a part of his religious community and his nation, and not ultimately with himself *as* an isolated human being, i.e., *as* an individual.[60] But for Schmitt, the problematic which is focussed in these various forms of the "as" of human Being is of no consequence; with regard to the state, he eliminates this problematic completely.

For him this "pluralism" has a merely negative meaning,[61] namely to deny the sovereign unity of the state; and he considers one's own Being-a-self and the decision about Being or Non-Being which is *always one's own* to be one's "private matter," though from a political standpoint such privacy simply demonstrates the individualistic-liberal character of bourgeois society. "The individual human being may die willingly for what he wants; like everything essential in an individual-liberal society, this is entirely a 'private matter,' i.e., it is a matter for one's free and unsupervised decision, which concerns nobody but oneself as the one who freely decides" (36/48).

Nonetheless, even Schmitt cannot get around the distinction between public and private,[62] and hence he also cannot get around the *connection between* them. For the enemy, understood politically, is "not the *private* opponent" but instead is "simply the *public* enemy," and the latter is a fighting totality. The enemy is *hostis*, but it is not *inimicus*.[n] As a private individual the human being has no political enemies,[63] since "for the individual as such there are no enemies with whom one would have to fight over life and death if one personally does not want to; in any case, to force him to fight against his will is, from the standpoint of the private individual, unfreedom and violence" (57/71). Hence the state's demand for the sacrifice of life is, "from the standpoint of the individualism of liberal thinking," "in no way to be achieved and grounded."[64]

[n]Translator's note: *Hostis*, which originally meant a stranger, came to signify an enemy or public foe, e.g., a traitor; *inimicus* signifies a private or personal enemy, in contrast to an enemy of the state. On this distinction, see *Der Begriff des Politischen*, p. 16f./ *The Concept of the Political*, p. 28f.

But with this antiliberal, purely polemical characterization of the decision which is always one's own, is there not some kind of clear positing, not to mention a solving, of the problem posed by the fact that there is always *one and the same* indivisible human being who must take part both in the political status of his people and in the affairs of his closest relatives and not finally in his own affairs alone? That in war political status is *de facto* "the measure" *for* all subordinate obligations, does not speak against but rather demonstrates the continuing existence of such obligations. War itself shows that, even in the exigent circumstance, human beings do not simply become the enemy of the enemy but instead retain their "private," apolitical qualities on both sides. The same human beings who in the midst of war were ready to kill one another, were able to become peaceful comrades who negotiated and conversed with one another and who nonetheless remained political enemies.[65] And the status of prisoners of war is simply an extreme case of this peaceful enmity.

But the fact that in general the private and public qualities of human beings do not fundamentally separate but instead combine by way of compromise, and that from out of this no serious conflict arises, does not mean that even here no exigency is possible which can function as an exception that sheds light on the rule. Even Schmitt takes this kind of potential exigency into consideration. It is simply as a consequence of his privatization of individual totality that, with respect to political exigency, he must demand the suspension of one's own decision regarding Being or Non-Being, which means the Being or Non-Being of others or even of oneself. In war there cannot be any right to blood vengeance, any more than an institution which lacks the sovereignty of the state is entitled to an *ius belli* [right to war]° or even to the declaration of a domestic *hostis*, since such an institution is entitled at most to a *ius vitae ac necis* [right to life and death].[66] The state also cannot permit its members to die for their beliefs or to commit suicide, when the political unity of those members demands the sacrifice of life. The extreme possibility of killing oneself or of letting oneself be killed *in a war*, so that one's own will-to-death creates the appearance of a heroic sacrifice for the whole, sheds light primarily on the case in which "*freedom* for death" is opposed to the "*sacrifice of life*," private existence is opposed to public existence, and one's own unity is opposed to political totality.[67] But at all times this problematic case is no less possible than a war which is beyond question, because it is

°Translator's note: *Ius belli* means "right to war" in the sense of the right to wage war; similarly, *ius vitae ac necis* means "right to life and death" in the sense of a right to make decisions regarding the life and death of other people.

essentially impossible that the one unity dissolve in the other or vice versa. Out of this difference between two equally primordial totalities, neither of which can subsist without the other, there results as the natural problem of politics the establishment of a common order which relates political unity and personal individuality.

In a radically decisionistic theory of the state, according to which the state is the political *status* of the people, this problem gets expressed in the fact that it must be asked how the "Führer" who decides in a sovereign manner and his "followers" are connected with one another.[P] Even here, mere polemics against the humanitarian concept of personhood and democratic "homogeneity"[68] cannot dispense with the *problem of human equality*.[69] Even Schmitt cannot avoid searching for a kind of equality which humanly authenticates and sustains the political unity between the one who leads and those who obey him. Schmitt seizes upon so-called *equality in kind* [*Artgleichheit*] as this kind of equality. For him this takes the place of equality before God, morality, and the law.

In a lecture on the spirit of modern political philosophy he said that the state previously treated unequals equally. On his view, the modern civil service law struggles against such treatment and toward a substantial equality in kind of the German people and its political leadership: for one cannot provide political leadership to those who are *foreign* in kind. Equality in kind is supposed to give an answer to the question whether the modern state is a constitutional state [*Rechtsstaat*]. On his view it is a just state [*gerechter Staat*] because it is sustained by the trust of a people who are equal in kind.

And yet in his concept of the political, Schmitt never gives a more precise specification of what is *distinctive* about this equality in kind. Only in one place does it become indirectly evident that he, like most of the others, is thinking here of a kind of *national* equality in the sense of race.[70] Thus his concept of the political is not merely antiliberal, but instead is also anti-Semitic; and it is both of these more than he will admit. For it is not simply that case that Schmitt is so anti*liberal* that he tolerates all groupings of whatever kind as long as they are "serious," but he is also so anti-*Semitic* that he advocates racial identity as the foundation of shared existence. And yet such identity is meant in an essentially polemical way.

[P]Translator's note: In this connection Schmitt employs the Latin *status* to suggest that the state is the political Being or the political situation of the people. *Der Begriff des Politischen*, p. 43 / *The Concept of the Political*, p. 55.

Führer literally means "leader"; in the following I have left it untranslated; unless otherwise indicated, I have rendered the related term *Führung* as "leadership."

Here Schmitt is thinking of the contrast between non-Aryans or Jews and so-called Aryans or non-Jews. And in fact there is no better example of a purely polemical concept: for what an "Aryan" is, can be defined only in terms of the fact that he is *not* a *non*-Aryan. Hence in a political state one's own "kind of Being," to which the fundamental distinction between friend and enemy is related, has as its implicit foundation an Aryan substantiality which gives it a semblance of content; and one's own "kind of Being" is meant polemically, in contrast to the essentially foreign kind exhibited by Being-non-Aryan.

And yet it is regrettable that this demand for equality in kind comes forth only in a kind of *Gleichschaltung*[q] that Schmitt carries out by altering a remark between the second and third editions [of *The Concept of the Political*]. The relevant passage reads as follows:

> Second edition (1932), p. 50 (*The Concept of the Political*, p. 63): "How long Hegel's spirit really resided in Berlin is open to question. In any case, the orientation which gained authority after 1840 . . . was that of a 'conservative' political philosophy, namely that of *Friedrich Julius Stahl*,[r] whereas Hegel found his way to Moscow by proceeding to *Lenin* by way of *Karl Marx*. There his dialectical method confirmed its concrete power in a new concrete concept of the enemy, namely that of the *class-enemy*; and the dialectical method transformed itself, together with everything else, namely legality and illegality, the state, and even compromise with the opponent, into a 'weapon' in this war. This actualization of Hegel is has its strongest life . . . in *Georg Lukács*."
>
> Third edition (1933), p. 44: "How long Hegel's spirit really resided in Berlin is open to question. In any case, the orientation which gained authority after 1840 . . . , was that of a 'conservative' political philosophy, namely that of *Friedrich Julius Stahl*. This conservative man switched his faith and his nationality [*Volk*], changed his name, and in accordance with this taught the Germans about piety, continuity, and tradition. He found the German Hegel 'hollow and untrue,' 'of bad taste,' and 'disconsolate.'"[71]

[q] Translator's note: *Gleichschaltung*, which means a synchronization or coordination, also refers specifically to a series of laws passed by the National Socialist government after 1933; the intent of these laws was to establish a highly centralized one-party state. In interpreting Löwith's use of the term *Gleichschaltung* here, the reader will find it illuminating to consider the status of the Jew or the "non-Aryan" in the National Socialist state.

[r] Translator's note: Friedrich Julius Stahl (1802–1861), whose surname was originally Jolson and who abandoned Judaism to become a Lutheran, was a Prussian legal philosopher and member of the *Unionsparlament* under Friedrich Wilhelm IV; Stahl was an opponent of liberalism and revolution (even though he did acknowledge the need for a sphere of private freedom) and an advocate of monarchy.

That in the third edition Schmitt is silent about deleting the outdated remark about Marx and the Marxist Jew Lukács and replacing it with a timely remark about the Prussian Jew Stahl, can become all the more conspicuous if we consider that in another connection, in a footnote regarding the Treaty of Versailles, he makes a new addition but says that it is "unchanged from the year 1927."[72]

But what follows fundamentally from the peripheral fact that a footnote has been altered so as to be timely? A kind of *confirmation* of Schmitt's claim that "politics," "as always," is "fate."[73] For the experience of the last war and the resulting events in German politics are in fact definitive for the manner in which Schmitt defines his time and the political in that time. So much is this the case that one must ask: is the manner in which the political gets understood by one of its active participants defined by "fate," or is this manner of understanding perhaps regulated by *factical occurrences*? But if one's own understanding and the accompanying concept are defined by the political occurrences of the time, then does not every concept and every idea necessarily, in Marx's sense, become "*ideology*"? In such a case the distinction between the dictatorship of Marxism and the dictum of a decisionistic political theory would be confined to the idea that Marx's theoritical critique relates all political and spiritual Being to the fundamental dialectical distinction between bourgeoisie and proletariat, while Schmitt's theoretical polemic relates such Being to the fundamental nondialectical distinction between the liberal and the sovereign state, i.e., between discussion and decision. In both cases, faith in the meaning of a conceptual [*begrifflich*] discussion gives way to a "theory of direct action."[74]

But this means that such understanding [*Begreifen*], which in itself is "political," fundamentally does not want to *understand* what the political is, but instead negates itself for the sake of a political decision. This inversion of philosophical insight into the essence of politics, so that such insight becomes an intellectual instrument of political action, occurred for the first time in a conscious and intentional manner in Marx's confrontation with Hegel. In Schmitt this same inversion is evident, though in relatively liberal form, in his thesis that all political concepts are necessarily "polemical"[75] because they are bound to a given "situation."[76] According to Schmitt there are no political concepts whatsoever that do not have in view "a concrete opposition," which is ultimately the exigency of one's relationship to the political enemy; there are no political concepts that are not bound to such a situation.[77]

For Schmitt the "unavoidable 'lack of objectivity' (should he not in fact *want* to avoid it?) of all political decisions" is simply the "consequence" [*Reflex*] of the friend-enemy distinction immanent in *all* political conduct and understanding."ˢ⁷⁸ But it makes no fundamental difference whether this gets expressed merely in the "meager forms and horizons of the filling of vacancies in party politics" or in the eminent form of Cromwell's will to annihilation, if from the start, even with regard to conceptualization, decision prevails as the highest authority, irrespective of whether such decision is manifest or veiled, radical or moderate.

In intellectual history the origin of this theory of decision, a theory which inverts the literal meaning of philosophy, lies in Kierkegaard's antiromantic thesis of the existential thinker and his passionate subjectivity, and in Marx's antibourgeois demand that theory become practical. Each thereby opposed himself to the entire inner and outer situation of his "rational" [*räsonnierenden*] epoch,ᵗ whose "first law" was that of indecisiveness, though they did so with different intentions and mutually opposed goals. For both, Hegel's spiritual completion of a two thousand year history becomes a "prehistory" prior to an extensive revolution and an intensive reformation. Both turn their concrete *mediations* into abstract *decisions*, in the one case in favor of the old Christian God and in the other in favor of a new earthly world. That Marx subjects the general and outward existential relationships of the masses to a decision and Kierkegaard subjects the inward existential relationship of the individual to himself to a decision, that Marx thinks *without* God and Kierkegaard does so *before* God—what these and other obvious differences have in common is that they have fallen into definite decline, together with the prevailing civil-Christian world.

Significantly, there are two "exceptions" which still characterize the "universal" of Being-human in the decay of this outdated world: on the one hand, the mass of the proletariat, which has been excluded from

---

ˢTranslator's note: The translator of *Der Begriff des Politischen* has translated "ist . . . nur der 'Reflex' der allem politischen Verhalten und Begreifen immanenten Freund-Feindunterscheidung" as "is only the reflex to suppress the politically inherent friend-enemy antithesis"; Schmitt's point, however, seems to be *not* that lack of objectivity is a *reaction against* the friend-enemy distinction, but rather that this lack *follows from* the primacy of the friend-enemy distinction. For Schmitt, all notions of morality, justice, and the like are *subject to* the underlying friend-enemy distinction; in fact, Schmitt's subjection of concepts like justice to what he calls the "exigent circumstance" is a focal point for Löwith's critique of his decisionism, as is implied in Löwith's claim that Schmitt's political theory cannot comprehend political organization in the sense of the *polis*.

ᵗTranslator's note: *Räsonnieren*, which comes from the French *raisonner*, can also mean to nag, grumble, find fault, or mock.

bourgeois society, guarantees the potential rehabilitation of Being-human; and on the other hand, the individuated Christian exception to prevailing Christendom guarantees the potential rehabilitation of Being-Christian. But the spiritual power with which they opposed themselves to this decay is not based simply on a decision in favor of decisiveness, but instead is based on the fact that both, in the face of the degradation and leveling of Being-human,[79] had faith in a highest court of appeal, i.e., in "God" and "humanity" respectively, as the *measure* for their decision.

With these two great opponents of Hegel's philosophy of absolute knowing there begins for the first time, though still within the broad horizon of classical German philosophy, the degeneration of good conscience into wisdom, into science, and into knowing, a degeneration which has subsequently become legitimate. Hence since that time all that has remained fundamental is this *one* difference: whether one still wants to understand anything at all or instead simply wants to "decide," whether with one's words one wants to make things manifest or instead wants to "encounter, fight, negate, and refute."[80] But such a polemical power of words, which are then necessarily catchwords, is something altogether different than the "power of an integrated knowing," from out of which there arises an order of human affairs rather than simply a nihilistic decision.

That Schmitt, in his 1934 essay *Über die drei Arten des rechtswissenschaftlichen Denkins* (*On the Three Forms of Legal Thinking*), does not simply dismiss the impersonal *normativism* of "thinking in terms of rules or laws" as he had done earlier, but also dismisses the personal and dictatorial *decisionism*, the thinking about decision, which he himself had proposed and now becomes an advocate of a "concrete" and specifically "German" transpersonal "*thinking about order* and *form*"[81]—at first blush this latest change in Schmitt's animated thinking would surely seem to overthrow everything he said previously, though in reality it simply confirms the thoroughly *occasional* character of his political thought. For it is simply a consequence of decision, which in itself is empty, if from what occurs *de facto* politically, decision happens to derive the sort of content which deprives decisionism as such of an object. If a state of political emergency is factically dealt with by a decisive act, then at the same time decisionism as a basic political *concept* becomes unnecessary.

Hence with this abandonment of decision, Schmitt in no way betrays himself; for if it does so anywhere, his thinking remains "true" to itself precisely in its passing from an extreme normativism (in his 1917 essay on *The Value of the State*) through the decisionistic concept of the political (in 1927) to his thinking about order (in 1934), inasmuch as it faithfully thinks along with what in each case devolves upon him in an unthinkable way in political situations. As "decisive" as the abnormal situation of the "exception" was previously, now the "normal" and stabilized situation and the "normal human being" become just as decisive for right and just political thinking.[82] The authoritative antithesis is no longer that of norm and decision, but rather that of norm and order.

In this way political concepts lose the essential character which they had previously claimed, namely the character of being polemical; they become essentially positive, in accordance with the new positive order of the state which follows from the political decision of the National Socialist revolution. The earlier notion of sovereign decision adapts itself, subsequent to its demise, to the newly emerging concrete order. Pure decisionism, as it was advocated in a classical manner by Hobbes, presupposes a "disorder" which can be brought into order only by means of some decision; but this decision itself now appears as one in favor of an ordered "communal life," the juridical expression of which is no longer thinking in the sense of a mere decision but instead is thinking about order (52).

In this sketch of "German development up to the present," what gets sketched out is the development of Schmitt's political thinking from 1917 to 1934—and this development is no different than Schmitt himself claims it to be when he makes a deprecating reference to his opponent Kelsen (15n1).[u] The only thing that is remarkable in this development is that Schmitt seems to consider it entirely unnecessary to point out this obligatory change in his notion of sovereign decision subsequent to *The Concept of the Political*, not to mention to justify it to the reader.

Postscript: On Martin Heidegger's Political Occasionalism and Friedrich Gogarten's Theological Occasionalism

Between the two world wars, the pathos of decision in favor of bare decisiveness had met with general approval. It paved the way for decision in favor of Hitler's decisiveness, and it made possible political overthrow in the sense of a "revolution of nihilism." But it was by no means confined to political decisionism; on the contrary, it equally characterized dialectical

---

[u]Translator's note: Hans Kelsen (1881–1973), an Austrian-American legal philosopher, was a neo-Kantian who sought to develop a legal system that makes no allowance for what Schmitt calls the exception; his *Hauptprobleme der Staatsrechtslehre* [Main Problems of International Law] (1911) advanced a "pure theory" of law according to which the law is supreme and independent of all extralegal values. Schmitt presents his critique of Kelsen's liberal political thought in chapter 2 of *Political Theology*.

theology and the philosophy of resolute existence. In the following supplement to the above 1935 discussion on Carl Schmitt,[v] this inner connection between political, philosophical, and theological decisionism[83] will be clarified with reference to Martin Heidegger[84] and Friedrich Gogarten.[w] *Being and Time*, which would appear to be an entirely apolitical work that does nothing but raise the question of Being, though within the horizon of time, appeared in the same year as Schmitt's *Concept of the Political*, and it was at the same time that dialectical theology exercised its greatest power of attraction.

In order to understand the contemporary historical background of Heidegger's radical impulses, it is useful to place them in the context of an expression from Rilke. In a letter from November 8, 1915, Rilke writes that, as regards faith in progress and humanity, the civil world has forgotten the "ultimate courts of appeal" of human life, i.e., the civil world has forgotten that it "was, from the very start, permanently overtaken by death and by God." In *Being and Time* (paragraph 63) death has this same sense of that "highest court of appeal" of our Being and capability which cannot be surpassed. Of course there is no talk of God in *Being and Time*. Heidegger had been a Christian theologian too long to be able to tell "stories about loving God" the way Rilke did. For him the one thing that is needful is the one question of Being as such and as a whole, a question in connection with which the Nothing and death are particularly illuminating.

Death is that Nothing in the face of which the radical finitude of our temporal existence manifests itself, or, as it is put in the Freiburg lectures around 1920:[x] it is "historiological facticity," whose pathos is resoluteness toward the assumption of one's ownmost Da-sein. "*Freedom toward death*," which in *Being and Time* is printed in italicized boldface, and on the basis of which the Dasein which is always one's own and is individuated unto itself achieves its "capacity-for-Being-whole," corresponds in political decisionism to the *sacrifice of one's life* for the total state in the exigency of war. In both cases the principle is the same: the radical return to some-

[v]Translator's note: The original version of "Der okkasionelle Dezisionismus von C. Schmitt," published in 1935 in the *Internationale Zeitschrift für Theorie des Rechts*, vol. 2 (under the pseudonym Hugo Fiala), did not include the discussions of Heidegger and Gogarten, which begin at this point in the text. These were added later, and the revised form of the essay first appeared in Löwith's *Gesammelte Schriften*, pp. 93–127 (now in *Sämtliche Schriften 8: Heidegger—Denker in dürftiger Zeit*, pp. 32–71).

[w]Translator's note: Friedrich Gogarten (1887–1967) was professor of theology in Breslau and Göttingen and a pioneer of dialectical theology, which saw a strict gulf between God and the world.

thing ultimate, namely the naked *that*-ness of facticity, i.e., the return to what remains in life when one does away with every kind of inherited life-content or *what*-ness.

Six years later, in a speech Heidegger gave as National Socialist rector in memory of Schlageter,[85] it was in accordance with this same principle that the highest court of appeal in *Being and Time* could be translated without further ado from the Dasein that is always one's own into something universal, though in its universality no less one's own, namely the "German Dasein." What appears as freedom toward death within the horizon of the Dasein that is always one's own can, within the horizon of popular community, appear as the sacrifice of one's life for one's nation.

In this pompous memorial speech it is said that Schlageter died the "hardest and greatest death" when this defenseless man was shot while his nation lay upon the soil degraded. "Alone and from out of himself, he had to present to his soul the image of the people's impending movement toward its honor and greatness, in order that he could die while having faith in this movement." And Heidegger asks: from where will this "firmness of the will" and "clarity of the heart" come? To this he responded with the "primitive rock" of the mountains of the Black Forest (Schlageter's home) and its autumnal clarity. According to Heidegger, these powers of the soil coursed through the will and the heart of this young hero.

In truth Schlageter was one of the many young Germans who were diverted from their path after the war, some of whom became Communists and some the opposite, as was superbly described by Ernst von Salomon in his novel *The City*.[y] Dissipated by the war and released from military service, they could no longer find their way back into civilian life; they joined a volunteer corps, so that there would be some place and someone against whom they could play out their lives in unbridled undertakings. The existential philosopher calls this a "Has To." "He *had to* go into the Baltics, he *had to* go to Upper Silesia, he *had to* go to the Ruhr," he *had to* fulfill the fate which he had chosen for himself. This is the extent

---

[x]Translator's note: Löwith is referring here to Heidegger's so-called "early" Freiburg lectures, namely those dating from the summer semester of 1919 to the summer semester of 1923 (volumes 56–62 of the *Gesamtausgabe*); after this period of teaching in Freiburg, Heidegger taught in Marburg for five years before returning to Freiburg in the winter semester of 1928–29.

[y]Translator's note: Ernst von Salomon (1902–1972), himself a member of a *Freikorps* unit which saw action in the Baltics and Oberschlesien from 1919 to 1921 and which took part in the Kapp-Putsch, wrote *Die Stadt* in 1932 and the better known *Der Fragebogen* [*The Questionnaire*] in 1951; he was a participant in the assassination of Walter Rathenau.

to which the *fatum* of ancient tragedy had deteriorated by the time of our inflationary period, at the hands of a philosopher!

A few months after this speech, Germany withdrew with aplomb from the League of Nations. The "Führer" called for a supplementary election, in order to make it known abroad that Germany and Hitler were the same. Heidegger had the Freiburg students march as a unit to the election room and register their approval of Hitler's decision *en bloc*. The "yes" to Hitler's decision seemed to him to be identical with the "yes" to one's "own Being"! The election proclamation he had issued as rector is entirely in the style of National Socialism; at the same time it is a popular departure from Heidegger's philosophy of resoluteness:

"German men and women! The German people has been called to a vote by the Führer. But the Führer asks nothing of the people. On the contrary, he is giving the people the most immediate possibility of the highest free decision: whether it—the whole people—wills its own Dasein, or whether it does not will this. This election is absolutely incomparable with all previous elections. What is unique about this election is the simple greatness of the decision to be made in it. But the inexorability of what is simple and ultimate will not endure any vacillation or hesitation. This ultimate decision extends to the furthest limit of the Dasein of our people. And what is this limit? It consists in the primordial demand of all Dasein, namely that it receive and save its own essence. . . . On November 12 the German people as a whole chooses *its* future. This future is bound to the Führer. The people cannot choose this future in such a way that it votes 'yes' on the basis of so-called extrapolitical considerations, without including in this 'yes' the Führer and the movement which is unconditionally devoted to him. There is no foreign politics nor even domestic politics. There is only the one will to the full Dasein of the state. The Führer has brought this will to full awakening and welded it into one single decision in the whole people. No one can stay away on the day on which this will is manifested!"[86]

With this emergence into publicness from out of that still half-religious individuation that in *Being and Time* was the standpoint for positing the question of Being generally, and with the resulting turnaround and application of ownmost Dasein and its "Has To" to the German fate and Dasein, formal "resoluteness," which produces its "toward which" first of all in the very act of resolution,[87] acquires historico-political content. The superb joke made up one day by a hearer of Heidegger's lectures—"I am

The Occasional Decisionism of Carl Schmitt 163

resolved; I just don't know upon what"—was received with unexpected seriousness, inasmuch as the energetic idling of the existentialia ("resolve upon oneself," "stand alone in the face of the Nothing," "will one's fate," "take oneself on") achieved some realization and entered into the universal, political "movement."

It was an Event that in the decisive moment of the German uprising Heidegger let himself be elected rector of Frieburg University, since in this critical time all the other universities did without the kind of "Führer" who could have filled such a position on the basis of his scientific achievement rather than merely on the basis of a party insignia. The bulk of the German intelligentsia were politically reactionary or indifferent. Heidegger had opposed the call to Berlin, succumbing to the temptation to be the Führer [zur Führung] of his own university.[z] His decision was of more than local significance and gained universal attention, for at that time Heidegger stood at the apex of his renown. The student body in Berlin demanded that every university go along with the "Gleichschaltung" which had taken place in Freiburg. Upon assumption of the rectorate, Heidegger delivered a speech on "The Self-Assertion of the German University."[88]

Compared with the countless brochures and speeches issued by the coordinated [gleichgeschalteten] professors following the overthrow, this speech is an ambitious one, a small masterwork of formulation and composition. Judged by the measure of philosophy it is highly suggestive, since it manages to make existential-ontological categories useful to the "commonly"-historical "moment" [Augenblick] in such a way as to make it seem as if the philosophical aims of these categories can and must go together *a priori* with the political situation, and as if the freedom of research can and must go together *a priori* with governmental force. "Labor service" and "armed service" become one with "knowledge service," so that at the end of the lecture one does not know whether one should attend to Diels' Presocratics or march with the SA [Sturmabteilung, "brown shirts" or "storm troopers"]. For this reason one cannot judge this speech as merely political nor as purely philosophical. Its weakness as a

---

[z]Translator's note: On several occasions Heidegger was asked to accept teaching posts at universities other than Freiburg; on two occasions he was asked to accept a post at the university in Berlin, and on one occasion he was invited to accept a position at the university in Munich. On each of these occasions he refused the "call" to vacate his position in Freiburg; for Heidegger's reasons for these refusals, see in particular "Schöpferische Landschaft: Warum bleiben wir in der Provinz?" in *Der Alemanne*, March 7, 1934, p. 1 (now in Schneeberger, *Nachlese zu Heidegger*, pp. 216–218 and Heidegger, *Aus der Erfahrung des Denkens*, pp. 9–13).

political speech is equal to its weakness as a philosophical discussion. It transposes Heidegger's philosophy of historical existence into German affairs; in this way Heidegger's will to gain influence gained ground for the first time, and his formal outline of the existential categories acquired decisive content.

The speech begins with a contradiction: *in opposition* to the threat being posed by the state to the independence of the universities, it deals with the "self-assertion" of the universities; and at the same time it rejects the "liberal" form of academic freedom and self-administration, *in order to subordinate these unconditionally* to the National Socialist scheme of "leadership" [*Führung*] and "following" [*Gefolgschaft*]. The rector has as his duty the spiritual leadership of the teachers and the students. But even he—the Führer—is at the same time one who is led, namely by the "spiritual mission of his people."[89] In what this spiritual mission consists, and by what means this mission is to become evident, remains indefinite. This mission is ultimately assigned by "fate," which one is supposed to will. Corresponding to this indefiniteness of the mission is the stress placed on its being "inexorable." And with a dictum which leaves no room for discussion, the fate of the people gets bound together with the destiny of the universities: the mission of the university is the same as that of the people. German science and German fate come to power in *one* "essential will" (9f./29f.).

The will to essence thereby gets tacitly equated with the will to power, since what is essential for the National Socialist standpoint is the will as such. Prometheus, the symbol of Occidental willing, is [seen here as] the "first philosopher" who should be followed. For the Greeks [according to this speech], with such a promethean willing European humans originally "arose opposite beings" so as to inquire after their Being, and this revolutionary uprising is characteristic of the "spirit" which falters in the face of the superior strength of fate but which is creative in this very impotence (11/31). Spirit [on this view] is not universal reason, nor understanding, nor intelligence, nor least of all *esprit*; instead it is a "knowing resolve" upon the essence of Being, and the true spiritual world is a "world of the most extreme and innermost danger" (14/33).

With soldierly strictness it is then demanded of the student that he "advance," as one who wills to know, to the "station of greatest danger," that he march, devote and expose himself, hold his ground, stick it out, and be generally resolved to assume that German fate which resides in Hitler (14f./34). The commitment to the Führer and the people, to their honor and destiny, is [on this view] one with knowledge service. And to Nietzsche's question whether Europe still wills itself or whether it no longer wills itself, the response is: "We will ourselves"; and [according to Heidegger] regarding the will to self-assertion—not merely that of the university, but on the contrary that of the whole German Dasein—the youthful force of the German people has already made a positive decision (19/38).

But in order to understand the "magnificence and greatness of this awakening" completely, [Heidegger says that] one must recall the wisdom of a word from Plato, which Heidegger translates (in a violently twisted manner): "Everything great stands in the storm!" (19/39).[90] This is the stormy note on which Heidegger's wisdom ended [in the rectorial speech]; and what young member of the SS [*Schutzstaffel* or "black shirts"] would not have felt himself addressed by this and been able to see through the Greek aura surrounding this very German storm? [According to Heidegger] even the community of German teachers and students is a community of struggle, and only in struggle does knowledge get advanced and safeguarded. In a lecture from this time it was said: every "Essence" discloses itself only to courage [*Mut*] and never to mere looking, and truth can be recognized only to the extent that one "demands" truth of himself [*sich* . . . "*zumutet*"]. Even the German "disposition" [*Gemüt*] got connected with this courage. Similarly [according to Heidegger] the enemy is not simply "present," but instead Dasein must *create* its enemy for itself in order that it not become impassive. [For Heidegger] everything which in general "is," is "governed by war," and where war and domination do not essence, there is decay. The essence essences in war.

Heidegger's leadership lasted only a year. Following a number of disappointments and difficulties he abandoned his "mission," so that he could once again oppose the new "anyone" ["man"] in the old manner and risk bitter remarks in his lecture courses, though this was not inconsistent with his substantial adherence to National Socialism as a religious movement of protest and negation. For the "spirit" of National Socialism had to do not so much with the national and the social as with the kind of radical resoluteness and dynamic that rejects all discussion and genuine communication because it relies exclusively on itself—on the (German) capacity-for-Being that is always one's own. Without exception, it is expressions of violence and resoluteness that characterize the vocabulary of National Socialist politics and Heidegger's speeches. Corresponding to the dictatorial style of politics is the apodictic in Heidegger's pathetic formulations. It is simply a distinction of degree rather than one of method which defines the internal differences among the followers, and in the end it is "fate" which justifies all willing and drapes upon it an onto-historical mantle.

Against this historico-political background, the specifically German sense of Heidegger's notions of Dasein becomes clear: existence and resoluteness, Being and capacity-for-Being, the interpretation of this capacity as one of fate and Having To, the insistence on the (German) capacity-for-Being that is "always one's own" and the constantly recurring words: discipline and force (one must "force" himself "upward" even to the "clarity of knowing"), hard, inexorable and strict, rigid and fierce (Dasein's "holding on fiercely"), holding one's ground and standing alone, devoting oneself and exposing oneself to danger; upheaval, awakening, and encroachment. These all reflect the *catastrophic manner of thinking* characteristic of the generation of Germans after the First World War. Least of all was their thinking concerned with "origin," "end," or "limit-situations." All these concepts and words were fundamentally expressions for the bitter and hard resoluteness of a willing which asserts itself in the face of the Nothing and which is proud of its contempt for happiness, reason, and sympathy.

The petty-bourgeois orthodoxy of the party was suspicious of Heidegger's National Socialism because the race question and the Jewish question play no role in it. *Being and Time* is dedicated to the Jew Husserl, the Kant book to the half-Jew Scheler. Heidegger's cast of mind did not seem to be in accord with the "Nordic cast," which is [supposedly] free of anxiety in the face of the Nothing.[91] On the other hand, the Germanist H. Naumann[92] managed to explain Teutonic mythology with the concepts of *Being and Time*, discovering "care" in Odin and the "anyone" in Balder![aa] Neither this approbation nor the aforementioned rejection can be taken seriously, because Heidegger's decision in favor of Hitler goes far beyond agreement with the party's ideology and program. He was and remained a "National Socialist," on the margins and in a state of individuation, though this individuation was by no means without influence. He was influential solely in virtue of the *radicalism* with which he placed the freedom of the Dasein that is German and always one's own upon the manifestness of the *Nothing*.[93]

In 1921 Friedrich Gogarten published a collection of essays and lectures under the title *Die religiöse Entscheidung* [*Religious Decision*].[94] As a Christian theologian and follower of Karl Barth he thought he knew what one

---

[aa]Translator's note: In Teutonic mythology, Odin (or Wotan) was the "All-father," i.e., the principal ruler of the gods as well as the spirit-god who was the source of spirit and the world. Balder was the son of Odin and Frigga, and was the summer sun-god. According to some accounts, Balder had the ability to make his adversaries speak gibberish.

has to decide in favor of, namely God as the "wholly Other,"[95] rather than in favor of the world, with its religion and culture, or in favor of the German people. For this reason he turns against Emil Fuchs, who as a Quaker sought to mediate Christian demands with social ones.[bb] But [for Gogarten] Christ's role as mediator between God and human beings forbids all mediation. If one does not degrade Christianity into a cultural phenomenon but instead grasps it as God's doing, then [on Gogarten's view] one can only place oneself in the middle between oneself and God, rejecting any mediation. [For him] it is a matter of resolutely rejecting even all religious inspirations and practices, experiences, virtues, and requirements, in order to place oneself in unconditional nakedness before God.

But how can one thus place oneself, as a human being, into the unconditional or, as Franz Overbeck put it, "into the air"?[cc] In response to that question which God is for us humans, there can be absolutely no answer, because there is no mediating relationship whatsoever between us and God. This question of all questions takes the ground out from under us, since church and religion, family, state, and national character, or whatever else one may specify, are none of them a means for finding God and standing unconditionally before Him.[96] But if this question deprives us of all ground because it places us outside of all being-conditioned, then [for Gogarten] this simply means that: it places us back into the *Nothing*, understood as that "origin" which is a "death which gives birth, an annihilation which creates" (30).

From this decisive standpoint, any peripheral consideration of the fate of the culture and the religion proper to it is just as insignificant for Gogarten as it was at that time for Heidegger, who wrote in reference to Kierkegaard: "At the least I *want* something different—but nothing much: viz., what I actively perceive to be 'necessary' in the current factical state of revolutionary change [*Umsturzsituation*], without any peripheral consideration of whether from out of this there will result a 'culture' or an acceleration of decline."[97] The distinction between Heidegger's

---

[bb]Translator's note: Emil Fuchs (1874–1970), professor of theology and religious sociology in Leipzig, was the leader of the "Religious Socialists" in Thüringen, a group that linked Christian faith and Marxist ideology. The subtitle of Gogarten's essay "Die religiöse Entscheidung" is "Offener Brief an Pfarrer D. Emil Fuchs [An Open Letter to the Minister Dr. Emil Fuchs]; see *Die religiöse Entscheidung*, p. 5ff.

[cc]Translator's note: Franz Overbeck (1837–1905) was a Lutheran theologian influenced by Nietzsche and Schopenhauer; he became increasingly critical of religion as a social institution, arguing that by its very nature Christianity cannot be accommodated within culture.

philosophical "destruction" of traditional metaphysics and Gogarten's theological dismantling of traditional theology down to something ultimate and radical consists simply in the fact that in the one case this something ultimate was the impending character of death and one's holding oneself into the Nothing, while in the other case it was one's standing before an unthinkable and inconceivable God in the sense of an "annihilation which creates." And just as Heidegger, in the "years of decision" (Spengler), allowed Dasein individuated in the face of the Nothing to carry over into a German Dasein in the face of Hitler, similarly Gogarten became a convert to a "German Christianity" after having previously rejected the idea that Christian faith in God has any national dimension, though after the war he was to swing back to the theological line sketched out by Bultmann.[dd]

Accompanying this return to his initial position is his renewed consideration of the problem of "*decision within the Nothing*."[98] For Gogarten as for Bultmann, faith gets reduced to a deliberate decision for or against faith as such, in which the human being wins or loses his "authentic Being." Faith in God, according to Bultmann,[99] is never a possession but instead is always a "decision." It sets us free from the world, which in its current form lacks the kind of order into which one could integrate oneself. Inasmuch as Gogarten's point of departure is a historiological reflection on the medieval order of creation, in which human beings were rigidly defined from the fall from grace up to the last judgment, he is aware that his understanding of faith as a "decision within the Nothing" is itself historically conditioned, namely by the absence of [*Nichts an*] reliable world-order in the contemporary human world. For the only order that is universally valid in the contemporary world is the scientific-technological order; only the specialist is familiar with this order and takes responsibility for it, whereas to the human being as human being it is entirely foreign.

The increasing rational objectification of human beings and their world offers no answer to the question of Being human, a question in which the question of God presents itself. There can be respons-ibility [*Ver-antwortung*] in the literal sense only when there is a word which asks insistently about me and to which I have to respond. The primordial question about human beings can come only from out of their origin, i.e., from that place where everything which constitutes our world is nothing

---

[dd]Translator's note: On Rudolf Bultmann, see "Heidegger: Thinker in a Destitute Time," note 15, p. 264.

[*nichts*]. This question comes from out of the Nothing, in the face of which the contemporary world places us. But precisely in coming forth in this way, this question encounters both the question of God and trusting faith. For unconditional trust [on Gogarten's view] means: letting loose of everything that one would like to hold on to. Faith trustingly lets itself loose into the Nothing, by detaching itself from all things in the world.

In this manner, Gogarten attempts to make apologetic use of "nihilism" and to show how the primordial question of God comes from out of the Nothing of the contemporary world and how from out of this comes the answer to the question of human beings. Of course the decisive question is whether human beings are of the world or of God. "That contemporary human beings . . . are the ones threatened by the Nothing, means that they stand in the most acute danger, in the face of the scientific-technological world and its superior force, of coming to despair of their Being-human. For such human beings, having faith in God can mean only that, more radically and resolutely than in resignation and despair, they expose themselves to the Nothing which opens itself up before them, and that, precisely in doing so, they seize upon their total dependence on God and thereby receive themselves as the ones who are of divine origin."[100]

Conscious of the fact that today the question of God and the response of Christian faith can no longer be advanced in the same manner as they were by earlier generations, Gogarten attempts to conceive of faith as a "decision within the Nothing." The inner connection between this theological decision in favor of faith, a decision that rests upon the Nothing, and philosophical and political decisionism is obvious. Their common heritage is the staunch conviction that all traditional goods and orderings, contents and measures, and the equating of the "world" with the historical human world, which is implicitly contained in these, have become null and void. But at the same time it is unmistakable just how much this theology and philosophy of decision has its spiritual prototype in Kierkegaard, whose merit was that he always understood his extreme position of existential decision as a "corrective" to his age, and that he explicitly rejected the idea that a temporally conditioned corrective could serve as a norm. Remarkably, neither Bultmann nor Gogarten ever saw his way to thematizing and settling his dispute with Kierkegaard; hence it will never become clear whether and to what extent their positions differ from Kierkegaard's desperate leap of faith.[101]

THREE

European Nihilism: Reflections on the Spiritual and Historical Background of the European War

Part I

The Unity of Europe and the Decline of That Unity

Europe is a concept that develops not from out of itself but rather from out of its essential contrast with Asia. The Greeks presumably took over the distinction between Europe and Asia from the Phoenicians, and on Assyrian monuments these two opposing concepts were found: "ereb" (the land of darkness or of the setting sun) and "asu" (the land of the rising sun). Europe is primordially and, as long as it remains true to itself, politically and spiritually a power that is opposed to the Asiatic. The German word *Abendland* ["West," literally "land of the evening" (tr.)] has a fuller sound. It signifies, in contrast to *Morgenland* ["East," literally "land of the morning" (tr.)], a movement toward the end, a movement which surely begins in the East but which completes itself in the West. "World-history goes from East to West, for Europe is simply the end of world-history, and Asia the beginning. . . . Here the external, physical sun rises, and it sets in the West; but in order that this occur, the inner sun of self-consciousness must ascend there, casting a higher kind of radiance,"[1] namely the radiance of absolutely free and hence critical spirit, whose dangers and greatness are as yet unknown to the East.

In Europe's adolescence, Hegel says (276), two adolescents developed the most lovely and free individuality: Achilles and Alexander the Great. "Achilles as the main figure in the Greeks' national undertaking against Troy . . . ; Alexander, who places himself at the head of the Greeks by following the example of Achilles, and who exacted the revenge which had been sworn against Asia." The adolescent deed of Alexander followed the manly deed of Caesar, who opened up the center of Europe by conquering Gaul. His followers established the Roman world-empire, which since then has been the historical ground upon which Europe moves. The heirs of Rome were to be the Roman Catholic Church and the "Holy Roman Empire of the German Nation," which officially confirmed its end only in 1806. But the first decisive break in the spiritual unity of Europe occurred long before this, with Luther's German protest against the universal authority of the Roman papacy. Europe's spiritual unity on the basis of the one and universal, i.e., "Catholic," Church and its Roman tradition was thereby called into question both religiously and politically. "Christendom or Europe," which Novalis was still celebrating in 1799, is, ever since the German Reformation, no longer a convincing reality but is instead—precisely as is Hölderlin's Hellenism—a longing born of need.

The unity of Europe, which distinguishes and demarcates the countenance and the mien of the European from all others, even if this unity is a shattered one, is neither geographic nor racial and is defined neither by "blood" nor by "soil." Geographically, Europe extends into Russia and Asia without a fixed, natural border, whereas America, in spite of its continental independence, is from the standpoint of culture and language more European than the southeastern and northeastern parts of Europe, which are populated by Slavic and half-Asian peoples. The white race of the Occident reaches far beyond Europe's borders, and foreign races reach far into Europe.[2] The crux of its unity can by no means be grasped in a material sense; it is a kind of shared feeling, willing, and thinking that has developed in the course of Europe's *history*, i.e., a definite way of conceiving and shaping itself and the world.

Europe is the European *spirit* and the shared safeguarding of that spirit. In this way Greece, in the Amphictyonic League,[a] shared the safeguarding of the Delphic cult in spite of the rivalry among its city-states; the Roman imperium safeguarded Hellas and Rome; and the medieval emperor safeguarded the Christian Occident. The political struggles of the Renaissance were spiritually united by the reawakening of and care for the Greek and Latin heritage; and the German humanism of Herder and Humboldt, of Schiller and Goethe, to which there corresponded no political structure, lived and moved within a shared faith in the *one* spirit of

[a]Translator's note: The Amphictyonic League was an association of Greek city-states for the preservation of the temples and cults of Apollo at Delphi and Demeter at Thermopylae.

European humanity. Subsequent to the decline of ecclesiastical tradition, the literary organ of the shared safeguarding of the unity of European spirit was an exchange of letters among the best minds in Europe (Erasmus, Leibniz, Voltaire, Diderot) which included all nations and which, upon a humanistic basis, replaced the earlier unity of religious education.

The last event of truly European significance was the French Revolution and Napoleon's attempt to unify politically and legally the European states and peoples. In reaction to his acts of violence against these many nations, the Congress of Vienna and the "Holy Alliance" produced the "Concert of Europe" which, as a "balance of power" or "European equilibrium," saved the fate of Europe whenever necessary. This was the last, weakest, and most problematic form of European unity, inasmuch as this compromise between conflicting national interests did not share any common idea, legislative process, or executive power. The Europe of the nineteenth century no longer lived with faith in a genuine mission; it simply disseminated its wares and its scientific-technological civilization in every direction.

Against this Europe of capitalist and imperialist undertakings, whose manners were lawless and whose spirit lacked a purpose, in the previous century a critique was directed for the first time by non-European peoples, which attacked Europe's innermost foundations. Subsequently the West saw itself in the critical mirror of Russia (Kirejewski,[b] Dostoevsky, and Tolstoy) and China (Ku-hung-ming),[3] after Voltaire had already broken apart the closed circle of the Christian Occident by appealing to the East (Confucius).[4] Of course Europe had already advanced a critique of itself, one more radical and open, more serious and penetrating, than the foreign critique. A phenomenon related to this self-critique is the migration of individual Europeans to Asia, their spiritual betrayal of Europe and their ill-fated love of an East which itself had already begun to become enslaved to progress. Lafcadio Hearn was one such extreme case, inasmuch as he attempted "to cross the concession line" between the two cultures and races.[5]

The European war from 1914 to 1918 did not put an end to the self-critique of the *fin de siècle* though it did put an end to its mood, to the extent that it was the end not simply of a century but rather of an entire epoch. In the midst of so much need and annihilation, it inspired the best

[b]Translator's note: Ivan Wassiljewitsch Kirejewski (1806–1856) was a Russian philosopher of religion and culture who studied with Hegel, Schelling, and Schleiermacher; he wrote on the tensions between Russia and Europe, and influenced Dostoevsky.

with the hope that precisely out of this shared need there could emerge a new shared good as well: a new order for Europe, through which its deflated concept might again come to life—even if this be first of all only in isolated individuals who, as a peaceful community, form the conscience of Europe.[6]

In German philosophy it was Scheler who posed most clearly the question of the meaning of the first European war: he says that this war must be either the beginning of Europe's rebirth or the beginning of its demise, since there is no third possibility. Nonetheless, his ideas on European solidarity end with the pessimistic conclusion that all bearers of European culture, including the churches, have failed entirely.

"The sacrifice of all shared investment in ethical measures and principles for making judgments about the kind of terrible events in the moral world which this war has brought with it, seems no longer capable of being overcome. At no time in the history of Western Europe subsequent to the decline of the medieval papacy, which was the last form of such universally revered authority, did it become as terribly clear as during this war what it means for Europe no longer to possess any supranational, commonly recognized authority—and this does not refer simply to the deplorable transgression against every limit imposed by international law. But with this it becomes equally clear that so-called presuppositionless . . . science's claim to take the place of the kind of spiritual European authority which contributes its moral weight and its sanctified tradition, has become so ephemeral, so unreliable and empty. . . . Expressions of every kind, the various exchanges of letters among the learned of the different European nations concerning war and warfare, indicated an intellectual and moral nadir, a clouding of judgment, a seeing of all things from the standpoint of the emotions of the masses [*durch Massenaffekte*]; this was all nourished by a press which in part just plain lied and in part suppressed all truth, and it was pushed to the point of grotesqueness by an inability . . . to secure . . . basic principles in the exchange of ideas which would be commonly recognized at least in Western Europe."

[According to Scheler] the war made it apparent

"that at this time in Europe there is no man, no place, and no authority which possesses the inner worth and moral weight to place it above the danger of partisanship and which also enjoys sufficient general respect and recognition that its pronouncements regarding the national obligations [*Gebundenheiten*] of spirit would touch the heart of Europe. This is the outlook of our time: every aspect has become dubious, in connection with each there prevails an unlimited number of conflicting opinions—and it is only the masses and power that confer some meaning."[7]

But even a man with the vision of Scheler, who had the courage in the midst of the war to speak openly of "The Causes of the Hatred of Germans,"[8] was susceptible to the mass emotions of the war to an extent that is made evident at the end of his book by the "Table of Categories of English Thinking," in which he analyzes English sanctimony or "cant" with a hostility that even today can hardly be surpassed.

Only the German collapse caused him to revise his ideas, to orient the "cultural reconstruction of Europe"[9] on Christian tradition as the common possession of the European peoples, and to advocate a Christian pacifism far removed from the "genius of war." In sharpest contrast to the "Pan-Germans," who had the arrogance to place Germany "über alles" and to annex as much of the others as possible, Scheler now advocated the viewpoint that the shared responsibility for the European war could be atoned for only by a shared penitence, reflection, and striving. A "conciliation" [*Ausgleich*] of European differences, and beyond that a balancing [*Ausgleich*] of Western spirit with the Eastern Christianity of Russia and with the wisdom of the East, is supposed to heal the wounds of a war whose meaning [according to Scheler] lies in its having brought a long-standing illness to the point of open outbreak.[c]

The factical events during the time following the war took the ground away from all attempts to reestablish Europe's spiritual and political ties, and those events showed all exchange and conciliation to be illusory. Because of to its civil war, Europe was further than ever before from becoming a new unity; indeed it had lost its war to Wilson and Lenin. Ever since, it hung in the balance between America and Russia, whose economic and political support it now had to seek in order to wage war within its own boundaries. Even the political victor of the last war, Clémenceau, could not remain blind to the insight that his triumph brings with it a misery (*Grandeur et misère d'une victoire*), while on the other hand Germany pronounced itself "undefeated in the field" and spoke of a "postponed" victory.

The fact of defeat was able only temporarily to reduce the strength of a consciousness which had been acquired in the course of four years of

[c]Translator's Note: On Scheler's essay "Man in the Era of Adjustment [*Ausgleich*]," see "The Occasional Decisionism of Carl Schmitt," note 79, p. 282.

battle; and the tragic result of the peace treaty and the League of Nations was, in spite of the disarmament, a "total mobilization."[d] To win the lost war after the fact is the simple, German formula for conceiving the continuation of the war, which only appeared to be concluded in 1918 to the extent that it ended in a senseless manner. Regarding the war there are the severe and prophetic words of a German poet: "Jubilation is not fitting: there will be no triumph. / Only many destructive events, without worth . . . . / The old God of battle is no more. / Diseased worlds suffer fever to the very end."[10] In fact, Europe as a whole was the one defeated.

But even the current war between Germany and England, whose antagonism repeatedly brought Europe before the abyss long before 1914,[11] is a war for Europe which directs itself *against* Europe. For whoever utters the last word in this war—old Europe will not exist again. Both of the opponents claim to stand for the shared spirit and the order of the one Europe, but in truth they are an *extra-European* and a *counter-European* power: England with the will to conserve what exists, and Germany with the will to revolution. Already in the last war people in Germany judged England to be the constitutive enemy of a new political formation of Europe, because its traditional political principle is based on its insularity and its concomitant claim to maritime supremacy, whereas both of these are incompatible with membership in a continental coalition of states.

"As long as England maintains its maritime supremacy, it will have to . . . view . . . the fate of every individual European state, indeed . . . the whole of Western Europe outside of itself, no differently than it views any non-European state in its political account of the world. Just this long will it bear within itself the radical contradiction of existence, namely that of being both a cultural part and a political outsider in the European community of states. As long as it is so preeminent in all possible respects in the world and its engagements far surpass all the European states, it can never, ever safeguard Europe's 'holiest goods.' For the sake of its interests in the world, it must . . . consign . . . all . . . European states to that phase in the anarchic form of world politics which is the ultimate root even of this war. . . .

[d]Translator's Note: See Ernst Jünger, "Die totale Mobilmachung," *Werke*, vol. 5 (Stuttgart: Ernst Klett, n.d.). Jünger was a prolific novelist and essayist; the National Socialists sought support for their ideals in his works (notably his *Der Arbeiter* (*The Worker*) and his World War I diaries *Stahlsturm* (*Storm of Steel*), though Jünger was eventually to criticize the movement for being "spiritually empty" in *Auf den Marmorklippen* (*On the Marble Cliffs*), 1939.

"Only if England were to become so limited in its maritime supremacy that it could not undertake a single world-political step before securing the accord of the European powers, could this position as outsider become transformed into the position of member in the community of European states. The principle of the 'method of equilibrium,' which for more than a century has . . . characterized . . . England's cant as the guarantee of tranquillity and peace in Europe, is, factually, the principle which in the long run will be absolutely lethal for the fate of Europe. . . . It is not the case that we want to exclude England from the unity of Europe, but on the contrary it politically excludes itself by means of its political methods; and it is we who must force it to heal all of Europe, and to adopt the standpoint of the 'good European' instead of posing imperialistically as a supra-European world power which takes Europe into account simply as one factor among others in its great economic-political accounting of the world. It is in the common interest of all European continental states that this force succeed."[12]

But on the other hand, we must also not overlook the fact that Germany is increasingly and ever more decisively distancing itself from the old Europe which is preserved in our Roman-Christian heritage. The German ideology in the writings of A. Rosenberg, A. Baeumler, and H. Heyse[e]—to name just a few names—is a decisive departure from the total European tradition, which gets covered up by being played out as a "nordically" interpreted Hellenism directed against Rome and Christendom. In contrast, Ernst Jünger expressed the anti-European meaning of the German war with his unique irony and cynical openness.

"We declared war on Europe—as if we were good Europeans gathered harmoniously with the others around a roulette wheel with only one color, namely the color for zero, which always lets the house win. We Germans

[e]Translator's note: Alfred Rosenberg (1893–1946) was an aide to Hitler who served as minister for the occupied eastern territories after 1941; in 1930 he wrote *Der Mythus des 20. Jahrhunderts* (*The Myth of the Twentieth Century*), which was a National Socialist manifesto. Alfred Baeumler (1887–1968) was a philosophy professor in Dresden and Berlin, and served as academic liaison to the Nazi party; he was charged with the ideological education of the party, and he led the Nazi appropriation of Nietzsche and the Nordic ideal, particularly through his publication of *Nietzsche, der Philosoph und Politiker* (*Nietzsche, Philosopher and Politician*) in 1931. Hans Heyse (1891–1976) was a neo-Kantian philosopher and professor in Breslau, Königsberg, and Göttingen; in *Idee und Existenz* (*Idea and Existence*) (1935) he argued that the Third Reich was determined by "basic values of tragic-heroic existence."

did not give Europe any chance to lose. But because we gave no chance of losing, in an essential sense we also offered nothing to win inasmuch as we played against the house with its own funds. Hence the result was the simultaneous inflation and depletion of what is European.... Great amusement at discovering that our stakes amounted to mere pocket change, that the most important reserves were not being mobilized into combat....

"We were hardly armed to the teeth, not to mention to our innermost heart and marrow. We had not at all learned how to speak our primoridal language yet—in order to do this we would first of all have had to enter school. This is why we were compelled to give the discussion a hypothetical, more superficial focal point: to this extent Europe was a working hypothesis in the space of which we could . . . hibernate and undergo pupation . . . in an acceptable manner. For our generation it is still necessary to take this hypothesis seriously, or to have taken it seriously at one time; today this is still one of the modes of access to German reality, and yet it also is no longer one; a penultimate nutshell which must be cracked. The European as 'great fashion,' like the Voltairism of Friedrich II.... We must learn to see Europe not as a category, but rather as a *German special case*. Finally: that apart from us, the Jews alone are the suspicious Europeans....

"Seen from the outside: we are not trusted. People are suspicious of secret military exercises and nocturnal advances, of rousing maneuvers between troops that are distinguished only by colored arm bands. These deployments of humanity into grouped columns, these little newspaper writers and bad novelists who in spite of everything allowed themselves to be schooled by the arch-Boche [*Erz-Boche*]^f Nietzsche—all of this, less the What than the How, points toward an internal secretion of the military tendency. One does not catch any kind of good scent—a *foetor germanicus* [Germanic stink] in which what seems to slumber is the aura of more chaotic battlefields to come. This is why humanity consistently attempts to see every Bushman as human before it will see us as human, and why (insofar as we are Europeans) our aversion to ourselves continually appears. Superb, but no sympathy for us! This is a position on the basis of which something can be accomplished. To take measure in this way from the secret standard of civilization, a standard which was preserved in Paris—for us this means to lose the lost war at its end, i.e. it means the consistent carrying out of a nihilistic act up to its necessary

---

^{f}Translator's note: "*Boche*," from the French *boche*, is a derogatory appellation for a German.

end-point. For a long time we have been marching toward a magical reference point which can be gotten beyond only by those who have at their disposal different, invisible sources of power. *Our* hope is tied to whatever is left over, left over because it cannot be measured in terms of what is European but instead provides the measure for itself."[13]

"The more Prussian or Bolshevist, the better" is the motto of this ecstatic manner of thinking, a clear special case of which is Europe. From this standpoint one must also evaluate Germany's alliance with Russia, which was anticipated by Rauschning already three years ago.[14] And this is how it was judged sixty years ago by Dostoevsky:

"In any case, one thing is clear: Germany needs us far more than we think . . . . The idea of a reunified Germany is great and proud and reaches back into the depths of centuries. But what does Germany want to share with us? The whole of Western humanity is its object, it has set aside the whole of the Western world of Europe for itself: instead of the Roman and romantic idea, here the Germanic idea is to assume the leadership. But to us, Russia, it leaves the East. It is left to two great peoples, us and them, to change the face of the whole world. It is neither human fancy nor human ambition which has invented this: the world itself determines things in this way."[15]

Together, Germany and Russia are revolutionizing the historical composition of the Eurasian continent: politically, economically, and spiritually.

The End of Ancient Europe

The destruction of the religious and moral unity of the Christian West began with the German Reformation, whereas the destruction of its political tradition began with the French Revolution. It continues with the Russian Revolution, inasmuch as Bolshevism is alive in Western Europe in the Jacobins,[g] and inasmuch as the events of 1789, 1848, and 1917 are part of *one* movement.

"We in Central Europe live under the [watchful] eye of the Russians. For a century their psychological gaze has seen through our great words and

---

[g]Translator's note: The Jacobins were originally a group of French revolutionaries in the 1790s, named for their meeting place, the Dominican monastery of St. Jacob in Paris.

our institutions; they possess sufficient vitality to marshal our knowledge and technology as weapons; their courage to live up to both rationalism and its opposite, their power to realize orthodoxy in good and in evil, are overwhelming. They have realized the connection between socialism and Slavicism, which Donoso Cortés prophesied in 1848 as the decisive event of the coming century.[h]

"The Russians have taken the European nineteenth century at its word, recognized its core, and derived the final consequences from its cultural premises. One always lives subject to the gaze of one's more radical brother, who forces one to take a practical conclusion to its end. Quite independent of the prognoses of foreign and domestic policy, one thing can definitely be said: that on Russian soil the antireligion of technicity was put into practice, and that here a state [*Staat*] comes into being which is more intensively national [*staatlich*] than a state of the most absolute prince ever was . . . . As a situation, all this can be understood only on the basis of the development of Europe during the last centuries; it perfects and surpasses ideas which are specifically European, and it exhibits, in a tremendous enhancement, the core of Europe's modern history."[16]

Both the French and Russian Revolutions turned the past into a *tabula rasa* and initiated a turning point in the history of Europe.

Carlyle called the French Revolution the "third act of world history" because for him, in relation to that revolution the whole history of Europe from the beginning of the Christian era on appeared as one single epoch, namely as the second act following the first act of antiquity.[i] He believed that European humanity has broken into anarchy and that it will take a number of "sordidly agitated" centuries before the old can be completely extinguished and something new can be established. Bonald and de Maistre in France, Burke in England, and Gentz in Germany gave expression in their counterrevolutionary writings, each in his own way, to nothing less than the insight that Europe stands at a critical turning point.[j]—Napoleon wanted to close the abyss that had started this revo-

[h]Translator's note: On Donoso Cortés, translator's note, p. 137.

[i]Translator's note: Thomas Carlyle (1729–1797) was an English author and critic of nineteenth-century materialism, which he identified with the decline of the West. He wrote *The French Revolution* (3 vols., 1837).

[j]Translator's note: Edmund Burke (1729–1797) was an Irish politician and opponent of the French Revolution; he wrote *Reflections on the Revolution in France* in 1790. Friedrich Gentz (1764–1832) was a Prussian military adviser who supported the French Revolution for a time but became critical of it, seeking to preserve European equilibrium by fighting against Napoleon; he translated Burke's *Reflections* into German. On Bonald and de Maistre, see translator's note, p. 143.

lution, but his attempt failed; and in the July Revolution of 1830 it became apparent that the Restoration that had taken place in the meantime was merely a moment between acts, and that starting in 1789 Europe found itself in an age of revolutions which even today has not yet come to an end.

In 1830 the German historian Niebuhr witnessed the onset of the kind of destruction that the world experienced around the third century: annihilation of prosperity, of freedom, education, and science.[k] Goethe concurred with him when he prophesied a coming barbarism and suggested that it is even already here, that "we are already in the midst of it." In a discussion from 1829 concerning Europe's situation, he said that the nineteenth century is not simply the continuation of the prior century but is instead the beginning of a new epoch. He saw the time coming when God will no longer have any joy in the world and will have to smash everything into a renewed creation. The ground of civil society and its sociability seemed to him to be destroyed, and he viewed the writings of Saint-Simon as the spirited blueprint for a radical annihilation of the prevailing order.[l]

He recognized the modern French literature that came his way to be a "literature of desperation" which forces upon the reader that which is opposed to everything that should be conveyed to human beings in the interest of some healing [*zu einigem Heil*]. "Its satanic business is to outdo ugliness, disgust, cruelty, and worthlessness in the extent to which it pushes all kinds of depravity into the realm of the impossible." [According to him] everything is now "ultra" and "transcends," in thinking as in doing.

"Nobody knows himself any more, nobody comprehends the element in which he resides and operates, nobody comprehends the material with which he works. There can be no talk of pure fatuousness; there is enough fatuous rubbish. Young people become agitated much too early, and then they get carried away in the whirlwind of time. Wealth and alacrity are what the world admires and what everyone strives for. Railroads, express mail services, steam ships, and every possible way of facilitating communication are what the educated world wants in order to overeducate

[k]Translator's note: Barthold Georg Niebuhr (1776–1831) was a German historian and statesman; he lectured on Roman history at the universities in Berlin and Bonn.

[l]Translator's note: Claude Henri de Rouvroy, Count of Saint-Simon (1760–1825), was a French social theorist who wrote on sociology, socialism, a united Europe, and pacifism; he advocated strict limits on private property ownership.

itself, though as a result it persists in its mediocrity. Of course it is also the result of universality that an average culture becomes base. This is genuinely the century for capable minds, for quick-witted, practical people who, equipped with a certain adroitness, feel their superiority over the masses even if they themselves are not capable of what is highest . . . . We will, together with perhaps just a few, be the last of an epoch which will not return very soon."[17]

This same epochal consciousness was spread among the Young Hegelians and the Young Germans. In 1830, in the introduction to his *Thoughts on Death and Immortality*, Feuerbach writes: "One who understands the language in which the spirit of world history speaks, cannot fail to recognize that our present is the copestone of a whole period in the history of humanity and is precisely thereby the starting point of a new life."[18] Immermann was of the opinion that the revolution of 1830 cannot be explained in terms of a material need,[m] but rather only in terms of a spiritual pressure similar to a religious movement, though what causes the movement is the political rather than faith.

Metternich foresaw a chaos,[n] the outbreak of which he sought through his political activity to defer for as long as possible. Of course at the Congress of Vienna the old system of nations had again triumphed over the seeds of the future, but Metternich did not have any illusions about the nature of his success, which was merely to cause a delay. "My most secret thought is that the old Europe is at the beginning of its end. Resolved to founder with it, I will know how to do my duty. The new Europe, on the other hand, is still in the process of becoming; between end and beginning there will be a chaos."

In 1846 Jakob Burckhardt resolutely detached himself from the political radicalism of his friends from his younger days,[19] and he henceforth confined himself to the learning of "Ancient Europe"—"turned backwards in order to rescue the learning of an earlier time, and turned forwards for the gay and indefatigable advocacy of spirit in a time which, in the absence of such advocacy, could sink to [the point of becoming oriented on] matter [to the exclusion of spirit]." [According to Burckhardt] no genuine social organism can be introduced into this aging Europe

[m]Translator's note: Karl Leberecht Immermann (1796–1840) was a German poet and theatrical producer.

[n]Translator's note: Klemens Wenzel Nepomuk Lothar Prince Metternich (1773–1859) was an Austrian statesman and opponent of the French Revolution who advocated "supranational monarchy."

anyway; this has been so ever since everything was set into motion by the unbridled will to change and to progress, whose optimism Burckhardt condemned as "reprobate." Because nothing is secure any more and everything has become provisional, the state must now strive to make all of its powers more completely unified and available. The national totalitarian state of the nineteenth century arises by means of a "centralization without right" modeled on the national despotism seen at the time of the Reign of Terror in the French Revolution. With the disappearance of a sense on the part of the governments and peoples that right had been religiously sanctified, the profane character of this right becomes all the greater, and in place of the dynasties there now rule "special authorities," individual leaders and usurpers who are supported by the masses and who are considered in every case to be "saviors."

[According to Burckhardt] when consciousness of constitutional and international law completely dies out, governments and peoples will agree that as much power as possible is necessary, whatever the cost. This situation results in a boundless augmentation of military power and of the national debt which such an augmentation requires, and these are considered to be national necessities. The state has learned from the industrialists how to exploit credit, and it defiantly maintains that the nation cannot cause credit to go bankrupt—"alongside all the swindlers there now stands the state as the great master-swindler." Ever since an ecumenical order has ceased to exist in Europe, the state has suppressed foreign groups within the population, and nationality has been misused as the sole means for establishing associations. In a decisive moment, the consciousness of a unified nation will outweigh even all social problems and especially the cultural unity of Europe. An unbounded *feel for business* goes hand in hand with the *feel for power*, the state becomes a large-scale manufacturer and a military despotism.

Hence [according to Burckhardt] something like the age of the Caesars in Rome is impending for Europe, an age on the horizon of which there lie great civil wars. On the basis of democratic leveling, [he says that] the state will once again obtain absolute power, with which it will command the masses to "shut their mouths." [For Burckhardt] there have never been pure questions of right when what is at issue is movements on the part of entire peoples, but in this case the world puts on a face which makes it seem "as if there were no longer any right nor any questions whatsoever." (But this despotism no longer wants to be driven by softhearted dynasties but instead by military commands which "can govern in an absolutely brutal manner," without regard for right, material welfare, popular sovereignty, or even for science.) Perhaps they will carry this quite far and will once again subjugate the European world, even to the point of absolutism.

Ever since 1840, the two pincers in which the so-called culture has found itself held have been the Fourth Estate from below and militarism from above. The ultimate end could then once again be an *imperium romanum*, after there have first been a number of Assurs, media [*Medien*], and Persias.º "*Terribles simplificateurs*" [terrible events which simplify] will come over the old Europe, and [according to Burckhardt] the character of all existence [*Dasein*] will become, even more so than it is already, a thoroughly ingrained military purposiveness, all the way down to the individual. But what is least expected will befall the workers: "a definite and controlled measure of misery, with promotion and in uniform, initiated and concluded on a daily basis amid the beating of drums, is what logically would have to come about."[20] [For Burckhardt] there is no talk of stopping on this path, and in Germany perhaps the sovereign power will for the first time don its *toga virilis*.P

The same ideas are found in the writings of Bruno Bauer, a radical student of Hegel.q In his book *Rußland und das Germanentum* [*Russia and the Germanic World*], which appeared in 1853, he characterizes the spiritual and political situation in the following way: "Oh how much of what was held dear by cultured people will have to be thrown overboard by them as spiritual 'luxuries'! and the new breed will grow up to be so distinctively different from the way we are . . . . 'Put your house in order' is the wisest thing that we all can do in the whole of Central Europe. Things are becoming different than they were."[21]

Kant's philosophical and political ideas still move within the limits of the French Revolution; in it he saw the highest guarantee of progress in the moral status of humanity, and it was on the basis of the experience of the French Revolution that he defined the task of history. Fichte had catered to German pride by portraying the Germans as the creative *Urvolk* [primordial people] and by linking the restoration of the rest of humanity to the Germans' self-assertion of their own essence. As a rec-

---

ºTranslator's note: Assur was the mythic national deity of Assyria; "media" in the present context seems to be an oblique reference to modes of commerce, sometimes signified by the German *Medien*.

PTranslator's note: A virilis was an outer garment worn by Roman youths who had reached their fifteenth or sixteenth year, to signify coming of age.

qTranslator's note: For a more detailed discussion of Bruno Bauer (1809–1882), see Löwith's *Von Hegel zu Nietzsche*, vol. 4; *From Hegel to Nietzsche*, pp. 105ff., 343ff.

ollection of past history, Hegel's completion of knowing is an end. He excluded from his account the possibility of a break with all of prior culture, and he did not permit the question of a new age to arise.

"All those German philosophers who gave the highest and purest expression to the outlook of their nation, thought only of the West—for them the East did not yet exist—for them a relationship of the Germanic world to Russia did not yet exist.

"And yet already in Kant's time Catherine the Great had established a dictatorship over the continent, a dictatorship which in power, influence, and world-historical significance far exceeded those of Charles V of Spain and Louis XIV of France" (2).

The question at present is "whether the Germanic world will survive the demise of the old civilization (for nothing is more certain than this demise), or whether the Russian nation alone will determine the new civilization—whether the age which is now beginning will be called the Russian age, or whether in conjunction with the Russian world the Germanic world will give this age its name" (71). "The German question and the Russian question are the only two living questions of the newer Europe—though the latter question is already so precisely formulated that an answer to it will precede the answer to the former, and the latter question is supported by an organization with power sufficient to specify the moment at which it wants to produce an answer and cut the Gordian knot."

In connection with the dissolution of Europe, Bauer also considers "The End of Philosophy" (44ff.) to be the natural conclusion of a historical development and the transition to a new organization of both the political and the spiritual world.

"Is it a mere accident that philosophy, to which the Germans have dedicated their best efforts during the last eighty years, should collapse at the same moment that Germany, with all its national assemblies, conferences, and deliberations about customs regulations, is seeking in vain the seat of its inner power, the very power which could organize Germany? Is it accidental that the dominating power with which philosophy subordinated to itself the individual sciences, the moral as well as the physical ones, is utterly destructive—that the supremacy which it previously manifested over the sciences should be called into question at the same moment that the nation which shook the West in the name of philosophy . . . lost its capacity for aggression? . . .

"Finally, is it accidental that at the same moment that the spiritual supremacy of the metaphysicians reached its end, a nation asserts dictatorship over the continent, dictatorship which from its inception remained foreign to the philosophical labors of the West, to which the metaphysics of the West offers no scruple, and which—we are thinking of the Russian nation—knows only one point of view, namely the practical? No! There is no doubt—the catastrophe which simultaneously befell the entire system of nations in Europe, contitutionalism, and metaphysics, is an internally related event" (45f.).

The universities, Bauer continues, have become insipid; their philosophy teachers simply recount antiquated systems and do not advance even one new idea that could, as before, move the world. The universal need of the time, a spiritual and economic "pauperism,"[22] has put an end to interest in metaphysical studies.

It is with justification that the number of students in the universities decreases each year, while the technical schools are thriving. The academies as well testify to the decline of general studies, inasmuch as they are adding to their numbers the most ordinary sorts of specialists.

"Populations that want to be able to subject nature once and for all need only the engineer, who grounds industrial arrangements in new and powerful principles or overcomes difficulties in working out means of communication; this is the man on whom populations confer their trust in their practical struggle with space and time; but they have neither the time nor the desire to listen to the disputes of the philosophers concerning the concepts of time and space, nor to be interested in the skill with which philosophers are able to bring about the transition from idea to nature. —And governments? The standing armies are their schools of philosophers, which in these times have united themselves toward the end of instructing the populations in the only system that is timely, namely that of calm and order. They now tolerate the teachers of the old metaphysics only in the universities, just as one tolerates an old ruin next to a new establishment only as long as pressing need does not demand its demolition."[23] —"And Europe is right. With this it is simply expressing the same thing that the German critique explained and began to carry out ten years earlier. If Europe has permanently turned away from metaphysics, then metaphysics has permanently been destroyed by the critique, and never again will the kind of metaphysical system be established that claims a place in the history of the culture" (49).

Instead, imperialistic dictatorships will become the master of Europe, and these will determine the answer to the question: "Russia or Europe?"

"The illusion of the March Revolution, namely that the time has come when the new fundamental principle of equal rights protects the members of the historical family of nations against earlier influences and protects them in their self-determination, and that these members will constitute themselves independently and will work together peacefully (an illusion which . . . announced itself in the attempts of individual governments, e.g., in the idea of national conferences and in the deliberations of peace conferences)—this illusion is just like all other ones which consider the time following the overthrow of prior limits on personal action to be an era of new freedom, as these are all illusions which are forced to dissolve by the recognition that there exists intense violence.

"All these illusions are like the illusion that sees in individualism, which is the result of the last sixty years of revolution, the solution and the whole, even though it is confronted every day with the fact that individualism is simply provisional and constitutes only *one side*, that it is attached by an iron law to its *opposite*, namely imperialism and dictatorship."

For the destruction of the old confederations and estates deprived the individual of his personal meaning as a member of definite groups and thereby subjected him to a "broadened system of centralization and the omnipotence of the whole." Since 1789 labor has been liberated—but in being unleashed, it is heading toward a more extreme centralization, one which will seize with an iron hand all the individual existences who felt content and protected in their previous captivity [*Abgeschlossenheit*], and which will force those existences either to submit to it or else to perish.

Once again there will come to prevail over human beings a law which—as in the old "military-theological world" of the French Revolution—will exercise discipline over human beings and will determine their feeling, thinking, and willing in accordance with firm measures. But still missing is the "historical science of law," which could lay hold of the emotional world of the masses in a manner similar to the manner in which it once brought about the old moral order. In this domain the eminence of the natural sciences has not yet been matched. Between traditional anarchy and the future form of society and domination, there are currently groundless individuals who anxiously ask "what now?" and who believe that their dissatisfaction, along with the present, contains the power of the future.

In France a decade later, Proudhon described the dissolution of Europe.[r]

"Today civilization is truly in a crisis, one that has but one sole analogy in history, namely the crisis which determined the rise of Christianity. All traditions have been exhausted, all faith worn out; on the other hand, the new program is not yet ready and has not yet penetrated into the consciousness of the masses. This is why there is now coming what I call dissolution. This is the most fruitful moment in the existence of human society. Everything is being brought together so as to make human beings, who want the Good, disconsolate: prostitution of conscience, triumph of mediocrity, confusion of true and false, trafficking in principles, baseness of the emotions, moral indolence, suppression of truth, rewards for lying . . . . I have few illusions and do not expect that already tomorrow, as if by the wave of a magic wand, there will be a rebirth in our land of candor in the expression of opinions, good faith on the part of the newspapers, morality in the government, reason in the citizens, and community spirit among the plebians. No, no; I can see no end to the decadence, and it will be no less in one or two generations, that is our lot . . . . I will see nothing but evil and I will die in complete darkness, in a befouled society marked by the corruption of the past . . . . Carnage will come, and the despondency produced by this blood bath will be fruitful. We will no longer see the works of the new age; we will fight in the night, and we must prepare ourselves to endure this life without too much sorrow while we do our duty. Let us stand by one another, let us call out to one another in the darkness; and as often as there is an opportunity to do so, let us be just."[24]

Another decade later, following the Franco-Prussian War, E. Renan's *La réforme intellectuelle et morale* [*Intellectual and Moral Reform*] appeared while in Germany Nietzsche was writing his *Untimely Meditations*; these are both diagnoses of the time and attempts to avoid the disintegration of things.[s] In the third *Meditation* ("Schopenhauer as Educator," 1874), the situation of Europe is described in a manner quite similar to Burchhardt's.

[r]Translator's note: On Proudhon, see "The Occasional Decisionism of Carl Schmitt," translator's note i.

[s]Translator's note: Ernest Renan (1823–1892) was a French philosopher of religion, Orientalist, and essayist.

Part I   191

"Now how does the philosopher see the culture of our time? Naturally quite differently than those philosophy professors who are satisfied with their state. When he thinks of the universal haste and the increasing speed with which things are falling, of the cessation of all contemplativeness and simplicity, it almost seems to him as if he were seeing the symptoms of a total extermination and uprooting of culture. The waters of religion are ebbing, and they are leaving behind swamps or ponds; the nations are again separating from one another in the most hostile manner, and they are trying to rip each other to shreds. The sciences, without any measure and pursued in the blindest spirit of *laissez faire*, are breaking apart and dissolving everything which is firmly believed; the edified classes and states are being swept along by a money economy which is enormously contemptible. Never was the world more a world, never was it poorer in love and good. The educated classes are no longer lighthouses or sanctuaries in the midst of all this turbulent secularization; they themselves become more turbulent by the day, more thoughtless and loveless. Everything, contemporary art and science included, serves the coming barbarism."[25]

"There are certainly forces there, prodigious forces, but ones which are wild, primordial, and completely merciless. One looks upon them with uneasy expectation, as one might look into the cauldron in a witch's kitchen: at any moment there can be flashes of lightning heralding terrible appearances. For a century we have been prepared for an absolutely fundamental cataclysm; and if there have been recent attempts to oppose this deepest modern tendency, namely the tendency to topple or explode things, with the constitutive power of the so-called nation-state, nonetheless for a long time to come even the nation-state will simply augment the universal insecurity and threatening atmosphere."[26]

"In the Middle Ages the hostile forces were more or less held together by the Church; and they were to some extent assimilated to one another by the strong pressure exerted by the Church. As the bond broke apart and the pressure diminished, each rebelled against the other. The Reformation declared many things to be . . . domains that should not be determined by religious thought; this was the price the Reformation had to pay in order to be able to live. . . . From that point on, the division continued to increase. Today almost everything on earth is determined by the most common and evil forces, by the egoism of acquisitors and military despots. In the hands of the latter, the state attempts, as does the egoism of the acquisitors, to organize everything anew from out of itself and to be the bond and the pressure for all those hostile forces; that is to say, the state wants human beings to idolize it in the same way that they previously idolized the Church. With what success? We have yet to witness this" (1:367f. / 150).

From Proudhon, Renan, and Nietzsche the path leads to Sorel, whose *Réflexions sur la violence* [*Reflections on Violence*] (1907) and *Illusions du progrès* [*Illusions of Progress*] (1908) characterize the spiritual dimension of the fascist movement.† Ever since the middle of the previous century, the construction of the history of Europe has not proceeded according to the schema of *progress*, but instead according to that of *decline*. This change began not at the end of the century but rather at its beginning, with Fichte's lectures *Über die Grundzüge des gegenwärtigen Zeitalters* [*On the Essential Characteristics of the Present Age*] (1804), which he saw as an age of "perfected iniquity." From there, there proceeds through European literature and philosophy an uninterrupted chain of critiques, critiques of contemporary issues as well as self-critiques, which decisively condition not simply the academic but the actual intellectual history between Hegel and Nietzsche. The state of Being in decline along with one's own time is also the ground and soil for Heidegger's "destruction," for his will to dismantle and rebuild, back to the foundations of a tradition which has become untenable.—What the First World War made universally apparent, those *knowledgeable* among the Europeans had seen coming for a century. The fact that such knowledgeable ones are always and everywhere a minority and are hardly known outside their own country, speaks not against them but rather against the vast majority, who are much too busy to know what is ultimately happening.

European Nihilism

In European Literature

In the midst of the frenzied progress in the domination and exploitation of the world by means of modern technology, which was invented in the nineteenth century, there developed among all the more refined minds of Europe both an awareness that their Dasein was aimless and a spiritual pes-

---

† Translator's note: Albert Sorel (1842–1906) was a French historian, professor at the Ecole des Sciences Politiques in Paris, and a member of the Académie Française.

simism; this pessimism seemed first of all to be mere fatigue, until Nietzsche gave nihilism the active label "logic of decadence," under whose sign we still live today. The German "awakening," in connection with which one fancies nihilism to be a thing of the past,[27] is the activated logic of decline and of dissolution, a "revolution of nihilism" as it was called by Rauschning.

Around the middle of the century, nihilism found its most significant expression in Flaubert and Baudelaire. After Flaubert had concluded *The Temptation of the Holy Antonius*, in which this holy one is tested by every article of faith and superstition ever thought of in this world, he proceeded to order and analyze the chaos in scientific education in the nineteenth century. He set about recording a catalog of human stupidity, a catalog that was supposed to be an ironic glorification of everything that counted as truth in the course of the age.

The result of this absurd study was the novel *Bouvard and Péuchet*. Two narrow-minded though good-natured and sensible bourgeois individuals, honestly struggling for higher edification, who had previously been office scribes, spend time on their fortuitously acquired estate wandering through the entire maze of amassed knowledge—from gardening, chemistry, and medicine to history, archaeology, politics, pedagogy, and philosophy—only to return in the end to their writing activity, producing excerpts from the books they had studied in vain. The entire work proceeds in the style of a *haute comédie*, moving through the realm of alienated edification and concluding with the absolute knowledge that our entire process of edification is senseless. In a few lines, doctrines of centuries-old standing are discussed, developed, and dismissed by being contrasted with other doctrines, which themselves are explained and annihilated with equal incisiveness and liveliness. Page by page, line by line, one sort of knowledge appears; at the same time, a different sort asserts itself and overturns the first, though this latter sort itself collapses when countered by the next sort.

In the sketch at the conclusion of this unfinished work, Péuchet offers a dark and Bouvard a rosy picture of the future of European humanity. According to the former, the human race, which has become inferior, is nearing its end, which will be a state of universal degeneracy. There are three possibilities: (1) Radicalism will destroy every connection with the past, the result being an inhuman despotism. (2) If theistic absolutism emerges victorious, then liberalism, which has been the source of humanity's satisfaction ever since the French Revolution, will die out and a cataclysm will ensue. (3) If the spasms that have been evident since 1789 should continue, then we shall be swept away by the power of their shock waves. In such a case there will no longer be ideals or religion or morality. In such a case America will have conquered the world. —In the opinion of the latter, Europe will become renewed by Asia; an unanticipated transportation technology will develop, with submarines and dirigibles, and new sciences will emerge that will enable human beings to put the powers of the universe into the service of civilization and, when the earth is spent, to emigrate to other stars. Together with need, evil will cease to be, and philosophy will become religion.

Dating from the same time as Flaubert's first outline of this novel is Baudeliare's outline of a poem concerning "The End of the World." A few fragments from this poem appeared under the title *Fusées* [*Threads*] three years after the February Revolution of 1848. Like almost all young intellectuals, Baudelaire took part in this uprising against the bourgeois order, caused by a thirst for revenge, a desire for destruction, and literary excitement. Later he objected to this rapture of 1848, though not on reactionary grounds but rather in order to remove himself all the more decisively from the prevailing social order and to place himself in isolation. In doing so, he experienced a kind of pleasurable dread at the prospect of reckoning the distance between himself and his time: "Lost in this ugly world, shoved about by the throng, I am like a tired person whose eyes see only disappointment and bitterness when they look back into the depths of years, and see in the future only a tempest which will bring nothing new, neither knowledge nor pain. If in the evening this person stole a few pleasant hours from fate, forgetting the past as much as possible, in accord with the present, tranquil in regard to the future, drunk with his coldbloodedness and his dandyism, and proud of not being as low as those who rush about, then as his eyes follow the smoke of his cigar he will say: what has it got to do with me, that *these consciences* have wound up where they are!"

What Goethe, with a quietly knowing vision, was able to predict on the basis of what is essential to good health, becomes intensified two centuries after his death into the apocalyptic images of the great tormented souls: of Baudelaire and Kierkegaard, Dostoevsky and Nietzsche. The descent of culture to a level of averageness, as it was foreseen by Goethe, is for Baudelaire a hellish crash into the Nothing from which only "artificial paradises" offer deliverance. "The world is approaching its end. It could continue to exist for only one reason: because it is still there. But how weak is this reason, compared with everything which points toward the opposite, i.e., compared with the question: What has the world got left to do under the heavens? If we assume that the world will continue to exist in a material sense: would this be an existence worthy of the name and of a place in history? I am not saying that the world is falling back into superstition and the quaint disarray of South American republics, nor that we might be returning to the condition of primitive wildness, in which we roam about the overgrown ruins of our civilization, gun in hand, looking for nourishment. No, for such adventure would presuppose a certain vital energy, an echo of primeval times. We will be a new example of the inexorable spiritual and moral laws, as well as their new victim: We will go to ruin at the hands of that which we thought would let us live. Technology will have Americanized us, and progress will impair the spiritual part of us, to such an extent that nothing in the bloodcurdling, wanton, and perverse dreams of the utopian thinkers will be capable of comparison with these positive facts.

"I call upon every thoughtful person to show me what remains of life. Religion—it is useless to speak of it and to search for remains of it; the only scandal in all this is that people go to the trouble to deny God. In principle, private property had already been abolished with the elimination of the right of primogeniture; but the time will come when humanity, like a vindictive cannibal, will snatch the last piece away from those who rightfully thought themselves the heirs of the Revolution. And even this will not be the greatest evil. . . . Universal ruin will not come to light exclusively or particularly through political institutions, universal progress, or whatever it may be called. It will become apparent in the baseness of our hearts. In the face of this do I still have to say that the small bit of politics which remains will offer its pathetic resistance to the all-embracing brutishness, and that those who govern, in order to maintain their position and to create a semblance of order, will of necessity have to invoke means which would cause our contemporary, embittered humanity to shudder?"

The image of the future of Europe that Flaubert and Baudelaire project is also advanced in the Russians' critique of Europe. In 1880 Dostoevsky wrote in his *Diary of a Writer*, as part of a polemic against Russian Occidentalists, that it is laughable to demand of the Russians that they transplant European institutions into Russia and catch up with the progress of the West, given that Europe has not yet dealt with any of its own problems and stands immediately before a horrible collapse. "The ant hill built long ago in Europe without a Church and Christianity (for the ideal of the Church has everywhere been lost there, the Church having been transformed into a state)—this ant hill has been overturned in that its foundation has been destroyed by the loss of everything universal and absolute."[28] What is supposed to be the sense of taking over from Europe institutions which are about to collapse there, institutions in which, even in Europe, the more intelligent individuals no longer have faith, while at the same time these institutions are being unthinkingly imitated by those Russians who are enthusiastic about Europe, as if what is comic in the order of civil society were the normal form of human unity.

In 1910, in the last year of his life, Tolstoy wrote the following radical critique of European civilization, which according to him is now corrupting not only Europe but also the Africans, the Indians, the Chinese, and the Japanese.

"Medieval theology and the moral corruption of Rome poisoned only their own respective people, and hence only a small portion of humanity; today electricity, railroads, and telegraphs are corrupting the whole world. Everyone appropriates these things; they cannot avoid appropriating them, and everyone is suffering in the same manner, forced in the same degree to change their way of life. Everyone is being put in a situation in which it is necessary to betray what is most important in their lives, to betray an understanding of life itself, to betray religion.

"What are machines supposed to manufacture? What are telegraphs supposed to transmit? What are schools, universities, and academies supposed to teach? What are assemblies supposed to discuss? What kind of news is supposed to be conveyed by books and newspapers? To whom and to what destinations are trains supposed to travel? What is supposed to be accomplished by millions of human beings who are drawn together and subjected to a highest power? For what purpose are hospitals, doctors, and pharmacists supposed to prolong life? . . .

"How easily do individuals, as well as whole nations, appropriate that which goes by the name civilization, genuine civilization! Graduate from the university, keep one's fingernails clean, use the services of a tailor and a hairdresser, travel abroad, and the most civilized kind of person has been realized. And with regard to nations: as many railroads, academies, factories, battleships, fortresses, newspapers, books, [political] parties, and parliaments as possible—and the most civilized kind of nation has been realized. This is why there are individuals and nations enough to attain civilization, but not enough to attain true enlightenment. The former is easy and is greeted with applause; the latter demands the exertion of our powers, and hence among the great majority it is always greeted with nothing but contempt and hatred, since it exposes the lie of civilization."

More and more documents of this kind could be found, leading up to the present. As the negation of existing civilization, nihilism was, even in the less apparent form of artistic analysis, skepticism, and irony, the only real belief among truly cultured individuals at the beginning of the twentieth century. It is not simply a result of the war, but on the contrary its presupposition. Most clearly conscious of this were those in the literary circle surrounding George.[u] The introduction to volume 3 (1912) of the *Jahrbuch für die geistige Bewegung* [*Yearbook for the Spiritual Movement*] edited by Gundolf and Wolters includes the following:

"Even clouded vision does not fail to see the universal bleakness which is spreading in spite of all the outward improvements, simplifications, and forms of entertainment, a bleakness which demands a comparison with the late Roman Empire. From the Kaiser to the lowliest worker, everyone senses that things cannot continue this way; and everyone admits this, at least with regard to those domains which do not touch them immediately. The sublime at this point is nothing more than the individual's concern for his station and his worldly possessions. No one still truly believes in the foundations of the current world situation. These alarmist hunches and suspicions are the most genuine feeling of the time; in contrast with this feeling, every hope which seeks to build a Something upon the Nothing appears desperate."[29]

To envision the Nothing of modern humanity by employing all the means of art and of spirit, had also been the task of the writer, in whose works the possibilities of the novel are exhausted. None of them give shape any more to an authentically human world; they simply analyze intellectual developments, mental reactions, and social relationships. Marcel Proust and André Gide, Thomas Mann and Aldous Huxley, André Malraux and D. H. Lawrence, Joyce and Céline—none of them give shape any more, as do the great novels from Cervantes to Dickens and from Balzac to Tolstoy, to a human cosmos; they simply convey a disheartening truth about human beings, in connection with which the human being as such disappears. "The modern psychological novel, fine and cultivated, concerns itself with the analysis of the unconscious, immerses itself in the flowing world of sensations and instincts, and at the same time becomes entangled to the extreme by a highly developed intellectuality. In this kind of novel, human beings are split up and torn apart by the power of the unconscious and the influence of the rational. Even the most talented

---

[u] Translator's note: On Stefan George, see translator's note p. 35.

modern novelists display a pronounced lack of creative fantasy; they either immerse themselves in themselves alone, or they dedicate themselves to the depiction of the evil reality which oppresses them."[30]

Similarly, modern natural science, and the technology for which it serves as the foundation, are taking human beings further and further away from the scope of their natural environment. And even modern philosophy and theology are dehumanizing human beings as such. Heidegger's concepts of Dasein allow human beings to disappear behind care, anxiety, and death, and all beings are simply a Being upon the ground of the Nothing. Barth's dialectical theology sees only powerlessness and sin in the creatural world; the human being is no longer a likeness of God, but instead his whole relationship to God becomes reduced to the abstract hearing of the Word, which is to be obeyed.

In German Philosophy

Hegel: Hegel concludes the history of spirit in old Europe.[31] To the extent that spirit, along the historical path of its "progress in the consciousness of freedom," finally achieves its full Being and knowing in Hegel, the history of spirit is completed in a dual sense. Hegel completes the history of spirit in the sense of the *greatest fullness*, in which everything that has happened or has been thought up to now gets combined into unity; but he also completes this history in the sense of an *eschatological end* [*endgeschichtlichen Endes*], in which the history of spirit finally grasps itself. "*Tantae molis erat se ipsam cognoscere mentem*" ["What a great endeavor it was for the mind to know itself"], the endeavor being 2,500 years of work on the part of spirit.[32] In this assertion from the conclusion to the *Lectures on the History of Philosophy*, it becomes apparent that Hegel's completion becomes ambiguous when he changes Virgil's "*romanam condere gentem*" ["to found the Roman nation"] into a "*se ipsam cognoscere mentem*" ["for the mind to know itself"].[v] This change means: The original founding of the Roman world-empire, this basis of Europe, required the same effort as was ultimately necessary for a final self-exploration in the empire of spirit. To the extent that, with knowing and willing, Hegel ended an epoch which had lasted two and a half millennia and precisely thereby opened up a new epoch, he in fact brought to an end the history of the Christian *logos*. A whole world of concepts, of language and edification, came to an end with Hegel's history of European spirit.

[v]Translator's note: The passage being discussed comes from Virgil's *Aeneid*, Book I, line 33.

Part I   199

The principle of eschatological construction grounds the progression [*Abschluß*] not only of phenomenology, the system of the *Encyclopedia*, and the "conclusion" or "end" [*Schluß*] of logic, but that of all particular modes of knowing as well. Both the history of the world, in the philosophy of history, and the history of philosophy and especially the history of art end with a completion [or fruition].[33] According to Hegel's periodization of the history of philosophy, his own system stands at the end of the third epoch. The first extends from Thales to Proclus, and encompasses the beginning and the decline of the ancient world.[w] At its complete highpoint in Proclus, the ancient reconciliation between the earthly and the divine worlds takes place.

The second epoch extends from the beginning of the Christian reckoning of time up to the Reformation. In the Reformation, the same reconciliation between the finite and the infinite takes place on a higher level; and in the third epoch, in philosophy from Descartes to Hegel, this reconciliation finally gets completed by the latter. In the same way as Proclus, Hegel now amalgamated the world of the *Christian logos* into the absolute totality of the concretely organized Idea, thereby concluding the whole of the three epochs. With reference to Proclus he remarks that such a unification of all systems into one all-encompassing, total system is no mere eclecticism, but rather is a deeper knowledge of the Idea as it must present itself "from time to time," i.e., at intervals of epochs. [Hegel says that] in Proclus, world-spirit stands on the verge of a great "change" before the absolute "break" [*Bruch*], i.e., before Christianity's encroachment [*Einbruch*] into the pagan world. Similarly, in a letter to Creuzer,[x] Hegel writes of the "enormous step" which is due especially to Proclus and which is the true turning point in ancient philosophy's transition to Christianity. [For Hegel] it is just such a step which must "now once again" be made, and for this reason nothing seems so timely to him as Creuzer's new edition of Proclus.

But what does this yield for Hegel's completion of philosophy? Indeed, it would seem to suggest that this completion must be a final step before a great change and a break with Christianity.[34] But then Hegel's completion of Christian philosophy is the same as it was in Proclus: a "coming to

---

[w] Translator's note: Proclus (410–485) was a Neoplatonist who followed Syrianus as the head of the School of Athens. Hegel discusses Proclus in his *Vorlesungen über die Geschichte der Philosophie* II, vol. 19, pp. 466ff.

[x] Translator's note: Georg Friedrich Creuzer (1771–1858) was a classical philologist and professor in Marburg, Leiden, and Heidelberg; he edited an edition of the works of Plotinus (Oxford, 1835).

terms with corruption." Its highest manifestation is simultaneous with the beginning of a decline, at a time when "everything is understood to be in a state of dissolution and of striving for something new."

Hegel gave no direct expression to this something new, which comes after the end of what is old, though he did give indirect expression to it. He thinks within a recollection of what has been, within the "old age of spirit," and at the same time within a questioning view forward to the possibility of a new land of spirit, though he explicitly leaves aside [any specification of] knowledge here.

Scant references to America, which since the beginning of the century was considered the land of the future, catch sight of the possibility that world-spirit could leave Europe. "America is thus the land of the future, in which, during the time which lies before us, . . . world-historical importance is supposed to manifest itself; for everyone bored by the historical arsenal of old Europe, it is a land of yearning. Napoleon is supposed to have said: *cette vieille Europe m'ennuie* [this old Europe bores me]. But what has happened there up to now is simply the reverberation of the old world and the expression of a foreign liveliness, and as a land of the future it is of absolutely no concern to us."[35] Similarly, Hegel concludes a remark about the coming significance of the Slavic world, which he understood as a "point of mediation" [*Mittelwesen*] in Christian Europe's struggle with Asia, with the statement that he is leaving this whole group out of consideration because up to now it has not presented itself as an independent moment in the sequence of reason's manifestations. "Whether this will occur in the future, is of no concern to us here."[36]

Hegel expresses himself in a less hesitant manner in a letter to a Russian student, the content of which has been passed along by Rosenkranz.[37] Europe, it is said there, has already become a sort of cage in which only two sorts of human being still seem to move freely: those who obstruct passage, and those who have sought out a place inside this cage where they need not take a stand either for or against the bars. But if things are such that one cannot truly unite oneself with the situation, then [for Hegel] it is more advantageous to live for oneself in good Epicurean manner and to remain a private person for oneself—an attitude which [on Hegel's view] is naturally that of a spectator but which nonetheless is also highly influential. To this European cage, Hegel opposes Russia's future. The other modern states seem already to have reached the aim of their development, and they may already have overshot their point of culmination, whereas Russia bears within itself "an enormous potential for the development of its intensive nature." —It is extremely hard to believe that Hegel, as Rosenkranz would have it, was simply making a joke here so as to cheer up his friend. On the contrary, it is precisely in this letter that he anticipated the mood of the coming time, after he himself had painted "grey upon grey" in *The Philosophy of Right*.

Marx and Kierkegaard: Of all Hegel's pupils, Marx and Kierkegaard comprehended in the most radical manner the end that was concluded in Hegel. Hence both confronted the question how one can proceed beyond that end. Their answer was: Not by means of a continuation of the path which Hegel pursued to its end; on the contrary, only by means of a decisive break with it can a new beginning be achieved. Marx carried out this break with the pure thinking of speculation in the name of social "praxis," and Kierkegaard did so in the name of ethical "conduct." Subsequent to this decisive turning point, German philosophy has lost the kind of good conscience that is oriented on the desire *to know*. Inasmuch as both recognized that Hegel's mediation of reason with reality lacked reality, they opposed to his *mediation* a *decision*: Marx for a new earthly world and Kierkegaard for the old Christian God; here they both, though each in a different direction, dissolve what exists and fight against their century. Kierkegaard's critique of the age (1846)[38] corresponds so precisely to the *Communist Manifesto* (1847)[39] that Marx's critique of the bourgeois-capitalist world and Kierkegaard's critique of the bourgeois-Christian world complement one another like the front and back sides of the same thing.

In his historical study of Louis Bonaparte, Marx characterized the epoch of the bourgeois revolution as one whose passions lacked truth and whose truths lacked passion. [For Marx] that epoch's world, which has become completely empty, persists solely through borrowing; its development is a constant repetition of the same tensing and relaxing; its oppositions are such that they sharpen themselves only to dull themselves; its history is without events, and its heroes are without heroic deeds. Its "highest law" [according to Hegel] is "indecisiveness."

With almost the same words, Kierkegaard comprehended this world within his critique of the present age, by using the term "leveling"; and he placed stress on the foundational distinctions themselves rather than on the razing of those distinctions. As concrete kinds of leveling, he analyzes the razing of the passionate disjunction between speaking and remaining silent down to irresponsible chatter; the razing of that between form and content down to a contentless lack of form; of that between Being-closed-off and Being-apparent down to representing; of that between love and dissoluteness down to passionless flirtation; of that between objective knowing and subjective conviction down to a nonbinding reasoning. To the bankruptcy of this antiquated world Marx opposed the mass of the proletariat, while Kierkegaard opposed to it one's individuated existence. Economic troubles seemed to him to have merely symptomatic significance: "they indicate that the European constitution has totally changed. In the future we will experience inner troubles—*secessio in montem sacrum* [withdrawl into the sacred mountain]."

More decisive than the economic, social, and political bankruptcy which is approaching Europe is [on Kierkegaard's view] its spiritual decline, the Babel caused by the high-speed output of the press. It would be best to let the noise of the age subside for an hour; but because this presumably will not come to pass, Europe [according to Kierkegaard] seeks to appeal to its "customers" [*Zeitgenossen*] in the language of finance: "saving, energetic and extensive saving!," i.e. a reduction to the elementary questions of human existence, to the naked question of existence as such, which for Kierkegaard was intrinsically the obverse of what Marx called the "life-size earthly question."

And in this way, on the basis of the same split with what exists, Marx's worldly critique of the bourgeois-capitalist world corresponds to Kierkegaard's equally radical critique of the bourgeois-Christian world, which is as foreign to Christianity in its origins as the bourgeois or civil state is to a *polis*. That Marx places the *outward* existential relations of the *masses* before a decision and Kierkegaard the *inward* existential relation of the *individual* to himself, that Marx philosophizes *without* God and Kierkegaard *before* God—these apparent oppositions have as a common presupposition the decay of existence along with God and the world. For both, so-called existence is no longer what it was for Hegel: plain "*existere*," as the emergence and advance of the inner essence into that existence which is appropriate to it; for Kierkegaard it is a retreat to a decision on the part of individual conscience, and for Marx it is a removal to a political decision concerning mass relations. On the basis of the same split with Hegel's rational world, they again divide what Hegel united. Marx decides on a humanitarian, "human" world, and Kierkegaard decides on a worldless Christianity which, "considered from the human standpoint, is inhuman," as he himself confessed.

If one considers the systematic and historical outcome of the spiritual events which follow Hegel, it becomes evident that Marx's economic analysis and Kierkegaard's experimental psychology belong together both conceptually and historically, and that they are an antithesis to Hegel. They conceived "what is" as a world determined by commodities and money, and as an existence defined throughout by irony and boredom. The "empire of spirits" in Hegel's philosophy becomes a ghost in a world of *labor* and desperation. Hegel's "Idea," extant in and for itself, becomes transformed [*verkehrt*] in Marx by a "German ideology," and in

Kierkegaard the "self-satisfaction" of absolute Spirit becomes transformed [*verkehrt*] by a "sickness unto death."^y For both, Hegel's completion of history becomes the end of the prehistory preceding an extensive revolution and a intensive reformation. His concrete mediations become transformed into abstract decisions, in favor of the old Christian God and a new earthly world. Hegel's active spirit gets replaced in Marx by a *theory* of social *praxis* and in Kierkegaard by a *reflection* on the part of inner *conduct*, and here both withdraw from theory as the highest human activity in relation to knowing and willing. As far as they remain from one another, they are closely related to one another in their common attack on what exists and in their departure from Hegel.

At the same time as Marx and Kierkegaard, all the other radical followers of Hegel made the negation of what exists into the principle of their thinking. Marx destroys the capitalist world; Kierkegaard intensifies the "absolute negativity" of romantic irony up to the point of leaping into faith; Stirner placed himself upon "Nothing"; Feuerbach says that we must be "absolutely negative" in order to create something new; and Bauer demands "heroic deeds from out of Nothing" as the presupposition of new worlds. "If the three greatest turning points in history were when Socrates, in opposition to theocracy, boasted about his *not*-knowing; when Christianity, opposing the empire, posited one's own soul above everything; and when Descartes commanded everyone to doubt—if these heroic deeds from out of Nothing created new worlds, then the final and most difficult intention which remains, namely the intention to will *nothing* or to will nothing of the old, will first grant to human beings complete dominance and mastery over the world."[40]

This philosophical negation also gave rise to a type of nihilist in literature, as is particularly well known from Turgenev and Gutzkov (*Die Nihilisten* [*The Nihilists*], 1853).[41] Of course, this nihilism does not yet possess the acuteness which Nietzsche gave to it by turning the "Romantic" nihilism of "weakness" into a nihilism of strength, and by drawing out of the experience of the last century those most extreme consequences which only today are proving themselves to be truly epoch-making. He judged the pessimism of the *fin de siècle* to be a mere "preliminary form of nihilism"; and the task which he set before himself was to take the feeling that our Dasein is without sense or value, and drive it to the point where it would change into the will to new values. But then nihilism is no longer a sign of decline and fatigue, but instead is an "active" nihilism of "strength" and of the increased power of spirit.[42]

^y Translator's note: *Verkehren* can also mean to pervert or to invert; Hegel's famous statement that philosophy is an "inverted world" is a translation of *verkehrte Welt*.

Nietzsche: In the first chapter of his last book, *Ecce Homo*, Nietzsche explains to the world the sense in which he is "something decisive and fateful" between two millennia, by appealing to his "dual heritage," i.e. [that he is descended from] "the highest and lowest rungs on the ladder of life."[43] He saw himself as decline and ascent, as end and beginning at the same time. This same double meaning, which characterizes his existence, also determines his concept of Europe: Europe is a world which at the same time is in decline and is first becoming; between these, though, there is no continuous transition but instead a fateful decision. Placed in tension within the contradiction between what is dying out and what is coming, Nietzsche had to be self-consciousness, a "decadent" with regard to what is dying out and a "premature birth" with regard to the coming century, i.e., a human being at the limit. As a consequence, in his time he was homeless in a distinctive sense. "Among the Europeans of today there is no lack of those who have the right to . . . call themselves homeless in a distinctive sense; it is precisely these that my 'gay science' takes to heart. For their lot is hard, their hope uncertain; it is a feat to devise consolation for them—but what does it help! We children of the future, how can we be at home in this present?"[44]

Such Europeans believe neither in the "ideals" nor in the "realities" of their decaying time, since they know that neither can have any substance. They want neither to conserve what has been and thereby be conservative, nor to work liberally for progress. On the contrary, they love danger and adventure. They contemplate new kinds of order, in which there is a new form of domination and slavery. "With all this, we must find ourselves ill at ease in an age which loves to busy itself with honor and consider itself to be the most human, mild, and righteous age that the sun has ever seen. It is bad enough that just these beautiful words inspire us with the ugliest thoughts, that in them we see only the expression of deep enfeeblement, of fatigue, of age, of decreasing energy" (section 377). The "good Europeans" live not in their own time but rather in past and coming centuries, removed from the present or untimely, as "the heirs of Europe, the rich but also excessively obligated heirs of millennia of European spirit; as such, they have also outgrown Christianity and are ill-disposed toward it" (section 377). They are sick of their time; and yet their concealed "yes," their will to a new faith, is stronger than their every "no." For they still possess the entire need and tension of spirit, which demands a new task and a goal.[45] But as long as this goal remains unclear, they would rather will the *Nothing* than not *will* at all.

For Nietzsche, the great goal is the Europeans' spiritual and political domination of the earth. In order for Europe be forced to this "great politics," which is at the same time a "war of spirits,"[46] it must be placed before the question "whether its will to decline 'wills,'" i.e., it is a matter of Europe itself overcoming its nihilism by willing itself once again as a whole and as something decisive.[47] This activated and "ecstatic" nihilism is a powerful force and hammer which compels degenerate nations and Russians to abdicate, and which gives rise to a new order of life. Nietzsche considered his doctrine of the eternal recurrence to be such a hammer and touchstone of the will to power and the will to life, a doctrine which demands of human beings that they affirm their Dasein at every instant, as if it were to recur eternally.[48]

This doctrine is a counterpoise against the experience of meaninglessness and aimlessness, which for its own part proceeds from a sickness suffered by the will which posits aims. Weakness of the will is greatest where a high culture has been established for a long time, as in France; and it is all the less where a culture lags behind and the barbarian still, or once again, lives under the mantel of edification, as in Russia, which is touched by European civilization in only a superficial way.[49]

But the more threatening Russia becomes, the more Europe will have to resolve upon becoming equally threatening and upon obtaining *one* will, by turning to a ruling class which, taking the long view, sets great goals for itself and trains the democratic masses to accept this aim. The time of petty national politics is past; Nietzsche prophesies that already the twentieth century, with the struggle for dominion over the earth, will force us to great, imperialistic national politics, and that in this connection Germany will have to "come to terms" quite seriously with England. "In other words, nobody believes any more that England is strong enough to carry on its old role for even fifty more years; the impossibility of getting rid of the government's *homines novi* [new infantry] is making it perish, and no such change of party can prepare the way for such protracted things: today one must first of all be a soldier in order that he not lose his credit when he is a salesman. Enough: in this as in other things, the next century will be found to follow in Napoleon's footsteps, in the footsteps of the first and most visionary human being of recent times."[50]

Standing armies, which became an enduring institution after the Napoleonic Wars, are merely a first sign of the military development of Europe. "Personal *manly* ability, the ability to love, is once again obtaining value; evaluations are becoming more physical, nourishment more carnal. Lovely men are again becoming possible. Pallid servility is past. The barbarian is *affirmed* in all of us, as is the wild animal. Precisely for this reason, there will be more to come from the philosophers."[51] In order to be able to struggle up to a new form, the European chaos stands in need of compulsion: one must have the choice between perishing and surviving. "A lordly race can grow upward only on the basis of terrible and violent beginnings. Problem: where are the *barbarians* of the twentieth century? Apparently they will become visible and will consolidate themselves only after enormous social crises—they will be the elements which are capable of the *greatest harshness against themselves* and which can guarantee the *longest willing*" (section 868). Nietzsche's faith in the future of Europe is based on its "masculinization"; and for him, Napoleon's St. Helena memoir was one of the most significant European documents,^z because the future would progress along those paths which Napoleon was the first to traverse when he attempted to unify Europe and thereby make it lord over the earth.

This political perspective stands not at the margins of Nietzsche's philosophy but rather at its middle. It is a consequence of his analysis of European nihilism and his counter-concept of the will, which replaces the "Thou Shalt" of Christian faith. In Nietzsche's perception and thought, the fate of Europe is one with himself, and the first section of the last chapter of *Ecce Homo* ("Why I am a destiny") ends with the statement: "Only beginning with me is there great politics on earth" and also that "war of spirits" which presupposes that one has recognized the origin and the consequences of the crisis of European humanity and Christian tradition. The letters from the time of his insanity are a reverberation and outburst of this will to define anew the fate of Europe; in them, Nietzsche invited the princes of Europe (n.b., excluding the House of Hohenzollern) and the Pope to a conference which was to take place in Rome. But even everything he produced when he was healthy is a constant war, from the *Untimely Meditations* to *The Antichrist*, opposed to everything that had previously been believed, demanded, and held sacred in Europe.

As an immoralist and "annihilator *par excellence*," he believed that he could create only by destroying,[52] true to the characteristics which Stirner attributes to the Germans generally in his critique of Bauer's *Trumpet*:[53]

"It is first of all and exclusively the German who reveals the world-historical calling of *radicalism*; now he alone is radical, and he alone is without wrong. None is as relentless and inconsiderate as he; for he does not just overthrow the existing world so that he himself can remain standing;

---

^zTranslator's note: After his defeat by Wellington at Waterloo, Napoleon was exiled to the island of St. Helena in the South Atlantic, where he wrote a memoir of his life in which he distorted the facts so as to idealize and bring a sense of coherence and unity to his actions.

he overthrows—himself. Where the German tears things apart, a God must fall and a world must perish. For the German, annihilating—creating and crushing the temporal—is his eternity." It is the decline of Christianity and its morality that Nietzsche wants to promote, since "one should also dethrone that which is falling."[54]

The positive side of this will to the decline of everything that exists is *The Will to Power* as a *Revaluation of All Values*, the first part of which (according to a final plan from the autumn of 1888) is *The Antichrist*. Zarathustra is the "conqueror of God and the Nothing," i.e., of the Nothing which has arisen out of the death of the Christian God, out of European nihilism. The will to power is a counter-will opposed to the sickness of willing which has been made sick by the fact that no God tells it any longer what it is supposed to do. This human will which has become godless must now be able to command itself, and for this it needs the greatest strength of a will which has been consigned to itself. Hence European nihilism, as Nietzsche understood it, is first of all a crisis of Christianity and ultimately a critical decision to will.

What Nietzsche describes in the preface to *The Will to Power* as the "first consummate nihilist of Europe" was in fact, as he maintained, the story of the future which is now our present. "I describe what is coming and what can no longer come differently: the emergence of nihilism. Already now this story can be told, for its very necessity is at work here. This history speaks in a hundred signs, this fate announces itself everywhere . . . . Our entire European culture has for a long time been moving with a tortured tension which grows from decade to decade, as if headed toward a catastrophe: restlessly, violently, precipitously, like a stream that wants *to reach its end*, that no longer reflects, that is afraid to reflect."[55]

In contrast, Nietzsche's reflection, by means of which he lived nihilism to the end and thought it to its end, sought with *The Will to Power* to give expression to a counter-movement which ought to dissolve this consummated nihilism, but which logically and substantively presupposes it. For him, nihilism is the logic of our former Christian-moral values thought to its end; it is a reaction to "God is the truth," and a love of "everything is false" and merciless. Together with the faith of the Christian religion, morality also perishes, as does the European humanity which is determined by both and which now no longer has any sanction.[56] But also nihilistic are the unavoidable consequences of modern science ("Since Copernicus, human beings have been rolling from the center toward X"),[57] the modern political-economic way of thinking, the historical sciences, and modern art—in short, everything points toward the devaluation of our highest values and toward the need for new ones.

Inasmuch as this radically conceived nihilism is the end of faith in God and morality, there follows as what is provisionally the only truth, the idea that "*nothing is true any more, but instead everything is permitted.*"[58] The freedom for everything and nothing resolved upon here is "the advantage of the time" in which we live. Morality is annihilated and "what remains is that I will," i.e., the power to will and to annihilate everything which can no longer will in this way and which no longer wills itself. Morality becomes replaced by the will to an end and hence by the will to the means toward that end.[59]

Nietzsche's ideas spiritually opened up the path for the Third Reich, though pathfinders always opened paths *for others* that *they themselves* did not traverse. Like no other philosopher of the last century, Nietzsche defines Germany's manner of political thought; and whoever has something to say in Germany today, is fundamentally under his spell. This dominant influence seems to be contradicted by the fact that Nietzsche was an opponent of the German Reich and said that *The Will to Power* was not written to favor Germany's imperial aspirations, but rather was exclusively a book for thinking; but [for him] the Germans of today are no longer thinkers, since today it is something else which impresses and entertains them.[60] And yet this personal rejection of an unwelcome endorsement changes nothing in the historical fact that Nietzsche, precisely as an opponent of everything that "Reich" meant, was situated within the scope of Bismarck's and Wagner's will to power, and that, as an untimely one, he was also timely and remained so.

With reference to Bismarck and Napoleon, he anticipated that the democratic leveling of Europe will one day extend to the point of dictatorial leadership. For "precisely those new conditions under which, on the average, . . . the human being will be rendered mediocre, a useful, industrious, . . . and handy herd animal—are apt in the highest degree to provide the origin of exceptional human beings of the most dangerous and attractive quality. . . . The democratization of Europe is at the same time an involuntary setup for the cultivation of *tyrants*—taking the word in every sense, including the spiritual."[61] Of course, for the emancipated masses it could be a kind of redemption and justification if someone were to come along and use them as the means to his ends. "The same conditions that drive the development of the herd animal forward, also drive the development of the leader-animal."[62]

Part II

Classical German Philosophy and the German Revolution

Whoever compares Nietzsche's attempt to philosophize "with a hammer" and hence to penetrate into the events of the time, with the speculation of German idealism, will see nothing but distance and contrast. And yet this contrast is not as radical as it first appears to be. In the end the distinction consists simply in the fact that Nietzsche deliberately anticipates the historical movement of Europe, whereas Kant, Fichte, Schelling, and Hegel developed ideas whose influence on German reality was only subsequent and indirect, if one leaves aside Fichte's *Addresses to the German Nation* (1808) and Hegel's revolutionary circle of pupils.

It is within this historico-political horizon that Heinrich Heine, in his *History of Religion and Philosophy in Germany* (1834), conceived the *political* consequences of the *spiritual* revolution that extends from Luther to Kant and beyond him to Hegel.[1] For "theoretical labors, I convince myself more every day, accomplish more in the world than do practical ones; if the realm of representation is revolutionized, then political reality will not endure."[2] In this sense Heine attempted, at the conclusion of his history of German philosophy (*Zur Geschichte der Religion und Philosophie in Deutschland*, 1834), to open the eyes of the French to the real revolution that could emerge from the Reformation and German philosophy:

"It seems to me that a methodical people like us had to begin with the Reformation, was able thereafter to become involved with philosophy, and was able only after the completion of philosophy to make the transition to political revolution. I find this order to be entirely rational. The heads that philosophy used for reflection can subsequently be decapitated to whatever ends the revolution chooses. But philosophy would never again have been able to make use of these heads if they had been decapitated by the revolution.

"But do not let yourselves be afraid, you German Republicans; the German revolution will not turn out milder and gentler for being preceded by Kantian critique, Fichtian transcendental idealism, or even natural philosophy. By means of these doctrines, revolutionary powers have developed which are simply waiting for the day when they can surge forth and fill the world with terror and admiration. Kantians will appear who have no use for piety, even in the world of appearances, and who, with sword and axe, will mercilessly uproot the ground of our European life in order to extirpate even the last roots of the past. Armed Fichtians will come on the scene who, in their fanaticism of the will, cannot be tamed through fear nor through self-interest . . . , indeed, such transcendental idealists would be even more inflexible in social upheavels than the first Christians were, since the latter endured earthly martyrdom in order thereby to achieve heavenly beatitude, whereas the transcendental idealist considers martyrdom itself to be empty semblance and is untouchable within the fortification of his own thought.

"But most terrible of all would be natural philosophers, who would be actively involved in a German revolution and would identify themselves with the very work of destruction. If the hand of the Kantian strikes its blows in a strong and sure manner because his heart is not moved by any traditional kind of reverence; if the Fichtian courageously defies every danger because for him it does not exist at all in reality; then the natural philosopher will be terrible in virtue of his alliance with the violent forces of nature, his ability to invoke the daemonic powers of old Teutonic pantheism, and the resulting awakening in him of a bellicosity like that found in the Germans of old, one which fights not in order to annihilate or to win but rather simply in order to fight. Christianity—and this is its greatest merit—placated that brutal Teutonic bellicosity to some extent, though it could not destroy it; and if one day that talisman which tames, namely the cross, should break apart, then that . . . insane, berserk rage will once again rattle forth about which the Nordic poets sing and say so much. That talisman is becoming brittle, and the day will come when it lamentably crumbles. . . . I advise you, you French, to conduct yourselves very peacefully when that happens, and by Jesus!

take care not to applaud. We could easily misunderstand all this and, in our impolite way, somewhat brusquely admonish you to be silent. . . .

"I mean well by you, and this is why I am telling you the bitter truth. You have more to fear from a liberated Germany than from the entire Holy Alliance together with all its Croatians and Cossacks . . . . I have never been able to comprehend what is really being alleged against you. Once, in a beer hall in Göttingen, a young German of old remarked that revenge must be taken on the French for Konradin von Stauffen, whom they beheaded in Naples. Surely you have long since forgotten this. But we forget Nothing. You see, if one day it should give us pleasure to pick a fight with you, we will not lack sound reasons. In any event, for this reason I advise you to be on your guard. Come what may in Germany, be it the rise to power of the Crown Prince of Prussia or of Doctor Wirth,[a] see that you always remain armed . . . . I mean well by you, and I was utterly alarmed when I recently heard of the intention of your ministers to disarm France."[3]

The Political Horizon of Heidegger's Existential Ontology

In Hegel's pupils, the revolutionary impulse of radical critique and speculation in German philosophy became immediately political. Feuerbach, Marx, Ruge, Bauer, Stirner, and Kierkegaard made actual use of Hegelian philosophy. The political and ecclesiastical reaction to the movement of the 1840s brought an end to that movement's radicalism, though it did not produce a spiritual movement which could have competed with that radicalism. The return to Kant, which began in the 1860s, was merely a way of avoiding confusion; here the problems posed by Hegel's pupils were shoved aside rather than solved. Only Nietzsche once again posited an influential beginning, in comparison with which the progress of academic philosophy remained meaningless until it received a new impulse from Heidegger, who led it out of its narrow-mindedness. From Heidegger's articulation of historicism, there resulted the thesis that human Dasein does not simply have a history but rather essentially is history, that in principle human Dasein is there as something finite or temporal.

On the basis of this orientation of Being on time and of Dasein on historicality, an explanation can also be found for Heidegger's partisanship for what factically occurred in Germany, for the events of the time. Of course, the political horizon of Heidegger's existential ontology does not touch on the entire substance of his doctrine of Being; at the same time,

[a]Translator's note: Johann Georg August Wirth (1798–1848) was a German revolutionary and editor of the *Deutsche Tribüne*, a liberal journal.

it is not simply a supplement which could be left aside. On the contrary, the political events of the time, precisely in virtue of their accidental character, are as much a part of the essence of "existence" as existence itself, as historical, stands upon the ground of "facticity." And if in the following I make only a few references to Heidegger's works, citing above all his addresses and letters, then this may be justified by the fact that the essential character of a philosophy of "historiological facticity" often manifests itself more in occasional and fortuitous remarks than in the convoluted form of a conceptually formalized system.

In order to understand the contemporary historical background of Heidegger's philosophy, it is useful to consider it in connection with a remark from Rilke and one from van Gogh.

A few statements from Rilke's letters[4] could without further ado be a motto for the understanding of Heidegger's work: the civil-bourgeois world has forgotten not only faith in progress and humanity, but also the "ultimate courts of appeal" in human life, namely that humanity "was outstripped both in advance and once and for all by death and by God." In Heidegger's *Being and Time* as well, the exclusive meaning of death is as an "unsurpassable court of appeal" for our Being and our capability. Naturally there is no longer any talk of God in Heidegger—he had been too much of a theologian to be able to tell "stories about loving God," as Rilke did. For him death is the Nothing in the face of which the finitude of our temporal existence becomes revealed or, as it was put in the first Freiburg lectures:[b] "historiological facticity."

The painter who, after the war, revealed to us most deeply the problem of our Being and of time, was van Gogh. "For semesters," Heidegger wrote to me in a letter in 1923, "a remark of van Gogh's has been accompanying me: 'I feel with all my strength that the history of human beings is precisely as it is in the case of wheat: if one is not put on earth in order to blossom, then one ends up getting milled in order to make bread.' Woe to the one who does not get ground up!" Instead of giving oneself over to the universal enterprise of education, as if one had been given the mission of "saving the culture," [according to Heidegger] one must, in a "radical dismantling and rebuilding" or a "destruction," acquire for oneself a firm conviction regarding "the one thing which is needful,"[5] without concerning oneself with the idle talk and the bustle of those sensible and enterprising people who reckon time with clocks.

In this search for the one thing which is needful and hence necessary, Heidegger oriented himself above all on Kierkegaard; nonetheless, he did

[b]Translator's note: See *Gesamtausgabe*, vols. 56–62 (1919–1923).

not want to be confused with Kierkegaard, because the motive and goal of his existential ontology was not "to draw attention to what is Christian" but rather to give a "formal indication" of worldly existence. "At the least I *want* something different—but nothing much: viz., what I actively perceive to be 'necessary' in the current factical state of revolutionary change [*Umsturzsituation*], without any peripheral consideration of whether from out of this there will result a 'culture' or an acceleration of decline."[6] For him, every philosophy of "culture" was an abomination, philosophical conferences no less so; the profusion of journals which appeared after the war excited his pathetic wrath, and even Werner Jaeger's *Antike* [*Antiquity*] seemed to him to be without purpose or use. With bitter severity he wrote that Scheler is "reviving" Eduard von Hartmann for the sake of variety,[c] whereas other scholars are retrieving an *ethos* and a *kairos* along with the *logos*. "And what will be the joke in the coming weeks? I believe that a madhouse has a clearer and more rational inner point of view than does this age."

As a consequence of this fundamental denial of everything that exists and of all programs for the reform of what exists, Heidegger also protested against the misinterpretation and the overestimation of his work, as if *he* had something "positive" and "new results" to give. "It is beginning to appear as if, by means of critique, something with suitable content might get opposed to what has been negated. And as if this task involved schooling, direction, ongoing activity, and completion." And yet it is *not* all this, but instead is confined to a critical and conceptual destruction of the philosophical and theological tradition; to this extent it is something remote, and it may be completely untouched by our enterprising present.[7] [According to Heidegger] one must instead be glad to stand outside of what is or is not well-received, for where things grow old so rapidly, there must be a lack of ground. —From out of this there later arose the attempt at a philosophy of "Being" and "time" by means of a "fundamental ontology," which drew together history from the Greeks to Nietzsche in terms of *one* question, in order to find a foundation-plan and ground in that which is simple and primordial.

That Heidegger's extraordinary success as an educator and the unusual influence of his hard-to-understand book drove Heidegger himself beyond the limitation he first had in mind and made a fashion out of him,

[c]Translator's note: Eduard von Hartmann (1842–1906) was a German philosopher influenced by Hegel and Schopenhauer; his principal writings include *Philosophy of the Unconscious* (3 vols., 1869), *Phenomenology of Moral Consciousness* (1879), and *Theory of the Categories* (1898).

was certainly against his own intention though it was also a natural consequence of his work as a transposed preacher. He influenced us not by anticipating a new system, but rather by means of the substantive indeterminacy and simple appeal of his philosophical willing, his spiritual intensity and concentration on "the one thing which is needful."

Only later did it become clear to us that this one thing was really nothing, a pure resoluteness whose object [*Wozu*] was not definite. "*I am resolved, I just do not know upon what*" was the fitting joke that a student once devised. The inner nihilism of this naked resoluteness in the face of the Nothing was concealed first of all by characteristics which allowed one to think of a religious concern, and in fact at that time Heidegger had not yet decisively detached himself from his theological heritage. During this time in Freiburg I remember having seen pictures of Pascal and Dostoevsky on his desk, and in a corner of his cell-like room there hung an expressionistic crucifix. At Christmas in 1920 he sent me Thomas à Kempis' *De imitatione Christi* [*Imitation of Christ*].[d] In 1925 it still seemed to him that spiritual life is present only in theology, in Barth and Gogarten. At that time he was most intimate with Bultmann, with whom he held a seminar on the young Luther. It was no small imposition on the students of theology to bring the pseudo-Christian categories of Heidegger's existential ontology together with their diverse theologies.

I find the key to Heidegger's godless theology in a letter from 1921, in which he characterizes his "I am" or his "historiological facticity" with the statement that he—in quotation marks—is a "Christian theo*logian*" (sic!), and that "both radical self-concern and the character of science" are present here; for [according to him] the scientific rigor of conceptual research accentuates his factical existence, which for him thereby becomes a problem of "facticity generally." Very few of us were able to grasp existentially this connection between personal pathos and conceptual passion. No doubt this was first understood by Catholic theologians like Przywara and Guardini,[e] who saw through Heidegger's presuppositions better than the rest of us.

---

[d]Translator's note: Thomas à Kempis (1380–1471) was a member of the Bretheren of the Common Life. *De imitatione Christi* is a famous devotional handbook which counselled "suffering with Christ" as the route to spiritual truth.

[e]Translator's note: Erich Przywara (1889–1972) was a Jesuit theologian interested in the relations between philosophy and religion; principal writings include *Analogia Entis* (1932) and *Polarity* (1933). Romano Guardini (1885–1968) was a German theologian and professor of the philosophy of religion in Breslau, Tübingen, and Munich; he was a leading advocate of the Catholic worldview in the philosophy of religion.

Even the implicit motto of his existential ontology came out of Luther: "*Unus quisque robustus sit in existentia sua*" ["Each may be strong in his own existence"], which Heidegger, lacking faith in Christ, Germanized by continually emphasizing that it is all a matter of "each doing what he can," of "the capacity-for-Being which is always one's own" or the "existentiell confinement to one's own, historiological facticity." At the same time he called this capacity a Having-To which has been called upon, and he also called it "fate." In 1921 he wrote to me: "I do only what I must and what I consider to be necessary, and I do this as I am able to—I do not slant my philosophical work toward cultural tasks for a universal present. I also do not have Kierkegaard's tendency. I work from out of my "I am" and my spiritual, indeed factical heritage. With this facticity, existence rages [*wütet*] (sic!)."

Whoever looks ahead from this standpoint to Heidegger's support of Hitler's movement, will find already in this earliest formulation of historical existence an intimation of his later link with political decision. It requires only one step beyond the still half-religious notion of individuation, and one step beyond the application of one's own Dasein and its Having-To to the proper "German Dasein" and its historical fate, in order to carry over the energetic idling of the existential categories ("resolve upon oneself," "stand alone in the face of the Nothing," "will one's fate," and "give oneself over to oneself") into the universal movement of German existence and then to destruct [*destruieren*] these categories upon political ground. And thus it is no accident if Heidegger's existential ontology corresponds to a political "decisionism" in Carl Schmitt,[8] a decisionism that shifts the "capacity-for-Being-a-whole" of the Dasein that is always one's own to the "totality" of the state that is always one's own. To the self-assertion of one's own Dasein corresponds the self-assertion of political existence, and to "freedom toward death" corresponds the "sacrifice of life" in the political exigency of war. In both cases the principle is the same, namely "facticity," i.e., what remains of life when one does away with all life-*content*.

Heidegger had twice received a call to Berlin, during the Weimar Republic (1930) and at the beginning of National Socialism (1933). He refused both times, and he gave his second refusal a kind of substantiation in terms of the "rootedness" of his spiritual existence. He published an essay in the newspaper *Der Alemanne* (March 7, 1934), which bore the challenging title: "Warum bleiben wir in der Provinz?" ["Why Do We Remain in the Provinces?"]. —After a short description of the ski hut in the Black Forest which Heidegger owns and where the inner circle of his pupils often spent comfortable weeks, there follows a polemical invective directed against the edified "city-dwellers" who come to the Black Forest during their vacations in order to "examine" and "enjoy" its beauty in an objective manner—two words which have a despicable ring for Heidegger, because they indicate idle behavior lacking in "action." [He says that] he himself never "examines" the landscape; instead it is his "work world," and the pace of his work is rooted in the events of this mountain world.

[According to Heidegger] it is not idle *theorein* or viewing, but rather the active praxis of caring existence, which discloses the Being of this world; and it is particularly when wild snow storms race around the hut, and everything is bedecked and enshrouded, that it is "high time" for philosophy. [For him] intellectual work must be as "solid" and "sharp-edged" as this dangerous mountain world, and philosophy is essentially no different than the work of the farmer. The essay ends with a sentimental story about an old farmer who simply shakes his head "no" when Heidegger tells him about his call to Berlin, and it concludes with the words: "inexorably *no!*" For what is this rooted Alemannian [Southern German] to do among the big shots and celebrities of Berlin?

All the essential concepts of existence are contained in this essay, which was intentionally written in a popular form. It is not difficult to see the relationship of these concepts to the ideology of National Socialism: one thanks God—as Mr. Goering loves to say[f] —that one is not "objective" where willing and action [*Einsatz*] are concerned. One denies— along with Nietzsche—enjoyment, happiness, and contentment, and instead affirms the toughness of fate and the rigor of work, which is supposed to be the same for the farmer and the scholar. The statement which is valid from Aristotle to Hegel, that philosophical seeing is the highest human activity because it is free from immediate needs, gets reinterpreted or denied by National Socialist existence and its philosophy.

It was an Event when Heidegger became Rector of Freiburg University in the decisive moment of the German revolution, inasmuch as in this critical time all the other universities did without the kind of "Führer" who could have filled such a position on the basis of his scientific achievement rather than merely on the basis of a party insignia. The bulk of the German intelligentsia was reactionary or indifferent. Heidegger had resisted the call to Berlin, succumbing to the temptation to be the

---

[f]Translator's note: Hermann Goering (1893–1946) was Reichsmarshall and second in command to Hitler until April 1945, when certain of his actions were held by Hitler to be treasonable. He was sentenced to death at Nuremberg but committed suicide before the sentence could be executed.

"Führer" of his own university. His decision was of more than local significance and gained universal attention. The student body in Berlin demanded that every university go along with the "*Gleichschaltung*" which had taken place in Freiburg. But on the other hand, a rejection of the Freiburg rectorate would not have failed to have repercussions, for at that time Heidegger stood at the apex of his renown. His decision came as a surprise to his students, because he had previously almost never expressed his opinion on political questions and no doubt had never been clear about them. Upon assumption of the rectorate, Heidegger delivered a speech on "The Self-Assertion of the German University."

Compared with the countless brochures and speeches issued by the coordinated professors following the overthrow, this speech is an ambitious one, a small masterwork of formulation and composition. Judged by the measure of philosophy it is highly suggestive, since it manages to make existential-ontological categories useful to the "commonly"-historical "moment" [*Augenblick*] (*Being and Time*, section 74) in such a way as to make it seem as if the philosophical aims of these categories can and must go together *a priori* with the political situation, and as if the freedom of research can and must go together *a priori* with governmental force. "Labor service" and "military service" become one with "knowledge service," so that at the end of the lecture one does not know whether one should attend to Diels' Presocratics or march with the SA [*Sturmabteilung*, "brownshirts" or "storm troopers"]. For this reason one cannot judge this speech as merely political nor as purely philosophical. Its weakness as a political speech is equal to its weakness as a philosophical discussion. It transposes Heidegger's philosophy of historical existence into German affairs, thereby giving that existence's will to efficacy a ground for the first time, so that the formal outline of the existential categories acquired decisive content.

The speech begins with a remarkable contradiction: *in opposition* to the threat being posed by the state to the independence of the universities, it deals with the "self-assertion" of the universities; and at the same time it rejects the "liberal" form of academic self-administration and freedom, *in order to subordinate these unconditionally* to the National Socialist scheme of "leadership" [*Führung*] and "following" [*Gefolgschaft*]. The rector has as his duty the spiritual leadership of the teachers and the students. But even he—the Führer—is at the same time one who is led, namely by the "spiritual mission of his people."[g] In what this spiritual mission consists, and

---

[g]Translator's note: On the meaning and the various interpretations of this passage, see translator's note, p.106; the passage is from Book 6 of the *Republic* (497d9) and literally means "all great things are precarious."

by what means this mission is to become evident, remains indefinite. This mission is ultimately assigned by "fate," which one is supposed to will. Corresponding to this indefiniteness of the mission is the stress placed on its being "inexorable." And with a dictum which leaves no room for discussion, the fate of the people gets bound together with the destiny of the universities: the mission of the university is the same as that of the people; German science and German fate come to power in *one* "essential will" (9f./29f.).

The will to essence thereby gets tacitly equated with the will to power, since what is essential for the National Socialist standpoint is the will as such. Prometheus, the symbol of Occidental willing, is [seen here as] the "first philosopher" who should be followed. For the Greeks [according to this speech], with such a promethean willing European humans originally "arose opposite beings" so as to inquire after their Being, and this revolutionary uprising is characteristic of the "spirit" which falters in the face of the superior strength of fate but which is creative in this very impotence (11/31). Hence spirit [on this view] is not universal reason, nor understanding, nor intelligence, nor least of all *esprit*; instead it is a "knowing resolve" upon the essence of Being, and the true spiritual world is a "world of the most extreme and innermost danger" (14/33). Danger is the authentic "calling" of human beings, Nietzsche said in *Zarathustra*.

With soldierly strictness it is then demanded of the student that he "advance," as one who wills to know, to the "station of greatest danger," that he march, devote, and expose himself, hold his ground, stick it out, and be generally resolved to assume that German fate which resides in Hitler (14f./34). The commitment to the Führer and the people, to their honor and destiny, is [on this view] one with knowledge service. And to Nietzsche's question whether Europe still wills itself or whether it no longer wills itself, the response is: "We will ourselves"; and [according to Heidegger] regarding the will to self-assertion—not merely that of the university, but on the contrary that of the whole German Dasein—the youthful force of the German people has already made a positive decision (19/38).

But in order to understand the "magnificence and greatness of this awakening" completely, [Heidegger says that] one must recall the wisdom of a word from Plato, which Heidegger translates (in a violently twisted manner): "Everything great stands in the storm!"[g] So stormy was the fading away of Heidegger's wisdom; and what young member of the SS [*Schutzstaffel* or "black shirts"] would not have felt himself addressed by this, assuming he possessed sufficient philosophical education, and been able to see through the Greek aura surrounding this very German storm? —[According to Heidegger] even the community of German teachers and students is a community of struggle, and only in struggle does knowledge get advanced and safeguarded. In a lecture from this time it was said: every "Essence" discloses itself only to courage [*Mut*] and never to mere looking, and truth can be recognized only to the extent that one "demands" truth of himself [*sich . . . "zumutet"*]. Even the German "disposition" [*Gemüt*] got connected with this courage. Similarly [according to Heidegger] the enemy is not simply "present," but instead Dasein must *create* its enemy for itself in order that it not become impassive. [For Heidegger] everything which in general "is," is "governed by war," and where war and domination do not essence, there is decay.

Heidegger's leadership lasted only a year. Following a number of disappointments and difficulties he abandoned his "mission," so that he could once again oppose the new "anyone" ["man"] in the old manner and risk bitter remarks in his lecture courses, though this was not inconsistent with his substantial adherence to National Socialism. For the "spirit" of National Socialism has to do not so much with the national and the social as with the kind of radical resoluteness and dynamic which rejects all discussion and genuine communication because it relies exclusively on itself—on the (German) capacity-for-Being which is always one's own. Without exception, it is expressions of power and resoluteness which characterize the vocabulary of National Socialist politics and Heidegger's philosophy. Corresponding to the dictatorial style of politics is the apodictic in Heidegger's pathetic formulations. It is simply a distinction of degree rather than one of method which defines the internal differences among the followers, and in the end it is "fate" which justifies all willing and drapes upon it an onto-historical mantle.

A month after Heidegger had delivered his speech, Karl Barth wrote his appeal to theology (*Theological Existence Today*) in opposition to the *Gleischschaltung* with the powers of the time. This text was and remained the only serious expression of spiritual resistance against that violent time. In order to be capable of taking an analogous step, philosophy would have to deal not with *Being and Time* but rather with the Being of *eternity*. But the salient point of Heidegger's philosophy consisted precisely in his having understood "time resolutely, on the basis of time," because even as a philosopher he was still enough of a theologian that he considered eternity to be identical with God—and the philosopher "knows nothing" of God. This negative commitment of Heidegger's philosophical time-problematic to the question of eternity in theology was expressed clearly only in a lecture from July 1924.[10]

Against this historico-political background, the specifically German sense of Heidegger's notions of Dasein becomes clear: existence and resoluteness, Being and capacity-for-Being, the interpretation of this capacity as one of fate and Having-To, the insistence on the (German) capacity-for-Being which is "always one's own" and the constantly recurring words: discipline and force (one must "force" himself "upward" even to the "clarity of knowing"), hard, inexorable and strict, rigid and fierce (Dasein's "holding on fiercely"), holding one's ground and standing alone, devoting oneself and exposing oneself to danger; upheaval, awakening, and encroachment. These all reflect the catastrophic manner of thinking characteristic of almost all people in Germany during the time following the war. Least of all was their thinking concerned with "origin," "end," or "marginal situations." All these concepts and words were fundamentally expressions for the bitter and hard resoluteness of a willing which asserts itself in the face of the Nothing and which is proud of its contempt for happiness and humanity.

Surely none of us could have anticipated in 1927, when Heidegger's *Being and Time* appeared, that six years later the death which is "always one's own" and which radically individuates, could be refashioned so as to herald the fame of a National Socialist hero.[h] And yet the leap from the ontological analysis of death to Heidegger's speech concerning Schlageter[11] is simply a transition from a Dasein which is always individuated to a Dasein which is always universal, though in this universality no less individuated, i.e., it is a transition to a German Dasein. In this affectedly pompous memorial speech it is said that Schlageter died the "hardest and greatest death" when this defenseless man was shot while his nation lay upon the soil degraded. "Alone and from out of himself, he had to present to his soul the image of the people's impending movement toward its honor and greatness, in order that he could die while having faith in this." And Heidegger asks: from where will this "firmness of the will" and "clarity of the heart" come? To this he responds with the "primitive rock" of the mountains of the Black Forest (Schlageter's home) and its autumnal clarity. According to Heidegger, these powers of the soil coursed through the will and the heart of this young hero.

In truth Schlageter was one of the many young Germans who were diverted from their path after the war, some of whom became commu-

[h]Translator's note: On Albert Leo Schlageter, see "The Occasional Decisionism of Carl Schmitt," note 85.

nists and some the opposite, as was superbly described by E. von Salomon in his novel *The City*. Dissipated by the war and released from military service, they could no longer find their way back into civilian life; they joined a volunteer corps, so that there would be some place and someone against whom they could play out their lives in unbridled undertakings. The existential philosopher calls this a "Has To." "He *had to* go into the Baltics, he *had to* go to Upper Silesia, he *had to* go to the Ruhr," he *had to* fulfill the fate which he had chosen for himself. This is the extent to which the *fatum* of ancient tragedy had deteriorated by the time of our inflationary period, at the hands of a philosopher.

A few months after this speech, Germany withdrew from the League of Nations. The "Führer" called for a supplementary election, in order to make it known abroad that Germany and Hitler were the same. Heidegger had the Freiburg students march as a unit to the election room and vote "yes" to Hitler's decision *en bloc*. (At other universities such as Marburg, one was still able to vote "yes" or "no"; the vote took place by secret ballot, though this was merely *pro forma*.) The "yes" to Hitler's decision seemed to him to be identical with the "yes" to one's "own Being."

The election proclamation he had issued as rector is entirely in the style of National Socialism; at the same time it is a popular departure from Heidegger's philosophy. The text was:

"German men and women! The German people has been called to a vote by the Führer. But the Führer asks nothing of the people. On the contrary, he is giving the people the most immediate possibility of the highest free decision: whether it—the whole people—wills its own Dasein, or whether it does not will this. This election is absolutely incomparable with all previous elections. What is unique about this election is the simple greatness of the decision which is to be made in it. But the inexorability of what is simple and ultimate will not endure any vacillation or hesitation. This ultimate decision extends to the furthest limit of the Dasein of our people. And what is this limit? It consists in the primordial demand of all Dasein, namely that it receive and save its own essence.

"In this way a boundary is established between what can be demanded of a people and what cannot. In virtue of this fundamental law of honor, the people preserves the worth and the decisiveness of its essence. It is neither ambition, nor a lust for fame, nor blind obstinacy, nor a striving for power, but rather the clear will to unconditional self-responsibility in bearing and mastering the fate of our people, that required our Führer to withdraw from the 'League of Nations.' This is *not* a turn away from the community of nations. On the contrary—with this step, our nation places itself under that essential law of human Dasein which every nation must follow if it wants to remain a nation. It is precisely on the basis of such unidirectional following in the face of the unconditional demand for self-responsibility, that there first develops the possibility of each taking the other seriously, in order thereby to affirm a community. The will to a genuine community of nations is as far removed from an unstable, non-binding world-brotherhood as it is from blind despotism. Such a will acts beyond this opposition. It forges the open and manly standing alone and standing together of peoples and states. . . .

"Our will to national self-responsibility wills that every nation find and protect the greatness and truth of its fate [*Bestimmung*]. This will is the highest guarantee of the security of nations; for it binds itself to the fundamental law of manly respect and unconditional honor. On November 12 the German people as a whole chooses *its* future. This future is bound to the Führer. The people cannot choose this future in such a way that it votes 'yes' on the basis of so-called extrapolitical considerations, without including in this 'yes' the Führer and the movement which is unconditionally devoted to him. There is no foreign politics nor even domestic politics. There is only the one will to the full Dasein of the state. The Führer has brought this will to full awakening and welded it into one single decision in the whole people. No one can stay away on the day on which this will is manifested!"[12]

After Heidegger spoke for the first time, in his Freiburg inaugural speech,[13] of the "ultimate greatness" of Dasein, which consists in its "boldly" wasting itself, extensive use is now made of heroic greatness. This characterizes Schlageter's death no less than it characterizes Hitler's decision to undertake a surprising coup and a bold separation; and yet this is not supposed to be a turn away from the community of European nations, but "on the contrary" is supposed to be the facilitation of a true community, in which every nation (on the pattern of Germany) stands alone precisely in order thereby to stand "together" as well!

A week before this election proclamation, Heidegger issued a widespread public appeal to the student body,[14] in which he said that the National Socialist revolution is bringing a "complete upheaval in our German Dasein." [According to Heidegger] the students must, in their will to knowledge, adhere to what is essential, simple, and great; and they must be staunch and pure in their demands, as well as clear and certain in their refusal, with respect to mobilizing aggressively and allowing the courage to grow which is necessary for saving the essence and for augmenting the power of the people. "Ideas" could not be the rules for the students' Dasein; instead, [according to Heidegger] Hitler alone is their law: "The Führer alone is the current and future German reality and law" (1/47). Hitler, Heidegger is supposed to have said even before the upheaval, is the only one of the elected Chancellors of the Reich to have "a vision [*Gesicht*]."

The petty-bourgeois orthodoxy of the party was suspicious of Heidegger's National Socialism because the race question and the Jewish question play no role in it. *Being and Time* is dedicated to the Jew Husserl, the Kant book to the half-Jew Scheler; and during the Freiburg years, we studied Bergson and Simmel under Heidegger's direction. Heidegger's cast of mind did not seem to be in accord with the "Nordic cast," which is [supposedly] free of anxiety in the face of the Nothing.[15] On the other hand, Professor H. Naumann managed to explain Teutonic mythology with the concepts of *Being and Time*,[16] discovering "care" in Odin and the "anyone" in Baldur!ⁱ Neither this approbation nor the aforementioned rejection can be taken seriously, because Heidegger's decision in favor of Hitler goes far beyond agreement with the party's ideology and program. He was and remained a National Socialist, similar to Ernst Jünger, on the margins and in a state of individuation, though this individuation was by no means without influence. He was influential solely in virtue of the *radicalism* with which he placed the freedom of the Dasein which is always one's own, and which is perhaps even always German, upon the manifestness of the *Nothing*.[17]

In light of Heidegger's substantial adherence to the National Socialist attunement and manner of thinking, it was inappropriate to criticize, as well as to offer excuses for, his political decision in isolation, rather than explaining it on the basis of the *principle* of his philosophy. Heidegger did not "misunderstand himself" when he supported Hitler;[18] on the contrary, anyone who did not comprehend how he could do this, did not understand him. A Swiss lecturer expressed regret that Heidegger let himself get involved "in the present day"[19]—as if a philosophy which explains Being on the basis of time and everydayness had nothing to do with the present day and with the time in which that philosophy arose and in which it exerts its influence. When this worshiper of Heidegger says that we must instead take exception to the "historically accidental character" of a set of ideas, rather than concentrating on the "ivory tower"

ⁱTranslator's note: On the figures of Odin and Baldur in Teutonic mythology, see "The Occasional Decisionism of Carl Schmitt," translator's note aa.

which elevates itself above these and into the "timeless," it is precisely as a pupil of Heidegger that one must counter him, by pointing out that no philosopher has oriented philosophy on the accident of "historiological facticity" as much as Heidegger, who precisely for this reason fell prey to facticity more than any other, when the decisive "moment" took place. The possibility of Heidegger's philosophical politics emerges not from a derailment which could be found regrettable, but rather from the principle underlying his conception of existence, a conception which "challenges" the "spirit of (the) time" in a dual sense.

But *the ultimate motivational basis for the will to overturning and awakening*, for the will to this politically strengthened youth movement from the time prior to the [First] World War, was *the consciousness of decay and demise*: European nihilism. And yet it is quite telling that this "European" nihilism was made a genuine theme for philosophy only by a German, namely Nietzsche, and that it was able to become active only in Germany. If we do not bear this will to destruction in mind, even the influence exerted on us by Heidegger's philosophical construction cannot be understood. I recall his letter of 1920, in which it was said that his work is independent of the peripheral consideration whether that work will give rise to a "culture" *or to an "acceleration of decline"!* The same idea returns in *Being and Time* (section 77), in the endorsement of a quotation which says that modern human beings have been "ready" ever since the Renaissance "to be buried."[20] Similarly, it was said in 1933 at the end of the rectorial address that it is too late to change old arrangements or add new ones, and that one must instead go back to the first beginnings of the Greeks in order to be able to begin anew in Europe. But [for Heidegger] there is the danger that, before we resolve upon this, the spiritual power of the West will fail and the West's joints will creak "when this moribund semblance of a culture collapses and rends every power into confusion."[21]

At that time Heidegger was still of the opinion that whether this takes place or not depends entirely on "whether or not we still and once again will ourselves" (19/29f.); and he was of the opinion that a positive decision has already been made in this connection by the followers of the Führer. Three years later, in his 1936 lecture on Hölderlin, Heidegger ends in an essentially more resigned way. Along with Hölderlin, he makes reference to "the time of the gods who have fled, and of the god who is coming."[22] But because the present age stands under this double "Not," namely the no-longer-Being-there of those who have fled and the not-yet-Being-there of the one who is coming, [according to Heidegger] it is essentially a needy and destitute time; and here there is no longer any talk of the "magnificence" of the 1933 awakening. [According to Heidegger] the poet of this time endures and stands firm in the Nothing of this night—an image which is reminiscent of the conclusion of Max Weber's lecture on *Science as Vocation*. "And what are poets for in a destitute time"? Even Heidegger may often have asked himself: what are philosophers for in a destitute time? The answer to this may be even more difficult for him than for his poet, for whom the gods were more than mere concepts of time.

The fascination that Heidegger inspired in us with his indefinite decisiveness and his merciless critique has not become detached from his person. It has now been twenty years since I came to Freiburg, but even today he is still capable of captivating his hearer with the enigmatic character of his lectures, and the influence of his teaching can be felt everywhere. —Raised as a Jesuit, he became a Protestant out of indignation, a Scholastic dogmatist through schooling, and an existentiell pragmatist from experience, a theologian on the basis of tradition and an atheist as a researcher; in the guise of a historian of his tradition, he was really a renegade against it. Existentiell like Kierkegaard while possessing the will-to-system of a Hegel, as dialectical in method as he was single-minded in content, making apodictic claims out of the spirit of negation, silent in response to others but uncommonly curious, radical regarding what is ultimate and inclined toward compromise in everything penultimate— this was the mixed effect that the man exerted on his pupils, who nonetheless remained captivated by him because he far exceeded all other university philosophers in intensity of philosophical willing.[23]

Germany—The Reich of Protest

The real key to understanding the German way of thinking and acting is German Protestantism in a broad sense. It is no accident that all of our great thinkers from Kant to Hegel and from Hegel to Nietzsche are Protestants. But Protestantism is the *"peccatum originale"* [original sin] not only of German philosophy,[24] but also of those specifically German actions whose source is the Prussian-Protestant spirit.[25] Nobody saw this basic character of protest on the part of the German nation more incisively than Dostoevsky, because as a Russian he had the free outlook that made it possible for him to recognize clearly the special position of the German reich within and opposite Europe.

"Germany has just *one* task, one which it had earlier and has always had. That is its *Protestantism*—not merely the form of this Protestantism as it developed under Luther, but rather its constant Protestantism, its *eternal protest*, first against the Roman world under Arminius, against everything that constituted Rome and the Roman mission; and later against everything that survived the transition from the old Rome to the new Rome, against all the nations that took over from Rome its form and its rudiments, against the heirs of Rome and against everything that constitutes this inheritance . . . .

"As the highest power, ancient Rome came up with the idea of a worldwide unification of human beings; and as the highest power, it believed that it could practically realize this idea in the form of a world monarchy. Nonetheless, this form collapsed in the face of Christianity—the form, though not the idea. For this idea is the idea of a whole European humanity, and on its basis European civilization has arisen; it lives for this alone. All that died was the idea of a *Roman* world monarchy, and it was replaced by the new ideal of an equally worldwide unification in Christ. . . .

"Since that time, in the Roman world this attempt has made constant progress and has been changing without interruption. With the development of this attempt, the most essential facet of the Christian principle has been almost completely lost. In finally having spiritually renounced Christianity, the heirs of the ancient Roman world also renounced the papacy. The world experienced the storm of the horrible French Revolution, which in principle had simply been a last version of the same ancient Roman formula for worldwide unification. But the new formula proved to be inadequate, and it did not come to fruition. There was even a moment when all the nations that had inherited the mission of ancient Rome came close to desperation.

"Of course the segment of society that had won political leadership in 1789, namely the bourgeoisie, triumphed and pronounced that there was no need whatsoever to proceed further. But all those minds which are ordained by the eternal laws of nature to remain in a state of perpetual unrest and to seek out a new formula for the ideal—they all thrust themselves upon the degraded and disenfranchised, upon everyone who had been given no place in the formula for universal unification that had been proclaimed by the French Revolution of 1789. They simply proclaimed a new word of their own, namely the need to unite humanity. And yet this was not for the purpose of allocating equality and rights to some particular quarter of humanity, so that the rest should serve as raw material and exploitable means for the welfare of this quarter of humanity; on the contrary, the need to unite all human beings was understood upon the foundation of universal equality and with an eye toward the shared enjoyment of the goods of this world by every individual, whatever these goods may turn out to be. They sought to fight for this solution with *all* means, i.e., not simply with the means of Christian civilization but rather without stopping at anything.

"Now what has Germany's role been during this whole time, in the course of all these two thousand years? From the first moment of its appearance in the historical world, the most characteristic and essential feature of this great, proud, and unique nation consisted in its never having wanted to unite itself, in its mission and its principles, with the most Western part of the European world, i.e. with all the heirs of the ancient Roman mission. For the entire two thousand years, it *protested* against this world; of course, it still had no word of its own to proclaim, no rigorously formulated ideal of its own to serve as a substitute for the ancient Roman idea, though it seems always to have been deeply convinced that it was in a position to proclaim this new word and to assume the leadership role for humanity. Already under Arminius it struggled with the Roman world, and then in the time of Roman Christianity it fought more fiercely than anyone with the new Rome for sovereignty.

"Finally the German nation protested in the most energetic and powerful way, by deriving its new formula for protest from the spiritual and most primordial foundations of the Germanic world: it proclaimed the freedom of inquiry and raised the flag of Luther. The break was horrible and touched the entire world; the formula for protest was found and had been perfected, although it still remained a negative formula and a new, *positive* word had not yet been spoken.

"After the Germanic spirit had spoken this new word of protest, it died out for a time; this occurred parallel to an identical weakening of its opponent's powers, the unity of which had previously been rigorously formulated. The most Western part of the world, under the influence of the discovery of America, the new science, and new principles, sought to transform itself into a new truth, to step into a new phase. When the first attempt at this transformation began during the French Revolution, the Germanic spirit became greatly perplexed, and for a long time it lost its faith in itself. It was unable to offer any objection to the new ideas of the most Western part of the European world. The time of Luther's Protestantism was past, but the idea of free inquiry had long since been taken up into science all over the world. The enormous organism of Germany felt more clearly than ever that, so to speak, it lacked a body and a form for self-expression. Around this time there arose in Germany the pressing need to consolidate itself, at least outwardly, into one whole harmonious organism, in the face of the coming phase in its eternal struggle with the most Western part of the European world. . . .

"Around this time Germany's genius comprehended that the German task—above all, before beginning anything, and before any attempt to utter a new word against its opponent's idea, an idea based on the old Catholic idea—consisted in forging its own political unity, in completing the creation of its own political organism, and only then to confront its old opponent face to face. And this is how it happened. After Germany had completed its unification, it thrust itself upon its opponent (France) and began a new period of struggle against it, a period which it introduced with 'iron and blood.' The work with iron has been completed; now it remains to perfect the matter spiritually."[26]

Afterword to the Japanese Reader

Peter the Great put Russia on the path that was taken by the entire Orient one hundred years later and on which it subsequently progressed: on the path of Europeanization, the goal being to break the hegemony of Europe. The European war of 1914 had the tendency to turn against Europe by using European technology and science; this tendency is still intensifying considerably, and respect for Europe is diminishing. The current resumption of the war that was stopped in 1918 will strengthen even more the turn away from the West. But to the extent that the advances learned and acquired from the West are getting used as means toward anti-European ends, the whole relationship of the Japanese to the West is necessarily discordant and *ambivalent*: one admires *and* loathes Western civilization; one often hears the claim that it is materialistic, and in making such a claim one demands idealism of oneself.[27]

The unmistakable undertone in the relationship of most Japanese to the West is a *renunciation of Europe*; this renunciation is all the more virulent the higher were one's initial, and now frustrated, expectations of Europe. This renunciation is aimed at Europe's spiritual condescension, economic exploitation, and political interference. In all areas one wants to be oneself again, i.e., purely Japanese, and to minimize as much as possible the influence of the foreign. But paradoxically, even this reflection on one's own essence and one's own task is an observance of European counsel. In his book *Japan: An Attempt at Interpretation*, Lafcadio Hearn cites a letter from Herbert Spencer to Baron Kaneko Kentaro and Count Ito from the year 1892, the content of which is in accordance with the nationalistic wishes of today's Japanese.[28]

In light of this situation, it may seem strange to my readers when a European outlines, in a Japanese journal, a history of European spirit that is grist for the mill of Japanese consciousness. For what could be more welcome to a Japanese patriot—and all Japanese are patriots, even the most broad-minded and freethinking[29]—than to hear from a European that the unity of Europe has decayed, that ancient Europe is at an end, and that our final word is a nihilism which has become active. But on the other hand, what could be more unwelcome for a European than to intensify the renunciation of Europe in a non-European country. Given that in spite of this I decided to write this essay and have it translated and thereby ran the risk that the reader, with half-pity for us Europeans and a sense of self-satisfaction for being Japanese, might misunderstand my open remarks as wind for his sail, it is necessary to include at the end a justification that cannot avoid also being a critique: a *justification of European self-critique* and a *critique of Japanese self-love*.

When in the latter half of the previous century Japan came into contact with us and took over our advances with admirable effort and feverish rapidity, our culture was already in decline, even though on the surface it was advancing and conquering the entire earth. But in contrast to the Russians of the nineteenth century, at that time the Japanese did not oppose themselves critically to us; instead they first of all took over, naively and without critique, everything in the face of which our best minds, from Baudelaire to Nietzsche, experienced dread because as Europeans they could see through themselves and Europe. Japan came to know us only after it was too late, after we ourselves lost faith in our civilization and the best we had to offer was a self-critique of which Japan took no notice.

Today it is only in America, Russia, and Japan that people still have faith in the idea of progress—in ancient Europe people had long since begun to doubt it. This is why it has to astonish us Europeans when a Japanese like R. Mori reckons *The Truth About Japan* (1886) against the measure of European progress, and when today's Japanese believe that in the course of the intervening fifty years the situation has so changed that my critique of Mori no longer captures it adequately.[30] But in reality, in the East people are so far from having come to terms with our problems that the observations I find regarding Japan in the older European literature (O. Lowell, B. H. Chamberlain, H. Bätz, etc.) still apply completely even today. The point in time when the Westernization of Japan began was, unfortunately, also the point in time when Europe recognized itself to be a problem without solution; and how should a foreigner be able to solve it? But after the beginning of Westernization, which has now become an incontrovertible fact, these questions remain: (1) *what* Japan took over from our civilization, and (2) *how* it took this over.

(1) What Japan took over from us was not, as it was in the Chinese culture's reception, the religious, scholarly, and moral foundation; rather, in the first instance it was our material civilization: modern industry and technology, capitalism, civil Right, military organization, and the scientific working methods that make all this possible, but by no means freedom and beauty, as R. Mori would like to think. Alongside all this, the genuine life of human beings, their way of experiencing and thinking, their morals and values, remained relatively unchanged. European *spirit* and the *history* without which it would not be what it is, were not taken over because they cannot be taken over, unless by means of an appropriation that intensively transforms them. But in spite of this *outward appearance* of Westernization, which must be conspicuous to every European, the *depth of its influence* is not to be overlooked. European civilization is not a garment one can don when the need arises and then take off again; on the contrary, it has the uncanny power to shape the body and even the soul of the one who wears it, in conformity with itself.

The assumption of Western institutions is certainly an outward appearance (and hence seemingly without danger) when one compares Western civilization in Japan with the Western civilization that is native to Europe, because it is only in Europe that technological civilization has a historical and spiritual ground on the basis of which it was able to develop inwardly, whereas the East simply took over the product as a finished result. But at the same time this outward appearance is more inward than it seems, since the modern achievements of Western civilization are never a mere means to an arbitrary end but instead define the entire life and living together of human beings and nations. Nobody can escape the inner consequences of the transformation of life by industry and technology, both of which are of service in the exigency of war. The breakdown of the old religious, moral, and social foundations is an inevitable consequence which no civilizing advance can obscure.

A modern Japan is (for the Europeans) a living self-contradiction, since what is modern in the West is not Japanese (*nippon seishin*), and what is genuinely Japanese is ages old. Whatever is still true culture in contemporary Japan, particularly simplicity, politesse, and beauty, is nothing new but rather something which preserves what is ancient. That in individual cases this opposition between old and new found a satisfactory resolution and sometimes reached a compromise which is acceptable on aesthetic and moral grounds even to Europe, simply confirms this rule.

Nonetheless the customary reaction in Japan to the problematic posed by this connection between us, who seem to be incompatible, is highly optimistic: one wants to preserve the best in what is Japanese and supplement it with Europe's best, thereby adding to the perfection of Japan the perfection of Europe (R. Mori), as if cultures could be combined in such a way that one brings home the good and leaves behind the bad, so as to surpass Europe. The Japanese loves to present as broad-mindedness his readiness to take over the best, wherever it may be; but alongside the modesty that distinguishes the Japanese so advantageously in civil life, this is by no means free of vanity and is even a matter of arrogance. In this connection one immediately thinks of the many Japanese wares on which "improved" appears, whereas in reality they are for the most part merely cheapened and worsened imitations of European or American wares. Yet it is not only wares but spiritual goods as well that one may seek to improve, by adopting the methods of our scientific thinking, imposing critical limits on them, and coming to the encouraging result that one does indeed understand the matter in somewhat greater depth and in greater complexity. The deeper ground for this naive trust in one's own superiority is Japanese self-love, which believes that Right and justice are embodied in Japan, the land of God.[31]

(2) The manner in which the Japanese for the most part takes over European thinking, seems questionable to us to the extent that we cannot see it as a pure appropriation. The appropriation of something other and foreign would presuppose that one can *alienate* or distance oneself from oneself, and that one then, on the basis of the distance one has acquired from oneself, makes what is other one's own as something foreign. The spiritual labor of appropriation has to be a kind of processing, in which the foreign object of our labor disappears as such.[32] In this way, the Greeks took a world whose roots were foreign and made it into their home. Of course they received the substantial beginnings of their religion, education, and social cohesion more or less from Asia, Syria, and Egypt; but they wiped out, transformed, processed, and changed what was foreign in this origin, they made something different out of it, to such an extent that what they, like us, value, acknowledge, and love in it is precisely what is essentially their own.[33]

This means that they were, in the Hegelian sense, with themselves or free in the other. There was knowledge in itself long before the Greeks, indeed of the highest order in the high cultures of the ancient Orient; but there was not the kind of free emergence from out of oneself and the consequent power of appropriation which proceeds from a free attitude toward oneself and the world. Only the Greeks, as the first-born Europeans, had panoramic eyes, as Burckhardt calls it,[34] i.e., the objective, concrete view of the world and oneself that can make comparisons and distinctions and that recognizes oneself in others. Their explorers and scholars had a universal interest in what is foreign just as they had an interest in themselves; their incisive and intelligent knowledge of the uniqueness of others goes hand in hand with their knowledge of themselves.

This character of free appropriation appears to me to be lacking for the most part in Japan. The students do indeed study our European books with dedication, and they understand them thanks to their intelligence; but they do not draw from their studies any consequences for themselves as Japanese. They do not make distinctions or comparisons between European concepts such as will, freedom, and spirit and what corresponds to these in their own lives, thinking, and speaking; or to put it more precisely, they avoid doing this. They learn what is foreign in itself, but they do not do so for themselves. They proceed into the text of a European philosopher as if doing so were a straightforward matter, without seeing the primordial foreignness of the philosopher's concepts in comparison with their own concepts; and for this reason they do not even have any impulse to transform what is foreign into something of their own. They do not come from others back to themselves; they are not free, or—to put it as Hegel does—they are not with themselves in Being-other.[35]

They live as if on two levels: a lower, more fundamental one, on which they feel and think in a Japanese way; and a higher one, on which the European sciences from Plato to Heidegger are lined up. And the European teacher asks himself: where is the step on which they pass from the one level to the other? In principle they love themselves as they are; they have not yet eaten from the (Christian!) tree of knowledge and lost their innocence, a loss which *places* human beings *beyond themselves* and makes them critical of themselves. Along with this comes an extreme sensitivity, a delicate sensitiveness, as Chamberlain puts it, whose flip-side is a touchiness that avoids the truth and that knows nothing of reasonable considerations. I doubt whether there are Japanese (but please correct me if I am wrong) who, like Baudelaire and Flaubert, Proudhon and Sorel, Wagner and Nietzsche, call themselves and their nation into question with the same stubborn incisiveness that is the case in Europe.

European spirit is not ultimately a spirit of critique that knows how to distinguish, compare, and decide. Of course, critique appears to be something wholly negative; but in itself it has a positive power of negating, which not only keeps in motion that which has been handed down and which exists, but also impels its further development. In fact critique is the principle underlying our progress, to the extent that it dissolves and propels, step by step, whatever exists. The Orient does not endure the kind of inconsiderate critique, either of itself or of others, in which all European progress is grounded. The very critique of what exists, of the state and nature, of God and human beings, of principles of faith and prejudices—this power of making distinctions, which embraces everything, calls it into question, doubts it, and investigates it, is a basic element of European life without which that life is unthinkable.

All the other characteristics of Europe are intimately connected with this capacity for critique: its movement through prevailing crises; its scientific spirit; its decisive thought and action; its direct mode of expression, even regarding what is unpleasant; its acknowledgment of consequences, and even its drawing of consequences; and above all, the individuality with which it unequivocally distinguishes itself. For only a human being who is an in-dividual, in the sense that he is indivisible regardless of what he is participating in, is capable of distinguishing and deciding so incisively and definitely between himself and God, between himself and the world, between himself and his people or nation, between himself and his fellow human beings, between himself and his own *moi haïssable* (Pascal), between truth and lie, between yes and no.

Hence the opposite of European spirit is: life in an attunement that blurs boundaries; a unity between human beings and the natural world that lacks an opposite because it is grounded in mere feeling;[36] the kind of commitment to parents, family, and state that has abandoned critique; a refusal to manifest and unmask oneself; the avoidance of logical consequences; compromise in dealings with human beings; the conventional observance of universally valid morals; and the indirect system of mediation,[37] which excludes the human being as an individual and does not allow him to act for himself, nor to speak about or for himself.

Hegel's characterization of Greek spirit captures the essence of Europe as well. It is an essentially anti-Asian spirit, because individuality is its universal substance. The universal as such has been overcome; immersion in nature has been sublated.[38] Greek spirit is varied in itself, and in a number of ways. It does not know uniformity; it lives in a dispersion and multiplicity, which correspond to the variety of Greek peoples and the agility of their spirit. For this reason Europe is the site of the richest creations and the home of all distinctions and oppositions.

In the same way that Hegel described Greek spirit, Burckhardt described European spirit. What is European is the exertion of *all* one's energies in monuments, in image and word, institution and party, down to the individual—the persistence of the spiritual on *all* sides and in *all* directions—the striving of spirit and everything in it to convey the message that we should not yield silently to world monarchies and theocracies like the *Orient*.[39] And this is why [for Burckhardt] there is always just one thing that is fatal for Europe: oppressive power, which makes everything uniform, be it the service of *one* state or *one* leveling intention, and regardless of whether the intention be political, religious, or social. Burckhardt believed that against such an oppressive power, Europe will always collect its last energies and find its rescuers in the face of the danger posed by political-religious-social forced unity and forced leveling, which threaten Europe's unique quality, viz. the multifaceted wealth of its spirit.

Nonetheless a decline of Europe is not to be expected; indeed Europe has subjected the entire earth to its progress: first America, then Russia, and finally the East, so that only now is Europe ascending on all sides. To Hegel, world history appears to punish lying, to the extent that for a century it has been retreating from the West to the East. But this new Europe, which is now spreading its annihilating civilization over the entire earth, so that it is no longer Homeric heroes and Christian knights but rather machines that are fighting with isolated human beings, is not the Europe of which I wrote, in which I take part as a German, and which I consider it valuable to disseminate through writing and teaching. Today there are Europeans in the old and true sense only here and there and in isolation. Only a few individuals in the current generation, which has endured the Second World War, possess in themselves an image of the Europe that gave our planet its primary spiritual color from the time of Homer and Virgil up to Dante and Shakespeare, Goethe and Hegel. The last German philosopher in whom European spirit was still alive was Nietzsche. In fact he stands on the border of the transition between the old and the new Europe, which according to Jünger, his most radical pupil, no longer exists as a German special case.

Two Letters from Martin Heidegger to Karl Löwith

Letter 1

August 19, 1921

Dear Mr. Löwith,

Your letter addresses two matters: (1) a self-justification on your part, and (2) the "correct" interpretation of "my philosophy." A year ago I told you from Messkirch what it is that I am looking for; and I told Becker the same thing[1] (about which I *never* would have spoken to another person), my motivation being simply the fact that you are inclined to earn a "doctorate" at the university. It makes no difference what people think of the title, how others attain it, etc.; for me the matter is *precisely as* serious as *it has to be for me.*

I am not in a position to judge the extent to which *this* inclination is related as an existential possibility to your attitude (which I find acceptable) about "scientific philosophy" (more about this below).[a] I have to take you as you present yourself to me—with which I am not saying that I have always seen you primarily and authentically as my "doctoral candidate." In connection with scientific work, I have (because I have greater concern for you than for others) a *certain* obligation to offer guidance. And even the "scientific conditions of life" are different than they are in "sciences." I am concerned not with a primary and isolated definition of philosophy—

---

[a] Translator's note: In the present remarks, *wissenschaftlich* has been translated as "scientific"; the German term signifies not only fields like natural science, but (as in the present discussion) the systematic pursuit of knowledge generally.

but rather only with the kind of definition that is related to the existential interpretation of facticity.

A discussion of the concept of philosophy in the detached sense is without purpose—and hence so is a discussion of "what is scientific."

I must now direct this talk at myself.

The discussion hinges first of all on the fundamental mistake that you and Becker make in measuring me (hypothetically or not) against standards like Nietzsche, Kierkegaard, Scheler, and various other creative and deep philosophers. You are free to do so—but in consequence it will have to be said that I am not a philosopher. I do not picture myself as an object of comparison; this is simply not my intention.

I do only what I must and what I consider to be necessary, and I do so as I am able; I do not slant my philosophical work toward cultural tasks for the sake of a "universal present." I also do not have Kierkegaard's inclination.

I work in a concretely factical manner, from out of my "I am"—from out of my spiritual, indeed factical heritage/milieu/life contexts, from out of that which thereby becomes accessible to me as the living experience in which I live. As existentiell, this facticity is no mere "blind Dasein"; Dasein is proper to existence, though this means that I live it—the "I must," about which one does not speak. With this *facticity of Being-thus*, i.e., with the historiological, existence rages; but this means that I live the inner obligations of my facticity just as radically as I understand them to be. Proper to this facticity of mine is—to state it briefly—my being a "Christian the*ologian*." In this there lies a definite radical concern for self, a definite radical scientific character—*in* this *facticity* there lies a rigorous objectivity; in it there lies "intellectual historical" historiological consciousness—and this is what I am in the life context of the *university*.

"Philosophizing" is connected with the university only in a factically existentiell manner, i.e., I do not maintain that there could be philosophy only *there* but rather that philosophizing has its own executive facticity [*Vollzugsfaktizität*], and hence its boundaries and limitations, precisely on account of its fundamental existentiell meaning in the university.

This does not exclude the possibility of a "great philosopher," a creative one, emerging from the universities; and it does not exclude the possibility that philosophizing in the university will be nothing but *pseudo-science*, i.e., neither philosophy nor science. What university philosophy is in such a case, one can demonstrate only in the course of his life.

Hence it cannot be determined which of the two of you understands me correctly—on whose side I stand; and what I am saying is not supposed to be a facile reconciliation, but on the contrary: you and Becker stand equally *distant* from me—only in different directions. It was always clear to me that you accept what is Christian just as little as does Becker, and I have never understood you to be seeking agreement in this connection—I have sought to influence you just as little as I have Becker. You each take something different to be what is essential in me; I do not, as you do here, make a distinction between the scientific, theoretically conceptual researching life and one's own life, and I do not consider these two to counterbalance one another. The essential manner in which my facticity becomes existentially articulated is scientific research—precisely as I conduct it. In this connection, for me the motive and goal of philosophizing is never to augment the store of objective truths, because the objectivity [*Objektivität*] of philosophy—as I understand and factically pursue it—is something of one's own. But the most rigorous objectivity [*Gegenständlichkeit*] of explication is not thereby excluded; rather, for me it lies within the meaning of my existing. Objective rigor pertains not to subject-matter—but rather to historiological facticity.

I can emphasize research, but the direction of my concern here is fundamentally different than Becker's. I take the person to be decisively important; but I do so within the possibilities for action which I alone honestly have at my disposal, without any intention to be creative and hence with the danger that in comparison with the greats I am threshing empty straw, assuming that on *my* own terms I am indeed threshing at all. Unfortunately, I know all too well that even this often fails to occur.

I readily believe that you are not able to bring together "theoretically" the How of my philosophizing with the direction of my concern. This Together is not a theme for theoretical unraveling. I cannot make my "I am" into something different, but can only seize upon it and be it in this or that way.

Even in connection with destruction,[b] I neither want nor envision an objectivity of the in-itself, for this serves to take one's own facticity and "twist it around"—if you like. It is simply a matter of whether a fictitious non-personality which understands everything accomplishes more than does going after things in such a way that taking hold of them depends on one's *being there himself in the process*. In such a case, objectively [*objektiv*] speaking one is one-sidedly dogmatic; but philosophically speaking one is in fact "absolutely" *objectively* [*gegenständlich*] *rigorous*.

[b] Translator's note: This is a reference to Heidegger's project of a "destruction" of the history of ontology, which he first discusses in section 6 of *Being and Time*.

Jaspers wrote to me and said that I have done him wrong in several ways.[2] My reply: Husserl and others have also said this—though for me this is simply a sign that I have at least *attempted* to take a stand, rather than fancifully listing the "results" of the book in an imaginary body of knowledge.

It is simply a matter of each doing what he can; ultimately he is there in the doing—unreflectively—even if he has a wholly "reflective" philosophy.

Perhaps I am much less objective than you. You are, to the extent that such expressions say something, an *objective* relativist; I, on the other hand, am a *dogmatic* subjective relativist, i.e., I push my "position" through—and am "unjust" toward others in the knowledge that I myself am "relative." But this interpretation is of no interest to me at all; I do not want to initiate a new direction in the history of philosophy.

What I want in my teaching at the university is: for human beings to *take a stand*. The old university cannot be overcome by making the "intellectualism" of fossilized lecturers laughable and by turning to individuals whom one considers to be richer, more lively, and deeper; instead it can be overcome only by returning to the origins of action in what has survived in contemporary facticity and by deciding for oneself what one can do. What will happen—whether we will still have universities in fifty years—who knows this—of course no institute lasts for eternity. But we do have one thing in hand, namely whether we will fret in moods and meditate on possible primordial cultures, or whether we will *sacrifice* ourselves and find our way back into our *existential* limitation and facticity rather than reflecting our way off into programs and universal problems. Things are going much too well for most young people today—especially from an intellectual standpoint; everything is available to them, and from early on—travel, literature, art, etc. I would not wish my student days on anyone, and yet I also would never part with them.

You have *not* misunderstood me, but there is *something* that you do not understand, as you yourself explained so well; to this I can only answer: I am not able to do otherwise without abandoning myself. For *you*, I think, this will suffice.

Becker misunderstood me because he, in a somewhat *isolated* manner, understood the same thing too *well*. Both are inconsequential. What is decisive is simply one thing: that we understand one another well enough that each of us is radically devoted to the last to the what and how of our understanding of the *unum necessarium*. We may be far removed from one another as regards "system," "doctrine," and "position"—but we are *together* in that one way in which humans are able to be genuinely together: in existence.

It is very good that you became agitated and vented your anger in your letter. I have just one objection: that, in comparison with the distinctness with which you interpret and measure me, you take me all too seriously.

But you must decide for yourself to what extent I "harm" or help you.

I cannot deal with people. And "leadership" always goes awry; I have nothing at all to say to you; what I told Becker about you is something that you heard from me *once*, though its direct effect was not your spontaneous resistance.

Do you want to come with Becker on Sunday evening?

Warm Regards
Your
Martin Heidegger

Letter 2

Todtnauberg
August 20, 1927

Dear Mr. Löwith,

I received your three letters and thank you for them.[3] I did not answer in the first days of August, because I first wanted to finish reading through your work. Nonetheless you were packed in my book box, which was in transit as freight for ten days. In the meantime Husserl invited me to Freiburg, where I stayed for a long time. I have been back for several days and have read a bit more of your work.

I accept it as your habilitation essay. It is quite essentially different than your first draft, both in its level of questioning and in its transparency of structure and linguistic expression.

Whether you agree with me substantively or not, is for me not a focal point for acceptance or nonacceptance; nor is the question whether or not you have understood all the fundamental tasks of my work. In your interest, I have simply indicated in marginal notes that in some places you have made your critique too facile and that you underestimate the difficulties of the problems and their presuppositions.

Your hidden attacks and supercilious jabs are part of the attunement in which one presents his first undertakings. After a decade such gestures subside, assuming that one is in a position to direct all one's passion intensively toward *the secure riverbed of one* exhaustive *life's work*.

I want to bring this matter before the faculty as soon as possible. The subsequent course of things depends on whether the open position is occupied and whether Freiling's habilitation is concluded.[4] In the latter matter a strong opposition has widely manifested itself, so that Jaensch did not conduct the affair as quickly as he had originally intended.[5] He hopes to push the matter through with the help of Mahnke as "schoolteacher";[6] because I understand nothing of the matter, neither of psychology nor of pedagogy, but also because I am concerned for your situation, I have decided to remain neutral even though doing so does not generally accord with my taste. And naturally I will not take part in shady dealings. To the extent that I have been able to sound things out, I do not believe that there will be serious opposition. Jaensch will surely become anxious when he notices that you "also" study anthropology, and his interpretation of the matter will be that you have been deployed by me against him. It is also possible that once the habilitation is underway, Hartmann will conduct opposing work with his friends.[c] But these are things that should not seriously disturb you. You will do well to reflect a bit on the themes for your trial lecture before the faculty and your public inaugural lecture.

I do not know whether an appointment has been made for the open position, since I departed on Sunday and have not heard anything from Marburg since then. The prominent men and their followers arrived rather late at the welcoming reception. There developed—*sit venia verbo*—such ... groveling around the minister[7] and Schmidt-Ott[8] that the whole thing sickened me. On the following day I would have stayed in my dressing gown from 9:00 in the morning until 4:00 in the afternoon. Physical exertion would have been tolerable; the emotional exertion was even worse. It is disgraceful how much banality and barbarism were manifested there. What ensued in the following two days was presumably even worse.

For the step you are venturing with your habilitation, you will surely be in the clear. One must be able to tolerate being passed over and must be in a position to wait. Especially today the whole thing is a game of chance. Natorp's high estimation of my Duns Scotus,[d][9] the fact that my teaching in Freiburg was effective, and the fact that I was taken for an indolent and harmless young man, are all accidents. Today I presumably would not become employed. He who wants something will always be contested; the result is that one gets defeated. But the fact that my days in Marburg are coming to an end is not the greatest misfortune. For you

---

[c] Translator's note: See note 12, p. 296.

[d] Translator's note: Paul Natorp (1854–1924) was one of the principal figures of the Marburg School of neo-Kantian philosophy.

there is the further question whether science is so central for you that you become an advocate of the university, or whether in your work you bring yourself to conclusions of the kind that Nietzsche drew.

It is best for us to discuss your work in person; I still do not hold sway over you sufficiently.

Regarding the Plessner affair,[10] I have only this advice: immediately demand the return of the manuscript without any comments. Ideally I would at the same time announce my withdrawal from the editorial board.[11] In your interest I will defer this until after your habilitation. Otherwise Hartmann,[12] as far as I know him, would definitely seek revenge by putting a spoke in your wheel at Marburg, even if this be done through Jaensch. Apparently reviews in Cologne primarily take the form of abuse from the "teacher," and in Cologne there are deep tendencies toward this. It is for such things that people have waste baskets.

I would like to respond briefly to what you have written about the problem of establishing an ontic foundation for philosophy as ontology: In the first place, I have emphasized *constantly*, almost to the point of monotony: the *equiprimordiality* of existence, thrownness, and falling, and correspondingly I have worked out the *Being* of Dasein as care. It is not the first ten pages that are the "point of departure" for fundamental ontology, but rather the entire treatise. At the same time I want to say: the analytic of Dasein is existential and hence guided by existence, and indeed precisely because only the "preparatory" analytic of Dasein (*not* ontological anthropology!) seeks to elucidate the understanding of Being that belongs to Dasein. It is a matter of explicating this understanding on the basis of Dasein. The question is: where and how shall I arrive at the horizon for the interpretation of *this understanding*. But understanding is characteristic of existence; it is for this reason that the existential is substantively and methodologically central, though in such a way that at the same time *the "totality" of the fundamental structure of Dasein emerges*. Of course, the "nature" of human beings is not something for itself and attached to "spirit." The question is: is there a possibility of acquiring from *nature* a ground and a guiding thread for the *conceptual* interpretation of Dasein, or of acquiring this from "spirit"—or from neither of these, but instead primordially on the basis of the *"totality"* of the constitution of Being, where, from a *"conceptual"* standpoint, *the existential* has a *priority as regards the possibility of ontology generally*. For *anthropological* interpretation, *as ontological*, can be conducted only on the basis of a clarified ontological problematic generally. This is why, in my eyes, Becker's way of posing the problem is grotesque and philosophically impossible. To make mathematical "existence" a problem and to say at the same time that the distinction between ontic and ontological is not essential and central, really means: not to know what one is doing and what one wants.

What I expected was naturally not an "application" of my investigations, but rather an independent fundamental exposition of the problem of mathematical existence on the basis of *what Becker takes to be the foundation of philosophy*. And yet there is no talk of this; instead, my questioning has been thrust onto an entirely false plane.

I too am of the conviction that ontology can be founded only ontically, and I believe that nobody before me explicitly saw and expressed this. But providing an ontic foundation does not mean *arbitrarily* pointing out and returning to something ontic; rather, the ground *for ontology* will be found only in such a manner that one knows what ontology is and lets it take itself down to the ground [*sich zugrunderichten*]. For me the problems of facticity persist just as they did in my early days in Freiburg—only they are much more radical, though they remain *within the perspectives* which guided me in Freiburg. It is no accident that I constantly occupied myself with Duns Scotus and the Middle Ages and also with Aristotle. And one cannot judge that work according to what was said in lectures or in recitation. I had to start by pursuing the fac*tical* in an extreme manner, in order to arrive at fac*ticity* as a problem generally. Formal indications, critique of the customary doctrine of the *a priori*, formalization, and the like are all still there for me, even if I do not speak of these now. I am truly not interested in my development; but if it gets talked about, one should not hastily piece it together as a product of lectures and what has simply been communicated here. Such a hasty examination completely forgets my central perspectives and motivations.

"What is understood by 'intelligibility' cannot be determined theoretically."[13] Certainly—but the question remains *whether* the psychoanalysis of philosophizing, the *ontic-psychological explanation of factical philosophizing* is *itself philosophy*, or whether it is and must be something different, so that the psychological question *can have meaning at all*.

Such analyses do not settle anything whatsoever for *productive knowledge and questioning*, but instead simply hinder and prevent these, and consolidate what is complex.

But when both Becker and you polemicize against me by combatting a subjectivism, I must confess that both Becker and you are characterologically much more "subjective," much more and more intensively self-absorbed than I am, and that from an ontic standpoint the "with-one-another" and the "nonvisual" are conditioned for both of you in a most subjective manner. It is mere pretense for you to believe that you think "more objectively."

Of course, ontically the two of you seem to bring something more objective than "existence" into consideration, and yet you are not in a position—based on the past, at least—*ontologically* to attain and to provide a foundation for the universal orientation which makes it possible to enter into the kind of crucial communication with prior philosophy that I am striving for.

I have always had *little* interest in psychoanalysis, because in a *fundamentally* philosophical sense it appears to me to be insufficiently relevant to the central problems. On the other hand, from the very beginning Becker and you have psychoanalytically redirected my hermeneutic of facticity and have pushed my work into perspectives within which it never moved.

Hence your *relationship to me*! can have changed *only from your side*, and it appears to have changed from the moment when you noticed that my *work*! does not proceed in the direction which you expected from the standpoint of your ontic interpretation.

Today my personal feelings toward you are no different than they were previously, leaving aside the respective differences which *were produced* by developments *in our work*! But for a long time now this has simply been a reason for me to wait and see, without pressure and solicitation, whether you will find the *secure* path *from the solidified position* of your own work and existence to a *genuine friendship*.

"Circles" are not friendships; this is clear from the fact that a day obviously comes when one has had quite enough of them.

With Warm Regards
From Your
Martin Heidegger

The light in my cabin failed, so that I had to write in near-darkness.

Notes

LÖWITH AND HEIDEGGER: AN INTRODUCTION

1. Karl Löwith, *From Hegel to Nietzsche: The Revolution in Nineteenth-Century Thought*, tr. David Green (New York: Columbia University Press, 1989); *Meaning in History* (Chicago: University of Chicago Press, 1949); *Max Weber and Karl Marx* (London: Allen and Unwin, 1982). See also *Nature, History, and Existentialism*, ed. A. Levinson (Evanston: Northwestern University Press, 1966). See also Leo Strauss' extremely favorable review of *From Hegel to Nietzsche*, in *Social Research* 8(4) (1941).

2. For a good discussion of Löwith's views in this regard, see Robert Wallace, "Progress, Secularization, and Modernity: The Löwith-Blumenberg Debate," *New German Critique* 22 (1981): 63–79. For an influential view that is contrary to Löwith's, see Hans Blumenberg, *The Legitimacy of the Modern Age*, tr. R. Wallace (Cambridge: MIT Press, 1983), especially, pp. 27ff.

3. For an important critique of Löwith's later thought, see Jürgen Habermas, "Karl Löwith: Stoic Retreat from Historical Consciousness," in *Philosophical-Political Profiles*, tr. F. Lawrence (Cambridge: MIT Press, 1981), pp. 79–98.

4. Hans-Georg Gadamer, *Truth and Method* (New York: Seabury, 1975), p. 481.

5. Löwith, "Welt und Menschenwelt," in *Sämtliche Schriften 1* (Stuttgart: Metzler, 1981), p. 294.

6. Ibid., p. 295.

7. Max Weber, "Science as a Vocation," in *From Max Weber: Essays in Sociology*, eds. H. Gerth and C. W. Mills (New York: Oxford University Press, 1946), p. 156.

8. Karl Löwith, "Curriculum Vitae," in *Mein Leben in Deutschland vor und nach 1933* (Stuttgart: Metzler Verlag, 1986), p. 147.

9. Karl Löwith, *Mein Leben in Deutschland*, pp. 42–43.

10. See Dieter Henrich, "Sceptico Sereno," in *Natur und Geschichte: Karl Löwith zum 70. Geburtstag* (Stuttgart: Kohlhammer, 1967), pp. 458–63.

11. Hans-Georg Gadamer, "Karl Löwith," in *Philosophical Apprenticeships* (Cambridge: MIT Press, 1985), p. 171.

12. Löwith, *Das Individuum in der Rolle des Mitmenschen* (Darmstadt: Wissenschaftliche Buchgesellschaft, 1969), p. 1.

13. Ibid., p. 2.

14. Herbert Marcuse, "The Struggle Against Liberalism in the Totalitarian Theory of the State," in *Negations: Essays in Critical Theory* (Boston: Beacon Press, 1968), p. 40. The Heidegger text, "German Students," may be found in Richard Wolin, ed., *The Heidegger Controversy: A Critical Reader* (Cambridge, Mass.: MIT Press, 1993), p. 46.

15. Hans Jonas, "Heideggers Entschlossenheit und Entschluss," in *Antwort: Martin Heidegger in Gespräch*, eds. G. Neske and E. Kettering (Pfullingen: G. Neske Verlag, 1988), pp. 226–27. In English, see *Martin Heidegger and National Socialism*, eds. Neske and Kettering (New York: Paragon House, 1991), pp. 197–205.

16. Hannah Arendt, "What is Existenz Philosophy?" *Partisan Review* 13, no. 1 (Winter 1946): 46.

17. Hannah Arendt and Karl Jaspers, *Correspondence* (New York: Harcourt Brace, 1992, p. 48).

18. Edmund Husserl, letter of May 4, 1933, in *Martin Heidegger und das "dritten Reich,"* ed. Bernd Martin (Darmstadt: Wissenschaftliche Buchgesellschaft, 1989), p. 149.

19. Hannah Arendt, "Martin Heidegger at Eighty," reprinted in *Martin Heidegger and National Socialism*, pp. 207–18 (see, however, especially the footnote on pp. 284–5). Of course, this quizzical argument that at base Nazism was a product of "thoughtlessness" and the actions of "thoughtless" men derived from her account of the Eichmann trial in *Eichmann in Jerusalem*. There, Arendt would coin the famous phrase, "the banality of evil" to characterize Eichmann and his fellow Nazi malefactors.

20. Löwith, *Mein Leben in Deutschland*, pp. 9ff.

21. Franz Neumann, *Behemoth: The Structure and Practice of National Socialism* (New York: Oxford University Press, 1944), pp. 135–36.

22. Löwith, "Les Implications politiques de la philosophie de l'existence chez Heidegger," *Les Temps modernes* 2, no. 14 (1946): 343–60. Other versions of text: an English translation of the article ("The Political Implications of Heidegger's Existentialism") may be found in *The Heidegger Controversy: A Critical Reader*, pp. 167–85.

I have explored the question of the differences between the two versions of existentialism proffered by Heidegger and Sartre in "Sartre, Heidegger, and the Intelligibility of History," *The Terms of Cultural Criticism* (New York: Columbia University Press, 1992), pp. 125–46.

23. See Hugo Ott, *Martin Heidegger: Unterwegs zu seiner Biographie* (Frankfurt: Campus Verlag, 1988), p. 307. See also the controversial biography by Victor Farias, *Heidegger and Nazism* (Philadelphia: Temple University Press, 1989).

24. The letter was first published in the *Frankfurter Allgemeine Zeitung*, January 1, 1994, p. 27.

25. Gadamer, "Das Sein und das Nicht-Sein," in Traugott König, ed., *Sartre: Ein Kongress* (Hamburg: Rowohlt, 1988), p. 37.

26. Heidegger, "Letter on Humanism," in *Basic Writings*, ed. D. Krell (New York: Harper Row, 1977), pp. 208, 213–14.

27. For an excellent account of Nietzsche's conception of "great politics," see Bruce Detwiler, *Nietzsche's Aristocratic Radicalism* (Chicago: University of Chicago Press, 1990).

28. Löwith, *Mein Leben in Deutschland*, pp. 44–45, 57.

29. See Heidegger, *An Introduction to Metaphysics*, tr. R. Mannheim (New Haven: Yale University Press, 1959), p. 199.

30. Löwith, "The Political Implications of Heidegger's Existentialism," pp. 182–83.

31. Nietzsche, *The Will to Power*, tr. W. Kaufmann and R. J. Hollingdale (New York: Vintage Press, 1969), p. 9.

32. Nietzsche, "Schopenhauer as Educator," in *Untimely Meditations* (Cambridge: Cambridge University Press, 1983), pp. 148–49.

33. Cited by Löwith below in "European Nihilism" ("The Political Horizon of Heidegger's Existential Ontology").

34. For an analysis of National Socialism as "revolution of nihilism" (written by a disillusioned former party member), see Hermann Rauschning, *The Revolution of Nihilism* (New York: Alliance, 1939).

35. See note 23. The literature on this subject, moreover, has become enormous.

36. Cited from Löwith, "The Political Horizon of Heidegger's Existential Ontology."

37. Heidegger's letter has been reprinted in *Telos* 72, 20, no. 2 (Summer 1987): 132.

38. Schmitt, *Der Begriff des Politischen* (Berlin: Duncker and Humblot, 1979), p. 67.

39. I discuss the relation between these two phases of Schmitt's development in "Carl Schmitt, Political Existentialism, and the Total State," in *The Terms of Cultural Criticism*, pp. 83–102; and in "Carl Schmitt: the Conservative Revolutionary Habitus and the Aesthetics of Horror," in *Labyrinths: Explorations of the Critical History of Ideas* (Amherst: University of Massachusetts Press, 1995).

40. On these points, see Heidegger's essays, "The Age of the World-Picture"

and "The Question Concerning Technology," in W. Lovitt, ed., *The Question Concerning Technology and Other Essays* (New York: Harper and Row, 1977).

41. Heidegger, "Hölderlin and the Essence of Poetry," in *Existence and Being* (Chicago: Regnery-Gateway, 1949), p. 287. See the following remarks from *Hölderlins Hymnen "Germanien" und "Der Rhein"* (Frankfurt: Klostermann, 1980), pp. 51–52: "The historical Dasein of nations—their emergence, flowering, and decline—originates from poetry; out of the latter [originates] authentic knowledge in the sense of philosophy; and from both of these, the realization of a Volk as Volk through the state—politics. This original, historical age of peoples is therefore the age of poets, thinkers, and state-founders, that is, of those who authentically ground and establish the historical Dasein of a Volk."

42. Heidegger, "Letter on Humanism," in *Basic Writings*, pp. 210, 216.

43. Heidegger, "The Word of Nietzsche: 'God is Dead,'" in *The Question Concerning Technology*, p. 112; emphasis added.

44. Löwith, "Heidegger: Thinker in a Destitute Time."

45. Reprinted in Wolin, *The Heidegger Controversy*, pp. 91–116.

46. Jaspers, "Letter to the Denazification Committee of Freiburg University, December 22, 1945," in *The Heidegger Controversy*, pp. 148–49.

ONE
Heidegger: Thinker in a Destitute Time

PREFACE

1. Nietzsche, *Sämtliche Werke: Kritische Studienausgabe*, ed. Giorgio Colli and Mazzino Montinari (Munich: Deutscher Tasschenbuch Verlag/De Gruyter, 1980), vol. 4, p. 101; *Thus Spoke Zarathustra* ("On the Gift Giving Virtue"), ed. Walter Kaufmann (New York: Viking, 1972), p. 78. Hereafter citation to the German edition of Nietzsche's works is to: *Kritische Studienausgabe*, plus volume and page number.

1. DASEIN RESOLUTE UNTO ITSELF, AND BEING WHICH ITSELF GIVES

1. On this see Otto Pöggeler, "Sein als Ereignis" in *Zeitschrift für philosophische Forschung* 13(4) (1959): 604f; see "Being as Appropriation," *Heidegger and Modern Philosophy*, ed. Michael Murray (New Haven, Yale University Press, 1978), pp. 84–115, where the cited passage is part of a section of the essay that has been omitted from the translation; *Der Denkweg Martin Heideggers* (Pfullingen: Neske, 1963); Eng.: *Martin Heidegger's Path of Thinking*, tr. Daniel Magurshak and Sigmund Barber (Atlantic Highlands, N.J.: Humanities Press International, 1987).

2. "Vom Wesen der Wahrheit," *Wegmarken* (2d ed.; Frankfurt-am-Main: Klostermann, 1978), p. 198; "On the Essence of Truth," *Basic Writings*, ed. David Krell (New York: Harper and Row. 1977), p. 140.

3. "Das Wesen der Sprache," *Unterwegs zur Sprache* (7th ed.; Pfullingen: Neske, 1982), pp. 157ff.; "The Nature of Language," *On the Way to Language*, tr. Peter D. Hertz (San Francisco: Harper and Row, 1982), pp. 57ff.

4. "Brief über den 'Humanismus,'" p. 353; "Letter on Humanism," in D. Krell, ed., *Basic Writings*, p. 234.

5. "Der Ursprung des Kunstwerkes," *Holzwege*, 6th ed. (Frankfurt: Klostermann, 1980), p. 48/ "The Origin of the Work of Art," p. 61f.; "Brief über den 'Humanismus,'" p. 352f./ "Letter on Humanism," p. 234.

6. "Der Urpsrung des Kunstwerkes," p. 39/ "The Origin of the Work of Art," *Poetry, Language, Thought*, tr. Albert Hofstadter (New York: Harper Colophon, 1971), p. 53.

7. *Sein und Zeit* (15th ed.; Tübingen: Niemeyer, 1979), p. 38; *Being and Time*, tr., John Macquarrie and Edward Robinson (NewYork: Harper and Row, 1962), p. 62.

8. "Die Sprache," *Unterwegs zur Sprache*, 7th ed., p. 30/ "The Nature of Language," *Poetry, Language, Thought*, p. 207.

9. "Brief über den 'Humanismus,'" p. 359/ "Letter on Humanism," p. 241.

10. "Das Ding," *Vorträge und Aufsätze*, 4th ed. (Pfullingen: Neske, 1978), p. 174/ "The Thing," *Poetry, Language, Thought*, p. 181. "Brief über den 'Humanismus,'" p. 358f./ "Letter on Humanism," p. 240f. Cf. "Das Ende der Philosophie und die Aufgabe des Denkens," *Zur Sache das Denkens*, 2d ed. (Tübingen: Niemeyer, 1976), p. 66/ "The End of Philosophy and the Task of Thinking," *On Time and Being*, tr. Joan Stambaugh (New York: Harper and Row, 1972), p. 59f.

11. "Zur Erörterung der Gelassenheit: Aus einem Feldweggespräch über das Denken," *Gelassenheit*, 7th ed. (Pfullingen: Neske, 1982), p. 64/ "Conversation on a Country Path About Thinking," *Discourse on Thinking*, tr. John M. Anderson and E. Hans Freund (NewYork: Harper and Row, 1969), p. 85.

12. "Nachwort zu: 'Was ist Metaphysik?'" in *Wegmarken*, 2d ed.

13. "Das Wesen der Sprache," *Unterwegs zur Sprache*, p. 189/ "The Nature of Language," p. 84.

14. "Nietzsches Wort: Gott ist tot," *Holzwege*, p. 207/ "The Word of Nietzsche: God is Dead," *The Question Concerning Technology and Other Essays*, tr. William Lovitt (NewYork: Harper and Row, 1977), p. 56.

15. "Der Spruch des Anaximander," *Holzwege*, p. 348/ "The Anaximander Fragment," in *Early Greek Thinking*, tr. David Farrell Krell and Frank Capuzzi (NewYork: Harper and Row, 1975), p. 40. [Translator's note: In the body of the present text, "Der Spruch des Anaximander" has been translated as "The Adage of Anaximander."]

16. "Brief über den 'Humanismus,'" p. 360/ "Letter on Humanism," p. 242.

17. Cf. E. Buddeberg, *Heidegger und die Dichtung: Hölderlin, Rilke* (Stuttgart, 1953, reprinted from *Deutsche Vierteljahrsschrift für Literaturwissenschaft und Geistesgeschichte*, vols. 26 and 27; Tübingen, 1952 and 1953); and B. Allemann, *Hölderlin und Heidegger* (Zurich/Freiburg i. Br., 1954). W. Muschg, *Die Zerstörung der deutschen Literatur* (Bern, 1956), pp. 93–109.

18. *Sein und Zeit*, p. 235n/ *Being and Time*, p. 278n.

1. Dasein Resolute Unto Itself . . .   251

19. "Nietzsches Wort: 'Gott ist tot,'" p. 245/ "The Word of Nietzsche: 'God is Dead,'" p. 94.

20. "Brief über den 'Humanismus,'" p. 323/ "Letter on Humanism," p. 205.

21. "Brief über den 'Humanismus,'" p. 360/ "Letter on Humanism," p. 242.

22. "Hölderlin und das Wesen der Dichtung," *Erläuterungen zu Hölderlin's Dichtung*, 5th ed. (Frankfurt: Klostermann, 1981), p. 47/ "Hölderlin and the Essence of Poetry," *Existence and Being*, tr. Werner Brock (Chicago: Regnery, 1949), p. 313. On a different foundation and with a different intention than Heidegger, Max Weber spoke of the world's loss of the gods on the basis of science; and he proposed not that we wait for the coming of God and the prophets, but rather that we satisfy the requirement of the day. Whoever cannot stand religious everydayness is to present a sacrifice to the intellect and return to the arms of the church.

23. "Brief über den 'Humanismus,'" pp. 311, 330, 357/ "Letter on Humanism," pp. 193, 213, 239. "Wozu Dichter?" *Holzwege*, p. 306; "What Are Poets For?" *Poetry, Language, Thought*, p. 132.

24. Cf. F. Hansen-Löve, "Parusie des Seins? Zu Martin Heideggers neuer Schrift 'Holzwege,'" in *Wort und Wahrheit*, vol. 5, Vienna, January 1950, pp. 60–68; M. Wandruszka, "Etymologie und Philosophie," in *Der Deutschunterricht*, vol. 4 (1958); H. Schweppenhäuser, "Studien über die Heideggersche Sprachtheorie," in *Archiv für Philosophie* 7 (1957): 279–324 and 8 (1958): 116–44.

25. Cf. "Brief über den 'Humanismus,'" p. 327/ "Letter on Humanism," p. 210; "Die Kehre," *Die Technik und der Kehre*, 5th ed. (Pfullingen: Neske, 1982), p. 42/ "The Turning," *The Question Concerning Technology and Other Essays*, p. 43; "Die Frage nach der Technik," *Vorträge und Aufsätze*, p. 33/ "The Question Concerning Technology," *The Question Concerning Technology and Other Essays*, p. 33 and p. 33n27; and especially "Wissenschaft und Besinnung," *Vorträge und Aufsätze*, p. 49/ "Science and Reflection," *The Question Concerning Technology and Other Essays* p. 164f.

26. "Brief über den 'Humanismus,'" p. 332/ "Letter on Humanism," p. 215.

27. "Brief über den 'Humanismus,'" p. 314/ "Letter on Humanism," p. 196.

28. "Zur Erörterung der Gelassenheit: Aus einem Feldweggespräch über das Denken," pp. 39, 62/ "Conversation on a Country Path About Thinking," pp. 66, 83.

29. The objection that it took a century for Hegel to be translated into English does not apply, since Hegel's *conceptual* creations still move in a wholly dialectical fashion within the language of traditional metaphysics and its rationality; and yet Heidegger's language disassociates itself from this very rationality, and as an "overcoming" of onto-theo-logy does not merely seek to avoid all conceptual determinacy but rather proceeds into a "saying non-saying."

30. "Hölderlin und das Wesen der Dichtung," p. 35/ "Hölderlin and the Essence of Poetry," p. 297.

31. *Einführung in die Metaphysik*, volume 40 of the *Gesamtausgabe* (Frankfurt-am-Main: Klostermann, 1983), p. 23; *An Introduction to Metaphysics*, tr. Ralph Manheim (New Haven: Yale University Press, 1959), p. 21.

32. "Wozu Dichter?" p. 315/ "What Are Poets For?" p. 141.
33. See "Der Spruch des Anaxamander," p. 317ff./ "The Anaximander Fragment," pp. 13ff.
34. "Was ist Metaphysik?" *Wegmarken*, p. 116/ "What Is Metaphysics?" *Basic Writings*, p. 107.
35. "Brief über den 'Humanismus,'" p. 228; "Letter on Humanism," p. 345.
36. "Nietzsches Wort: 'Gott ist tot,'" p. 214/ "The Word of Nietzsche: 'God Is Dead,'" p. 62.
37. "Nietzsches Wort: 'Gott ist tot,'" pp. 206, 260/ "The Word of Nietzsche: 'God is Dead,'" pp. 54, 109f.
38. "Die Frage nach der Technik," p. 32/ "The Question Concerning Technology," p. 28; "Die Kehre," p. 40/ "The Turning," p. 42.
39. "Überwindung der Metaphysik," p. 69; "Overcoming Metaphysics," in *The End of Philosophy*, tr. Joan Stambaugh (New York: Harper and Row, 1073), p. 86.
40. "Zur Erörterung der Gelassenheit" p. 30f./ "Conversation on a Country Path," p. 59f.
41. The expression "constellation" is used in contrast to the mere "situation" of human beings, the *condition humaine*.
42. "Gelassenheit," in *Gelassenheit*, pp. 22, 24/ "Memorial Address," *Discourse on Thinking*, pp. 54f.
43. "Wissenschaft und Besinnung," p. 43/ "Science and Reflection," p. 157.
44. *Being and Time*, section 6.
45. The following reflections have sometimes been misunderstood to mean that I want to show that Heidegger falsified his original point of departure in an illegitimate way, although it was explicitly emphasized that his "turning" has its own kind of logic inasmuch as the formulation of the question reverses within itself; in connection with this reversal a "shift in emphasis" takes place that is just as decisive as it is "subtle," namely from Dasein as resolved to itself and asserting itself before the nothing to Being which itself gives, for the understanding of which the Dasein which is always one's own was first of all the "foundation" though it later has only to correspond to the claim of Being and hence is no longer fundamental.

The turning has, as Walter Schulz has explained ("Über den philosophiegeschichtlichen Ort Martin Heideggers," *Philosophische Rundschau* 1 [1953/54]: 90ff.) a double aspect: it is a *further thinking* on the path which has been entered upon, in which the path of thinking is in itself nonetheless *transformed* dialectically. Our critique of the turning is not concerned with this transformation as such, but rather with the fact that in Heidegger's portrayal of himself the reinterpretation of essential concepts remains indiscernible and gets concealed in such a way as to give rise to the appearance that Heidegger actually completed the turning prior to the turning and simply did not yet express it clearly.

The turning is also not simply about an altered "mood," since if attunement is as essential to the disclosedness of Dasein as it is in *Being and Time* then the turn-

1. Dasein Resolute Unto Itself . . .

ing must also be about the substantive content of the analyses and not merely about their tone. On this cf. Heinrich Ott, *Denken und Sein: Der Weg Martin Heideggers und der Weg der Theologie* (Zollikon, 1959), pp. 76ff. Heidegger's own interpretation of the "turning" is included in his preface to William J. Richardson, *Heidegger: Through Phenomenology to Thought* (The Hague: Nijhhoff, 1963).

46. On this cf. Karl Löwith, "M. Heidegger und F. Rosenzweig. Ein Nachtrag zu *Sein und Zeit*," in *Heidegger—Denker in dürftiger Zeit: Zur Stellung der Philosophie im 20. Jahrhundert, Sämtliche Schriften*, vol. 8 (Stuttgart: J. B. Metzler, 1984), pp. 72–101.

47. "Der Feldweg," (Frankfurt: Klostermann, 1953); also in *Aus der Erfahrung des Denkens (1910–1976)*, vol. 13 of the *Gesamtausgabe* (Frankfurt: Klostermann, 1983), pp. 87–90; "The Pathway," trs. Thomas F. O'Meara, O.P., *Listening: Current Studies in Dialog* 2, no. 2 (Spring 1967): 88–91.

48. *Sein und Zeit*, p. 324/ *Being and Time*, p. 370f.

49. *Holzwege*, page immediately preceding table of contents.

50. "Der Spruch des Anaximander," p. 344/ "The Anaximander Fragment," p. 36.

51. "Brief über den 'Humanismus'" p. 339/ "Letter on Humanism" p. 222; "Einleitung zu: 'Was ist Metaphysik?'" *Wegmarken*, 2d ed., p. 369/ "The Way Back Into the Ground of Metaphysics," in *Existentialism from Dostoevsky to Sartre*, ed. and tr. Walter Kaufmann (Cleveland: Meridian Books, 1969), p. 214.

52. "Brief über den 'Humanismus,'" p. 340/ "Letter on Humanism," p. 223.

53. *Sein und Zeit*, p. 437/ *Being and Time*, p. 487f.

54. *Sein und Zeit*, p. 3/ *Being and Time*, p. 22.

55. The first indication of the problem of the ontic-ontological difference, i.e., of the distinction between Being and beings, which is developed in *Being and Time*, is already contained in Heidegger's habilitation essay on *Die Kategorien- und Bedeutungslehre des Duns Scotus*, where it is said in the final chapter that a philosophy of living spirit cannot be content with the "spelling out of reality" (of beings) but rather must aim beyond the totality of the knowable and toward a breakthrough into true actuality and the actual truth. *Frühe Schriften* (Frankfurt: Klostermann, 1972), p. 348. For this it is necessary to bring new meaning to the dimension of the soul which extends into the "transcendent" and which gave the Christian philosophy of the middle ages its orientation, in contrast to the two-dimensional modern way of life and its "superficial breadth," lacking rootedness in the absolute spirit of God and in the transcendent "primordial relation of the soul to God." *Frühe Schriften*, p. 351.

If one translates "true actuality" and "actual truth" as "truth of Being" and "Being of truth," the dimension of "spiritual life" that extends into the transcendent as "*ek-sistence*," "God" as "Being," and the "becoming lost" of contemporary humans in the "substantive breadth of the sensible world" as falling into the world and abandonment of Being, then one can recognize the later Heidegger in his habilitation essay. Even the dialectical "correspondence" between Being and human existence is already sketched out distinctly in a language still conditioned by a philosophy of life and of value. To wit, transcendence is not supposed to signify an unconditional removal of the subject but rather only the one pole of a "correlative" life context, so that the positing of value does not gravitate exclusively into the transcendent but instead rests in the individual, so to speak, via the reflection of the transcendent, in spite of the weight of the other side of this correlation.

If one may assume with Heidegger that essential thinking always thinks only *one* thought and that in every thinker of stature the essential thought is there already from the start, then the analytic of Dasein resolved upon itself, which reaches its acme in the doubly emphasized "freedom toward death" (*Sein und Zeit*, p. 266/ *Being and Time*, p. 311), would signify only an *intermediate stage* and Heidegger's "turning" toward Being/ which itself gives, would be a return to his theological beginning.

56. "Der Spruch des Anaximander," p. 340/ "The Anaximander Fragment," p. 33.

57. "Brief über den 'Humanismus,'" p. 339/ "Letter on Humanism," p. 222.

58. "Wozu Dichter?" pp. 292ff./ "What Are Poets For?" pp. 118ff.; "Einleitung zu: 'Was ist Metaphysik?'" p. 363/ "The Way Back Into the Ground of Metaphysics," p. 209.

59. *Sein und Zeit*, p. 38/ *Being and Time*, p. 62.

60. *Sein und Zeit*, sections 7 and 83.

61. *Sein und Zeit*, p. 12/ *Being and Time*, p. 32.

62. "Brief über den 'Humanismus,'" p. 339/ "Letter on Humanism," p. 222.

63. "Was ist Metaphysik?" *Wegmarken*, p. 121/ "What Is Metaphysics?" *Basic Writings*, p. 112.

64. On this cf. Karl Löwith, *Wissen, Glaube, Skepsis* (*Sämtliche Schriften*, vol. 3), ch. 4: "Schöpfung und Existenz"; and Eugen Fink, *Alles und Nichts*, 1959, pp. 196ff.

65. "Nachwort zu: 'Was ist Metaphysik?'" *Wegmarken*, 2d ed., p. 305.

66. "Was ist Metaphysik?" p. 116f.; "What Is Metaphysics?" p. 108.

67. In a retrospective reinterpretation conducted thirty years after *Being and Time*, it is said that "understanding of Being" is supposed to mean "that human beings, in accordance with their essence, stand in the open of the projection of Being and endure this understanding." In the same way there is a turning in the meaning of "attunement," which in *Being and Time* signifies the disposition of one's own Dasein and later signifies the "voice of Being," which attunes and determines our attentive corresponding. *Was ist Das—Die Philosophie?* 8th ed. (Pfulllingen: Neske, 1984), p. 29.

68. "Die Kehre," *Die Technik und die Kehre*, p. 39/ "The Turning," *The Question Concerning Technology and Other Essays*, p. 39.

69. "Die Kehre," p. 38/ "The Turning," p. 38. Cf. *Identität und Differenz*, p.

1. Dasein Resolute Unto Itself . . .   255

18f. / *Identity and Difference*, tr. Joan Stambaugh (New York: Harper and Row, 1969), p. 31.

70. "Logos," *Vorträge und Aufsätze*. p. 209/ "Logos," *Early Greek Thinking*, p. 67f.

71. "Zur Seinsfrage," *Wegmarken*, 2d ed., pp. 379–419; *The Question of Being*, tr. with an intro. by Jean T. Wilde and William Kluback (New Haven: College and University Press, 1958).

72. *Was Heißt Denken?* (4th ed.; Tübingen, Niemeyer, 1984), p.73f.; *What Is Called Thinking?* tr. J. Glenn Gray (New York: Harper Colophon, 1968), p. 79. Cf. *Unterwegs zur Sprache*, p. 188/ *On the Way to Language*, p. 83.

73. "Das Wesen der Sprache," *Unterwegs zur Sprache*, p. 215/ "The Nature of Language," *On the Way to Language*, p. 107. Cf. "Der Weg zur Sprache," p. 267/ "The Way to Language," p. 135.

74. "Brief über den 'Humanismus,'" p. 333/ "Letter on Humanism," p. 216.

75. Section 7, "The Phenomenological Method of Investigation."

76. "Der Spruch des Anaximander," p. 332/ "The Anaximander Fragment," p. 26.

77. "Brief über den 'Humanismus,'" p. 329/ "Letter on Humanism," p. 211.

78. "Einleitung zu: 'Was ist Metaphysik?'" p. 365/ "The Way Back into the Ground of Metaphysics," p. 210.

79. *Sein und Zeit*, p. 220/ *Being and Time*, p. 263.

80. In the *Introduction to Metaphysics* the same thought is expressed in the following way: humans—the "most uncanny" of all essences—can deny Being the possibility of appearing. "This arrogance (which in truth is the highest acknowledgment) is part of the violence of what is most uncanny: to overpower the evident dominion by denying all openness in the face of that dominion, to become a match for it to the extent that its omnipotence is closed off from the place for its appearance. But for Dasein, the denial of such openness in the face of Being means nothing other than: the surrender of its essence. This requires: departing from Being, or rather never entering into Dasein. . . . Here the most uncanny possibility of Dasein becomes apparent: in the most extreme act of violence against itself, to break the ascendancy [*Übergewalt*] of Being. Dasein does not have this possibility as an empty way out, but rather *is* this possibility, to the extent that it is." *Einführung in die Metaphysik*, p. 185f. / *An Introduction to Metaphysics*, p. 176f.

81. *Sein und Zeit*, p. 230/ *Being and Time*, p. 272.

82. See "Einleitung zu: 'Was ist Metaphysik?'" p. 367f. /"The Way Back Into the Ground of Metaphysics," p. 212; *Einführung in die Metaphysik,* pp. 171f. and 213f. / *An Introduction to Metaphysics,* pp. 162f. and 204f.; "Der Spruch des Anaximander," p. 361ff. /"The Anaximander Fragment," p. 51ff.; "Die Frage nach der Technik," pp. 37f. /"The Question Concerning Technology," p. 33f.; "Überwindung der Metaphysik," p. 95 /"Overcoming Metaphysics," in *The End of Philosophy*, p. 110; *Was heißt Denken?* pp. 114ff. / *What Is Called Thinking?* pp. 186ff.; "Der

Satz der Identität," *Identität und Differenz*, pp. 20ff. /"The Principle of Identity," in *Identity and Difference*, pp. 32ff.; *Der Satz vom Grund* (Pfullingen: Neske, 1978), pp. 146 and 157/ *The Principle of Reason*, tr. Reginald Lilly (Bloomington: Indiana University Press, 1991), pp. 86 and 93; "Zur Erörterung der Gelassenheit," pp. 64ff. /"Conversation on a Country Path," pp. 84ff.; *Unterwegs zur Sprache*, pp. 30, 155, 197, 254, 260f. /"Language," p. 207, *On the Way to Language*, pp. 54, 91, 123f., 129f.

83. "Brief über den 'Humanismus,'" p. 342/ "Letter on 'Humanism,'" p. 224.

84. On this cf. Karl Löwith, "Mensch und Geschichte," now *Sämtliche Schriften*, vol. 2: *Weltgeschichte und Heilsgeschehen* (Stuttgart: Metzler, 1983), pp. 346–76; "Natur und Humanität des Menschen," and "Die Sprache als Vermittler von Mensch und Welt," in Karl Löwith, *Gesammelte Abhandlungen: Zur Kritik der geschichtlichen Existenz* (Stuttgart: Kohlhammer, 1960).

85. Theodor Litt, "Die Weltbedeutung des Menschen," in *Zeitschrift für philosophische Forschung* 4 (1949).

86. *Kant und das Problem der Metaphysik*, 4th ed. (Frankfurt: Klostermann, 1973), p. 222/ *Kant and the Problem of Metaphysics*, tr. James S. Churchill (Bloomington: Indiana University Press, 1975), p. 236.

87. *Kant und das Problem der Metaphysik*, p. 239/ *Kant and the Problem of Metaphysics*, p. 254.

88. "Brief über den 'Humanismus,'" p. 336f. / "Letter on Humanism," p. 219f.

89. "Nachwort zu: 'Was ist Metaphysik?'" p. 305.

90. "Einleitung zu: 'Was ist Metaphysik?'" p. 371/ "The Way Back into the Ground of Metaphysics," p. 215.

91. "Hölderlin und das Wesen der Dichtung," p. 39/ "Hölderlin and the Essence of Poetry," p. 302.

92. "Andenken," *Hölderlins Dichtung*, p. 145.

93. "Der Urpsrung des Kunstwerkes," *Holzwege*, p. 64/ "The Origin of the Work of Art," *Poetry, Language, Thought*, p. 78.

94. Hölderlin, "Die Wanderung," second strophe; cf. "Andenken," pp. 145ff.

95. "Der Urpsrung des Kunstwerkes," p. 62/ "The Origin of the Work of Art," p. 76.

96. "Der Feldweg," p. 90/ "The Pathway," p. 91.

97. "Einleitung zu: 'Was ist Metaphysik?'" p. 361/ "The Way Back Into the Ground of Metaphysics," p. 207.

98. "Einleitung zu: 'Was ist Metaphysik?'" p. 363/ "The Way Back Into the Ground of Metaphysics," p. 209; "Brief über den 'Humanismus,'" p. 327f. / "Letter on Humanism," p. 221.

99. "Wozu Dichter?" *Holzwege*, p. 293/ "What Are Poets For?" *Poetry, Language, Thought*, p. 119.

100. *Was Heißt Denken?* p. 74/ *What Is Called Thinking?* p. 79f.

101. "Brief über den 'Humanismus,'" p. 314/ "Letter on Humanism," p. 196.

102. *Sein und Zeit*, p. 25/ *Being and Time*, p. 47.

1. Dasein Resolute Unto Itself . . . 257

103. "Die Kehre," pp. 43ff. / "The Turning," pp. 45ff. Cf. "Logos," pp. 214ff. / "Logos," pp. 72ff.

104. *Was ist Das—Die Philosophie?* p. 23.

105. "Was ist Metaphysik?" p. 105 / "What Is Metaphysics?" p. 97. *Kant und das Problem der Metaphysik,* p. 221 / *Kant and the Problem of Metaphysics,* p. 235.

106. See "Brief über den 'Humanismus,'" pp. 329, 333 / "Letter on Humanism," pp. 211f., 216.

107. Cf. Max Müller, *Existenzphilosophie im geistigen Leben der Gegenwart* (Heidelberg: F. H. Kerle, 1949), p. 75f. In a manner different than Müller's, Walter Schulz sought to illuminate the contradiction in the afterwords to the fourth and fifth editions of "What Is Metaphysics?" as a dialectical identity, in order to conclude his discussion with the lapidary assertion: "The fourth and fifth editions mean the same thing" ("Über den philosophiegeschichtlichen Ort Martin Heideggers," p. 212f.). Schulz is certainly right when he emphasizes that it would be nonsensical to reflect on Being and Dasein as if they were two objectively opposed media between which commerce takes place. But he is wrong when he misconstrues their "standing opposite" by maintaining that one can reflect on the relation between Being and extant Dasein only on the basis of the latter, because "Being" is nothing other than the meaning of Being for me [*mein Seinssinn*—literally "my sense of Being"—tr.]. "The meaning of 'empty Dasein' is the nothing, and the meaning of 'extant Dasein' is Being." It is on this basis that the apparent contradiction in Heidegger's assertions regarding the relationship between Being and beings is to be understood and resolved. Both assertions are, from different standpoints, assertions of my "self-understanding."

Against this view it should be noted that the nonobjectivity of Being which essences, like the nonobjectivity of Dasein which exists, so little excludes the "mutual opposition of Being and the human essence" (*Der Satz vom Grund,* p. 158 / *The Principle of Reason,* p. 94) that Heidegger characterizes this standing opposite precisely as *the* "destining of Being" and says on the other hand of humans that they *are* precisely "the relation of correspondence" ("Der Satz der Identität," p. 18 / "The Principle of Identity," p. 31). Without such a "mutual opposition" there could be no correspondence, and humans and Being could not be "assigned to one another." The To-one-another excludes their being the same and embraces their distinctness.

Hence when Heidegger crossed out the word "Being" in "The Question of Being" in order to dispel the view that Being is something ab-solute, something which subsists as free for itself, and something that is not dependent on us humans nor something "needing" us (this "supposition" *sustaining everything,* we are assured by Schulz, is "correct"!), he thereby says something entirely different than in Schulz's interpretation, according to which Being is supposed to be simply the meaning of Being for me or the "*pure* condition" of my power and impotence. A Being that eventuates us and assigns itself to us, that exerts a claim upon us and pre-thinks and addresses us and grants us grace, can be neither the mere meaning of Being for me nor a concept for reflection in transcendental philosophy. In the midst of its relation and withdrawl, it must in itself eventuate and make a claim, and it must be distinguished from human Dasein. But on a certain level of reflection, interpretive acumen appears to become incapable of acknoweldging a simple and evident distinction within a relation.

Heidegger himself characterizes the unresolvable distinction between Being and the human essence with the words "correspondence" and "assignment" of the one to the other. This two-sided assignment, which only from a distance is reminiscent of the onesidedly existential concept of Dasein as "always one's own" and "authentic," is grounded for its own part in the "relationship" of all relationships. At first Heidegger called this relationship the "domain of the relation" ("Vom Wesen der Wahrheit," *Wegmarken*, p. 182 /"On the Essence of Truth," *Basic Writings*, p. 124) and in the "Letter on Humanism" he called it the equivalent of "Being" because it, like Being, in itself maintains ek-sistence ("Brief über den 'Humanismus,'" p. 329 /"Letter on Humanism," p. 211); and Heidegger now calls it the "Event," though he does not simply equate Being and Event. There is nothing to say about the Event [*Ereignis*] except that it "inheres" [*eignet*] ("Der Weg zur Sprache," p. 259 /"The Way to Language," p. 128).

Already in the lecture on "The Thing," there was talk of the "rondo [*Reigen*—this also suggests a marriage dance (tr.)] of the event." The unity of the "fourfold," of sky and earth, mortals and immortals, "essences as the eventuating mirror-play of those which are in each other's simple trust." ("Das Ding," *Vorträge und Aufsätze*, p. 173 /"The Thing," *Poetry, Language, Thought*, p. 180.) "The intersection [*Vierung*—literally "fouring" in the sense of a unified foursome—tr.] essences as the worlding of world. The mirror-play of world is the rondo of the Event. Therefore the rondo does not first embrace the Four as a circle. The rondo is the ring that joins [*ringt*] by playing as the mirroring. By eventuating, the rondo clears the Four into the radiance of their simplicity. The ring radiantly unifies the Four, everywhere open to the puzzle of their essence. The gathered essence of the mirror-play of the world, which joins in this way, is the Gather-ring [*das Gering*]. In the Gather-ring of the ring that mirrors and plays, the Four nestle into their essence, on which they are all in accord and which is nonetheless specific to each. Nestling in this way, they ordain the world, worlding in a way which ordains." "Das Ding" p. 173/ "The Thing," *Poetry, Language, Thought* p. 180.

One may ask whether one can take this thought-play with words quite seriously without becoming comical even to himself. Whereas Ludwig Wittgenstein's "language games" examine language as an inadequate instrument with respect to scientific exactness, Heidegger's driving seriousness treats language as useless conversation with oneself, "for philosophical problems arise when language *goes on holiday* [*feiert*]." Wittgenstein, *Philosophische Untersuchungen*, (Frankfurt-am-Main: Suhrkamp, 1977), Paragraph 38, p. 39/ *Philosophical Investigations*, tr. G. E. M. Anscombe (New York: Macmillan, 1968), p. 19.

108. "Nachwort zu: 'Was ist Metaphysik?" p. 304. Cf. "Was ist Metaphysik?" p. 113/ "What Is Metaphysics?" p. 105.

109. "Nachwort zu: 'Was ist Metaphysik?'" pp. 307–9.
110. "Platons Lehre von der Wahrheit," *Wegmarken*, p. 235f./ "Plato's Doctrine of Truth," in *Philosophy in the Twentieth Century*, ed. William Barrett and Henry Aiken (NewYork: Random House, 1962), p. 269f.
111. "Brief über den 'Humanismus,'" p. 350/ "Letter on Humanism," p. 232.
112. Cf. the motto from Novalis at the end of Heidegger's habilitation essay: "Everywhere we seek the unconditioned [*das Unbedingte*] and always find only things [*Dinge*]." "Die Kategorien und Bedeutungslehre des Duns Scotus," *Frühe Schriften*, p. 341.

2. HISTORY, HISTORICALITY, AND DESTINING OF BEING

1. "Die Zeit. Vortrag gehalten am 26.VII.24 vor der Marburger Theologenschaft." Unpublished *Nachschrift* prepared by Karl Löwith; published in an English-German edition as *The Concept of Time*, tr. William McNeill (Oxford: Blackwell, 1992), pp. 1–2 and 1E–2E.
2. What for us is missing in Heidegger's publications to date is not so much the second part of *Being and Time* as division three on "Time and Being," which had been planned in the first part—*Sein und Zeit*, p. 39/ *Being and Time*, p. 63f.—and which was to have brought the turning from "Being and *Time*" to "*Time* and Being."
3. "Hölderlin und Wesen der Dichtung," p. 47/ "Hölderlin and the Essence of Poetry," p. 313.
4. "Holderlin und Wesen der Dichtung," p. 47/ "Holderlin and the Essence of Being," p. 313.
5. "Der Spruch des Anaximander," p. 323/ "The Anaximander Fragment," p. 18.
6. "Nietzsches Wort: 'Gott ist tot,'" p. 206/ "The Word of Nietzsche: 'God is Dead,'" p. 54. On this cf. Gerhard Krüger, "M. Heidegger und der Humanismus: Zur Auseinandersetzung mit den Schriften 'Platons Lehre von der Wahrheit' und 'Brief über den Humanismus,'" in *Studia Philosophica* 9 (1949): 126f. In Heidegger's judgment, even Hegel's historical thinking is rooted in common world-time. For Hegel, "spirit" does indeed essentially fall into time in order to unfold in it, but spirit itself is not temporal. Time has no power over the "Notion," but instead the latter is the power of time, and for Hegel true time is the present understood in Aristotelian terms as a revolving eternity. In contrast to Hegel, Heidegger says that spirit does not first fall into time but rather exists as the primordial bringing about [*Zeitigung*] of temporality.
7. *Sein und Zeit*, p. 384/ *Being and Time*, p. 435.
8. *Being and Time*, Division 2, chapter 5.
9. *Sein und Zeit*, pp. 249ff., 425/ *Being and Time*, pp. 293ff., 477.
10. *Die Selbstbehauptung der deutschen Universität: Rede, gehalten bei der feierlichen Übernahme des Rektorats der Universität Freiburg i. Br. am 27.5.1933. Das Rektorat 1933/34: Tatsachen und Gedanken* (Frankfurt-am-Main: Klostermann, 1983);

"The Self-Assertion of the German University," in *The Heidegger Controversy: A Critical Reader*, ed. Richard Wolin (Cambridge: MIT Press, 1993), pp. 29–39.

11. "[Bekenntnis zu Adolf Hitler und dem nationalsozialistischen Staat]," *Nachlese zu Heidegger*, p. 150/ "Declaration of Support for Adolf Hitler and the National Socialist State (November 11, 1933)," *The Heidegger Controversy*, p. 52.

12. On this see Karl Löwith, "Les implications politiques de la philosophie de l'existence chez Heidegger" in *Les Temps Modernes* (November 1946 and August 1948); cf. Löwith, *Sämtliche Schriften*, vol. 2: *Weltgeschichte und Heilsgeschehen* (Stuttgart: J. B. Metzlersche Verlagsbuchhandlung, 1983), pp. 473ff. and 614ff.; cf. also Karl Löwith, "Der okkasionelle Dezisionismus von Carl Schmitt," translated below as "The Occasional Decisionism of Carl Schmitt."

13. Karl Barth, *Theological Existence To-Day! (A Plea for Theological Freedom)*, tr. R. Birch Hoyle (London: Hodder and Stoughton, 1933), p. 9.

14. "Der Spruch des Anaximander," p. 332f./ "The Anaximander Fragment," p. 26f.

15. See Heidegger's rectorial address (Breslau, 1933). On this cf. Guido Schneeberger's *Ergänzungen zu einer Heidegger-Bibliographie: Mit vier Beilagen und einer Bildtafel* (Bern: 1960), pp. 13ff. Only at one point in the writings from the years 1936 to 1946 ("Überwindung der Metaphysik," *Vorträge und Aufsätze*, p. 86, "Overcoming Metaphysics," p. 102) did Heidegger call into question his own assumption of this "mission," though he did so only indirectly, namely with respect to the National Socialist leadership. For because the will to will denies every goal in itself, though not as the anarchy of catastrophe which this will is or can appear to be, it legitimates itself with talk of a "mission" and a "fate." Later, the one charged with a mission by a historical fate becomes one who is "needed" by Being and language and who attentively belongs into the "Event."

16. In E. Barlach (Darmstadt, 1951).

17. "Brief über den 'Humanismus,'" p. 332/ "Letter on Humanism," p. 215.

18. "Die Kehre," p. 44/ "The Turning," p. 47.

19. Already Heidegger's habilitation essay on Duns Scotus closes with a reference to the need for a confrontation with Hegel's historiological *Weltanschauung* of living spirit. There it is said in an entirely Hegelian way: "Spirit can be grasped only when the entire fullness of its accomplishments, that is its *history*, becomes sublated in it, where along with this constantly growing fullness in its philosophical conceptualization an ever-improving means for the living conceptualization of the absolute spirit of God is given." *Frühe Schriften*, p. 350. With this concept of living spirit, an insight is to be opened up into the inner belonging-together of history and philosophy, change and absolute validity, time and eternity.

20. "Der Spruch des Anaximander," p. 319/ "The Anaximander Fragment," p. 14.

21. *Einführung in die Metaphysik*, p. 53/ *An Introduction to Metaphysics*, p. 50.

22. *Der Satz vom Grund*, pp. 143ff./ *The Principle of Reason*, pp. 84ff.

2. History, Historicality, and Destining of Being 261

23. In a discussion of Heidegger's "Letter on Humanism" (*Sinn und Form*, Berlin, 1949), Georg Lukács took a position on Heidegger's assessment of communism. Heidegger stands the relationship between common and authentic history on its head by transforming actually extant history into a mythologized pseudo-history of Being. The opposition between traditional metaphysics of beings and the originary thinking of Being simply repeats the conflict, characteristic of the age of capitalism, between "civilization" and "culture" (Spengler) or between "spirit" and "soul" (Klages). Of course Heidegger recognizes the inner belonging-together of the private and public spheres of modern life, both of which are far removed from an essential Being-human, though he attempts an illusory escape into a third dimension which, under the title "Being," leads into the nameless Nothing. Hence social reality remains just as closed off from the "essential" thinking of Heidegger as from the private existentialism of Jaspers and Sartre. [See translator's note i, p. 81.]

24. *Sein und Zeit*, p. 22 / *Being and Time*, p. 44.

25. "Die Selbstbehauptung der deutschen Universität," p. 19 / "The Self-Assertion of the German University," p. 38.

26. "Hölderlin und das Wesen der Dichtung," p. 47 / "Hölderlin and the Essence of Poetry," p. 314.

27. "Der Spruch des Anaximander," p. 321f. / "The Anaximander Fragment," p. 17.

28. "Der Spruch des Anaximander," p. 321f. / "The Anaximander Fragment," p. 17.

29. "Nietzsches Wort: 'Gott ist tot,'" p. 259f. / "The Word of Nietzsche: 'God is Dead,'" p. 109.

30. "Wozu Dichter?" pp. 291ff. / "What Are Poets For?" pp. 117ff.

31. "Platons Lehre von der Wahrheit," pp. 216ff. / "Plato's Doctrine of Truth," pp. 257ff.

32. On this cf. Gerhard Krüger's critical remarks on Heidegger's interpretation of Plato in "M. Heidegger und der Humanismus," p. 126f. and H.J. Krämer, *Arete bei Platon und Aristoteles*, Heidelberger Akademie der Wissenschaft, 1959, p. 555.

33. "Nietzsches Wort: 'Gott ist tot,'" p. 216 / "The Word of Nietzsche: 'God is Dead,'" p. 64.

34. E. Vietta, *Die Seinsfrage bei M. Heidegger*, Stuttgart, 1950, p. 22.

35. "Der Spruch des Anaximander," p. 324; "The Anaximander Fragment," p. 19. Cf. Otto Pöggeler, "Sein als Ereignis" p. 629 ("Being as Appropriation," *Heidegger and Modern Philosophy*, p. 112), where it is said that the binding character of Heidegger's thinking does not derive from substantive evidence but rather is supposed to develop on the basis of conveying "the Event" and enduring a destining. When "binding character" is understood in this way, all critical verifiability is *a priori* rejected by Heidegger and his adherents. Then what is ultimately true is whatever is timely in the sense that it suitably corresponds to a destin-

ing—as if the destining of a history, understood as it has always been, could in each case instruct us as to what is true and what is false.

36. *Being and Time*, sections 48 and 49.

37. Later, in the lecture on "The Origin of the Work of Art," nature is distinguished as "earth" from the historical world. It is that toward which and in which historical humans ground their dwelling in the world. Earth itself is essentially "that which withdraws" and which first of all comes into the openness of a world through the work of humans. Again, a few years later Heidegger speaks of the favor that permeates [*durchwalten*—literally "to rule (or to preside, or to be) throughout" (tr.)] "earth and sky" and which grants something that remains. In a lecture on "The Thing," "world" is the "fourfold" of "sky and earth, divinities and mortals." The "worldliness of the world," understood existentially, is as distinct from the four world-regions of the "fourfold" as the Being-toward-death, which is always one's own, is distinct from the later talk of humans as "mortals," talk which seizes upon the Greek experience of Being-human and which nonetheless is fundamentally distinct from that experience inasmuch as it lacks the presence of immortal gods.

38. *Sein und Zeit*, p. 65/ *Being and Time*, p. 94.

39. *Being and Time*, section 11.

40. "Vom Wesen des Grundes," p. 154n/ *The Essence of Reasons*, German-English edition, tr. Terence Malick (Evanston, Ill.: Northwestern University Press, 1969), p. 81n.

41. "Brief über den 'Humanismus,'" pp. 323f., 338/ "Letter on Humanism," pp. 206, 221. In the "Letter on Humanism" it is said that our "scarcely conceivable" bodily relatedness to animals points toward an essential distance between organic nature and ek-sistent human nature, which is so immeasurable that in relation to it the essence of the divine stands closer to us. "Brief über den 'Humanismus,'" p. 323/ "Letter on Humanism," p. 206.

42. "Vom Wesen der Wahrheit," *Wegmarken*, p. 187/ "On the Essence of Truth," *Basic Writings*, p. 129.

43. On this see Heidegger's interpretive translation of Aristotle's *Physics* B1 in *Il Pensiero* 3, nos. 2 and 3 (1958) (now *Wegmarken*, pp. 237ff.). Cf. *Der Satz vom Grund*, p. 187 (*The Principle of Reason*, p. 112f.), where the "unsaid" in the Greek word *aion* (Heraclitus, Fragment 52) is translated as "destining of Being."

44. See "Wie wenn am Feiertage . . . ," *Erläuterungen zu Hölderlins Dichtung*, 5th ed., pp. 49–77, especially pp. 56ff. and 63ff.

45. Cf. Gerhard Krüger, "M. Heidegger und der Humanismus," p. 125.

46. "Brief über den 'Humanismus,'" pp. 328, 333, 359f./ "Letter on Humanism," pp. 210, 216, 241f.

47. "Brief über den 'Humanismus,'" p. 328/ "Letter on Humanism," p. 210.

48. See Max Müller, *Existenzphilosophie im geistigen Leben der Gegenwart*, pp. 38ff. and 53ff. Of course it is correct that what is distinctive in Heidegger's thinking lies precisely in this fusion of essence and history, though this does not

mean that the problem posed by historiological consciousness has been solved but rather that it has been made more pressing. We are not indebted to Heidegger for a new eternal truth beyond the temporality of Being and the historicality of essence, and hence for a "synthesis of absoluteness and relativity," which Müller justifies by suggesting that on the one hand modern historiological consciousness can no longer be retracted and that on the other hand we must seize upon the question of essence in a *philosophia perennis*; rather, we are indebted to Heidegger for making new demands through the intensity of his questioning.

49. Already in his critique of Husserl and Heidegger (*Lebensphilosophie und Phänomenologie*), G. Misch pointed out this remarkable ahistoricality in Heidegger's concept of happening, in order to validate Dilthey's historical concept in contrast to the "Adamitic" concept of happening in *Being and Time*.

50. On this cf. Karl Löwith, *Weltgeschichte und Heilsgeschehen*, and the lecture on "Natur und Geschichte" in *Neuer Rundschau* 1 (1951), now in *Sämtliche Schriften* 2: 7ff. and 280ff.

51. "Der Spruch des Anaximander," p. 317/ "The Anaximander Fragment," p. 51.

52. "Brief über den 'Humanismus,'" p. 336/ "Letter on Humanism," p. 219.

53. On this cf. Karl Löwith, *J. Burckhardt, der Mensch inmitten der Geschichte* (Lucerne: 1956); now *Sämtliche Schriften*, vol. 7: *Jacob Burckhardt* (Stuttgart: Metzler, 1984); and "Mensch und Geschichte," *Sämtliche Schriften*, vol. 2: *Weltgeschichte und Heilsgeschehen*, pp. 346–76 (originally *Gesammelte Abhandlungen*, chapter 5, pp. 152–78).

3. THE INTERPRETATION OF THE UNSAID IN "NIETZSCHE'S WORD 'GOD IS DEAD'"

1. "Nietzsches Wort: 'Gott ist tot,'" pp. 207, 263; "The Word of Nietzsche: 'God is Dead,'" pp. 56, 112.

2. "Brief über den 'Humanismus,'" pp. 312f., 350ff.; "Letter on Humanism," pp. 194f., 232ff.

3. *Kritische Studienausgabe*, vol. 9 (Nachlaß, 1880), p. 52.

4. *On the Genealogy of Morals*, ed. Walter Kaufmann (New York: Random House, 1989), Third Essay, section 24. Cf. *Kritische Studienausgabe*, vol. 11 (Nachlaß, 1884), pp. 88, 95, 155; *Kritische Studienausgabe*, vol. 4, p. 340; *Thus Spoke Zarathustra*, ed. Walter Kaufmann (New York: Viking, 1978), p. 274.

5. *On the Genealogy of Morals*, Third Essay, section 24; *Beyond Good and Evil*, ed. Walter Kaufmann (New York: Random House, 1989), section 210.

6. *Ontologie (Hermeneutik der Faktizität)*, volume 63 of the *Gesamtausgabe* (Frankfurt-am-Main: Klostermann, 1988).

7. "Die Frage nach der Technik," p. 22; "The Question Concerning Technology," p. 19.

8. "Der Spruch des Anaximander," p. 324; "The Anaximander Fragment," p. 19.

9. "Nachwort zu: 'Was ist Metaphysik?'" p. 302.
10. In *M. Heideggers Einfluß auf die Wissenschaften* (Bern: 1949), p. 73ff.
11. Cf. *Concluding Unscientific Postscript*, Book Two, part two, ch. 3.
12. *Sein und Zeit*, p. 145/ *Being and Time*, p. 185.
13. *Sein und Zeit,* pp. 149ff./ *Being and Time,* pp. 190ff.
14. See H. Kuhn, "Heideggers 'Holzwege,'" in *Archiv für Philosophie* (Stuttgart, 1952), vol. 4, no. 3, pp. 253–69. What is conducted explicitly is a self-interpretation through the text of another in Heidegger's interpretation of Kant's *Foundations of Metaphysics*. This is supposed to help bring Heidegger's interpretation to its own "more primordial possibility"; but in actuality it helps Heidegger in substantiating historically the questioning of *Being and Time* with regard to what Kant may have wanted to say, and it helps him in setting aside all prior understandings of Kant as nonprimordial. On this see H. Levy, "Heideggers Kantinterpretation; zu Heideggers Buch: Kant und das Problem der Metaphysik," in *Logos*, vol. 21 (Tübingen, 1932), pp. 1–43.
15. Rudolf Bultmann, "Das Problem der Hermeneutik," in *Glauben und Verstehen*, vol. 2, 1952, p. 228. [Translator's note: Rudolf Bultmann (1884–1976) was an existentialist Protestant theologian who taught at Marburg.] Cf. Hans-Georg Gadamer, "Vom Zirkel des Verstehens," in *Martin Heidegger zum siebzigsten Geburtstag: Festschrift* (Pfullingen: Neske, 1959), pp. 24–34. Against these, cf. Heidegger's remark on the "superficiality" [*Vordergründigkeit*] of talk of the circle in "Aus einem Gespräch von der Sprache," *Unterwegs zur Sprache*, 7th ed., pp. 134 and 150f./ "A Dialogue on Language," *On the Way to Language*, pp. 39 and 50f.
16. We are leaving aside the special possibility and necessity of interpreting something that has been said with special reference to something thath has not been said, namely when the genuine thought has intentionally been left unexpressed, concealed, or masked in order within a public context to address only the secret initiates. This is always the case when, as a result of ecclesiastical or political persecution, that which is genuine in a publication can be said only *privatim*, between the lines, so that from the very start the interpretation must distinguish between the exoteric and the esoteric meaning of an assertion. On this see Leo Strauss, *Persecution and the Art of Writing* (New York: Free Press, 1952).
17. *Being and Time*, section 26. On this see Karl Löwith, "Das Individuum in der Rolle des Mitmenschen," in *Sämtliche Schriften*, vol. 1, pp. 9ff., especially section 21.
18. *Sein und Zeit*, p. 250f./ *Being and Time*, p. 294.
19. See the preface to the second edition of Heidegger's book on Kant: *Kant und das Problem der Metaphysik*, 4th ed. (Frankfurt: Klostermann, 1973), p. xiv; *Kant and the Problem of Metaphysics*, tr. James S. Churchill (Bloomington: Indiana University Press, 1975), p. xxv. At the end of section 35 (German, p. 196; English, p. 207), the necessity of violence is grounded in the idea that an interpretation depends not on understanding what an author said explicitly, but rather on "wresting" from him what he did not say but "meant to say." In order to do so,

3. The Unsaid in "Nietzsche's Word 'God Is Dead'" 265

one must entrust oneself to the concealed passion of a work and let oneself be forced into saying the unsaid. Hence the interpretation that forces the text gets justified by a force that is supposed to proceed from out of the text to be interpreted. A two-sided force takes the place of an interpretation that critically distinguishes itself from one's own opinion of the text.

20. "Hegels Begriff der Erfahrung" (1942/3), *Holzwege*, pp. 111–204; *Hegel's Concept of Experience* (New York: Harper and Row, 1970).

21. "Wozu Dichter?" pp. 284ff., 308f.; "What Are Poets For?" pp. 110f., 133ff.

22. This is a specifically Greek idea, which is explained in Herodotus, *Histories* Book VII, chapter 10 and also comes to words in Nietzsche's poem "Pinie und Blitz" ["Pine and Lightning"], in *Kritische Studienausgabe*, vol. 10, p. 107.

23. "Nietzsches Wort 'Gott ist tot'"/ "The Word of Nietzsche: 'God is Dead.'"

24. "Wer ist Nietzsches Zarathustra?" *Vorträge und Aufsätze*, pp. 97–122; "Who Is Nietzsche's Zarathustra?" *The New Nietzsche: Contemporary Styles of Interpretation*, ed. David B. Allison (Cambridge: MIT Press, 1986), pp. 64–79.

25. *Sein und Zeit*, p. 329f. / *Being and Time*, p. 378.

26. Friedrich Nietzsche, "Unzeitgemäße Betrachtungen, Zweites Stück: Vom Nutzen und Nachtheil der Historie für das Leben," *Kritische Studienausgabe*, vol. 1, p. 258; *Untimely Meditations*, p. 67 [where it is called a "threefold relationship"].

27. *Sein und Zeit*, p. 396; *Being and Time*, p. 448.

28. "On the Use and Disadvantages of History for Life," *Kritische Studienausgabe*, vol. 1, p. 248f.; *Untimely Meditations*, p. 60f.

29. *Kritische Studienausgabe*, vol. 4, p. 31; *Thus Spoke Zarathustra*, p. 27.

30. See Nietzsche, *Großoktavausgabe*, vol. 19 (*Philologica*, vol. 3, 1913), p. 184f.

31. Cf. "Das größte Schwergewicht" (section 341) in *The Gay Science*, tr. Walter Kaufmann (New Yori: Vintage, 1974).

32. *Thus Spoke Zarathustra*, "At Noon."

33. Cf. *Kritische Studienausgabe*, vol. 1, pp. 256f., 261, 330f.; *Untimely Meditations*, pp. 66f., 69, 120f.

34. *Kritische Studienausgabe*, vol. 4, p. 278; *Thus Spoke Zarathustra*, p. 221.

35. *Kritische Studienausgabe*, vol. 1, p. 330; *Untimely Meditations*, p. 120.

36. *Kritische Studienausgabe*, vol. 1, p. 334; *Untimely Meditations*, p. 123. Cf. *Großoktavausgabe*, vol. 9 (*Nachlaß*, 1871/2), p. 377f.

37. "Fatum und Geschichte" and "Willensfreiheit und Fatum" (1862), *Gesammelte Werke, Erster Band: Jugendschriften, 1858–1868. Dichtungen, Aufsätze, Vorträge, Aufzeichnungen und philologische Arbeiten* (Munich: Musarion, 1921), vol. 1, pp. 60–69.

38. Poem "Ruhm und Ewigkeit" ["Fame and Eternity"], which Nietzsche had planned as the conclusion to *Ecce Homo*, *Kritische Studienausgabe*, vol. 6, p. 402.

39. "Wozu Dichter?" *Holzwege*, p. 316/ "What Are Poets For?" *Poetry, Language, Thought*, p. 142.

40. "Nietzsches Wort 'Gott ist tot,'" p. 216/ "The Word of Nietzsche: 'God is Dead,'" p. 64; "Der Spruch des Anaximander," *Holzwege*, p. 321f./ "The Anaximander Fragment," *Early Greek Thinking*, p. 16f.

41. "Die Selbstbehauptung der deutschen Universität," p. 13/ "The Self-Assertion of the German University," p. 33.

42. Paragraph 125 of *The Gay Science*; cf. "Nietzsches Wort: 'Gott ist tot,'" pp. 210ff./ "The Word of Nietzsche: 'God is Dead,'" p. 59f.

43. "Nietzsches Wort 'Gott ist tot,'" p. 248/ "The Word of Nietzsche: 'God is Dead,'" p. 97f.

44. *Erläuterungen zu Hölderlins Dichtung* (5th ed.; Frankfurt: Klostermann, 1981), p. 8.

45. In a lecture on *The Fundamental Problems of Phenomenology* from 1927, it is said more clearly: "Hence we do not simply want to, but instead must, understand the Greeks better than they understood themselves, and only thus shall we acutally possess our inheritance. Only then is our own phenomenological research more than a patchwork and not simply an accidental alteration and improvement or worsening." Cf. *Die Grundprobleme der Phänomenologie, Gesamtausgabe*, vol. 24 (Frankfurt: Klostermann, 1975), p. 157; *The Basic Problems of Phenomenology*, tr. Albert Hofstadter (Bloomington: Indiana University Press, 1982), p. 111.

46. "Nietzsches Wort 'Gott ist tot,'" p. 229/ "The Word of Nietzsche: 'God is Dead,'" p. 76. Cf. the opening statements of "Plato's Doctrine of Truth." Heidegger proceeds like a depth psychologist, though for him it is this very manner of "analysis" that lies most distant: from out of what is said he hears something unsaid, which is the genuine if concealed motivation for what is said, viz., original acts of misconduct that have been forgotten and that, as original, determine and surpass in advance all subsequent human destinings by unconsciously defining the entire history of life—until a healing one comes, who ventures to "repeat" the long history of this destining.

To the impersonal "it" of the unconscious corresponds the anonymous "it" of Being and Eventuating. Freud and Heidegger both appropriate the self-conscious "I" from a deeper relationship, to the extent that they heed something that withdraws and that is unsaid in that which shows itself and which is said, something which comes to language in a nonarbitrary manner in the play of the association of ideas.

What is also methodically related to psychoanalysis is the way in which Heidegger, by means of an *argumentatio ex privativo*, defeats possible counterarguments in advance by incorporating them into his own presuppositions. Whoever denies, for example, that what "is there" is simply the prejudice of an interpreter, must admit that he must necessarily think in this manner, but only because he has fallen into the "anyone," which refuses to go beyond what is there. The existential-ontological interpretation is correct in every case, because opposition to it only proves itself to spring from a "deficient mode" of what is to be demonstrated.

47. "Der Spruch des Anaximander," *Holzwege*, p. 365; "The Anaximander Fragment," *Early Greek Thinking*, p. 55f.

48. *Die Selbstbehauptung der deutschen Universität*, p. 13 / "The Self-Assertion of the German University," p. 33.

49. See the poems from his youth (*GesammelteWerke*, Musarion ed., vol. 1): "Du hast gerufen—Herr, ich komme" (1862, pp. 72–73), "Vor dem Kruzifix" (1863, pp. 122–24), "Gethsemane und Golgatha" (1864, pp. 187–88), "Dem unbekannten Gott" (1863/64, p. 254), and the poem from "The Magician" in *Zarathustra* (*Kritische Studienausgabe*, vol. 4, pp. 313ff./ *Thus Spoke Zarathustra*, pp. 252ff.).

50. "Nietzsches Wort: 'Gott ist tot,'" pp. 255, 262/ "The Word of Nietzsche: 'God is Dead,'" pp. 105, 112. Cf. Karl-Heinz Volkmann-Schluck, "Zur Gottesfrage bei Nietzsche," in *Anteile. Zu Heideggers 60. Geburtstag* (Frankfurt-am-main: Klostermann, 1950), pp. 212–34, where the attempt is made to show that Nietzsche's tidings of the death of God are an expression of the piety which, with Heidegger, rejects that belief in an *extant* God that is a product of the forsakenness of Being.

51. *Sein und Zeit*, p. 306n./ *Being and Time*, p. 354n.ii.

52. "Vom Wesen des Grundes," p. 157n/ *On the Essence of Reasons*, p. 91n.

53. "Nietzsches Wort: 'Gott ist tot,'" p. 263/ "The Word of Nietzsche: 'God is Dead,'" p. 112.

54. "Der Spruch des Anaximander," p. 367/ "The Anaximander Fragment," p. 57.

55. "Der Spruch des Anaximander," p. 348/ "The Anaximander Fragment," p. 40 [where the translators render "das böse Geschick des Seins" as "the baneful destiny of Being"].

56. "Die Zeit des Weltbildes," *Holzwege*, 6th ed., p. 74/ "The Age of the World Picture," *The Question Concerning Technology and Other Essays*, p. 116.

57. "Die Frage nach der Technik," p. 40; "The Question Concerning Technology," p. 35. On this see Karl Löwith, *Wissen, Glaube und Skepsis: Zur Kritik von Religion und Theologie, Sämtliche Schriften*, vol. 3, (Stuttgart: J. B. Metzler, 1984).

58. "Nietzsches Wort: 'Gott ist tot,'" p. 215/ "The Word of Nietzsche: 'God is dead,'" p. 63.

59. *Kritische Studienausgabe*, vol. 6, p. 318/ *Ecce Homo*, in *On the Genealogy of Morals*, tr. Walter Kaufmann (New York: Vintage, 1969). p. 278f.

60. "Nietzsches Wort: 'Gott ist tot,'" p. 209/ "The Word of Nietzsche: 'God is Dead,'" p. 57.

61. "Die Zeit des Weltbildes," *Holzwege*, p. 74/ "The Age of the World Picture," *The Question Concerning Technology and Other Essays*, p. 116f.

62. *On the Genealogy of Morals*, Second Essay, section 24.

63. *Großoktavausgabe*, vol. 16 (*The Will to Power*), pp. 422 and 425; vol. 12 (*Nachlaß*), p.406. I would like to point out that already in 1935 I published an interpretation along these lines of Nietzsche's philosophy as a *Philosophy of the*

Eternal Return of the Same, which appeared in 1956 in an expanded edition—*Nietzsches Philosophie der ewigen Wiederkehr des Gleichen* (Stuttgart: Kohlhammer, 1956).

64. "Nietzsches Wort: 'Gott ist tot,'" pp. 213, 227, 258/ "The Word of Nietzsche: 'God is Dead,'" pp. 61, 75, 108.

65. "Wie die 'wahre Welt' endlich zur Fabel wurde," *Kritische Studienausgabe*, vol. 6, p. 80f.; "How the 'true world' finally became a fable," *The Portable Nietzsche*, ed. and trans. Walter Kaufmann (New York: Penguin, 1982), p. 485f.

66. "Nietzsches Wort: 'Gott ist tot,'" p. 259f./ "The Word of Nietzsche: 'God is Dead,'" p. 109.

67. *Kritische Studienausgabe*, vol. 4, p. 249; *Thus Spoke Zarathustra*, p. 199.

68. "Nietzsches Wort: 'Gott ist tot,'" p. 214/ "The Word of Nietzsche: 'God is Dead,'" p. 62.

69. Cf. "Brief über den 'Humanismus,'" *Wegmarken*, p. 345; "Letter on Humanism," *Basic Writings*, p. 228.

70. See *inter alia Kritische Studienausgabe*, vol. 4, p. 209/ *Thus Spoke Zarathustra*, p. 66; *Die Fröhliche Wissenschaft*, sections 1 and 357/ *The Gay Science*, pp. 73ff. and 304ff.; *Kritische Studienausgabe*, vol. 6, p. 96f./ *Twilight of the Idols* (in *The Portable Nietzsche*), p. 500f.

71. *Kritische Studienausgabe*, vol. 4, p. 209; *Thus Spoke Zarathustra*, p. 66.

72. Nietzsche's poem "An Goethe" [To Goethe], *Kritische Studienausgabe*, vol. 3, p. 639.

73. Nietzsche's poem "Sils-Maria," *Kritische Studienausgabe*, vol. 3, p. 649. The final aphorism of *The Will to Power* has survived in two very different formulations, the first of which (Nietzsche, *Großoktavausgabe*, vol. 16, p. 515/ *The Will to Power*, p. 550) does not end with the expression "will to power" but instead understands self-willing, or blessing, from the standpoint of the eternal return, as a "willing again and again" of oneself.

74. See *Was heißt Denken?* p. 47/ *What Is Called Thinking?* p. 109. See also "Wer ist Nietzsches Zarathustra?" p. 122/ "Who Is Nietzsche's Zarathustra?" p. 79.

75. *The Will to Power*, section 708. The final statement, "Consequently philosophical pessimism is to be counted among comical things," is a reference to Dühring's book *Der Wert des Lebens* [*The Value of Life*], to which Nietzsche repeatedly refers in a polemical manner. [Translator's note: The German economist-philosopher Eugen Dühring (1833–1901) argued for the purification of capitalism on the basis of a material substratum, and was thereby the object of attack by Marx and Engels. He wrote *Der Wert des Lebens* in 1865.]

76. *The Will to Power*, section 708. Cf. *Kritische Studienausgabe*, vol. 4, p. 254; *Thus Spoke Zarathustra*, p. 202f.

77. Section 707. Cf. "Über Wahrheit und Lüge im außermoralischen Sinne," *Kritische Studienausgabe*, vol. 1, pp. 873–90; "On Truth and Lies in a Nonmoral Sense," *Philosophy and Truth: Selections from Nietzsche's Notebooks of the Early 1870s*,

ed. and tr. Daniel Breazeale (Atlantic Highlands, N.J.: Humanities Press, 1992), pp. 79–97.

78. "Nietzsches Wort: 'Gott ist tot,'" p. 254/ "The Word of Nietzsche: 'God is Dead,'" p. 103.

79. Modern subjectivity philosophically "completed" itself already in Fichte, when he translated the absolute "I" into "God" as that which alone is absolute; in doing so, he introduced the turn which would be made by Hölderlin, Schelling, and Hegel. Corresponding to this in Schelling and Hegel is a comparable critique of Descartes's "annihilation of nature" or of spirit: Hegel, "Über das Wesen der philosophischen Kritik überhaupt, und ihr Verhältnis zum gegenwärtigen Zustand der Philosophie insbesondere," Suhrkamp Theorie Werkausgabe (Frankfurt: Suhrkamp, 1982), vol. 2, p. 184. And it is in a dispute with Fichte that the concept of "nihilism" appeared for the first time (Friedrich Heinrich Jacobi, Werke, vol. 3, p. 44).

80. "Nietzsches Wort: 'Gott ist tot,'" pp. 234, 251/ "The Word of Nietzsche: 'God is Dead,'" pp. 83, 100; "Wozu Dichter," Holzwege, p. 284f./ "What Are Poets For?" Poetry, Language, Thought, p. 110f.

81. Kritische Studienausgabe, vol. 6, p. 86; Twilight of the Idols, p. 490.

82. The Will to Power, section 715.

83. "Nietzsches Wort: 'Gott ist tot,'" p. 234/ "The Word of Nietzsche: 'God is Dead,'" p. 83.

84. Section 1059; Kritische Studienausgabe, vol. 11 (Nachlaß), pp. 632 and 656; Kritische Studienausgabe, vol. 11 (Nachlaß), pp. 640–41 against Descartes.

85. Kritische Studienausgabe, vol. 4, p. 261; Thus Spoke Zarathustra, p. 208.

86. Morgenröte, section 575, Kritische Studienausgabe, vol. 3, p. 331; Daybreak: Thoughts on the Prejudices of Morality (trs. R. J. Hollingdale (Cambridge: Cambridge University Press, 1987), p. 229.

87. "Brief über den 'Humanismus,'" Wegmarken, 2d ed., p. 174; "Letter on Humanism," Basic Writings, p. 223.

88. "Nietzsches Wort: 'Gott ist tot,'" p. 222/ "The Word of Nietzsche: 'God is Dead,'" p. 70.

89. Kritische Studienausgabe, vol. 11 (Nachlaß, 1884), p. 88.

90. Kritische Studienausgabe, vol. 6, p. 340; Ecce Homo, p. 301.

91. Kritische Studienausgabe, vol. 4, pp. 197ff.; Thus Spoke Zarathustra, pp. 155ff.

92. Kritische Studienausgabe, vol. 6, p. 340; Ecce Homo, p. 301.

93. Kritische Studienausgabe, vol. 4, pp. 345, 402; Thus Spoke Zarathustra, pp. 278, 323.

94. "Nietzsches Wort: 'Gott ist tot,'" p. 253/ "The Word of Nietzsche: 'God is Dead,'" p. 102.

95. "Der Spruch des Anaximander," Holzwege, p. 328f./ "The Anaximander Fragment," p. 22.

96. "Fatum und Geschichte" and "Willensfreiheit und Fatum" (1862), *Gesammelte Werke*, musarion ed., vol. 1, pp. 60–69.

97. "Nietzsches Wort: 'Gott ist tot,'" p. 249/ "The Word of Nietzsche: 'God is Dead,'" p. 98f.

98. "Die Zeit des Weltbildes," p. 92/ "The Age of the World Picture," p. 135.

99. Cf. "Nietzsches Wort: 'Gott ist tot,'" p. 247f./ "The Word of Nietzsche: 'God is Dead,'" p. 97.

100. "Wozu Dichter?" p. 315; "What Are Poets For?" p. 141.

101. "Der Spruch des Anaximander," p. 368/ "The Anaximander Fragment," p. 58.

102. That even Fichte, Kierkegaard, and Marx anticipated that which saves in the change brought about by an "utter sinfulness," a "sickness unto death," and a total "alienation," does not make this manner of thinking truer about anything, but rather simply proves what deep roots it has in the theological dialectic of sin and grace.

103. *Kritische Studienausgabe*, vol. 4, p. 194; *Thus Spoke Zarathustra*, p. 152.

104. *Holzwege*, p. 316/ "What Are Poets For?" p. 142.

4. ON THE CRITICAL APPRAISAL OF HEIDEGGER'S INFLUENCE

1. *Wegmarken*, p. 123/ *The Essence of Reasons*, p. 3.

2. *Einführung in die Metaphysik*, p. 134/ *An Introduction to Metaphysics*, p. 126.

3. *Sein und Zeit*, p. 385/ *Being and Time*, p. 437.

4. "Deutsche Studenten," *Nachlese zu Heidegger*, p. 136/ "German Students," *The Heidegger Controversy*, p. 47.

5. "For questioning is the piety of thinking." "Die Frage nach der Technik," *Vorträge und Aufsätze*, p. 40; "The Question Concerning Technology," p. 35.

6. "Der Feldweg," p. 90/ "The Pathway," p. 91.

TWO

The Occasional Decisionism of Carl Schmitt

THE OCCASIONAL DECISIONISM OF CARL SCHMITT

1. Carl Schmitt's *Der Begriff des Politischen* first appeared in the *Archiv für Sozialwissenschaft und Sozialpolitik*, vol. 58 (1927): 1–33. It then appeared in a second edition, together with his discussion of the age of neutralizations ["Das Zeitalter der Neutralisierungen und Entpolitisierungen"], in *Wissenschaftliche Abhandlungen und Reden zur Philosophie, Politik, und Geistesgeschichte* (Munich: Duncker and Humboldt, 1932), vol. 10; reprinted in 1963 by Duncker and Humboldt, Berlin, with a preface and three corollaries; and it appeared in a final, third edition in 1933 [Hamburg: Hanseatische Verlagsanstalt]. Unless otherwise noted, I am citing the second edition. [Translator's note: *Der Begriff des Politischen* has been translated as *The Concept of the Political*, tr. George Schwab (New Brunswick, N.J.: Rutgers University Press, 1976); Schwab's translation is based on the second edition of *Der Begriff des Politischen*.]

2. The second edition of each of these essays is being cited here. [Translator's note: See *Politische Romantik*, 2d ed. (Munich and Leipzig: Duncker & Humboldt, 1925; 1st ed. 1919), translated as *Political Romanticism*, tr. Guy Oakes (Cambridge: MIT Press, 1986); and *Politische Theologie: Vier Kapitel zur Lehre von der Souveränität*, 2d ed. (Munich: Duncker & Humboldt, 1934; 1st ed. 1922), translated as *Political Theology: Four Chapters on the Concept of Sovereignty*, tr. George Schwab (Cambridge: MIT Press, 1985.]

3. "Das Zeitalter der Neutralisierungen und Entpolitisierungen," in *Der Begriff des Politischen*, 2d ed., pp. 74ff.

4. "The generation of Germans that preceded us was seized by an attunement of cultural decline which was expressed already before the World War and which did not need to wait for the collapse of 1918 and Spengler's *Decline of the West*. In Ernst Troeltsch, Max Weber, and Walther Rathenau one can find numerous expressions of such an attunement. . . . Once one had abstracted first from religion and theology and then from metaphysics and the state, it now seemed that everything cultural was abstracted from and that the neutrality of cultural death was arrived at." "Das Zeitalter der Neutralisierungen und Entpolitisierungen," p. 78f. [Translator's note: Ernst Troeltsch (1865–1923), a Protestant theologian and historicist thinker, sought to address spiritual crisis and disillusionment by developing a "formal logic of history" and a "material philosophy of history"; he was also a political propagandist during the First World War and a political analyst during the Weimar Republic. Walter Rathenau (1867–1922) was a German industrialist, statesman, and philosopher; he organized Germany's economy during the First World War and, as foreign minister and minister of reconstruction in the Weimar government, administered reparations payments under the Treaty of Versailles. In *Die Neue Wirtschaft* [The New Economy], written in 1918, Rathenau argued that unrestricted capitalism had undergone an irreversible decline and that "the new economy" should establish a balance between industrial self-government and state control.]

5. "Das Zeitalter der Neutralisierungen und Entpolitisierungen," p. 80.

6. *Der Begriff des Politischen*, p. 27/ *The Concept of the Political*, p. 39.

7. *Der Begriff des Politischen*, p. 58/ *The Concept of the Political*, p. 71f.; "Das Zeitalter der Neutralisierungen und Entpolitisierungen," pp. 72ff.

8. "Das Zeitalter der Neutralisierungen und Entpolitisierungen," p. 73.

9. *Der Begriff des Politischen*, pp. 14 and 26/ *The Concept of the Political*, pp. 26 and 38.

10. *Politische Romantik*, p. 225/ *Political Romanticism*, p. 160.

11. "Das Zeitalter der Neutralisierungen und Entpolitisierungen," p. 70. Cf. *Politische Romantik*, p. 21/ *Political Romanticism*, p. 15f.

12. *Politische Romantik*, p. 16/ *Political Romanticism*, p. 12. Cf. *Politische Romantik*, p. 141/ *Political Romanticism*, p. 99.

13. Carl Schmitt, *Th. Däublers Nordlicht* (1916), p. 10f.

14. *Politische Romantik*, p. 141/ *Political Romanticism*, p. 99.

15. "Only in a society which had dissolved into individualism was the aesthetically productive subject able to transpose the spiritual center into itself, i.e., only in a bourgeois world which spiritually isolates the individual, refers the individual back to itself alone, and encumbers the individual with the burden which was previously divided up hierarchically in various functions within a social order. In this society it is left to the private individual to be his own priest. . . . Romanticism and romantic phenomena have their ultimate root in this private priesthood." *Politische Romantik*, p. 26/ *Political Romanticism*, p. 20.

16. *Politische Romantik*, p. 87/ *Political Romanticism*, p. 59.

17. "This is a destructive concept, since everything that confers consistency and order on life and events . . . is incompatible with the notion of the merely occasional. Where what happens now and then and by accident becomes a principle, something emerges which is greatly superior to such binding forces . . . in Malebranche's philosophy, for example, God is the final and absolute court of appeal, and the entire world and everything that occurs in it is a mere occasion [*Anlaß*] for His exclusive efficacy. This is a grand picture of the world, one which builds up God's superiority to . . . fantastic proportions. This attitude, which is characteristic of occasionalism, can continue to subsist with something else taking the place of God as the highest court of appeal and foundational factor, for example the state or even the individual subject; in romanticism the latter is the case"—and in Schmitt's antiromanticism the former is the case! *Politische Romantik*, p. 22f. / *Political Romanticism*, p. 17.

18. "The 'teacher of oppositions' [namely Adam Müller—K.L.] was incapable of seeing an opposition unless it was an aesthetic contrast. Neither logical distinctions nor moral judgments of value nor political determinations are possible for him. The most important source of political vitality, namely faith in right and outrage over wrong, does not exist for him." *Politische Romantik*, p. 177/ *Political Romanticism*, p. 129. Cf. *Die geistesgeschichtliche Lage des heutigen Parlamentarismus* (2d ed.; Munich/Leipzig: Duncker & Humboldt, 1926), p. 68; *The Crisis of Parliamentary Democracy*, tr. Ellen Kennedy (Cambridge: MIT Press, 1988), p. 56.

19. "In spite of irony and paradox, a constant dependence is evident. In the narrowest area of its specific productivity, namely in the lyrical- and musical-poetic, subjective occasionalism may find a small island of free creativity, though even here it is unconsciously subject to the power which is nearest and strongest; and the superiority of this occasionalism over the present, taken in the merely occasional sense, suffers a most ironic reversal: everything romantic is in servitude to other, nonromantic energies, and ascendancy over definition and decision becomes transformed into a servile compliance with foreign power and foreign decisions." *Politische Romantik*, p. 228/ *Political Romanticism*, p. 162.

20. Above all see Kierkegaard, *The Concept of Irony* and *The Present Age*; Marx, "The Eighteenth Brumaire of Louis Bonaparte," 1852.

21. On this see Kierkegaard, "Das Eine, was not tut," in *Zeitwende*, vol. 3, no. 1, 1927.

22. *Die geistesgeschichtliche Lage des heutigen Parlamentarismus*, p. 68f. / *The Crisis of Parliamentary Democracy*, p. 56f.

23. Truly moral categories like "loyalty," "inner discipline," and "honor" define Schmitt's political thinking only after his departure from decisionism, in his new essay *Über die drei Arten des rechtswissenschaftlichen Denkens* (*On the Three Forms of Jurisprudential Thinking*), 1934, p. 52.

24. *Politische Theologie*, p. 11 / *Political Theology*, p. 5.

25. Against this cf. p. 62 of Schmitt's *Über die drei Arten des rechtswis-*

senschaftlichen Denkens, where on the contrary the "concrete reality of a life-relation" is now supposed to be understood on the basis of concepts of natural order that are oriented on the *normal* situation.

26. *Politische Theologie*, p. 22 / *Political Theology*, p. 15.

27. Kierkegaard, *Entweder-Oder*, vol. 2, 1913, pp. 285ff. / *Either-Or*, vol. 2, tr. Walter Lowrie (Princeton: Princeton University Press, 1974), pp. 334ff.

28. *Politische Theologie*, p. 49 / *Political Theology*, p. 36.

29. Preface to the second edition, *Politische Theologie*, p. 8 / *Political Theology*, p. 3.

30. "Das Zeitalter der Neutralisierungen und Entpolitisierungen," p. 81.

31. "There is an original conception which is peculiar to the German romantics: the eternal conversation; Novalis and Adam Müller proceed within this as the authentic realization of their spirit. The Catholic political philosophers, who are referred to in Germany as romantics because they were conservative or reactionary . . . would surely have considered an eternal conversation to be the product of a horrible comic imagination. For what their counterrevolutionary political philosophy emphasizes is the consciousness that the times demand a decision; and with an energy that increases to the highest extreme between the revolutions of 1789 and 1848, the concept of decision comes to occupy the center of their thinking. Wherever the Catholic philosophy of the nineteenth century manifested itself in spiritual actuality, it expressed some form of the idea that a great alternative is imposing itself which no longer permits any mediation . . . . Every one of them formulates a great Either-Or, the rigor of which sounds more like dictatorship than like an eternal conversation." *Politische Theologie*, pp. 69 and 80 / *Political Theology*, pp. 53 and 63.

32. *Politische Theologie*, p. 71 / *Political Theology*, p. 55f. In contrast to this *determination [Entscheidung] of* the will, it seems for Schmitt that "the fate of democracy is to neutralize itself in the problem of *forming* a will." But at the same time he also emphasizes the potential compatibility between democracy and dictatorship in Bolshevism and fascism, in terms of the contrast they share to the bourgeois liberalism of the parliamentary state. *Die geistesgeschichtliche Lage des heutigen Parlamentarismus*, pp. 37 and 64; cf. pp. 22, 34, 41 / *The Crisis of Parliamentary Democracy*, pp. 28 and 51f.; cf. pp. 16, 25f. and 31f.

33. *Politische Theologie*, p. 72 / *Political Theology*, p. 56.

34. *Die geistesgeschichtliche Lage des heutigen Parlamentarismus*, pp. 13 and 61ff. / *The Crisis of Parliamentary Democracy*, pp. 35 and 48ff.

35. *Politische Theologie*, p. 74 / *Political Theology*, p. 57.

36. Cf. *Die geistesgeschichtliche Lage des heutigen Parlamentarismus*, pp. 65 and 75 / *The Crisis of Parliamentary Democracy*, pp. 53 and 63, where reference is made to ultimate evidence in Marx's socialist faith.

37. *Politische Theologie*, p. 83 / *Political Theology*, p. 66.

38. *Politische Theologie*, p. 83 / *Political Theology*, p. 66.

39. In relation to this modern nihilism, Hobbes' realistic "pessimism," with

The Occasional Decisionism of Carl Schmitt 275

which Schmitt thinks he is closely allied (*Der Begriff des Politischen*, pp. 46ff. / *The Concept of the Political*, pp. 58ff.), is a kind of faith in the progress offered by a potential restriction on the state of nature; and yet Schmitt, in contrast to Hobbes, affirms this state of nature precisely *for being* a *status belli* [state of war]. The only person to figure out modern nihilism philosophically was Nietzsche, who was the first to recognize that modern human beings, who no longer have faith in anything and who no longer know "for what purpose" they exist, "*would rather will Nothing than not will at all*." Nietzsche, On the Genealogy of Morals, Third Essay, section 28. The will "itself" gets "saved" by this nihilism of strength.

This nihilism, which has become active, is also characteristic of the early writings of Ernst Jünger, to whom Schmitt sometimes refers. In Jünger's diary *Das abenteuerliche Herz* [*The Adventurous Heart*] from 1929, the following statements are made:
"One may never find out one's reason for existing, as all so-called purposes can be mere pretenses for the sake of definition; but *that* one exists . . . is what matters." "Thus it happens that our time demands one virtue above all others: that of *decisiveness*. It is a matter of being able to will and to believe, quite apart from the particular content in terms of which this willing and believing presents itself. This is the way today's communities are; the interplay of the extremes is more vehement than ever." "But what is going on today in all struggles over flags and symbols, over laws and dogmas, and over order and systems, is simply a sham. Your very aversion to these squabbles . . . betrays the fact that it is not answers but rather more pointed questions, not flags but rather fighters, not order but rather uprisings, and not systems but rather human beings, of which you are in need." "For a few years we worked in a rigidly nihilistic manner with dynamic forces and, dispensing with even the slightest trace of authentic questioning, we attacked the foundations of the nineteenth century, i.e., our own foundations; and only at the very end did the means and the men of the twentieth century become apparent. We declared war on Europe—as if we were good Europeans gathered harmoniously with the others around a roulette wheel with only one color, namely the color for zero, which always lets the house win. We Germans did not give Europe any chance to lose. But because we gave no chance of losing, in an essential sense we also offered nothing to win inasmuch as we played against the house with its own funds."

"This is a position on the basis of which something can be accomplished. To take measure in this way from the secret standard of civilization, a standard which was preserved in Paris—for us this means to lose the lost war at its end, i.e., it means the consistent carrying out of a nihilistic act up to its necessary end point. For a long time we have been marching toward a magical reference point which can be gotten beyond only by those who have at their disposal different, invisible sources of power. *Our* hope is tied to whatever is left over, left over because it cannot be measured in terms of what is European but instead provides the measure for itself."

In Jünger this confident nihilism knows itself to be in accord with decisive anarchism, which acts in a solitary and withdrawn manner. "This activity tailors itself to that juncture which I call the magical reference point, a point through which we shall pass and upon which both nothing and everything depends."

40. Schmitt's neutral manner of talking about *the* political gives rise to the impression, in a way similar to Kierkegaard's talk of *the* aesthetic and religious, that the political is a specific subject area, even though it is precisely not supposed to be such a thing. But the deeper reason for this indeterminacy of formulation may be that Schmitt in fact *can* not specify what is proper to the political, unless what is proper to it be a totality which goes beyond all determinate subject areas and which neutralizes every one of them in the same manner, though it does so in a direction opposite to that seen in depoliticization. On Schmitt's view, the positive meaning of the total state emerges exclusively from out of the polemical negation of the neutral state, i.e., of the liberal state. And hence such a total state does not gather together the concrete moments of civil society "*universally*," as it does in Hegel's conception of the state, but instead it totalizes both state and society, on the basis of political exigency. *Der Begriff des Politischen*, p. 12/ *The Concept of the Political*, p. 24.

41. *Der Begriff des Politischen* pp. 20ff. and 34/ *The Concept of the Political*, pp. 32ff. and 46.

42. *Politische Romantik*, p. 22/ *Political Romanticism*, p. 16f.

43. *Der Begriff des Politischen*, 3d ed., p. 23f.

44. *Der Begriff des Politischen*, p. 14, 3d ed., 8/ *The Concept of the Political*, p. 26.

Hugo Grotius (Hugeianus de Groot, 1583–1645) was a Dutch jurist and scholar whose *De Jure Belli ac Pacis* (*On the Law of War and Peace*), written in 1625, laid the foundations of modern international law.

45. On this, cf. Leo Strauss' critical remarks on Schmitt's *The Concept of the Political*: "Anmerkungen zu Carl Schmitt, Der Begriff des Politischen," in *Archiv für Sozialwissenschafte und Sozialpolitik* 67, no. 6 (1932): 732–49; "Comments on Carl Schmitt's *Der Begriff des Politischen*," in *The Concept of the Political*, pp. 81–105.

46. *Der Begriff des Politischen*, p. 21/ *The Concept of the Political*, p. 33.

47. On this cf. Schmitt's new essay *Staatsgefüge und Zusammenbruch des zweiten Reichs* [*The State Structure and Collapse of the Second Reich*], 1934, where this formal belligerence is given a historical content by the introduction of the thesis that the Prussian soldier-state is the only true substance of the German Reich.

48. *Der Begriff des Politischen*, p. 46f. and 54/ *The Concept of the Political*, pp. 58f. and 67; against this cf. Schmitt's earlier characterization of war in *Th. Däublers Nordlicht*, p. 63. "The phenomenon of the political can be grasped only in relation to the real possibility of groupings of friend and enemy, irrespective of what kind of religious, moral, aesthetic, or economic evaluation of the political results from these. . . . A war need not be something pious, something

morally good, or something remunerative;* today it is probably none of these. This simple knowledge is generally obscured by the fact that religious, moral, and other oppositions can become intensified into political oppositions and give rise to the decisive grouping in a war in terms of friend or enemy. But if it should come to such a grouping in a war, the authoritative opposition is no longer purely religious, moral, or economic, but instead is political. Then the question is always simply whether or not such groupings of friend and enemy are present as a real possibility or actuality, irrespective of which human motives are sufficiently strong to bring them about." *Der Begriff des Politischen*, p. 23f./ *The Concept of the Political*, p. 35f. Cf. *Der Begriff des Politischen*, p. 31/ *The Concept of the Political*, p. 43f.

In the third edition, the clause following the asterisk reads as follows: "In a time which morally or economically veils its metaphysical oppositions, it is probably none of these." *Der Begriff des Politischen*, 3d ed., p. 18f. Hence the possible meaning of war is, even in relation to our own time, related to metaphysical oppositions, even though the distinctively polemical mark of all of Schmitt's writings is his denial that the theological, the metaphysical, the moral, and the economic can serve as the measure for the authentically political.

49. *Der Begriff des Politischen*, pp. 15 and 25/ *The Concept of the Political*, pp. 27 and 37.

50. "The political can draw its power from the most varied domains of human life, from religious, economic, moral, and other oppositions; it does not designate a subject area of its own, but instead simply designates the *degree of intensity* of an association of human beings, whose motives can be of a religious, national (in the ethnic or cultural sense), economic, or other kind. At different times these motives give rise to different commitments and divisions." *Der Begriff des Politischen*, p. 26/ *The Concept of the Political*, p. 38.

51. Heidegger, *Sein und Zeit*, sections 9 and 29.

52. *Der Begriff des Politischen*, p. 25/ *The Concept of the Political*, p. 37.

53. On this cf. Leo Strauss, "Anmerkungen zu Carl Schmitt, Der Begriff des Politischen," especially the excellent summary on p. 748; "Comments on Carl Schmitt's *Der Begriff des Politischen*," in *The Concept of the Political*, p. 102f.

54. *Der Begriff des Politischen*, p. 54f./ *The Concept of the Political*, p. 67f.

55. *Oliver Cromwell's Letters and Speeches*, Carlyle edition (NewYork: Dutton, 1907), pp. 149ff.; cf. *Der Begriff des Politischen*, p. 55/ *The Concept of the Political*, p. 68.

56. *Der Begriff des Politischen*, p. 16n/ *The Concept of the Political*, pp. 28–9n.

57. *Der Begriff des Politischen*, p. 15/ *The Concept of the Political*, p. 27.

58. In the characterization of the friend as "of the same kind and allied," this ambiguity becomes immediately apparent. *Der Begriff des Politischen*, 3d ed., p. 8.

59. In the essay *Der Wert des Staates und die Bedeutung des Einzelnen* [*The Value of the State and the Meaning of the Individual*] (1917), in which Schmitt still advocates an extremely normative-juridical conception of the omnipotence of the state, it

is said that the state is not a human construction but that on the contrary the state makes a construction out of every human being.

"Through the acknowledgment of the suprapersonal dignity of the state ... the single, concrete individual disappears. For the state is a servant either of the individual or of Right. Since only the latter is correct, the state is prior to the individual, just as Right is prior to the state; and just as the continuity of the state proceeds only from Right, the continuity of the individual who lives in the state flows only from the state.

"The state is ... the sole subject of the ethos of Right; it alone has a duty to Right in the eminent sense. The concrete individual, on the other hand, is subject to the force of the state; the individual's duty and authority are simply the reflex of this force.... For the state, the individual as such just happens to be the bearer of the sole essential task, of the definite function, which the individual has to carry out. Hence in principle the state cannot consider anyone to be irreplaceable nor to be untenable, and in terms of this general phenomenon of the functionary ..., of the official, the meaning of the state could be given a much deeper explanation than if we degrade the state to the level of a *negotiorum gestor* [business functionary] for a 'personality' which is all that is of importance" (p. 85f.).

60. On this cf. Karl Löwith, *Das Indivuum in der Rolle des Mitmenschen*, in *Sämtliche Schriften*, vol. 1, pp. 9ff.

61. *Der Begriff des Politischen*, p. 28f./ *The Concept of the Political*, p. 40f.

62. Ever since Rousseau, the political form of this distinction within human Dasein has been that of *citoyen* and *bourgeois*. Even Marx appeals to this in his critique of Hegel's political philosophy, in order to show that "the merely political state" is the public form of—bourgeois privacy!

63. *Der Begriff des Politischen*, p. 40/ *The Concept of the Political*, p. 51.

64. *Der Begriff des Politischen*, p. 57/ *The Concept of the Political*, p. 71. Against this, cf. Wilhelm von Humboldt, *Gesammelte Werke*, vol. 1, ch. 5.

65. An analogous situation is present today in the problem of the Jews, a problem which has become political and whose characteristic case is that of anti-Semites who are friendly toward Jews; these are people who publicly are enemies of Judaism and who privately are friends of Jews (on this cf. Schmitt's dedication to his *Verfassungslehre* [Constitutional Theory] and his study on Däubler's *Nordlicht*). Schmitt's position on this becomes evident indirectly through the manner in which he explains the relationship of political exigency to the Christian Commandment to love one's enemy. From the fact that the statement reads "*diligete inimicos vestros*" he concludes that it refers not to the *hostis* but rather only to the private enemy (*Der Begriff des Politischen*, p. 17; *The Concept of the Political*, p. 29.) Hence the Christian requirement in no way touches on the fundamental political distinction. But this means that Schmitt reduces, in good liberal fashion (and in a way that contradicts his own conception in *Römischer Katholizismus und politische Form* [Roman Catholicism and Polit-

ical Form] (1925, p. 39), the absolute demand of the Christian religion to the relativity of a private concern.

But in reality, from the fact that the Christian Commandment (in the Latin translation of the *Vulgate*) is not related, even as a special case, to the *hostis*, something quite different follows: this Commandment, as a total determination of human beings, must be the measure for the human being's *whole* relationship to the world. In his worldly way, the Christian knows neither enemies nor friends, be these private or public, for in each case his manner of relating to friend and enemy is different than that of the pre-Christian heathen. One who is in the world as if he were not of this world, one for whom it is not war but rather the Last Judgment that is the decisive exigency, can in principle not distinguish between private and public enemies. On this cf. Schmitt, *Verfassungslehre*, 1928, p. 158 and Thieme, *Religiöse Besinnung*, final edition of 1933, pp. 45ff. [Translator's note: (1) *Diligete inimicos vestros* means "love your enemy" (or "honor him who is not a friend"). (2) The *Vulgate* is Jerome's translation of the Bible.]

66. *Der Begriff des Politischen*, p. 35f./ *The Concept of the Political*, p. 47: "An association of humans that wanted to reject these consequences of political unity would not be a political association, since it would be rejecting the possibility of deciding authoritatively on whom it sees and treats as an enemy."

67. "Now as soon as a war breaks out, with it there breaks out among the noblest of a people a desire which naturally has been kept secret: they thrust themselves with delight into the new danger of *death*, because in this self-sacrifice for the fatherland they think that they have permission which they have sought for a long time—permission to *avoid their goal*: for them war is a detour to suicide, though it is a detour with a good conscience." Nietzsche, *The Gay Science*, aphorism 338 (*Kritische Studienausgabe* 3:567f.; *The Gay Science*, p. 270).

68. *Der Begriff des Politischen*, p. 41f./ *The Concept of the Political*, p. 53f; *Die geistesgeschichtliche Lage des heutigen Parlamentarismus*, pp. 16ff., 20/ *The Crisis of Parliamentary Democracy*, pp. 10ff., 14.

69. On this cf. Schmitt, *Verfassungslehre*, p. 226ff.; against this, cf. Haecker, *Was ist der Mensch?*, 1933, pp. 21ff. and 71ff.

70. On this cf. Schmitt's earlier judgment, from 1916, regarding the "romanticism of racial doctrines" in *Th. Däubler's Nordlicht*, p. 14.

71. Precisely as did the German Schopenhauer!

72. *Der Begriff des Politischen*, p. 59, 3d ed., p. 54/ *The Concept of the Political*, p. 73. An analogous "improvement" is made between the second and third editions of *The Concept of the Political* (*Der Begriff des Politischen*, 2d ed., p. 63, 3d ed., p. 58/ *The Concept of the Political*, p. 76f.) in the critique of Franz Oppenheimer's conception of the state, and it is done in such a way that the innocent reader would not naturally be brought to the idea that Schmitt's new addition might have been made *after* the victory of the National Socialist revolution; for it surely would be remarkable if it is only after 1933, at the time of the third edition, that these social "strata" advocated by Oppenheimer are "becoming entrenched" even

further in spite of the fact that the military and the bureaucracy are "not yet" accessible to them! But when Schmitt continues by saying that it is "really not permissible and neither morally nor psychologically nor least of all scientifically appropriate to make definitions simply by means of moral disqualifications," one can only agree with him, particularly inasmuch as such a disqualification can pertain just as much to the sovereign state as to liberal society.

But the principle underlying *all* the changes in the various editions is always that of an occasionalism which characterizes Schmitt's decisions, which are situation-bound and hence in every case polemical.

[Translator's note: Franz Oppenheimer (1864–1943) was a professor of sociology in Frankfurt and an advocate of "liberal socialism," which among other things sought to redress social discontent by prohibiting large-scale private property ownership and promoting cooperative group ownership and peaceful commerce. Schmitt's criticism of Oppenheimer centers on the latter's claim that "society, as a sphere of peaceful justice, stands infinitely higher than the state." *Der Begriff des Politischen*, p. 63 / *The Concept of the Political*, p. 77.]

73. *Der Begriff des Politischen*, p. 64 / *The Concept of the Political*, p. 78.

74. *Die geistesgeschichtliche Lage des heutigen Parlamentarismus*, p. 76 / *The Crisis of Parliamentary Democracy*, p. 64.

75. When Schmitt thinks that he has found the "first polemical-political definition of the bourgeois" in Hegel's critique of civil society, he is forgetting that Hegel's state in no way polemically negates civil society and its principle, namely individualism, but instead positively "sublates" [*aufhebt*] these within itself. For Hegel so-called individualism is not, as it is for Marx *and* Schmitt, a mere feature of civil society, but instead it is based on the Christian principle of the "right of absolute subjectivity," i.e. the principle of the "infinitely free personality" of the individual, a principle which had not yet gained recognition in the "merely substantial" state of antiquity. Cf. *Philosophy of Right*, section 185 (*Grundlinien der Philosophie des Rechts oder Naturrecht und Staatswissenschaft im Grundrisse. Mit Hegels eigenhändigen Notizen und den mündlichen Zusätzen, Werke in zwanzig Bänden*, vol. 7, Frankfurt: Suhrkamp Theorie Werkausgabe, 1982), p. 342; *Hegel's Philosophy of Right*, tr. T. M. Knox (London: Oxford University Press, 1967), p. 124; *Encyclopedia*, section 163, Zusatz 1 (*Encyclopädie der philosophischen Wissenschaften im Grundrisse (1830). Erster Teil. Die Wissenschaft der Logik. Mit den mündlichen Zusätzen*, vol. 8, Frankfurt: Suhrkamp Theorie Werkausgabe, 1979), pp. 311ff.; *Hegel's Logic. Being Part One of the Encyclopedia of the Philosophical Sciences (1830)*, tr. William Wallace (Oxford: Clarendon Press, 1975), p. 227f.; and *Encyclopedia*, section 482 (*Encyclopädie der philosophischen Wissenschaften im Grundrisse (1830). Dritter Teil. Die Philosophie des Geistes. Mit den mündlichen Zusätzen*, vol. 10, Frankfurt: Suhrkamp Theorie Werkausgabe, 1983), p. 301f.; *Hegel's Philosophy of Mind. Being Part Three of the Encyclopedia of the Philosophical Sciences (1830)*, tr. William Wallace, *Zusätze* tr. A. V. Miller (Oxford: Clarendon Press, 1978), p. 239f.

76. *Der Begriff des Politischen*, p. 18 / *The Concept of the Political*, p. 30.

77. "Words like state, republic, society, class, and also: sovereignty, constitutional state, absolutism, dictatorship, planning, neutral or total state, etc., are unintelligible if one does not know who *in concreto* is supposed to be encountered, fought, negated, and refuted with such words. This polemical character dominates above all the linguistic use of the word 'political' itself, regardless of whether one posits the opponent as 'apolitical' . . . or whether one instead wants to disqualify and denounce him as 'political' so as to elevate oneself as 'apolitical' . . . over against him." *Der Begriff des Politischen*, p. 18f./ *The Concept of the Political*, pp. 30ff.; *Die geistesgeschichtliche Lage des heutigen Parlamentarismus*, p. 32/ *The Crisis of Parliamentary Democracy*, p. 24.

78. *Der Begriff des Politischen*, p. 19/ *The Concept of the Political*, p. 32.

79. In Kierkegaard's critique of the present age, this is the constantly recurring *ethical* expression for what Schmitt refers to in a *political* connection as "neutralization" and what Scheler, in a lecture from 1927 which Schmitt seizes upon in a polemical manner [in "Das Zeitalter der Neutralisierungen und Entpolitisierungen," p. 77], refers to in a *cultural* connection as "adjustment [*Ausgleich*]." Max Scheler, "Der Mensch im Weltalter des Ausgleichs," originally published in *Politische Wissenschaft (Ausgleich als Schicksal und Aufgabe)* (Berlin: Veröffentlichung der deutschen Hochschule für Politik, 1929); later in *Philosophische Weltanschauung* (Bonn: Cohen, 1929; 2d ed. Dalp Taschenbücher, vol. 301, Bern: Francke, 1954; 3d ed., revised, 1968). Now in Scheler's *Gesammelte Werke*, vol. 9: *Späte Schriften*, ed. Manfred Frings (Bern: Francke, 1976); translated as "Man in the Era of Adjustment," in *Philosophical Perspectives*, tr. Oscar A. Haac (Boston: Beacon, 1958). In these various ways of naming a state of affairs which is one and the same but is nonetheless ambiguous, a fundamental difference in interpretation announces itself, one which is as revealing as the difference that Schmitt exhibits between the two political concepts of "tribute" and "reparation." *Der Begriff des Politischen*, pp. 18–19n/ *The Concept of the Political*, pp. 31–32n.

80. *Der Begriff des Politischen*, p. 18/ *The Concept of the Political*, p. 31.

81. Thinking about order is first characterized as "institutional" thinking in the preface to the second edition of *Political Theology* (*Politische Theologie*, pp. 7ff./ *Political Theology*, pp. 2ff.); on this cf. his new essay [*Staatsgefüge und Zusammenbruch des zweiten Reichs*, 1934], p. 57f.

82. *Über die drei Arten des rechtswissenschaftlichen Denkens*, pp. 10, 22f., 56.

83. On this see Count Krockow's recent sociological discussion *Die Entstehung, eine Untersuchung über E. Jünger, C. Schmitt, M. Heidegger* (1958), in which theological decisionism is nonetheless not taken into account.

84. In connection with the following remarks, cf. the author's more complete discussion in *Les Temps Modernes*, 1947 ["Les implications politiques de la philosophie de l'existence chez Heidegger," in *Les Temps Modernes* 2, no. 14 (November 1946): 343–60; "The Political Implications of Heidegger's Philosophy," in *The Heidegger Controversy: A Critical Reader*, ed. Richard Wolin (Cambridge: MIT Press, 1993), pp. 168–85; discussion with Alphonse de Waehlens in *Les Temps*

Modernes 2, no. 22 (July 1947): 115–27]. The unpublished German version was written in 1939 and is being employed in part here (cf. "Der europäische Nihilismus. Betrachtungen zur Vorgeschichte des europäischen Krieges" in *Sämtliche Schriften 2:Weltgeschichte und Heilsgeschehen*, pp. 473–540 and 614–17; "European Nihilism: Reflections on the Spiritual and Historical Background of the European War," this volume). [Translator's note: For an explanation regarding the various versions and places of publication of Löwith's *Les Temps Modernes* essay, see the introductory note to "The Political Implications of Heidegger's Existentialism" in *The Heidegger Controversy*, p. 167f.]

85. Albert Leo Schlageter (1894–1923) was a student at Freiburg University who had participated in the revolts against the French occupation army after the First World War, was shot for sabotage [by the French occupation army in the Ruhr on May 26, 1923], and was canonized by National Socialism. Heidegger's speech, "Schlageterfeier der Freiburger Universität [Freiburg University's Celebration of Schlageter]," appeared in the *Freiburger Studentenzeitung* [*Freiburg Student Newspaper*] on June 1, 1933, p. 1 [now in Schneeberger, *Nachlese zu Heidegger*, pp. 47–49, translated as "Schlageter" in The Heidegger Controversy, pp. 40–42; this speech was first published in *Der Alemanne. Kampfblatt der Nationalsozialisten Oberbadens*, May 27, 1933, p. 6—tr.].

86. "Deutsche Männer und Frauen!" in the *Freiburger Studentenzeitung*, November 10, 1933, p. 1 (now in Schneeberger, *Nachlese zu Heidegger*, pp. 144–146); translated as "German Men and Women," in *The Heidegger Controversy*, pp. 47–49.

87. *Sein und Zeit*, p. 298/ *Being and Time*, p. 345. In a discount edition, Alfred Bäumler (*Männerbund und Wissenschaft*, 1934, p. 108) popularized the resoluteness toward resolution analyzed by Heidegger. For him action does not mean deciding *in favor of something*, but instead signifies simply "taking a direction" in virtue of a "fateful mission." In contrast, the decision in favor of something that one has recognized as right because one knows what one wants, is "secondary." For a criticism, see M. Marcuse, "Der Kampf gegen den Liberalismus in der totalitären Staatsauffassung," in *Zeitschrift für Sozialforschung*, vol. 3, 1934, pp. 187f.

88. "Die Selbstbehauptung der deutschen Universität," Breslau, 1933. *Die Selbstbehauptung der deutschen Universität: Das Rektorat, 1933/34; Tatsachen und Gedanken* (Frankfurt: Klostermann, 1983); "The Self-Assertion of the German University," in *The Heidegger Controversy*, pp. 29–39.

89. "Die Selbstbehauptung der deutschen Universität," p. 9/ "The Self-Assertion of the German University," p. 29.

90. In truth it means: "That which is noble is for the most part endangered." [Translator's note: On the meaning and the various interpretations of this passage, see translator's note, p. 106; the passage is from Book 6 of the *Republic* (497d9) and literally means "all great things are precarious."]

91. See A. Hoberg, *Das Dasein des Menschen*, 1937.

92. H. Naumann, *Germanischer Schicksalsglaube*, 1934.

93. "Einleitung zu: 'Was ist Metaphysik?'" p. 375f. / "The Way Back Into the Ground of Metaphysics," p. 219f. From the same "spirit of the time" comes Hans Freyer's lecture, inspired by the youth movement, on "Das geschichtliche Selbstbewußtsein des 20. Jahrhunderts" ["The Historical Self-Consciousness of the Twentieth Century"] (Veröffentlichungen der Abteilung für Kunst- und Kulturwissenschaft, 1. Reihe: Vorträge, Heft 3, Verlag Heinrich Keller, Leipzig, 1937), in which "decision" gets self-consciously played out in opposition to historical "development." [Translator's note: Hans Freyer (1887–1969) was a neo-Hegelian professor of sociology in Kiel, Leipzig, and finally Münster; his major works include *Weltgeschichte Europas* [The World-History of Europe] (1948) and *Schwelle der Zeiten* [Threshold of the Times] (1965).]

94. Friedrich Gogarten, *Die religiöse Entscheidung* (Jena: Eugen Diedrichs, 1921).

95. Gogarten, "Die Kirche," in *Die religiöse Entscheidung*, pp. 77, 81.

96. Gogarten, "Religion und Volkstum," in *Die religiöse Entscheidung*, p. 25.

97. Letter, 1920.

98. *Eckart*, April–June edition, 1952.

99. "Die Krise des Glaubens" (1931), in *Glaube und Verstehen*, vol. 2.

100. Gogarten, *Die religiose Entscheidung*.

101. On this see Karl Löwith, *Wissen, Glaube und Skepsis* (*Sämtliche Schriften* 3), ch. 3.

THREE
European Nihilism: Reflections on the Spiritual and Historical Background of the European War

PART 1

1. Hegel, *Vorlesungen über die Philosophie der Geschichte*, [Lectures on the Philosophy of History], *Suhrkamp Theorie Werkausgabe* (Frankfurt: Suhrkamp), vol. 12, p. 134.

2. On this see Max Scheler, *Der Genius des Krieges und der deutsche Krieg* [The Genius of War and the German War] (Leipzig: Verlag der weissen Bücher, 1915), pp. 285ff.; now in Scheler, *Collected Edition* (Berne, Frankfurt: 1954–), vol. 4.

3. Ku-hung-ming, *Chinas Verteidigung gegen die Ideen Europas* [China's Defense Against the Ideas of Europe], 1911.

4. Voltaire, *Essai sur les moeurs et l'esprit des nations* [Essay on the Manners and the Spirit of Nations], 1757; on this see Kaegi's discussion in the journal *Corona*, 1937/38, vol. 1.

5. Hearn first became critical of Japan in his last book, *Japan: An Attempt at Interpretation* (New York: Macmillan, 1904). On this cf. *More Letters from Basil Hall Chamberlain to Lafcadio Hearn and Letters from M. Toyama, Y. Tsubouchi, and Others* (Tokyo: Hokuseido Press, 1937), pp. 135 and 142.

6. A splendid indication of this European outlook is found in Rilke's letters from 1914 to 1926 and in Hugo von Hofmannsthal's essays, *Die Berührung der Sphären* [The Touching of the Spheres], 1931.

7. Scheler, *Der Genius des Krieges*, pp. 322, 323.

8. Scheler, *Die Ursachen des Deutschenhasses: Eine nationale pädagogische Erörterung* (Leipzig: Wolff, 1917; 2d revised ed., Leipzig: Der Neue Geist Verlag, 1919).

9. Scheler, *Vom Ewigen im Menschen: Religiöse Erneuerung* (Leipzig: Der Neue Geist, 1923), vol. 1, pp. 204ff.; now in Scheler, *Collected Edition*, vol. 5; *On the Eternal in Man*, tr. Bernard Noble (London: Student Christian Movement Press, 1960).

10. Stefan George, *Der Krieg*, 1916.

11. On this see Benedetto Croce, *Geschichte Europas im 19. Jahrhundert*; in English, *The History of Europe in the Nineteenth Century*, tr. Henry Furst (New York: Harcourt, Brace, 1933), ch. 10, "International Politics, Activism, and the World War (1871–1914)."

12. Scheler, *Der Genius des Krieges*, pp. 311f. 313f.

13. Ernst Jünger, *Das abenteuerliche Herz* [The Adventurous Heart], (Berlin: 1929), pp. 186ff.

14. Hermann Rauschning, *Die Revolution des Nihilismus*, 1938, pp. 409 and 458ff.; *The Revolution of Nihilism: Warning to the West*, trs. E. W. Dickes (New York: Alliance Book Corp., 1939), pp. 220, 257ff. [Translator's note: Hermann Rauschning (1887–19??) was a politician and opponent of National Socialism.]

15. Dostoevsky, *Politische Schriften* (Munich: R. Piper, 1917; 2d ed., 1922), p. 489.

16. Carl Schmitt, "Das Zeitalter der Neutralisierungen und Entpolitisierungen," p. 66. Cf. Oswald Spengler, *Jahre der Entscheidung* [Years of Decision], 1933, p. 69.

17. Goethe, letter to Karl Friedrich Zelter, June 6, 1825, *Goethes Briefe und Briefe an Goethe* (Hamburger Ausgabe), 6 vols., ed. Karl Robert Mandelkow (Munich: C. H. Beck, 1988), vol. 4, p. 146.

18. Ludwig Feuerbach, *Werke*, vol. 3, p. 8f.; cf. *Briefe*, vol. 1, pp. 406ff., 349, and 365.

19. On the following, see the detailed discussion of Burckhardt's conception of history in my book *Jacob Burckhardt: Der Mensch Inmitten der Geschichte* (Stuttgart: Kohlhammer, 1966; originally published 1936), now *Sämtliche Schriften*, volume 7.

20. Burckhardt, letter to Friedrich von Preen, 1871.

21. Bruno Bauer, *Rußland und das Germanentum* (Berlin: Neudruck der Ausgabe, 1853, Scientia Verlag Aalen, 1972).

22. *Rußland und das Germanentum*, p. 42; cf. part 3 of Bauer's *Vollständige Geschichte der Parteikämpfe in Deutschland während der Jahre 1842–46*, 3 vols., 1847.

23. *Rußland und das Germanentum*, p. 47f.

24. Pierre Joseph Proudhon, *Du Principe fédératif* (1863).

25. Nietzsche, "Unzeitgemässe Betrachtungen III: Schopenhauer als Erzieher," *Kritische Studienausgabe*, vol. 1, p. 366; "Schopenhauer as Educator," *Untimely Meditations*, tr. R. J. Hollingdale (New York: Cambridge University Press, 1984), p. 148.

26. "Schopenhauer als Erzieher," 1:367/ "Schopenhauer as Educator," 149.

27. In this regard a characteristic document is Gottfried Benn's 1933 tract

Nach dem Nihilismus [After Nihilism]. [Translator's note: Gottfried Benn (1886–1956) was a German poet influenced by Nietzsche; for a time during the Third Reich, he was a staunch advocate of the subordination of the individual to the "total" state.]

28. F. M. Dostoevsky, *The Diary of a Writer*, tr. Boris Brasol (Santa Barbara, Calif.: Peregrine Smith, 1979), p. 1003.

29. *Jahrbuch für die geistige Bewegung*, ed. Friedrich Gundlof and Friedrich Wolters (Berlin: Verlag der Blätter für die Kunst, 1912), vol. 3, p. iii.

30. Nicolas Berdyaev, *The Fate of Man in the Modern World* (Ann Arbor: Ann Arbor Paperbacks/University of Michigan Press, 1963), p. 35.

31. A thoroughgoing explanation and exposition of what is merely sketched out here is contained in my book *Von Hegel zu Nietzsche: Der revolutionäre Bruch im Denken des 19. Jahrhunderts*, *Sämtliche Schriften*, vol. 4; *From Hegel to Nietzsche: The Revolution in Nineteenth-Century Thought*, tr. David E. Green (New York: Columbia University Press, 1991).

32. Hegel, *Vorlesungen über die Geschichte der Philosophie III*, vol. 20, p. 455.

33. Hegel, *Suhrkamp Theorie Werkausgabe*: vol. 13 (*Aesthetics I*), pp. 22ff, and 139; vol. 14 (*Aesthetics II*), p. 234ff.; vol. 15 (*Aesthetics III*), p. 572f.

34. On the crisis in Christianity, see *Philosophie der Religion*, ed. Lasson, 1929, vol. 3, pp. 229ff.

35. Hegel, *Vorlesungen über die Philosophie der Geschichte*, vol. 12, p. 114.

36. Ibid., pp. 422, 500.

37. Rosenkranz, *Hegels Leben*, p. 304f.

38. Compare with Kierkegaard's "The Present Age," his essay "Das Eine, was not tut" ["The One Thing Which is Needful"], *Zeitwende* 3, no. 1 (1927).

39. On this see his essay "The Revolution of 1848 and the Proletariat."

40. Bauer, *Rußland und das Germanentum*, pp. 121 and 77.

41. On the connection between Russian nihilism and Marxism, see K. Nötzel, *Die soziale Bewegung in Rußland* [The Social Movement in Russia], 1923, pp. 170ff.

42. Nietzsche, *Kritische Studienausgabe*, vol. 12 (*Nachlaß 1885–86*), pp. 125ff.; *The Will to Power*, "Towards an Outline," ed. Walter Kaufmann (New York: Random House, 1968), p. 7f.

43. Nietzsche, *Kritische Studienasugabe*, vol. 6, p. 264; *On the Genealogy of Morals, Ecce Homo*, ed. Walter Kaufmann (New York: Vintage, 1969), p. 222.

44. *The Gay Science*, tr. Walter Kaufmann (New York: Random House, 1974), section 377.

45. Nietzsche, *Kritische Studienausgabe*, vol. 5, p. 13; *Beyond Good and Evil*, ed. Walter Kaufmann (New York: Random House, 1989), p. 3f.

46. Nietzsche, *Kritische Studienausgabe*, vol. 6 (*Ecce Homo*), p. 366/ *On the Genealogy of Morals, Ecce Homo*, p. 327.

47. Nietzsche, *The Will to Power*, section 1054; cf. *Großoktavausgabe* (Leipzig: Kröner, 1910–26), vol. 16, p. 420.

48. On this see my book *Nietzsches Philosophie der ewigen Wiederkehr des Gleichen* [Nietzsche's Philosophy of the Eternal Recurrence of the Same] (Stuttgart: Kohlhammer, 1956 (now *Sämtliche Schriften*, vol. 6).

49. Nietzsche, *Kritische Studienausgabe*, vol. 5, pp. 138ff.; *Beyond Good and Evil*, pp. 129ff.

50. Nietzsche, *Kritische Studienausgabe*, vol. 11 (*Nachlaß*, 1885), p. 584.

51. Nietzsche, *The Will to Power*, section 127.

52. See *Thus Spoke Zarathustra*, part 1, "On War and Warriors" and part 3, "On Old and New Tablets," ed. Walter Kaufmann (New York: Random House, 1968). These two chapters already contain the entire German ideology of the present.

53. Bruno Bauer, *Die Posaune des jüngsten Gerichts über Hegel* [The Trumpet of the Last Judgment Regarding Hegel], 1841.

54. Nietzsche, *Kritische Studienausgabe*, vol. 4, p. 261; *Thus Spoke Zarathustra*, "On Old and New Tablets," p. 209.

55. Nietzsche, *Kritische Studienausgabe*, vol. 13 (*Nachlaß*, 1887–1888), p. 189; *The Will to Power*, p. 3.

56. On this see *On the Genealogy of Morals*, third essay, section 27.

57. Nietzsche, *Kritische Studienausgabe*, vol. 12 (*Nachlaß*, 1885–86), p. 127; *The Will to Power*, p. 8. Cf. *On the Genealogy of Morals*, third essay, section 25.

58. See *On the Genealogy of Morals*, third essay, section 24; cf. *Kritische Studienausgabe*, vol. 11 (*Nachlaß*, 1884), pp. 88, 95, 155.

59. *The Will to Power*, section 880.

60. Nietzsche, *Kritische Studienausgabe*, vol. 12 (*Nachlaß*, 1887), p. 450; *Briefe*, vol. 1, p. 534.

61. *Beyond Good and Evil*, section 242; cf. *The Will to Power*, section 128.

62. *The Will to Power*, section 956; cf. sections 954ff.

PART 2

1. See also J. E. Spenle, *La pensée allemande de Luther à Nietzsche* [German Thought from Luther to Nietzsche], Paris, 1934.

2. Hegel, letter to Niethammer, October 28, 1808, *Briefe*, vol. 1, p. 194; *Hegel: The Letters*, trs. Clark Butler and Christiane Seiler (Bloomington: Indiana University Press, 1984), p. 179.

3. Heinrich Heine, *Werke*, 4 vols., ed. Helmut Schanze (Frankfurt: Insel, 1968), vol. 4, pp. 162ff; "Concerning the History of Religion and Philosophy in Germany," *Heinrich Heine: Selected Works*, tr. and ed. Helen M. Mustard (New York: Random House, 1973), pp. 416ff.

4. Rilke, *Briefe von 1914–21*, p. 89f.

5. Cf. Rilke: "It seems to me as if only one thing, one thing which has ultimate validity, the one thing that is needful, gives me justification for verbal expression."

6. Heidegger, letter, 1920.

7. Heidegger, letter, 1924.

8. On this see Hugo Fiala (pseudonym for Karl Löwith), "Politischer Dezisionismus [Political Decisionism]," in *Internationale Zeitschrift für Theorie des Rechts*, 1935, vol. 2.

9. "Die Selbstbehauptung der deutschen Univeristät," in *Die Selbstbehauptung der deutschen Univeristät das Rektorat, 1933/34:Tatsachen und Gedanken* (Frankfurt; Klostermann, 1993), p. 9; "The Self-Assertion of the German University," *The Heidegger Controversy: A Critical Reader*, ed. Richard Wolin (Cambridge: MIT Press, 1993), p. 29.

10. Heidegger, "Der Begriff der Zeit" [The Concept of Time]. [Translator's note: published in an English/German edition, tr. William McNeill (Oxford: Blackwell, 1992).]

11. "Schlageterfeier der Freiburger Universität" [Freiburg University's Celebration of Schlageter], *Freiburger Studentenzeitung*, June 1, 1933. Now in *Nachlese zu Heidegger: Dokumente zu seinem Leben und Denken*, ed. Guido Schneeberger (Bern: 1962), pp. 47–49; translated as "Schlageter" in *The Heidegger Controversy*, pp. 40–42.

12. "Deutsche Männer und Frauen!" ["German Men and Women"] in the *Freiburger Studentenzeitung*, November 10, 1933. Now in Nachlese zu Heidegger, pp. 144–46/ The Heidegger Controversy, pp. 47–49.

13. "What Is Metaphysics?" 1929.

14. "Deutsche Studenten," Freiburger Studentenzeitung, November 3, 1933, p. 1; now in Schneeberger, *Nachlese zu Heidegger*, p. 135; "German Students," in *The Heidegger Controversy*, p. 46f.

15. See A. Hoberg, *Das Dasein des Menschen*, 1937.

16. *Germanischer Schicksalsglaube*, 1934.

17. "Einleitung zu: 'Was ist Metaphysik?'" p. 375f. / "The Way Back Into the Ground of Metaphysics," p. 219f.

18. See the article by H. Kunz in the *Zürcher Zeitung*, January 3, 1938.

19. See the controversy between H. Barth and E. Staiger in the *Zürcher Zeitung*, January 1936.

20. Heidegger, *Sein und Zeit*, 15th ed. (Tübingen: Niemeyer, 1979), p. 401; *Being and Time*, tr. John Macquarrie and Edward Robinson (New York: Harper and Row, 1962}, p. 453 [citing Count Yorck].

21. "Die Selbstbehauptung der deutschen Universität," p. 19/ "The Self-Assertion of the German University," p. 38.

22. Heidegger, "Hölderlin und das Wesen der Dichtung," *Erläuterungen zu Hölderlins Dichtung*, 5th ed., p. 47; "Hölderlin and the Essence of Poetry," *Existence and Being*, 1949, p. 313.

23. The Japanese reader may be surprised that I subject my "sensei" to such a sharp and public critique. But even this critique of my own teacher is simply a special case of that fundamentally critical attitude that characterizes the European spirit. For us, gratitude toward one's teacher is not incompatible with the sharpest disagreement with him; on the contrary, we will often subject to the

most rigorous critique precisely that from which we have learned the most. In principle, a critique of one's teacher is at the same time a critique of oneself, since it signifies the pupil's act of distinguishing and separating himself from his past, which has been conditioned by his teacher. One must also see this kind of indirect critique of oneself in Schelling's radical polemic against Fichte, in Hegel's against Schelling, in Marx's and Kierkegaard's against Hegel, and in Nietzsche's against Wagner.

24. See Nietzsche, *The Antichrist*, aphorism 10 and H. Ball, *Zur Kritik der deutschen Intelligenz* (Bern, 1919).

25. See Nietzsche's statement regarding Frederick the Great in *Beyond Good and Evil*, aphorism 209.

26. Dostoevsky, *Diary of a Writer*, May-June 1877, pp. 727ff. [following Löwith's rendering of the passage].

27. On this see Chamberlain's excellent remark to Hearn (letter, June 17, 1894) in *More Letters from Basil Hall Chamberlain to Lafcadio Hearn*, p. 135.

28. Lafcadio Hearn, *Japan: An Attempt at Interpretation*, pp. 529ff.

29. See Chamberlain's letter to Hearn, October 22, 1893, *More Letters from Basil Hall Chamberlain to Lafcadio Hearn*, p. 108: "Patriotism comes before everything, before Christianity, before humility, before even fair play and truth."

30. In the journal *Dosetsu*, no. 14 (1938).

31. See the famous poem by Fujita Toko.

32. On this see Hegel's analysis of theoretical edification (*Gymnasialrede*, September 29, 1809), *Suhrkamp Theorie Werkausgabe*, 20 vols. (Frankfurt: Suhrkamp: 1982), vol. 4, p. 320f.

33. Hegel, *Vorlesungen über die Philosophie der Philosophie I, Suhrkamp Theorie Werkausgabe*, vol. 18, p. 174; cf. *Vorlesungen über die Philosophie der Geschichte*, *Suhrkamp Theorie Werkausgabe*, vol. 12, p. 237.

34. See Burckhardt's lecture "Über das wissenschaftliche Verdienst der Griechen" [On the Greeks' Service to Knowledge], *Gesamtausgabe*, vol. 14, p. 234.

35. An occasion and impetus for Japan to distinguish and critique itself, one which is natural because it recommends itself both geographically and historically, is offered not by Europe, which is most distant and Christian, but only by China. In order that Japan be brought back to itself and at the same time be placed beyond itself by the spiritual consequences of its military and political conflict with China, in the first instance this may have to be brought about in a decisive manner by an other—an event that has as many opportunities as dangers for an insular culture. In Europe, on the other hand, the need to compare oneself with others, to distinguish oneself from them, and thereby to become critical of oneself was always present, because Europe contains a variety of different nations, which immediately border on one another.

36. The unity and uniformity of Japanese culture, which lacks an opposite, has a positive basis in the development of well-established traditions. But within this uniform homogeneity, an infinite variety of minute variations and modifica-

tions of unchanging basic forms has developed. To the European eye and ear these appear to be more or less insignificant, because our senses seize less on such perceptible nuances than on decisive oppositions; or to use a metaphor, because the spiritual air of our lives is drier than in the humid climate of Japan, where the firm and clear forms of colors and things merge together as if in a foggy vapor which enshrouds and penetrates everything. Whoever has seen the marble temples on the barren rock of the Acropolis and the wooden shrines in the forest of Ise, will understand what I mean here.

37. An excellent characterization of the Japanese insistence upon mediators in all decisive matters in political and private life is given, from the European viewpoint, by E. Lederer in Japan-Europa, 1929, pp. 77f., 119f., and 232.

38. *Vorlesungen über die Philosophie der Geschichte*, vol. 12, p. 277.

39. Burckhardt, *Gesamtausgabe*, vol. 7, pp. 368ff.

Two Letters from Martin Heidegger to Karl Löwith

Editor's Note: The two letters from Martin Heidegger to Karl Löwith were written at decisive points in Löwith's youthful philosophical existence. On both occasions, Löwith was on the verge of completing a major step of his university career: the letter of August 19, 1921, was written as Löwith was in the process of finishing a dissertation under Heidegger's tutelage; the letter of August 20, 1927, as Löwith neared completion of his habilitation, also written under Heidegger's direction.

Both documents are of more than passing interest. The first letter, for example, offers exceptional insight concerning Heidegger's self-understanding as a thinker in relation to the philosophical tradition (Kierkegaard, Nietzsche, Husserl, etc.). The point is especially relevant with regard to the lucid justification it contains of the existential standpoint from which, according to Heidegger, all authentic philosophical inquiry must proceed. Moreover, one should also note Heidegger's telling criticism of the "pseudo-science" characteristic of contemporary academic philosophy. With the second letter, we are accorded a unique view concerning Heidegger's self-understanding as a teacher of philosophy.

The letters were first published in *Zur philosophischen Aktualität Heideggers: Symposium der Alexander von Humboldt-Stiftung vom 24–28 April 1989 in Bonn-Bad Godesberg*, vol. 2, eds. Dietrich Papenfuss and Otto Pöggeler (Frankfurt: Klostermann, 1990). They are translated here with the permission of the publisher. To date, Löwith's letters to Heidegger remain unpublished.

1. Oskar Becker, philosopher and mathematician (1889–1964). Received

doctorate at Leipzig in 1914 and habilitation at Freiburg in 1922. Followed Heidegger as Husserl's assistant in 1923; professor at Freiburg in 1928, and professor at Bonn in 1931. Author of *Mathematische Existenz*, in *Jahrbuch für Philosophie und phänomenologische Forschung*, vol. 8 (Halle, 1927), pp. 441–809, investigations concerning the logic and ontology of mathematical phenomena.

2. Heidegger's critical review of Jaspers' *Psychologie der Weltanschauungen*, which Heidegger renounced at the time of its publication. Cf. letter from Jaspers to Heidegger, August 1, 1921: "I would very much like to talk with you about your critique, which I have now read carefully. . . . I found several judgments to be unjust." Cf. also Heidegger's letter of reply to Jaspers, August 5, 1921: "Husserl as well has said that I do you wrong in several ways; for me this is simply proof that I have at least *attempted* to take a stand."

3. Letters from Karl Löwith to Martin Heidegger, August 2, 10, and 17, 1927.

4, Heinrich Freiling completed his doctorate in 1923 with Erich Jaensch in Marburg with the work *Über die räumliche Wahrnehmung der Jugendlichen in der eidetischen Entwicklungsphase* [The Spatial Perceptive of Adolescents in the Phase of Eidetic Development], in *Zeitschrift für Sinnespsychologie*, vol. 55 (Leipzig: 1923).

5. Erich Rudolf Jaensch, born 1883 in Breslau. Lecturer at Strassbourg in 1911, professor at Halle in 1912, professor of psychology at Marburg in 1913. *Zur Analyse der Gesichtswahrnehmungen* [On the Analysis of Facial Perception], 1909; *Über die Wahrnehmung des Raumes* [On the Perception of Space], 1911; *Über den Aufbau der Wahrnehmungswelt und ihre Struktur im Jugendalter* [On the Construction of the Perceptual World and Its Structure in Youth], 1923.

6. Dietrich Mahnke (1884–1939). Doctorate in philosophy at Freiburg in 1922, lecturer at Freiburg in 1926. A pupil of Husserl, professor at Marburg in 1927. Mahnke had been a teacher.

7. Carl Heinrich Becker (1878–1932), orientalist and Prussian Politician. Professor in Heidelberg, Hamburg, Bonn, and Berlin. In the Prussian Ministry of Culture starting in 1916; Prussian minister of culture in 1921 and from 1925 to 1930.

8. Friedrich Schmidt-Ott (1860–1936). Doctor of theology, philosophy, and medicine; doctor of engineering; Prussian cultural politician in the Ministry of Culture starting in 1895; minister of culture 1917–1918; in 1920 he founded the Emergency Association for German Science, of which he was president until 1934.

9. Heidegger's habilitation essay, *Die Kategorien- und Bedeutungslehre des Duns Scotus* [The Doctrine of Categories and Meaning in Duns Scotus], first published by J. C. B. Mohr (Paul Siebeck), Tübingen, 1916.

10. Helmuth Plessner, born 1892, in Wiesbaden. Doctorate 1916, habilitation at Cologne 1920, professor at Cologne from 1926 to 1933, later at Groningen (Holland). Professor in Göttingen starting in 1945.

11. *Philosophischer Anzeiger: Zeitschrift für die Zusammenarbeit von Philosophie und*

Einzelwissenschaft [The Philosophical Gazette: Journal for the Collaboration of Philosophy and the Individual Sciences], edited by Heinrich Plessner. Plessner edited the journal "in conjunction with" numerous scientists and philosophers, among them Nicolai Hartmann and Martin Heidegger.

12. Nicolai Hartmann, 1882–1950. Doctorate in philosophy at Marburg 1907, habilitation at Marburg 1909, professor at Marburg beginning in 1920. Full professor at Marburg 1922, Cologne 1925, Berlin 1931, Göttingen 1945. *Grundzüge einer Metaphysik der Erkenntnis* [Foundations of a Metaphysics of Knowledge], Berlin, 1921; *Ethik* [Ethics], Berlin, 1926; *Zur Grundlegung der Ontologie* [The Foundation of Ontology], Berlin, 1935; *Philosophie des Natur* [Philosophy of Nature], Berlin, 1950.

13. Quotation from Löwith's letter of August 2, 1927.

Index

Academic freedom, 164, 217
Actuality, 76
Aestheticization, in Schmitt's theory, 140
Alexander the Great, 173–74
America, 200, 229, 234
Anarchism, 145
Anaximander, *see under* Heidegger
Anthropomorphism, 3
Anti-Semitism, 9, 278–79n.65; in Schmitt's political theory, 154
Arendt, Hannah, 6, 9, 11, 14
Aristotle, 37, 48, 82, 92, 94, 98, 242; Nietzsche's relationship to, 110–11, 115
Aryan, in Schmitt's political theory, 154–55
Asia, 175; Japan, 228–32
Atheism, 225; Nietzsche's, 115
Augmentation, in Nietzsche's philosophy, 120, 122
Augustine, Saint, 67–68, 94–95, 134; *Soliloquia*, 134

Authenticity, 4; of happenings, 75; individual and political, 18; National Socialism's potential for, 7
Authority, Schmitt's concept of, 142, 144, 150, 159

Baeumler, Alfred, 179
Balance of power, European, 175
Barth, Karl, 75–76, 166, 198, 214, 219; *Theological Existence Today*, 75, 219
Baudelaire, Charles, 193–95; "End of the World, The," 194; *Fusées*, 194
Bauer, Bruno, 186–88, 203, 206, 211; *Russia and the Germanic World*, 186
Becker, Oskar, 235–39, 241–43
Becoming, in Nietzsche's philosophy, 120–21
Being, 21–22, 33, 36–38; abandonment of, 77; and beings, 66–68, 76, 93, 102; Dasein and, 53–54, 57–58, 63–68, 257n.107; decline,

Being (*Continued*)
192; destiny, 57, 60; dialectic of correspondence, 64; epochal character, 76; eschatology, 71; *es gibt*, 54, 78; essence, 53, 72; and experience of the Nothing, 51; finite temporality, 59–60; as foundation, 64; God and, 112–13; history, 60, 71, 82, 88, 92; human essence and, 53, 63; interpretation of, 46–49, 52, 97; Kierkegaard's saying of, 98; meaning of, 40–41, 45–47; nature and, 88–89; in Nietzsche's philosophy, 110, 122, 124; as the Other, 67; presence, 53; revelation and concealment, 113; sacrifice for protection of truth of, 52; source of, 62; temporality and historicality, 60–61; thinking and, 79, 113; time and, 60, 98, 108, 127, 133, 211; traditional metaphysics, 63; as *transcendens*, 23, 66, 126–27; truth and, 54–57, 59, 61, 67–68; truth of, 45, 72, 81, 97, 133; value and, 119, 124; *see also* Dasein
Being-a-self, 42
Being-at-the-end, 71
Being-free-for-death, 73
Being-from-out-of-itself, 65
Being-in-itself, 52, 67
Being-in-the-world, 23, 39, 55, 73, 86, 134; National Socialism and, 18; temporal structures, 59
Being-on-the-way, 46, 61–62, 65, 70
Being-present, 61
Being-present-at-hand, 51
Being-toward-death, 4–5, 92
Being-toward-the-end, 72, 74, 86, 92
Being-with-others, 6, 74
Benn, Gottfried, 43
Bonald, Louis-Gabriel-Ambroise de, 143, 182

Bourgeoisie, 140, 144, 147, 152, 226; Marx's critique of, 201–2
Bultmann, Rudolf, 103, 168–69, 214
Burckhardt, Jakob, 95, 184–86, 232, 234

Capacity-for-Being, 57, 100, 102, 105, 107, 215, 220; Dasein and, 75; German, 166
Capacity-for-Being-a-whole, 101–2, 105, 108, 161, 215
Chamberlain, Basil Hall, 229, 232
Child, Nietzsche's view of, 108
China, critique of Europe, 175
Christ, in Nietzsche's philosophy, 114–15
Christianity, 2, 46, 58, 78, 82–83, 85, 92–95, 116, 133; Barth's reflections on, 75; decisionism of Donoso Cortés, 145–46; eternal truths, 59; and European cultural reconstruction, 177; and European unity, 226; Gogarten's theological decisionism, 166–69; in Hegel's history of philosophy, 199; Kierkegaard's critique of, 97–98, 142–43, 201–2; love, 125–26, 279n.65; Nietzsche's understanding of, 114–15, 117, 206–7; in political philosophy, 157–58; and Teutonic bellicosity, 210
Circle of understanding, 102–3
Clearing, the, 87, 89, 91, 93
Common sense, Heidegger's attacks on, 35
Communism, 79, 181; *see also* Marx, Karl
Concert of Europe, 175
Congress of Vienna, 175, 184
Conscience, 82
Corporate state, 138
Correctness, Heidegger's derivation of meaning of, 40–41

Index

Corresponding, dialectic of, 64–66
Counterrevolution, political philosophy of the, 144
Co-world (*Mitwelt*), 5–6
Creation, 51, 95, 117
Cromwell, Oliver, 150–51
Culture, hostility to, 16

Danger, 218, 220
Dasein, 4–5, 7, 17–18, 23, 38–39, 241; Being and, 53–54, 57–58, 63–68, 257n.107; Being and truth and, 59; and Being-in-itself, 52; as Being-in-the-World, 134; capacity-for-Being and, 75; death and, 73; essence of, 49; existence, 49, 66; existing, and Being, 47; experience of burden, 49; facticity, 51; fate and, 74; as foundation, 64; freedom of, 223; grounding of, 33; and heroic greatness, 222; historicality, 72, 92–93, 107–8, 211; meaning and meaninglessness, 45; nature in, 87; Nietzsche's understanding of, 108, 116; ontic-ontological priority of, 48–49; projection, 47, 50; resolve, 42; temporality, 59–60, 78; throwness, 50–51; truth and, 54–57; understanding and, 55, 100, 102, 105; wholeness, 73; world-history and, 73; *see also* German Dasein
Death, 34, 42, 49, 57, 59–60, 62, 86, 92, 101, 105, 160, 212, 220; anticipation of, 73; freedom toward, 74; in Gogarten's theory, 168; in Schmitt's theory, 146–47, 153
Death of God, 4, 106, 110–12, 114–16, 118, 123, 134, 207
Decision, 84, 159
Decisionism, 8, 18, 159; *see also* Political decisionism; Theological decisionism
Democracy: German right-wing intellectuals' view of, 14; Nietzsche's reflection on, 208; in political theology, 143
Denken, see Thinking.
Descartes, Réne, 82, 86, 93, 122–23
Destining of Being, 60, 64, 69, 72, 74–79, 81, 83–84, 92–94
Destitute time, 69–70, 84, 99
Destruction, 18, 35, 80, 192, 212, 215, 224, 237
Dialectic, 63–64
Dialectical theology, 159–60, 198
Dictatorship, 187–89; Nietzsche's reflection on, 208; Schmitt's concept of, 19, 144–45
Dilthey, Wilhelm, 72, 86, 99, 130
Donoso Cortés, Juan María de la Salud, 138, 143–46, 182
Dostoevsky, Fyodor, 16, 175, 181, 195; critique of Germany, 225–28; *Diary of a Writer*, 195
Duns Scotus, John, 99, 240, 242

Elucidation of texts, 111–12
Enemy, 165, 219; Schmitt's concept of, 19, 152–53
Enemy-friend distinction, Schmitt's notion of, 19–20, 147–51, 155–56
Enframing, 36
England, 177–79; Nietzsche's view of, 205
Equality, Schmitt's concept of, 154–55
Error, 77–78
Eschatology, 2, 38–39, 70–71, 73, 81–82, 85, 93, 198
Essence: ground of, 91; *see also* Human essence
Eternal return, Nietzsche's concept of, 120, 123–24, 205
Eternal truths, 59–60, 62
Eternity, 60, 69, 82, 219–20; Nietzsche's concept of, 108–9, 124

Europe: Asia, contrast with, 173; concept of, 173; disunity and decline, 176, 181–92, 234; foreign critique, 175; Kierkegaard's view of spiritual decline of, 202; Nietzsche's reflection on, 204–7; post-World War I, 177–80; self-critique, 175; unity, 174–75, 226

European nihilism. *see* Nihilism

Event, 33, 53

Ever-extant, Greek notion of, 69

Exception, the: Kierkegaard's notion of, 142; Schmitt's concept of, 142

Existence, 57, 66; Heidegger's philosophical politics and, 224; of human Dasein, 49–50; Kierkegaard's Christian definitions of, 97–98; in "Letter on Humanism," 50; resoluteness and, 75; temporal, and the problem of history, 73; understanding and, 100; value and, 119

Existentialism, 35; nihilism of Heidegger's, 17; political, 8, 10, 19–20; pro-fascist reading of Heidegger's, 7; and Sartre, 11, 13

Existential ontology: *Being and Time* as study in, 15, 21; political consequences of Heidegger's doctrine, 211–25

Facticity, 20, 47, 50–51, 73, 215, 242

Faith, 113–14, 116; Gogarten's concept of, 168–69

Fall, the, 78, 95

Farias, Victor, 10, 18; *Heidegger and Nazism*, 10

Fate, 74, 76, 78, 165–66, 215, 217–20, 222; Schmitt's concept of, 156; self-chosen, 75

Feuerbach, Ludwig, 6, 184, 203, 211; *Principles of a Philosophy of the Future*, 6; *Thoughts on Death and Immortality*, 184

Fichte, Johann Gottlieb, 186, 192, 209–10; *On the Essential Characteristics of the Present Age*, 192

Finitude, 59–60; and eternity, 47

First World War, *see* World War I

Flaubert, Gustave, 193, 195; *Bouvard and Péuchet*, 193; *Temptation of the Holy Antonius, The*, 193

Forgottenness of Being, 93–94, 111, 115, 126, 129

Freedom, 87, 223; Nietzsche's understanding of, 116; of the self, 42

Freedom toward death, 160–61, 215; in Schmitt's political theory, 147, 153

Freiburg University: election proclamation, 162, 221–22; Heidegger as rector of, 163, 165, 216–17, 219–22; inaugural speech, 106, 163–65, 217–19

French literature: Goethe's critique of, 183; nihilism, 193–95

French Revolution, 175, 181–83, 185–86, 189, 226–27

Friend-enemy distinction, *see* Enemy-friend distinction

Fundamental ontology, 47, 63, 100, 213, 241

Futurism, 70, 85

Gadamer, Hans-Georg, 2, 5, 13

George, Stefan, 35, 131, 196

German Dasein, 75, 161, 165–66, 168, 215, 218, 220, 222

German Reformation, *see* Reformation

Germany, 186–87; alliance with Russia, 181; Christianity, 168; Dostoevsky's critique of, 225–28; in Nietzsche's political thought, 208; post-World War I, 177–80, 220; World War I, 179–80

God, 34, 46, 55, 58, 66–69, 83, 219;

Index

Being and, 112–13; Gogarten's theological decisionism, 167–69; in Nietzsche's teaching, 117, 119; revelation and concealment, 113–14; and time, 70; *see also* Death of God

Goethe, Johann Wolfgang von, 94, 183, 194

Gogarten, Friedrich, 160, 166–69, 214

Greece, 174; appropriation of foreign thinking, 231–32

Greek philosophy: Heidegger's reappropriation of, 42–43; history, understanding of, 70–72, 85–86; time, 94

Greek spirit, 233

Happiness, 82–83

Having-To (Has-To), 161–62, 166, 215, 220–21

Healing, 34–35, 39, 70, 81, 126

Hearn, Lafcadio, 175, 228; *Japan: An Attempt at Interpretation*, 228

Hegel, Georg Wilhelm Friedrich, 35–38, 40, 52, 63–64, 71, 73, 79, 83, 92–93, 98–99, 130, 155, 157, 186, 209, 234; death of God, 115–16; on Europe's adolescence, 173; Greek spirit, characterization of, 233; history of spirit, 198–200, 202; individualism, 281n. 75; revolutionary impulse of pupils, 211

works: *Encyclopedia of the Philosophical Sciences*, 98; *Lectures on the History of Philosophy*, 198; *Philosophy of Right, The*, 200

Heidegger, Martin: "Analytic of Dasein," 97; anti-intellectual stance, 14; basis of political thought, 7–8, 10, 13–15, 17–18, 25; Being and Nothing, 60; Being essencing, 66; Dasein and Being, relationship of, 65; denazification commission, 11, 24; difficulty in understanding, 36; facticity, problem of, 51; Husserl, treatment of, 9, 166; influence, 128–34, 213–14, 225; Löwith, letters to, 235–43; Löwith's encounter with and critique of, 4, 14, 17–18, 20–25; manner of thinking, 96; National Socialism, adherence to, 6–9, 14–15, 25, 161–66, 216–25; political consequences of philosophy of, 211–25; political decision, 75–76; political occasionalism, 159–66; truth of Being, 55; turning, 21, 44, 47, 69; *see also* Freiburg University, Heidegger as rector of

WORKS: "Anaximander Fragment, The," 43, 55, 71, 90, 106, 112; •*Being and Time*, 15, 21, 131–33; Being as *transcendens*, 66; capacity-for-Being, 105; Dasein and Being, 53–54, 57–58; Dasein and understanding, 55; death, 34, 160–61, 212; dedication, 166, 223; essence of Dasein, 49; essential categories and concepts, 17–18; eternal truths, 59, 62; existence of Dasein, 49–50; facticity, 51; fate and resoluteness, 74; finitude of Dasein, 59; grounding of history, 78; hermeneutics, 99; historical-political reading, 18; historical time, 69; history, 86; history of ontology, destruction of, 80; human subjectivity, fundamental analysis of, 48; inauthentic existence, 5; interpretation of Being, 46–49; introduction, 98, 126–27; Kierkegaard acknowledged in, 38; language, understanding of, 39; later writings compared to, 64–65; misunderstandings of, 129; *Mitsein*, 4;

Heidegger, works (*Continued*)
nature, 86–87; Nietzsche, interpretation of, 107; nihilism, 17; phenomenon and logos, 54; philosophical perspective, 22–23; resolve, 8, 42; second part, 33; systematic structure, 36; Teutonic mythology and, 223; time, understanding of, 73; title, 44; truth and Being, 55–57; understanding of Being, 52–53;
—"Conversation on a Country Path," 44, 62, 134; "Hegel's Concept of Experience," 106; "Hermeneutics of Facticity," 97; *Holzwege*, 44, 55, 76, 80; Nietzsche, interpretation of, 107, 110; *Introduction to Metaphysics, An*, 51, 79;
•"Letter on Humanism," 13, 23, 35, 39, 132; Being and Dasein, 53, 58; essence of Dasein, 49; forest keeper, 45; healing, 34; historical thinking, 78; homelessness, 60; thinking, 67; thrown character of projection, 50;
—"On the Essence of Ground," 87, 113, 130; "On the Essence of Truth," 55, 87; "On the Question of Being," 53; "Origin of the Work of Art, The," 262n.37; *Principle of Reason, The*, 132; "Self-Assertion of the German University, The," 75–76, 80, 163–65, 217–19; "Thing, The," 262n.37; "What Are Poets For?" 106; *What Is Called Thinking?* 53, 107; "What Is Metaphysics?" 118; "Who Is Nietzsche's Zarathustra?" 107; "Why Do We Remain in the Provinces?" 215–16
Heraclitus, 64, 92
Heyse, Hans, 179
Historicality, 64, 72–75

Historical thinking, 70, 76, 78
Historicism, 2, 14, 24, 71–72, 85, 91–93, 107, 211
Historiological consciousness, 99, 236
Historiological facticity, 212, 214–15, 224
Historiological relativism, 72, 91–93, 97
Historiological thinking, 94
Historiology, 72, 84–86, 88; interpretation of texts, 105; Nietzsche's critique of, 107–9
History, 71–79, 81, 83–94; essential ground, 94–95; Greeks' understanding of, 70–71; Heidegger's derivation of meaning of, 40
History of Being (*Seinsgeschichte*), 21, 71, 88, 93–94
Hitler, Adolf, 162, 164, 222–23
Hölderlin, Friedrich, 22, 37, 39, 41, 43, 61, 70, 88–91, 94, 133, 174, 224; **works**: "Andenken," 61; "Patmos," 43
Holy, the, 34, 70, 81, 89–90
Human essence, 49, 53, 64, 70, 85, 95, 105; Being and, 57–58, 63, 65, 68; change in, 75; and truth of Being, 56–58, 61
Humanism, 48, 174–75
Human nature, 92; Greeks' understanding of, 70
Husserl, Edmund, 4, 9, 166, 223, 238–39

Imperialism, 188–89, 205
In-connection-with-which, in Heidegger's historical thinking, 70–71
Individual, in Schmitt's political theory, 151–54
Individualism, 189; Hegel's concept of, 281n.75
Interpretation, process of, 99, 101–6

Japan, 228–32
Jaspers, Karl, 9, 24, 97, 103–4, 238
Jews, 9–10, 223; Jünger's assessment of, 180; in Schmitt's political theory, 154
Jünger, Ernst, 18, 178n., 179, 223, 234

Kant, Immanuel, 24, 59–60, 92, 186–87, 209–11
Kehre, see Turn
Kierkegaard, Søren Aabye, 4–5, 24, 38, 62, 71–72, 80, 211; critique of the present age, 200–203; decisionism, 141–42, 157, 169; exception and universal, 142; existence, concept of, 100; Heidegger's orientation on, 212–13; indirect communication of existence, 97; Nietzsche's relationship to, 111, 115
Knowledge service, mission of the universities as, 163–64, 218

Law, 185, 189, 223
Life, in Nietzsche's philosophy, 121–22
Linguistic thinking, Heidegger's, 37, 39–42
Logos, 54, 198–99
Love, Heidegger's derivation of meaning of, 40
Löwith, Karl: *From Hegel to Nietzsche*, 1; *Karl Marx and Max Weber*, 1; *Meaning in History*, 1; "My Life in Germany Before and After 1933," 10; "Political Implications of Heidegger's Philosophy of Existence, The," 11
Luther, Martin, 174, 215, 227

Maistre, Joseph Marie Comte de, 143–44, 182

Marx, Karl, 2, 43, 71, 83, 155–56, 200–203, 211; decisionism, 141, 157; *Communist Manifesto* (Marx and Engels), 201
Metaphysics, 44, 63; end of, 114, 187–88; history of, 79, 81–83, 92, 94, 99; Nietzsche's, 117, 125; in Schmitt's political theory, 143
Metaphysics of value, Nietzsche's philosophy as, 120
Militarism: in Burckhardt's theory, 185–86; in Nietzsche's system, 205; Teutonic bellicosity, Heine's notion of, 210–11; *see also* War
Modernity, 84, 122–23
Moment of vision, 71–72, 74, 76, 78, 91
Morality, in Nietzsche's philosophy, 207–8
Mori, R., 229–31; *Truth About Japan, The*, 229
Müller, Adam, 138, 140

Napoleon, 175, 182, 200, 205–6, 208
National Socialism (Nazism), 80; authenticity, potential for, 7; and Being-in-the world, 18; German Dasein and, 75; Heidegger's commitment to, 6–9, 14–15, 25, 166; Heidegger's election proclamation (1933), 162; mission of the universities, 164; nihilistic spirit, 17; relationship of Heidegger's concepts to, 216–25; Schmitt's support of, 18; spirit of, 165; total politicization, 138; unhomogeneousness of, 10
Natural science, 197
Nature, 85–91, 93–94
Naumann, H., 166, 223
Nazism, *see* National Socialism
Neutralization, in Schmitt's theory, 138, 140

Nietzsche, Friedrich Wilhelm, 38, 63, 78, 80–82, 92, 190, 209, 211; eternal recurrence of Being, 61; Heidegger's interpretation of, 103–4, 106–27; historiology, 84, 107–9; Jaspers' interpretation of, 103–4; nihilism, 15–16, 192, 203–8, 224; and old and new Europe, 234; suffering, Nietzsche's understanding of, 114–15; superman, 2; suprahistorical position, Nietzsche's, 109–10; truth, 97

works: *Antichrist, The*, 115, 206–7; *Dawn, The*, 110; *Ecce Homo*, 115, 203, 206; "Fame and Eternity," 123; "Fate," 109; "Freedom of the Will," 109; "History," 109; "On the Use and Disadvantage of History for Life," 107; "On the Vision and the Riddle," 124; "Schopenhauer as Educator," 190; *Thus Spoke Zarathustra*, 108–10, 114–17, 119, 121–24, 218; *Untimely Meditations*, 16, 19, 107–9, 190, 206; *Will to Power, The*, 15, 110, 116, 118–22, 207–8

Nihilism, 2, 15–17, 43, 71, 78, 81, 95, 224, 229; in European literature, 192–98; existential, of Germany in late 1920s, 20; in German philosophy, 198–208; in Gogarten's theory, 169; Nietzsche's concept of, 116–18; political decisionism, 159; in Schmitt's political theory, 146, 151

Nothing, the, 46, 51–52, 223, 225; death as, 160; Gogarten's concept of, 167–69; in Nietzsche's teaching, 116–17; in Schmitt's theory, 140, 146

Occasionalism, in Schmitt's political theory, 137, 144, 158
Ontic-ontological, 48, 66–67

Onto-historical thinking, 77, 79–80, 86, 92–93, 98
Ontology, 48, 98, 241–42; destruction of history of, 80; fundamental, 47, 63, 100, 213, 241
Open, the, 89, 93
Order: in Gogarten's theory, 168; in Schmitt's theory, 158–59
Other, the, 6, 67

Parusie (parousia), 62, 70, 93
Pascal, Blaise, 86, 114, 116
Physis, 85–86, 88–91, 93, 120; Nietzsche's concept of, 109
Plato, 21–22, 37, 43, 48, 82–83, 92, 98; Christian Platonism, 117; mistranslation, in Heidegger's rectorial address, 106, 165, 218; political theory, 144
Poetry, 22, 37
Political Being, Schmitt's concept of, 147, 150, 152
Political decisionism, 159, 215; Schmitt's theory of, 18–20, 137–38, 140–47, 154–59
Political existentialism, Schmitt's doctrines of, 19–20
Political philosophy, 75–76; Schmitt's theory, 137–59
Political romanticism, 137, 139–41, 144, 147
Political theology, 137, 143
Present, the, 71, 74–75, 80, 83
Preservation, in Nietzsche's philosophy, 120, 122
Progress, 83, 229, 233–34
Projection, 47, 50; understanding and, 100
Proletariat, 2, 157, 201
Prometheus, 164, 218
Protestantism, German, 225–26
Proudhon, Pierre Joseph, 145, 189
Prussian-Protestant spirit, 225
Psychoanalysis, 243

Index 303

Public and private, in Schmitt's political theory, 152–53

Racial identity, in Schmitt's political theory, 19–20, 154
Reason, 21, 23, 82–83, 113
Reformation, 174, 181, 191, 199, 227; political consequences, 209
Region, Heidegger's derivation of meaning of, 41
Religious motive, in Heidegger's thinking, 37–38, 82, 133
Resoluteness, 8, 42, 57, 73–76, 78, 162, 214, 219; death and, 160; existence and, 75; Heidegger's derivation of meaning of, 40; of National Socialist politics, 165
Revolution of 1848, 140, 144, 194
Rilke, Rainer Maria, 33–34, 81–82, 106, 160, 212
Roman Catholic Church, 174
Roman Empire, 174, 226
Romanticism, 139–41; *see also* Political romanticism
Rosenberg, Alfred, *Myth of the Twentieth Century, The*, 139n., 179
Rosenkranz, Johann Karl Friedrich, 83, 200
Russia, 181–82, 187–88, 228–29, 234; critique of Europe, 175, 195; Hegel's view of, 200; Nietzsche's view of, 205; worker-state, 138
Russian Revolution, 181–82, 188

Sacrifice of life, 215; *see also* Freedom toward death
Salomon, Ernst von, 161, 221; *City, The*, 161, 221
Salvation, 82
Sartre, Jean-Paul, 11, 35, 50, 100; Heidegger's letter to and opinion of, 12–13; *Being and Nothingness*, 12–13
Scheler, Max, 166, 176–77, 213, 223, 282n.79; "Causes of the Hatred of Germans, The" 177; "Table of Categories of English Thinking," 177
Schelling, Friedrich Wilhelm Joseph von, 83, 209
Schlageter, Albert Leo, 161, 220, 222
Schleiermacher, Friedrich Ernst Daniel, 107
Schmitt, Carl, 8, 18–20, 215; political theory, 137–59;
works: *Concept of the Political, The*, 19, 137, 139, 155; *Crisis of Parliamentary Democracy, The*, 19; *Dictatorship from the Beginnings of the Modern Idea of Sovereignty to the Proletarian Class Struggle*, 141; *On the Three Forms of Legal Thinking*, 158; "Place of Contemporary Parliamentarianism in Intellectual History, The," 141; *Political Romanticism*, 137; *Political Theology*, 19, 137, 141; *Value of the State, The*, 158
Schulz, Walter, 257n.107
Seinsgeschichte, *see* History of Being
Seyn, 34
Shepherd of Being, 45, 50, 63–64, 68
Sorel, Albert, 191; *Reflections on Violence*, 192
Sovereignty, Schmitt's concept of, 143
Spengler, Oswald, 81
Spirit, 98, 218; history of, 71, 198–200, 202
Stahl, Friedrich Julius, 155–56
State, 77; in Burckhardt's theory, 185; Nietzsche's critique of, 191; Schmitt's concept of, 138–39, 146, 150, 152, 154, 278n. 59
Stirner, Max, 203, 206, 211
Subjectivity, 47–48, 60, 63–64, 82, 85, 92
Suicide, 56, 153
Suprasensible world, 82–83, 110, 126–27

Technology, 43–44, 88, 192, 197, 234; Heidegger's derivation of meaning of, 39; politicization of the state and, 138, 140
Temporality, 59–60, 73–74, 78, 94, 108, 133; *see also* Time
Teutonic mythology, 166, 223
Theological decisionism, Gogarten's theory of, 160, 166–69
Theology, 34, 37, 83, 114, 214; time, 94; *see also* Political theology
Thinking (*Denken*), 22–23, 37–38, 46, 63–64, 67–68, 76, 84, 96–97; faith and, 113–14; German, after World War I, 166; Heidegger's derivation of meaning of, 40–41; history and, 78–79, 92
Third Reich: Heidegger's defense of, 77; Nietzsche's political thought and, 208; *see also* National Socialism
Throwness, of Dasein, 50–51
Time, 24, 44, 76, 83, 93–94, 219; Being and, 98, 108, 127, 133; Dasein and temporality, 59, 73; finite, 60; and God, 70; Greek philosophers' understanding of, 39; nature and, 89; philosopher's understanding of, 69; and truth of Being, 61; what is essential for, 62–63
Time of decision, 74–75, 224
Timidity, 60–61
Tolstoy, Leo, 175, 196
Total mobilization, 18
Total state, 20, 140
Tradition, 73
Truth, 35, 37, 45, 55–56, 59, 62, 68, 76, 82, 85, 92, 126, 219; of Being, 47, 54, 61, 72; Cartesian definition of, 122–23; development of, 99; essence of, 88; freedom and, 87; happening of, 72, 93; Heidegger's derivation of meaning of, 39, 41; history and, 92; Nietzsche's view of, 97, 123, 208; precipitous epochs of, 72; protection of Being, 64
Turgenev, Ivan Sergeyevich, 16, 203
Turn (*Kehre*), in Heidegger's thought, 21, 44, 47, 69

Understanding, 99–105
Universal, the, Kierkegaard's notion of, 142

Value, Nietzsche's concept of, 82, 117–24
Vico, Giambattista, 86, 93, 139
Volk (people), poetry and the, 22

War, 165, 219; freedom toward death, 161; in Schmitt's political theory, 142, 146–53; *see also* World War I
Weber, Max, 3, 25, 43, 225; "Science as a Vocation," 3, 225
Whence, in Heidegger's historical thinking, 70–71
Whither, in Heidegger's historical thinking, 70
Will, 119–20, 124–26, 218–19, 224; Nietzsche's notion of, 204–8
Will to power, 164, 205, 207, 218
Wisdom, Nietzsche's concept of, 109
Withdrawal, 53
Worker-state, 138
World, 2–3, 5, 86–87; in Nietzsche's philosophy, 121
World-history, 73–74, 76, 79–82, 93–94
World-moment-of-vision, 78
World-need, 78, 84
World-night, 80–81, 83
World-order, 168
World-picture, 21
World-spirit, 79, 200
World War I, 175–77, 179, 192, 228; postwar Europe, 177–78